THE LEROI JONES/AMIRI BARAKA READER

THE
LEROI JONES /
AMIRI BARAKA
READER
by Amiri Baraka

EDITED BY WILLIAM J. HARRIS
in collaboration with Amiri Baraka

THUNDER'S
MOUTH
PRESS

Contents © 1960, 1961, 1963, 1964, 1965, 1966, 1967, 1968, 1969, 1970, 1971, 1972, 1975, 1979, 1980, 1981, 1984, 1985, 1987, 1989 by Amiri Baraka

Preface © 1991 by Amiri Baraka

Introduction, chronology, and editor's notes © 1991 by William J. Harris

First edition.

First printing, 1991.

Published by Thunder's Mouth Press

54 Greene Street, Suite 4S

New York, NY 10013

Grateful acknowledgement is made for permission to reprint the following materials:

Excerpt from "The LeRoi Jones Press Conference." © 1967 by Pacifica Radio Archives. Reprinted by permission of Pacifica Radio Archives.

Excerpt from the audio track of *Nationtime Gary*, a documentary film by William Greaves. © 1973 by William Greaves Productions, Inc. Reprinted by permission of William Greaves Productions, Inc.

Excerpt from "A Black Poet/Amiri Bararka; interviewed by Paul Vangelisti." © 1976 by Pacifica Radio Archives. Reprinted by permission of Pacifica Radio Archives.

Excerpt from "Amiri Baraka on Politics, Poetry, and the Blues," an interview with Amiri Baraka by David Barmassian. © 1984 by David Barmassian and the Pacifica Radio Archives. Reprinted by permission of David Barmassian and the Pacifica Radio Archives.

Portions of the introduction by William J. Harris, from the Contemporary Authors New Revision Series, Volume 26. Hal May and James G. Lesniak, editors. © 1989 by Gale Research Inc. Reprinted by permission of the publisher.

Library of Congress cataloging-in-publication data:

Baraka, Imamu Amiri, 1934–

    The LeRoi Jones/Amiri Baraka reader / edited by William J. Harris.

—1st ed.

    Includes bibliographical references.

    ISBN 1-56025-006-2 : $24.95 — ISBN 1-56025-007-0 (pbk.) : $13.95

    1. Afro-Americans—Literary collections. I. Harris, William J.,

1942–   . II. Title.

PS3552.A583A6   1991

818'.5409—dc20   90-25689
                                                       CIP

Text design by Loretta Li.

Manufactured in the United States of America.

For my wife, AMINA
and our children
OBALAJI, RAS, SHANI, AMIRI & AI

Contents

Preface to the Reader

The first book I published was called "Preface . . ." Now, some thirty years later, I find myself writing another Preface, now more clearly serving as both "anchor" (as in relay races) to one motion, and as "1st leg" to another, further motion.

This Reader should give some further description of my own changing and diverse motion, of where I been and why, and how I got to where I was when I next "appeared" or was heard from. In the literary sense, it has always been somewhat difficult to "appear" or be heard from — some times more difficult than others. In the last decade, it has been exceptionally difficult, except if you could actually listen to me talking.

The typology that lists my ideological changes and so forth as "Beat-Black Nationalist-Communist" has brevity going for it, and there's something to be said for that, but, like notations of Monk, it doesn't show the complexity of real life.

"You mean that's not accurate?" Dick or Dixie Dugan wd counter.

"Well, yes and no," I'd drawl, acknowledging with an easy dismissal any mental disclaimer needed to sound so Zennish.

But the truth is that in going toward and away from some name, some identifiable "headline" of one's life, the steps are names too, but we ain't that precise yet. We go from step 1 to step 2 and the crushed breath away from the "given" remains unknown swallowed by its profile as what makes distance. But there is real life between 1 and 2. There is the life of the speed, the time it takes, the life there in, in the middle of, the revelation, like perception, rationale and use. To go from any where to any there.

Hopefully, there is enough motion — movement — in these works to show not only the letter increments identifying change but the minute organic calibration breaths go going gone been gone contain. From here to there and the how you gots in the middle.

What does need hammering away at is the reason that I have not been on the scene recently. As a young person of confused but definite energy and perception, I could publish like a scatter gun of quasi-defined sensitivity, though sometimes even at odds with my self. The bohemian rootlessness and quick draw aspect (actually the safety net for the Castle dwellers, who can see no matter how loud you get, you still don't know the whole story) would give way more and more to what was at first, I thought, the shadow of an earlier life, but it was the dimension of myself I had to learn, to complete the rationale. The explanation.

Black Nationalism was an emotional historical fulfillment. Like that shadow, it was the rest of myself I had yet to get together, and so used in the way does a mouth to ear text from way back, not understanding that the whole telling of that, the whole memory, begets a wholer step 3 self. Malcolm X, Robert Williams, Cuba, The Black Arts were fires burning the stone, giving up the living touching heart of me, to myself, and to whoever was out there, the rush of feelings held in by education, socialization—but what was real and could be touched. And so it rushed out, armed with the seen, the understood, the resisted ugliness of all they stacks around our hearts hoping to stifle the funk.

And so struggle, change, struggle, unity, change, movement and more of, the movement, the motion. The work reflects my life and ideas of that. All of it a whole—realized or half realized or some way station.

When we declared the need for:

1. An art that is recognizably Afro American
2. An art that is mass oriented that will come out the libraries and stomp
3. An art that is revolutionary, that will be with Malcolm X and Rob Williams, that will conk klansmen and erase racists

we meant this not only with the fervor and new fire of youth, but with the certainty and necessity of our realest history. This intention remains today.

All of the oaths I swore were sincere reflections of what I felt— what I thought I knew and understood. But these beliefs change, and the work shows this too. From the cultural nationalist steeped in violent bitterness against the "white eyes" there was yet a deeper commitment that could be harnessed as organization. I joined and helped create organizations, political and cultural, to work at the social transformation I sought. I wrote poetry and essays and plays and stories towards this end as well. It was, and I am still certain of this, part of the same work.

In organization, in finding mutual commitment, in the actual world, there is the materialization of the ideas. In Newark, with Spirit House, or the Committee for Unified Newark or the Congress of African People or the Revolutionary Communist League (MLM) it was the same thrust, and this information is literary as well. That is, I write from my own deepest feelings, and the political forms of my life, whether the Black Power Conference or National Black Assembly or African Liberation Support Committee, are at least as cogent and authentic as writing about or inspired by it!

I became a Communist through struggle, the intensity of realized passion, and understood, and finally stood under, as a force, my ideological clarity, like a jet stream, a nuclear force of reason, from way back, birth black, history fueled, experience directed. Finally I understood that to characterize my ideology as hate whitey is accurate since the only whitey is system and ideology, that whitey is a class and the devil what do d evil. Though, for sure "white" peepas (and what is that "white" when everybody's mama is black?) has been socialized to be hierarchical monsters, and rainbow smaller b's and petty b's have had the likewise "classic," "judeo-xtian," "greco-roman," "intelligent" (like Larry Bird), "upscale," "straight" (as opposed to kinky) gibberish degreed in their caps and tattooed in their feeling skin like gowns.

But still it was easier to be heard from with hate whitey than hate imperialism! The retrograde trend of ideology means to tell us struggle is old hat, black is old hat, communism is dead, and nothing matters. Greed does not need consistent objection and analysis of its changing same ol ugliness. To grow a younger set of weasels, the old weasels do not need our resistance. They go back in history to erase us, imperialism must be Elvis Presley to our Big Mama Thornton's Dis'd and Covered (they call it *Discovered*!)

As of October 1990 we are poised on the brink of a war that Robert Redford told us about several years ago in the last minutes of "Three Days of the Condor" e.g., "it's about oil, isn't it?"

(The villain nods, once, now terrified)

"Are we planning to invade the middle east?"

(Again the same single head shake up and down)

In the Sisyphus Syndrome of American life, the African American people roll the huge stone of slavery up off them through consistent struggle but also with continuous revolutionary outbursts. Then at another point the villains conspire to push it back down on upon us. Hopefully never as far down as before. We are in the down-the-slope motion now. The Supreme Court is now peopled largely with "ugs" wearing cellophane klan lids. Since the deaths of Malcolm, Martin, and the brothers Kennedy, the U.S. has been in the slowly tightening grip of would be creators of the new international corporate state. What we struggled for they have attacked, undermined, ridiculed, and even grown blackus retrogradus to oppose (from soul of Sowell so to speak) our self-determination and a U.S. peoples' democracy.

My writing reflects my own growth and expansion, and at the same time the society in which I have existed throughout this longish confrontation. Whether it is politics, music, literature, or the origins of language, there is a historical and time/place/condition reference that will always try to explain exactly why I was saying both how and for what.

AMIRI BARAKA
October 1990

Editor's Note

Amiri Baraka and I have jointly made the selections in this collection; I made an initial list, and through a series of conversations we arrived at the final list. Since Baraka is a process artist—one who reflects the daily "zoom" of his life in his art—I have arranged his work chronologically, and broken it up into four periods: the Beat Period (1957–1962), the Transitional Period (1963–1965), the Black Nationalist Period (1965–1974), and the Third World Marxist Period (1974–   ). These divisions are defined in my introduction, but a few words on the dates are in order here. I start the first period with 1957, because it is the year that Baraka arrived in Greenwich Village. I begin the second with 1963, because that year marks the approximate beginning of his serious doubts about white bohemia. I start the third with 1965, since that was the year Malcolm X was killed, and marked the beginning of a period when Baraka declared his opposition to white society and moved uptown to Harlem, where he declared himself a black cultural nationalist. I begin the last with 1974, because that is the year that Baraka pronounced himself a Marxist-Leninist.

Yet not everything works out neatly. Each of Baraka's books reflects not only the "present moment," but also the moments leading up to that moment. For example, in a volume like *Home* he not only records his Black Nationalist "present," but also includes the essays—arranged chronologically—that led up to that time. Therefore, it seems to me that the attitudes and thought expressed in a particular piece are more meaningfully reflected in the date that a piece was first published in book form rather than in its date of composition or date of publication in a magazine or journal. (There are exceptions to this rule, and I have noted these in the introductions to particular pieces.)

In considering the totality and span of Amiri Baraka's work it may seem paradoxical, but it is nonetheless true, that continual change is a reflection of an essential integrity and unity—as it is the reflection of a process of development.

Finally, I would like to take the opportunity to offer some special thanks: to Amiri Baraka for producing a major body of work, to

Michael Schwartz for being a demanding and energetic editor, to D. H. Melhem for giving good advice, and to Susan K. Harris for being my intellectual comrade.

WILLIAM J. HARRIS
October 1990

Introduction

Poet, dramatist, essayist, and critic, Amiri Baraka (formerly LeRoi Jones) is a major contemporary author. As both theorist and practitioner he was the cental figure, "the acknowledged father" as the poet Haki R. Madhubuti (Don L. Lee) called him, of the 1960s' Black Arts Movement, a literary movement dedicated to racially focused art. Acting as an energetic artist-critic-spokesman, Baraka almost single-handedly changed both the nature and the form of post–World War II Afro-American literature. In addition to being a prime influence on other poets and dramatists of his time, Baraka has also created an original body of work that belongs in the forefront of innovative avant-garde writing, regardless of ethnic background. As a contemporary American artist Baraka must be ranked with the likes of John Coltrane, Ralph Ellison, Norman Mailer, Toni Morrison, and Thomas Pynchon.

That his abilities transcend particular artistic milieus is suggested by the fact that although the Black Arts Movement is moribund, Baraka's influence and creativity persevere. While being the most famous figure of that movement may have overshadowed his ongoing achievement, at present he is producing work in a variety of genres, including poetry and drama; he is now engaged in what is perhaps his most original and important work. His influence extends into the 1990s; it is evident not only in the expected continuation of black nationalist themes in the work of such figures as Jayne Cortez and Ntozake Shange, but also in the work of mainstream personages like Alice Walker and Toni Morrison, and that of younger figures like the filmmaker Spike Lee, the poet Thulani Davis, and the critic Greg Tate. In essence, Baraka and the Black Arts Movement have had a profound and lasting philosophical and aesthetic impact on all postintegrationist black art; they have turned black art from other-directed to ethnically centered. Thus the contemporary Afro-American artist writes out of his or her own culture and, moreover, is self-consciously an Afro-American. Therefore, when Arnold Rampersad claims in The Kaleidoscopic Torch, the most recent and comprehensive collection of critical essays on Baraka, that he "stands with [Phillis] Wheatley, [Frederick] Douglass, [Paul Laurence] Dunbar, [Langston] Hughes, [Zora Neale] Hurston, [Richard] Wright and [Ralph] Ellison as one of the eight figures . . . who have significantly affected the course of African American literary culture," he does not overstate the case.

Yet Baraka is not only a major author but he is also an exceedingly controversial one. He is one of those mavericks, who, like Allen Ginsberg and Norman Mailer, have produced large bodies of work that are extremely critical of American civilization. Perhaps even more so than Ginsberg and Mailer, Baraka continues to be an irritant to the American literary establishment. In fact, Baraka may be the most difficult American author to evaluate dispassionately since the modernist poet Ezra Pound, another writer whose work still evokes volatile critical response. Like Pound, Baraka has dared to bring radical politics into the world of literature and to deliver his explosive ideas in an inflammatory style.

It is not surprising, then, that critical opinion about Baraka is highly divided. For example, Kimberly Benston asserts in *Baraka: The Renegade and the Mask*: "Imamu Amiri Baraka is one of the foremost American artists of our century." On the other hand, Stanley Kauffmann says in *Dissent* that Baraka is "the luckiest man of our times, a writer who . . . would be less than lightly held if he did not happen to be a Negro at this moment in American history." The centrality of race to Baraka's art seems to be problematic for some critics. Furthermore, he is an avant-garde writer whose variety of forms — including poetry, drama, music criticism, fiction, literary criticism, autobiography, and political and personal essays — makes him difficult to categorize, while his stormy history clouds critical objectivity. No armchair artist, he has gone through a series of dramatic stages, from wild Beatnik ranting against the square world in the late 1950s through the early 1960s, to black cultural nationalist renouncing the white world from the mid-sixties through early seventies, to Marxist-Leninist rejecting monopoly capitalism since the mid-seventies. In this introduction I can only give a hint of the richness and variety of this extraordinary artist's long and distinguished career.

The Beat Period (1957–1962)

During his Beat period, when he was known as LeRoi Jones, Baraka lived in New York's Greenwich Village and Lower East Side, where he published important little magazines such as *Yugen* and *Floating Bear* and socialized with such bohemian figures as Ginsberg, Frank O'Hara, and Gilbert Sorrentino. He was greatly influenced by the white avant-garde: Charles Olson, O'Hara, and Ginsberg, in particular, shaped his conception of a poem as being exploratory and open in form. Donald Allen records in *The New American Poetry: 1945–1960* Baraka's Beat-period views on form: "There must not be any preconceived notion or design for what a poem ought to be. 'Who knows what a poem ought to sound like? Until it's thar' says Charles Olson . . . & I follow closely with that. I'm not interested in writing sonnets, sestinas or anything . . . only poems."

Baraka's first book, *Preface to a Twenty Volume Suicide Note*, has met with general critical approval. In *The New Poets: American and British Poetry since World War II*, M. L. Rosenthal says that the early Jones/Baraka "has a natural gift for quick, vivid imagery and spontaneous humor, and his poems are filled with sardonic or sensuous or slangily knowledgeable passages." Theodore Hudson, in *From LeRoi Jones to Amiri Baraka: The Literary Works*, observes: "All things considered, *Preface* was an auspicious beginning for LeRoi Jones the poet." However, sometimes the positive critical response to the early work comes at the expense of the later poetry. Lloyd Brown represents such a position when he announces in *Amiri Baraka*: "The scurrilities and general lack of control are a major drawback in the later collections, especially the black nationalist and socialist verse. But, despite the monotony that plagues the style of the first two volumes they remain Baraka's most consistently successful collections of poetry."

At first glance *Preface* looks like a typical product of integrated bohemia; in fact, it ends: "You are / as any other sad man here / american." Yet there is a "blues feeling" throughout, that is, an infusion of black culture and reference. The reader can hear the "moaning . . . [of] Bessie Smith" in the book's lines, although blackness is not its principal focus. As David Ossman reports in *The Sullen Art: Interview with Modern American Poets*, Baraka remarked in early 1960: "I'm fully conscious all the time that I am an American Negro, because it's part of my life. But I know also that if I want to say, 'I see a bus full of people,' I don't have to say, 'I am a Negro seeing a bus full of people.' I would deal with it when it has to do directly with the poem, and not as a kind of broad generalization that doesn't have much to do with a lot of young writers today who are Negroes." This view proved to be transitory. With the Civil Rights movement, Martin Luther King, and the black political upsurge of the late 1960s, Baraka's attitude toward race and art changed; he found that being a Negro wasn't some abstract and generalized stance but was integral to his art. Furthermore, with the coming of ethnic consciousness came political consciousness and the slow and painful rejection of bohemia.

In July 1960 Baraka visited Castro's Cuba. In *The Autobiography of LeRoi Jones/Amiri Baraka*, Baraka refers to this visit as "a turning point in my life." While in Cuba he met forceful and politically commited Third World artists and intellectuals who forced him to reconsider his art and his apolitical stance. They attacked him for being an American; he tried to defend himself in "Cuba Libre," an essay reprinted in *Home: Social Essays*, by saying: "Look, why jump on me? . . . I'm in complete agreement with you. I'm a poet . . . what can I do? I write, that's all. I'm not even interested in politics." The Mexican poet, Jaime Shelley, answered him: "You want to cultivate your soul? In that ugliness you live in, you want to cultivate your soul? Well, we've got millions of starving people to feed, and that moves me enough to make poems out of." Finally, the Cuban revolution impressed Baraka as an alternative to the unanchored rebellion of his bohemian friends at home. In Cuba the young intellectuals seemed to be doing something concrete to create a better and more humane world. Baraka felt that the Cuban government, unlike that of the United States, was actually being run by young intellectuals and idealists. This trip was the beginning of Baraka's radical political art and his identification with Third World artists.

Although Baraka started publishing in the late 1950s, he did not achieve fame until the 1964 publication of his play *Dutchman*, which won the *Village Voice's* Obie Award. Werner Sollors notes in *Amiri Baraka/LeRoi Jones: The Quest for a "Populist Modernism"* that Norman Mailer called it "the best play in America." Baraka's most famous work, it has often been reprinted and performed, including a British film version by Anthony Harvey. (The play also provides scenes for Jean-Luc Godard's movie *Masculine-Feminine*.) In *Dutchman* Baraka no longer presents the melancholy hipster world where, as he declared in *Preface*, "Nobody sings anymore," but instead a realm where an angry young man fights for his ethnic identity and his manhood. Lula, the symbolic agent of the white state, sent out to find the latent murderer in the assimilated middle-class Negro Clay, locates and kills him. The play is highly stylized, reflecting the 1960s movement to propel black literature away from naturalism, the principal mode from the 1940s to 1960s, to a more experimental avant-garde art. A character in Baraka's play *The Slave* speaks for the author when he says: "the worst thing that ever happened to the West was the psychological novel." In a 1979 *New*

York Times Book Review Darryl Pinckney commends Baraka's skill as a playwright: "He is a highly gifted dramatist. Much of the black protest literature of the 60s now seems diminished in power, even sentimental. But *Dutchman* immediately seizes the imagination. It is radically economical in structure, striking in the vivacity of its language and rapid shifts of mood."

The Transitional Period (1963–1965)

The Dead Lecturer, Baraka's second book of poetry, is the work of a black man who wants to leave white music and the white world behind. It is a book written in a period that marked a time of changing allegiances, from bohemian to black. As civil rights activities intensified, Baraka became more and more disappointed with his white friends; in fact, the word "friends" becomes ironic in this second volume. In "*Black Dada Nihilismus*," for example, he realizes that he must "Choke my friends / in their bedrooms" to escape their influence and vision. To elude Western metaphysical domination Baraka must call up the dark gods of the black soul; he demands violence in himself and his people to escape the white consciousness. He no longer wants to be the Dead Lecturer; he wants life. In this book of poetry he attempts to reject the "quiet verse" of the Beat Generation and claim the black chant of political commitment.

This blackening and politicalization of Baraka's art is formal as well as thematic. The poetic line becomes longer as the verse imitates the chant. In the poem "Rhythm and Blues," Baraka reveals that he does not want to become a martyr for Western art. Richard Howard, writing in the *Nation*, finds the Baraka of *The Dead Lecturer* "much surer of his own voice. . . . These are the agonized poems of a man writing to save his skin, or at least to settle in it, and so urgent is their purpose that not one of them can trouble to be perfect." Howard understands Baraka's pain. In a negative review of *The Dead Lecturer* in *Salmagundi*, M. L. Rosenthal makes an important statement which anticipates the far more political art of Baraka's Black Arts and Marxist periods: "No American poet since Pound has come closer to making poetry and politics reciprocal forms of action." Rosenthal perceives that Baraka wants his poems to act on the world; as Baraka wrote to his friend, Black Mountain poet Edward Dorn, in a 1961 letter: "'Moral earnestness' . . . ought [to] be transformed into action. . . . I know we think that to write a poem, and be Aristotle's God is sufficient. But I can't sleep. . . . There is a right and a wrong. And it's up to me, you, all of the so called minds, to find out. It is only knowledge of things that will bring this 'moral earnestness.'"

Baraka had joined the Beat Generation because he regarded its members as spiritual outsiders who were against white middle-class America. Yet over the years he became disillusioned with this apolitical avant-garde that refused to take action in the world. Disengagement was no longer enough for Baraka who notes in the essay "Cuba Libre": "The rebels among us have become merely people like myself who grow beards and will not participate in politics. Drugs, juvenile delinquency, complete isolation from the vapid mores of the country, a few current ways out. But name an alternative here." Baraka wanted an alternative to bohemianism.

During this transitional period Baraka produced two fine works, his only serious efforts in fiction: *The System of Dante's Hell*, a novel, and *Tales*, a collection of short stories. As Sollors points out, the sections of the novel parallel the themes and even passages found in *Preface, Dead Lecturer*, and the early uncollected poems. Although *System* was published in 1965 it was mostly written in the early 1960s. Baraka commented on the book and the times to Kimberly Benston in an interview published in *Boundary 2*: "I was really writing defensively. I was trying to get away from the influence of people like Creeley and Olson. I was living in New York then and the whole Creeley-Olson influence was beginning to beat me up. I was in a very closed circle—that was about the time I went to Cuba—and I felt the need to break out of the type of form that I was using then. I guess this was not only because of the form itself but because of the content which was not my politics."

Tales, published in 1967, treats the years 1963 through 1967, a time of radical change in Baraka's life, and reflects the themes of the poetry in *Black Magic*, which also appeared in 1967. Both works try to convey a sense of ethnic self away from the world of white culture. In *Conscientious Sorcerers: The Black Postmodernist Fiction of LeRoi Jones/Baraka, Ishmael Reed and Samuel R. Delany*, Robert Elliot Fox remarks on Baraka's fiction: "However, the essential energy linking these two works—which recount and reevaluate his life up to that time—is a relentless momentum deeper into blackness. These fugitive narratives describe the harried flight of an intensely self-conscious Afro-American artist/intellectual from neoslavery of blinding, neutralizing whiteness, where the arena of struggle is basically within the mind." In *Tales* Baraka describes the posture and course he wishes to adopt: that of "The straight ahead people, who think when that's what's called for, who don't when they don't have to. Not the Hamlet burden, which is white bullshit, to always be weighing and analyzing, and reflecting." Baraka wants action, and the story "Screamers" casts action in musical terms. For Baraka dance and music are associated with vitality and political action. In this tale blacks riot in the streets because of the wild music of Lynn Hope, a jazz saxophonist: "We screamed at the clear image of ourselves as we should always be. Ecstatic, completed, involved in a secret communal expression. It would be the sweetest revolution, to hucklebuck into the fallen capital, and let the oppressors lindy hop out." In the 1960s Baraka was the pioneer of black experimental fiction, probably the most important since Jean Toomer, who had written during the Harlem Renaissance of the 1920s. In the 1970s and 1980s Baraka was joined by a band of younger experimental black writers, including Ishmael Reed, Clarence Major, Charles Johnson, Ntozake Shange and Xam Wilson Cartier.

During the early 1960s Baraka composed his major social-aesthetic study of black music in America, *Blues People: Negro Music in White America*. A history, it begins in slavery and ends with contemporary avant-garde jazz (John Coltrane, Ornette Coleman, and Cecil Taylor). Baraka argues that since Emancipation the blues have been an essential feature of black American music and that this form was born from the union of the American and the African experience; as Baraka says, "Undoubtedly, none of the African prisoners broke out into 'St. James Infirmary' the minute the first of them was herded off the ship." *Blues People* gave Baraka an opportunity to meditate on a profound and sophisticated art form created by blacks and to do so during a time when he was trying to find a model for his own art that was not white avant-garde. Although he later retracted his evaluation, he had temporarily rejected black literature as mediocre and middle-brow. In his *Home* essay "The Myth of 'Negro Literature,' " he declares: "Only in music, and most notably in blues, jazz, and spirituals, i.e., 'Negro Music,' has there been a significantly profound contribution by American Negroes." In the *New York Times Book Review*, Jason Berry calls Baraka "an eloquent jazz critic: his 1963 study, *Blues People: Negro Music in White America* is a classic." Furthermore, Clyde Taylor maintains in James B. Gwynne's *Amiri Baraka: The Kaleidoscopic Torch*, "The connection he nailed down between the many faces of black music, the sociological sets that nurtured them, and their symbiotic evolutions through socio-economic changes, in *Blues People*, is his most durable conception, as well as probably the one most indispensable thing said about black music."

Although *Blues People* is his only sustained study of Afro-American music, Baraka has published two other collections containing important essays on the subject: *Black Music*, written from a cultural nationalist perspective, and *The Music: Reflections on Jazz and Blues*, written from a Marxist one. In *Black Music* Baraka crystallizes the idea of John Coltrane as the prime model for the new black art: "Trane is a mature swan whose wing span was a whole world. But he also shows us how to murder the popular song. To do away with weak Western forms. He is a beautiful philosopher." Brown asserts: "As an essayist Baraka's performance is decidedly uneven. The writings on music are always an exception. As historian, musicological analyst, or as a journalist covering a particular performance Baraka always commands attention because of his obvious knowledge of the subject and because of a style that is engaging and persuasive even when the sentiments are questionable and controversial." In *The Kaleidoscopic Torch* Joe Weixlmann states: "Baraka's expertise as an interpreter of Afro-American music is, of course, well-known. Had he never done any belletristic writing or political organizing, he would be remembered as the author of *Blues People* . . . and *Black Music*."

The Black Nationalist Period (1965–1974)

In 1965, following the assassination of black Muslim leader Malcolm X, Baraka left Greenwich Village and the bohemian world and moved uptown to Harlem and a new life as a cultural nationalist. He argued in "The Legacy of Malcolm X, and the Coming of the Black Nation" (collected in *Home*) that "black People are a race, a culture, a Nation." Turning his back on the white world, he established the Black Arts Repertory Theater School in Harlem, an influential model that inspired black theaters throughout the country. In 1967, he published his black nationalist collection of poetry, *Black Magic*, which traces his painful exit from the white world and his entry into blackness.

His exorcism of white consciousness and values included a ten-year period of professed hatred of whites, and most especially Jews. His poetry from this time contains provocative phrases, such as the following from a work that he later repudiated as anti-Semitic: "I got the extermination blues, jewboys." In his autobiography, Baraka relates an apocryphal incident from this time, which conveys the uncompromising intensity of his hostility: "A woman asked me in all earnestness, couldn't any whites help? I said, 'You can help by dying. You are a cancer. You can help the world's people with your death.'"

Baraka's autobiography also provides a retrospective explanation for this anti-white hostility: "We hated white people so publicly, for one reason, because we had been so publicly tied up with them before . . . I guess, during this period, I got the reputation for being a snarling, white-hating madman. There was some truth to it, because I was struggling to be born, to break out from the shell I could instinctively sense surround[ing] my own dash for freedom."

This time marked a period of thorough disassociation from liberals, bohemians, and whites in general, due, he has written, to his perception of their inability and their refusal to take the political action he saw as essential. "A POEM SOME PEOPLE WILL HAVE TO UNDERSTAND," (published in the poetry collection *Black Magic* in 1969, and included in this reader) reflects this renunciation, as it places political action and political art in direct opposition to bohemianism and art for art's sake, proclaiming, "We want poems that kill." In the poem's final declaration, Baraka gave words to his feeling of urgency and impatience towards those he perceived of as standing in the way when he asked: "Will the machinegunners please step forward?"

After a year in Harlem, he returned home to his birthplace, Newark, New Jersey, where he continued his cultural nationalist activities. In 1967 he changed his name from LeRoi Jones to the Bantuized Muslim appellation Imamu ("spiritual leader," later dropped) Ameer (later Amiri, "prince") Baraka ("blessed"), as confirmation of his pride in his blackness.

While in Harlem Baraka had become the main theorist of the Black Aesthetic, defined by Houston Baker in *Black American Literature Forum* as "a distinctive code for the creation and evaluation of black art." The aesthetician felt that the black artist must express his American experience in forms that spring from his own unique culture and that his art must be evaluated by standards that grow out of his own culture. Baraka writes in "Expressive Language," an essay in *Home*: "Words' meanings, but also the rhythm and syntax that frame and propel their concatenation, seek their culture as the final reference for what they are describing of the world." In "And Shine Swam On," an essay in *Black Fire: An Anthology of Afro-American Writing*, Larry Neal, the brilliant Black Arts Movement theorist and writer, provides one of the central statements of the Black Aesthetic: "The artist and the political activist are one. They are both shapers of the future reality. Both understand and manipulate the collective

myths of the race. Both are warriors, priests, lovers and destroyers."
In his *Home* essay, "State/meant" Baraka declares fiercely: "The
Black Artist's role in America is to aid in the destruction of America
as he knows it. His role is to report and reflect so precisely the nature
of the society, and of himself in that society, that other men will be
moved by the exactness of his rendering and, if they are black men,
grow strong through this moving, having seen their own strength,
and weakness; and if they are white men, tremble, curse, and go
mad, because they will be drenched with the filth of their evil." In
a less rhetorical fashion, Fox presents the goals of the contemporary
black artist: "The radical inversion of Western systems of belief and
order (that black artists) engage in can be termed 'mytho-clasm,' the
drastic demystification of ideological signs that have been turned
into false universals. . . . Their praxis as artists involves counter-
ing the hegemonic (authoritarian) code inscribed by the master culture with alternatives of discourse and desire (transformational
longings)." Or, as Baraka writes in his essay "The Legacy of Malcolm
X," "The song title 'A White Man's Heaven Is a Black Man's Hell'
describes how complete an image reversal is necessary in the West."

In *Understanding the New Black Poetry: Black Speech and Black
Music as Poetic References*, Stephen Henderson observes, "[Baraka]
is the central figure of the new black poetry awakening"; in an essay
collected in *Modern Black Poets*, Arthur P. Davis calls him "the high
priest of this new Black literary renaissance and one who has done
most to shape its course." Baraka dominated the Black Arts Period
of the late 1960s both as a theorist and artist. He was the main artist-
intellectual responsible for shifting the emphasis of contemporary
black literature from an integrationist art conveying a raceless and
classless vision to a literature rooted in the black experience. The
Black Arts Era, both in terms of creative and theoretical writing, is
the most important one in black literature since the Harlem Renaissance. No post–Black Arts artist thinks of himself or herself as simply being a human being who happens to be black; blackness is central to his or her experience and art. Furthermore, Black Arts had its
impact on other ethnic groups and primarily through the person of
Baraka. The Native American author Maurice Kenny writes of Baraka in *The Kaleidoscopic Torch*: "He opened tightly guarded doors
for not only Blacks but poor whites as well and, of course, Native
Americans, Latinos and Asian-Americans. We'd all still be waiting
the invitation from the *New Yorker* without him. He taught us all
how to claim it and take it." In *The Kaleidoscopic Torch* Clyde
Taylor says of Baraka's poems of the Black Arts period: "There are

enough brilliant poems of such variety in *Black Magic* and *In Our Terribleness* to establish the unique identity and claim for respect of several poets. But it is beside the point that Baraka is probably the finest poet, black or white, writing in this country these days." However, the response to the poetry was not all favorable. In *With Eye and Ear*, the avant-garde critic and poet Kenneth Rexroth contended: "In recent years he [Baraka] has succumbed to the temptation to become a professional Race Man of the most irresponsible sort. . . . His loss to literature is more serious than any literary casualty of the Second War."

In 1966 Baraka published *Home*, an important book of essays, in which the reader sees Baraka becoming "blacker" and more radical in each essay. The collection includes the famous "Cuba Libre," which documents his trip to Cuba and his awakening to Third-World conceptions of art and political activism. A spiritual autobiography written at its author's fullest powers, *Home* assumes the same importance in Baraka's career as *Advertisements for Myself* does in Mailer's. The poet Sterling D. Plumpp observes in *The Kaleidoscopic Torch* that he regards *Home* as a major work "for its forthrightness and daring courage to call for 'revolutionary changes,' [and moreover it] . . . is unsurpassed for its seminal ideas regarding black art which is excellent and people-centered."

Baraka's years in Greenwich Village had made him a master of avant-garde technique that he utilized in his own work and passed on to younger black artists such as Nikki Giovanni and Haki Madhubuti. Ironically, avant-garde ideas of form cohered perfectly with the new black artist's need to express his or her own oral traditions; the free verse and the eccentric typography of the white avant-garde were ideal vehicles for black oral expression and experience. Unlike Harlem Renaissance poets—such as Claude McKay, who constantly battled the rigid, archaic form of the English sonnet replete with nineteenth-century diction and conventions to express 1920s black American language and life—the Black Arts poet had the flexibility of contemporary forms, forms committed to orality and polyrhythms. In a 1971 issue of *Black World* Dudley Randall observes: "The younger poets have a teacher of great talent, and while they think they are rejecting white standards, they are learning from LeRoi Jones, a man versed in German philosophy, conscious of literary traditions . . . who uses the structure of Dante's *Divine Comedy* in his *The System of Dante's Hell* and the punctuation, spelling and line divisions of sophisticated contemporary poets." Arnold Rampersad maintains in *American Book Review*: "Among all the major writers who helped to wean younger black writers away from imitation and compulsive traditionalism and toward modernism, Baraka has been almost certainly the most influential. . . . In speaking of his modernizing influence on younger black poets, one does not mean that Baraka taught them to imitate or even to admire the verse of Pound and Eliot, Stevens and Williams, Ginsberg and Kerouac, all of whose poetry he himself attempted to absorb. More than any other black poet, however, he taught younger black poets of the generation past how to respond poetically to their lived experience, rather than to depend as artists on embalmed reputations and outmoded rhetorical strategies derived from a culture often substantially different from their own."

The Third World Marxist Period (1974–   )

In 1974, dramatically reversing himself, Baraka rejected black nationalism as racist and became a Third World Socialist. He declared, in the New York Times: "It is a narrow nationalism that says the white man is the enemy. . . . Nationalism, so-called, when it says 'all non-blacks are our enemies,' is sickness or criminality, in fact, a form of fascism." Since 1974 he has produced a number of Marxist poetry collections and plays, including Hard Facts, Poetry for the Advanced and What Was the Relationship of the Lone Ranger to the Means of Production? He has also published a book of Marxist essays, Daggers and Javelins. The goal of his socialist art is the destruction of the capitalist state and the creation of a socialist community. Baraka has stated: "I think fundamentally my intentions are similar to those I had when I was a Nationalist. That might seem contradictory, but they were similar in the sense I see art as a weapon, and a weapon of revolution. It's just now that I define revolution in Marxist terms. I once defined revolution in Nationalist terms. But I came to my Marxist view as a result of having struggled as a Nationalist and found certain dead ends theoretically and ideologically, as far as Nationalism was concerned and had to reach out for a communist ideology." His socialist art is addressed to the black community, which has, he believes, the greatest revolutionary potential in America.

Baraka's socialist works have not fared well in the establishment press. In the New York Times Book Review Darryl Pinckney comments that Baraka has "sacrificed artistic vitality on the altar of his political faith. . . . his early work is far better than his recent efforts: he now seems content to express his Marxism in the most reductive, shrill propaganda." Fox, in his 1987 study, says, "The Marxist work is intellectually determined, whereas the cultural-nationalist pieces are emotionally felt." On the other hand, E. San Juan, an exiled Filipino leftist intellectual, writes in *The Kaleidoscopic Torch* that he finds the *Lone Ranger* "the most significant theatrical achievement of 1978 in the Western hemisphere." Weixlmann sensitively responds in *The Kaleidoscopic Torch* to the tendency to categorize the radical Baraka instead of analyze him: "At the very least, dismissing someone with a label does not make for a very satisfactory scholarship. Initially, Baraka's reputation as a writer and thinker derived from a recognition of the talents with which he is so obviously endowed. The assaults on that reputation have, too frequently, derived from concerns which should be extrinsic to informed criticism."

As the critical climate cools, critics will find merit in the recent poetry, especially the long "In the Tradition (for Black Arthur Blythe)" and the ongoing epic about African-American history, "Why's/Wise," both accomplished works. (In these pages the reader will find "In the Tradition" in its totality and *Wise* generously excerpted.) Also with the 1984 publication of *The Autobiography* Baraka has joined the great tradition of the black autobiography, which runs from Frederick Douglass to W. E. B. Du Bois to Richard Wright to Malcolm X. Like other authors in this tradition, in the act of making sense of his life, Baraka makes sense of American culture. Arnold Rampersad comments on Baraka and his *Autobiography* in *The Kaleidoscopic Torch*: "His change of heart and head is testimony to his honesty, energy, and relentless search for meaning, as demonstrated recently once again with the publication of his brilliant *The Autobiography of LeRoi Jones*."

In a piece on Miles Davis in *The Music: Reflections on Jazz and Blues*, Baraka quotes the contemporary trombonist, Craig Harris: "Miles is gonna do what Miles wants to do. And everbody else can follow if they feel like it." Like Davis, Baraka is going his own way; he is an original, and others can follow if they like. He is a black writer who has taken the techniques and notions of the white avant-garde and made them his own; like the great bop musicians before him, he has united avant-garde art with the black voice, creating a singular expressive mode. Baraka has created a major body of art, not by trying to blend into the Western tradition, but by trying to be true to himself and to his culture. He speaks out of a web of personal and communal experience, minimizing the so-called universal features he shared with the white world and focusing instead on the black cultural difference—what has made the black experience unique in the West. From this experience Baraka fashions his art, his style, and his distinctive vision of the world.

WILLIAM J. HARRIS

Chronology

1934   EVERETT LEROY JONES is born in Newark, New Jersey, October 7, to Coyette ("Coyt") LeRoy Jones, a future postal supervisor, and Anna Lois Jones, a future social worker.

1951   graduates with honors from Barringer High School in Newark; attends Rutgers University (Newark) on scholarship.

1952   begins spelling his first name in frenchified form, LeRoi; transfers to Howard University, "the capstone of Negro education," in Washington, D.C.

1954   flunks out of Howard; serves in the United States Air Force, eventually attaining rank of sergeant.

1957   is discharged "undesirably" from the service; settles in New York's Greenwich Village and is influenced by the post–World War II avant-garde, most notably Allen Ginsberg, Frank O'Hara, and Charles Olson.

1958   marries Hettie Cohen and they co-edit the avant-garde literary journal *Yugen* (1958–63).

1960   visits Castro's Cuba, which initiates him into thinking of art as political.

1961   publishes *Preface to a Twenty Volume Suicide Note*; co-edits *Floating Bear* (1961–63) with Diane di Prima.

1963   publishes *Blues People: Negro Music in White America*; wins a Whitney Fellowship. John F. Kennedy and Medgar Evers are assassinated; four young black girls are murdered in a bombing of a church in Birmingham, Alabama.

1964   sees his play *Dutchman* produced and wins an Obie; *The Dead Lecturer*, a collection of poetry, appears; civil rights activists James Chaney, Andrew Goodman, and Michael Schwerner are killed in Mississippi.

1965   leaves Greenwich Village and Hettie Cohen in the wake of the assassination of Malcolm X; moves uptown to Harlem, declaring himself a black cultural nationalist, that is, one who is committed to black people as "a race, a culture, a nation"; organizes and directs the Black Arts Repertory Theater-School; wins a Guggenheim Fellowship; publishes *The System of Dante's Hell*, his only novel; returns "home," to Newark, New Jersey.

1966   marries Sylvia Robinson, now known as Amina Baraka; publishes *Home: Social Essays*.

1967   assumes the Bantuized Muslim name Imamu ("spiritual leader," later dropped) Ameer (later Amiri, "Prince") Baraka ("blessed"); teaches at San Francisco State University and associates with Ron Karenga, the founder of the cultural nationalist organization, US; is injured while being arrested on charges of unlawfully carrying weapons and resisting arrest during the Newark riots; is convicted of a misdemeanor, sentenced to a three-year jail term, conviction is reversed on appeal; publishes his only collection of short stories, *Tales*.

1968   publishes *Black Music*; co-edits *Black Fire*, a seminal anthology of African-American literature, with Larry Neal.

1969   *Black Magic*, his first volume of black culturalist poetry, appears.

1970   assists black candidate Kenneth Gibson in his mayoralty campaign in Newark; major organizer and participant in the "Pan-African" Congress of African Peoples in Atlanta.

1972   major organizer of and participant in the National Black Political Convention in Gary, Indiana.

1974   categorically rejects black nationalism; proclaims his conversion to international socialism ("Marxism–Leninism–Mao Tse-tung Thought") — Third World Marxism — in "Toward Ideological Clarity," published in *Black World*.

1975   publishes his first Marxist poetry collection, *Hard Facts*.

1979   begins teaching in the Africana Studies Department at SUNY, Stony Brook; is arrested in Greenwich Village after two policemen intercede in a dispute between him and his wife; sentenced to 48 consecutive weekends in a Harlem halfway house where he writes *The Autobiography of LeRoi Jones/Amiri Baraka*.

1981   wins Rockefeller Foundation Fellowship and National Endowment for the Arts Fellowship.

1982   edits the magazine *The Black Nation*(1982–86).

1984   becomes full professor and publishes *Autobiography*.

1987   along with Toni Morrison and Maya Angelou eulogizes James Baldwin during a funeral service at the Cathedral of St. John the Divine in New York; *The Music: Reflections on Jazz and Blues* appears.

1988   attends the Democratic National Convention in Atlanta as a reporter for *Essence* magazine.

1989   wins the American Book Awards' Lifetime Achievement Award and the Langston Hughes Award, given by the City College of New York.

1990   becomes involved in curricular reform of the Newark public schools; begins to co-write the autobiography of Quincy Jones; *The Life and Life of Bumpy Johnson*, a musical drama in collaboration with Max Roach, is staged.

THE BEAT PERIOD (1957–1962)

I had the *New York Times* under my arm. I was in civilian clothes and I remember I was reading *The New Yorker*. I'd stopped at a bench and sat down near a square. It was quiet and I could see a long way off toward the newer, more Americanized part of the city, the Condado Beach section, where I could only go if in uniform, so they would know I was an Americano and not a native. I had been reading one of the carefully put together exercises *The New Yorker* publishes constantly as high poetic art, and gradually I could feel my eyes fill up with tears, and my cheeks were wet and I was crying, quietly softly but like it was the end of the world. I had been moved by the writer's words, but in another, very personal way. A way that should have taught me even more than it did. Perhaps it would have saved me many more painful scenes and conflicts. But I was crying because I realized that I could never write like that writer. Not that I had any real desire to, but I knew even if I had had the desire I could not do it. I realized that there was something in me so *out*, so unconnected with what this writer was and what that magazine was that what was in me that wanted to come out as poetry would never come out like that and be *my* poetry. . . .

— From *The Autobiography of LeRoi Jones/Amiri Baraka*

∎∎∎∎∎∎∎∎∎

Preface to a Twenty Volume Suicide Note

(for Kellie Jones, born 16 May 1959)

Lately, I've become accustomed to the way
The ground opens up and envelopes me
Each time I go out to walk the dog.
Or the broad edged silly music the wind
Makes when I run for a bus . . .

Things have come to that.

And now, each night I count the stars,
And each night I get the same number.
And when they will not come to be counted,
I count the holes they leave.

Nobody sings anymore.

And then last night, I tiptoed up
To my daughter's room and heard her
Talking to someone, and when I opened
The door, there was no one there . . .
Only she on her knees, peeking into

Her own clasped hands.

Hymn for Lanie Poo

Vous êtes de faux Négres

—RIMBAUD

O,
these wild trees
will make charming wicker baskets,
the young woman
the young black woman
the young black beautiful woman
said

These wild-assed trees
will make charming
wicker baskets.

(now, I'm putting words in her mouth . . . tch)

1

All afternoon
we watched the cranes
humping each other
dropped
our shadows
onto the beach
and covered them over with sand.

Beware the evil sun . . .
turn you black

turn your hair

crawl your eyeballs

rot your teeth.

All afternoon
we sit around
near the edge of the city

                    hacking open
                    crocodile skulls
                    sharpening our teeth.

The god I pray to
got black boobies
got steatopygia

make faces in the moon
make me a greenpurple &
maroon winding sheet.
                        I wobble to
                        the edge of the water

give my horny yell
& 24 elephants
stomp out of the subway
with consecrated hardons.

(watch out for that evil sun
turn you black)
                    My fireface

my orange
and fireface
squat by the flames.
She had her coming out party
with 3000 guests
from all parts of the country.
Queens, Richmond, Togoland, The Cameroons;
A white hunter, very unkempt,
with long hair,
whizzed in on the end of a vine.
(spoke perfect english too.)

"Throw on another goddamned Phoenecian,"
I yelled, really getting with it.

John Coltrane arrived with an Egyptian lady.
he played very well.

"Throw on another goddamned Phoenecian."

We got so drunk (Hulan Jack
brought his bottle of Thunderbird),
nobody went hunting
the next morning.

2

o,
don't be shy honey.
we all know
these wicker baskets
would make wild-assed trees.

Monday, I spent most of the day hunting.
Knocked off about six, gulped down a couple of monkey foreskins, then took in a
flick. Got to bed early.

Tuesday, same thing all day. (Caught a
mangy lioness with one tit.) Ate.
Watched television for awhile. Read the
paper, then hit the sack.

Wednesday, took the day off.
Took the wife and kids to the games.
Read Garmanda's book, "14 Tribes of
Ambiguity," didn't like it.

Thursday, we caught a goddamn ape.
Must've weighed about 600 pounds.
We'll probably eat ape meat for the
rest of the month. Christ, I hate
ape meat.

Friday, I stayed home with a supposed
cold. Goofed the whole day trying to
rethatch the roof. Had run in with
the landlord.

We spent the weekend at home.
I tried to get some sculpting done,

but nothing came of it. It's impossible to be an artist and a bread
winner at the same time.
Sometimes I think I oughta chuck
the whole business.

3

The firemasons parade.

(The sun is using this country
as a commode.

Beware the sun, my love.)

The firemasons are very square.
They are supposed to be a civic
and fraternal organization, but
all they do is have parades and
stay high. They also wear funny
looking black hats, which are
round and have brims. The firemasons are cornballs.

4

Each morning
I go down
to Gansevoort St.
and stand on the docks.
I stare out
at the horizon
until it gets up
and comes to embrace
me. I
make believe
it is my father.
This is known
as genealogy.

5

We came into the
silly little church
shaking our wet raincoats
on the floor.
It wasn't water,
that made the raincoats
wet.

> The preacher's
> conning eyes
> fired when he saw
> the way I walked to-
> wards him; almost
> throwing my hips out
> of whack.
> He screamed,

He's wet with the blood of the lamb!!

And everybody
got real happy.

6

(die schwartze Bohemien)

They laught,

and religion was something

he fount in coffee shops, by God.

It's not that I got enything

against cotton, nosiree, by God

It's just that . . .

> Man lookatthatblonde
>
> > whewee!

I think they are not treating us like

Mr. Lincun said they should

                or Mr. Gandhi

For that matter. By God.

          ZEN

is a bitch! Like "Bird" was,

              Cafe Olay

for me, Miss.

           But white cats can't swing . . .

Or the way this guy kept patronizing me—

like he was Bach or somebody

             Oh, I knew

John Kasper when he hung around with shades . . .

             She's a painter, Man.

It's just that it's such a drag to go

Way uptown for Bar B Cue,

            By God . . .

How much?

        7

About my sister.

        (O, generation revered
        above all others.
        O, generation of fictitious
        Ofays
            I revere you . . .
            You are all so beautiful)

my sister drives a green jaguar
my sister has her hair done twice a month

my sister is a school teacher
my sister took ballet lessons
my sister has a fine figure: never diets
my sister doesn't like to teach in Newark
   because there are too many colored
   in her classes
my sister hates loud shades
my sister's boy friend is a faggot music teacher
   who digs Tschaikovsky
my sister digs Tschaikovsky also
it is because of this similarity of interests
that they will probably get married.

> Smiling & glad/in
> the huge & loveless
> white-anglo sun/of
> benevolent step
> mother America.

In Memory of Radio

Who has ever stopped to think of the divinity of Lamont Cranston?
(Only Jack Kerouac, that I know of: & me.
The rest of you probably had on WCBS and Kate Smith,
Or something equally unattractive.)

What can I say?
It is better to have loved and lost
Than to put linoleum in your living rooms?

Am I a sage or something?
Mandrake's hypnotic gesture of the week?
(Remember, I do not have the healing powers of Oral Roberts . . .
I cannot, like F. J. Sheen, tell you how to get saved & rich!
I cannot even order you to gaschamber satori like Hitler or
   Goody Knight

& Love is an evil word.
Turn it backwards/see, see what I mean?
An evol word. & besides

who understands it?
I certainly wouldn't like to go out on that kind of limb.

radio shows

Saturday mornings we listened to *Red Lantern* & his undersea folk.
At 11, *Let's Pretend*/& we did/& I, the poet, still do, Thank God!

What was it he used to say (after the transformation, when he
      was safe
& invisible & the unbelievers couldn't throw stones?) "Heh,
      heh, heh,
Who knows what evil lurks in the hearts of men? The Shadow
      knows."

intro to the show

O, yes he does
O, yes he does.
An evil word it is,
This Love.

nostalgia for a time when evil/badness only existed in radio shows

Look for You Yesterday, Here You Come Today

Part of my charm:
                    envious blues feeling
                    separation of church & state
                    grim calls from drunk debutantes

Morning never aids me in my quest.
I have to trim my beard in solitude.
I try to hum lines from "The Poet In New York".

People saw metal all around the house on Saturdays. The Phone
                                                rings.

terrible poems come in the mail. Descriptions of celibate parties
                              torn trousers: Great Poets dying
                              with their strophes on. & me
                              incapable of a simple straight-
                              forward anger.

It's so diffuse
being alive. Suddenly one is aware
        that nobody really gives a damn.
        My wife is pregnant with her child.
        "It means nothing to me", sez Strindberg

An avalanche of words
could cheer me up. Words from Great Sages.
        Was James Karolis a great sage??
        Why did I let Ora Matthews beat him up
        in the bathroom? Haven't I learned my
        lesson.

I would take up painting
if I cd think of a way to do it
better than Leonardo. Than Bosch.
Than Hogarth. Than Kline.

Frank walked off the stage, singing
"My silence is as important as Jack's incessant yatter."

I am a mean hungry sorehead.
Do I have the capacity for grace??

To arise one smoking spring
& find one's youth has taken off
for greener parts.

A sudden blankness in the day
as if there were no afternoon.
& all my piddling joys retreated
to their own dopey mythic worlds.

The hours of the atmosphere
grind their teeth like hags

                (When will world war two be over?)

I stood up on a mailbox
waving my yellow tee-shirt
watching the grey tanks
stream up Central Ave.

All these thots
are Flowers Of Evil
cold & lifeless
as subway rails

the sun like a huge cobblestone
flaking its brown slow rays
primititi

once, twice,. My life
seems over & done with.
Each morning I rise
like a sleep walker
& rot a little more.

All the lovely things I've known have disappeared.
I have all my pubic hair & am lonely.
There is probably no such place as BattleCreek, Michigan!

Tom Mix dead in a Boston Nightclub
before I realized what happened.

People laugh when I tell them about Dickie Dare!

What is one to do in an alien planet
where the people breath New Ports?
Where is my space helmet, I sent for it
3 lives ago . . . when there were box tops.

What has happened to box tops??

O, God . . . I must have a belt that glows green
in the dark. Where is my Captain Midnight decoder??
I can't understand what Superman is saying!

THERE MUST BE A LONE RANGER!!!

*   *   *   *

but this also
is part of my charm.
A maudlin nostalgia

that comes on
like terrible thoughts about death.

How dumb to be sentimental about anything
To call it love
& cry pathetically
into the long black handkerchief
of the years.

> "Look for you yesterday
> Here you come today
> Your mouth wide open
> But what you got to say?"

> —part of my charm

> old envious   blues feeling
> ticking like   a big cobblestone
>   clock.

I hear the reel running out . . .
the spectators are impatient for popcorn:
It was only a selected short subject

F. Scott Charon
will soon be glad-handing me
like a legionaire

My silver bullets all gone
My black mask trampled in the dust

& Tonto way off in the hills
moaning like Bessie Smith.

Notes for a Speech

> African blues
> does not know me. Their steps, in sands
> of their own

land. A country
in black & white, newspapers
blown down pavements
of the world. Does
not feel
what I am.
              Strength
in the dream, an oblique
suckling of nerve, the wind
throws up sand, eyes
are something locked in
hate, of hate, of hate, to
walk abroad, they conduct
their deaths apart
from my own. Those
heads, I call
my "people."
                (And who are they. People. To
                concern
myself, ugly man. Who
you, to concern
the white flat stomachs
of maidens, inside houses
dying. Black. Peeled moon
light on my fingers
move under
her clothes. Where
is her husband. Black
words throw up sand
to eyes, fingers of
their private dead. Whose
soul, eyes, in sand. My color
is not theirs. Lighter, white man
talk. They shy away. My own
dead souls, my, so called
people. Africa
is a foreign place. You are
as any other sad man here
american.

From *New American Poetry*

How You Sound??

"HOW YOU SOUND??" is what we recent fellows are up to. How *we* sound; our peculiar grasp on, say: a. Melican speech, b. Poetries of the world, c. Our selves (which is attitudes, logics, theories, jumbles of our lives, & all that), d. And the final . . . The Totality Of Mind: Spiritual . . . God?? (or you name it) : Social (zeitgeist) : or Heideggerian *umwelt*.

MY POETRY is whatever I think I am. (Can I be light and weightless as a sail?? Heavy & clunking like 8 black boots.) I CAN BE ANYTHING I CAN. I make a poetry with what I feel is useful & can be saved out of all the garbage of our lives. What I see, am touched by (CAN HEAR) . . . wives, gardens, jobs, cement yards where cats pee, all my interminable artifacts . . . ALL are a poetry, & nothing moves (with any grace) pried apart from these things. There cannot be closet poetry. Unless the closet be wide as God's eye.

And all that means that I *must* be completely free to do just what I want, in the poem. "All is permitted": Ivan's crucial concept. There cannot be anything I must *fit* the poem into. Everything must be made to fit into the poem. There must not be any preconceived notion or *design* for what the poem *ought* to be. "Who knows what a poem ought to sound like? Until it's thar." Says Charles Olson . . . & I follow closely with that. I'm not interested in writing sonnets, sestinas or anything . . . only poems. If the poem has got to be a sonnet (unlikely tho) or whatever, it'll certainly let me know. The only "recognizable tradition" a poet need follow is himself . . . & with that, say, all those things out of tradition he can use, adapt, work over, into something for himself. To broaden his *own* voice with. (You have to start and finish there . . . your own voice . . . how you sound.)

For me, Lorca, Williams, Pound and Charles Olson have had the greatest influence. Eliot, earlier (rhetoric can be so lovely, for a time . . . but only remains so for the rhetorician.) And there are so many young wizards around now doing great things that everybody calling himself poet can learn from . . . Whalen, Snyder, McClure, O'Hara, Loewinsohn, Wieners, Creeley, Ginsberg &c. &c. &c.

Also, all this means that we want to go into a quantitative verse . . . the "irregular foot" of Williams . . . the "Projective Verse" of Olson. Accentual verse, the regular metric of rumbling iambics, is dry as slivers of sand. Nothing happens in that frame anymore. We can get nothing from England. And the diluted formalism of the academy (the formal culture of the U.S.) is anaemic & fraught with incompetence & unreality.

1959

THE TRANSITIONAL PERIOD (1963–1965)

So as I wrote that article, "LeRoi Jones Speaking," there came over me this most terrific sense of purpose and focus. It rose up within me like my grandfather's ghost. Yeh, I was some colored bohemian liberal living on the Lower East Side in hedonism heaven, yet I could not sound like that. What the "fame" *Dutchman* brought me and raised up in me was this absolutely authentic and heartfelt desire to speak what should be spoken for all of us. I knew the bullshit of my own life, its twists and flip-outs, yet I felt, now, some heavy *responsibility*. If these bastards were going to raise me up, for any reason, then they would pay for it! I would pay these motherfuckers back in kind, because even if I wasn't strong enough to *act*, I would become strong enough to SPEAK what had to be said, for all of us, for black people, yes, particularly for black people, because they were the root and origin of my conviction, but for anyone anywhere who wanted Justice!

The article was really, then, a commitment to struggle. I said, "Let them know this is a fight without quarter, and I am very fast." Brash, arrogant, sophomoric, but it was smoke from a moving vehicle! There now began in my downtown environs and elsewhere a dervish of forums, speakouts, intellectual shootouts, not just in reflection of my own mind's motion but as reflection of what the whole society had become and was still to become.

—From *The Autobiography of LeRoi Jones/Amiri Baraka*

Blues People is Baraka's most comprehensive study of black music. He locates the music in its social and historical context, tracing it from slave times to the avant-garde scene of the early 1960s. Baraka has asserted that close examination of black music will reveal "the essential nature of the Negro in this country . . . as well as something about the essential nature of this country." Baraka is highly regarded as a music critic. As Joe Weixlmann has observed: "Had he never done any belletristic writing or political organizing, he would be remembered as the author of *Blues People . . .* and *Black Music*."

—wjh

African Slaves/American Slaves: Their Music

It is a comparatively short period of history that passes between the time, when Richard Francis Burton could say of African music that "it is monotonous to a degree, yet they delight in it," or when H. E. Krehbiel could ask (1914), "Why savages who have never developed a musical or other art should be supposed to have more refined aesthetic sensibilities than the peoples who have cultivated music for centuries, passes my poor powers of understanding . . ."[1] until the time (1920) when a great mass of white Americans are dancing a West African (Ashanti) ancester dance they know as the "Charleston."

Jazz is commonly thought to have begun around the turn of the century, but the musics jazz derived from are much older. Blues is the parent of all legitimate jazz, and it is impossible to say exactly how old blues is—certainly no older than the presence of Negroes in the United States. It is a native American music, the product of the black man in this country; or to put it more exactly the way I have come to think about it, blues could not exist if the African captives had not become American captives.

The immediate predecessors of blues were the Afro-American/ American Negro work songs, which had their musical origins in West Africa. The religious music of the Negro also originates from

21

the same African music. However, while the general historical developments of Negro secular and religious music can be said to be roughly parallel, i.e., they follow the same general trends in their development, and in later forms are the result of the same kind of accultural processes, a Negro religious music contingent on Christianity developed later than the secular forms. An Afro-American work song could come about more quickly in slavery than any other type of song because even if the individual who sang it was no longer working for himself, most of the physical impetuses that suggested that particular type of singing were still present. However, Africans were not Christians, so their religious music and the music with which they celebrated the various cultic or ritualistic rites had to undergo a distinct and complete transfer of reference.

For the African in the United States there was little opportunity for religious syncretism (the identification of one set of religious dogma or ritual with analogous dogma or ritual in a completely alien religion). In the essentially Catholic New World cultures, the multitudes of saints were easily substituted for the many *loa* or deities in the various West African religions. But in Protestant America this was not possible.

So the music which formed the *link* between pure African music and the music which developed after the African slave in the United States had had a chance to become exposed to some degree of Euro-American culture was that which contained the greatest number of Africanisms and yet was foreign to Africa. And this was the music of the second generation of slaves, their work songs. The African slave had sung African chants and litanies in those American fields. His sons and daughters, and their children, began to use America as a reference.

As late as the nineteenth century, pure African songs could be heard and pure African dances seen in the Southern United States. Congo Square, in New Orleans, would nightly rock to the "master drums" of new African arrivals. In places like Haiti or Guiana, these drums still do remind the West that the black man came from Africa, not Howard University. But in the United States pure African sources grew scarce in a relatively short time after the great slave importations of the eighteenth century.

The work song took on its own peculiar qualities in America for a number of reasons. First, although singing to accompany one's labor was quite common in West Africa, it is obvious that working one's own field in one's own land is quite different from forced labor in a foreign land. And while the physical insistence necessary to suggest a work song was still present, the references accompanying the work changed radically. Most West Africans were farmers and, I am certain, these agricultural farm songs could have been used in the fields of the New World in the same manner as the Old. But the lyrics of a song that said, "After the planting, if the gods bring rain / My family, my ancestors, be rich as they are beautiful," could not apply in the dreadful circumstance of slavery. Secondly, references to the gods or religions of Africa were suppressed by the white masters as soon as they realized what these were — not only because they naturally thought of any African religious customs as "barbarous" but because the whites soon learned that too constant evocation of the African gods could mean that those particular Africans were planning on leaving that plantation as soon as they could! The use of African drums was soon prevented too, as the white man learned that drums could be used to incite revolt as well as to accompany dancers.

So the work song, as it began to take shape in America, first had to be stripped of any purely African ritual and some cultural reference found for it in the New World. But this was difficult to do within the African-language songs themselves. The diverse labors of the African, which were the sources of this kind of song, had been funneled quite suddenly into one labor, the cultivation of the white man's fields. The fishing songs, the weaving songs, the hunting songs, all had lost their pertinence. But these changes were not immediate. They became the realized circumstances of a man's life after he had been exposed sufficiently to their source and catalyst — his enslavement.

And this is the basic difference between the first slaves and their offspring. The African slave continued to chant his native chants, sing his native songs, at work, even though the singing of them might be forbidden or completely out of context. But being forbidden, the songs were after a time changed into other forms that weren't forbidden in contexts that were contemporary. The African slave might have realized he was losing something, that his customs and the memory of his land were being each day drained from his life. Still there was a certain amount of forbearance. No one can simply decree that a man change the way he thinks. But the first black Americans had no native cultural references other than the slave culture. A work song about fishing when one has never fished seems meaningless, especially when one works each day in a cotton field. The context of the Africans' life had changed, but the American-born slaves never knew what the change had been.

It is impossible to find out exactly how long the slaves were in America before the African work song actually did begin to have extra-African references. First, of course, there were mere additions of the foreign words—French, Spanish or English, for the most part, after the British colonists gained power in the United States. Krehbiel lists a Creole song transcribed by Lafcadio Hearn, which contains both French (or patois) and African words (the italicized words are African):

Ouendé, ouendé, macaya!
Mo pas barrasse, macaya!
Ouendé, ouendé, macaya!
Mo bois bon divin, macaya!
Ouendé, ouendé, macaya!
Mo mange bon poulet, macaya!
Ouendé, ouendé, macaya!
Mo pas barrasse macaya!
Ouendé, ouendé, macaya!
Macaya!

Hearn's translation was:

Go on! go on! eat enormously!
I ain't one bit ashamed—eat outrageously!
Go on! go on! eat prodigiously!
I drink good wine!—eat ferociously!
Go on! go on! eat unceasingly!
I eat good chicken—gorging myself!
Go on! go on! etc.

It is interesting to note, and perhaps more than coincidence, that the portions of the song emphasizing excess are in African, which most of the white men could not understand, and the portions of the song elaborating some kind of genteel, if fanciful, existence are in the tongue of the masters. But there was to come a time when there was no black man who understood the African either, and those allusions to excess, or whatever the black man wished to keep to himself, were either in the master's tongue or meaningless, albeit rhythmical, sounds to the slave also.

Aside from the actual transfer or survival of African words in the songs and speech of the early slaves, there was also some kind of syntactical as well as rhythmical transfer since Africans and their descendants tended to speak their new languages in the same manner as they spoke their West African dialects. What is called now a "Southern accent" or "Negro speech" was once simply the accent of a foreigner trying to speak a new and unfamiliar language, although it was characteristic of the white masters to attribute the slave's "inability" to speak perfect English to the same kind of "childishness" that was used to explain the African's belief in the supernatural. The owners,when they bothered to listen, were impressed that even the songs of their native American slaves were "incomprehensible" or "unintelligible." However, as Herskovits says of early Afro-American speech:

". . . since grammar and idiom are the last aspects of a new language to be learned, the Negroes who reached the New World acquired as much of the vocabulary of their masters as they initially needed or was later taught to them, pronounced these words as best they were able, but organized them into aboriginal speech patterns. Thus arose the various forms of Negro-English, Negro-French, Negro-Spanish and Negro-Portuguese spoken in the New World, their "peculiarities" due to the fact that they comprise European words cast into an African grammatical mold. But this emphatically does not imply that those dialects are without grammar, or that they represent an inability to master the foreign tongue, as is so often claimed."[2]

A few of the "unintelligible" songs are not as unintelligible as their would-be interpreters would have it. For instance, Mr. Krehbiel lists as "unintelligible" two "corn songs"—songs sung while working the corn fields. Only a fragment of one song remains, the words "Shock along, John." It seems to me incredible that Krehbiel could not see that *shock* is the word *shuck*, meaning to strip the corn of its outer covering, which is what the slaves did.

> Five can't ketch me and ten can't hold me—
> Ho, round the corn, Sally!
> Here's your iggle-quarter and here's your count-aquils—
> Ho, round the corn, Sally!
> I can bank, 'ginny bank, 'ginny bank the weaver—
> Ho, round the corn, Sally!

All of the above seems obvious to me except the third and fifth lines. But *iggle* is, of course, *eagle*, and an eagle quarter was American money. It would also seem that *count* in the phrase "your count-aquils" is either a reference to that money or the count of merchandise being harvested—in this instance, the corn. *Aquil* could be either an appropriation of the Spanish *aquí*, meaning *here*, or more likely an appropriation of the French word *kilo*, which is a term of measure.

Another less "obscure" song of probably an earlier period:

Arter you lub, you lub you know, boss. You can't broke lub. Man can't broke lub. Lub stan'—he ain't gwine broke—Man heb to be very smart for broke lub. Lub is a ting stan' just like tar, arter he stick, he stick, he ain't gwine move. He can't move less dan you burn him. Hab to kill all two arter he lub fo' you broke lub.[3]

Though the above should be considered an American song, it still retains so much of the African that it might be difficult for some people to understand. Yet I think the references quite American. But now, however, by *African*, I do not mean actual surviving African words, but rather the African accent and the syntactical construction of certain West African dialects. It is relatively easy to see the connection in the syntax of this song and the literal translation into English of African phrases. For example, the literal English rendering of an Ashanti (Twi dialect) phrase meaning "to calm a person" is "cool he heart give him." (And here, I think, even the word *cool* should bear further consideration.)

African speech, African customs, and African music all changed by the American experience into a native American form. But what was a pure African music? Were there similarities between African and European music before the importation of the slaves? What strictly musical changes occurred to transform African music into American? How did this come about?

The role of African music in the formulation of Afro-American music was misunderstood for a great many years. And the most obvious misunderstanding was one that perhaps only a Westerner would make, that African music ". . . although based on the same principles of European music, suffers from the African's lack of European technical skill in the fashioning of his crude instruments. Thus the strangeness and out-of-tune quality of a great many of the played notes." Musicologists of the eighteenth and nineteenth centuries, and even some from the twentieth, would speak of the "aberration" of the diatonic scale in African music. Or a man like Krehbiel could say: "There is a significance which I cannot fathom in the circumstance that the tones which seem *rebellious* [my italics] to the negro's sense of intervallic propriety are the fourth and seventh of the diatonic major series and the fourth, sixth and seventh of the minor." [4] Why did it not occur to him that perhaps the Africans were using not a diatonic scale, but an African scale, a scale that would seem ludicrous when analyzed by the normal methods of Western musicology? Even Ernest Borneman says: "It seems likely now that the common source of European and West African music was a simple non-hemitonic pentatone system. Although indigenous variants of the diatonic scale have been developed and preserved in Africa, modern West Africans who are not familiar with European music will tend to become uncertain when asked to sing in a tempered scale. This becomes particularly obvious when the third and seventh steps of a diatonic scale are approached. The singer almost invariably tries to skid around these steps with slides, slurs or vibrato effects so broad as to approach scalar value."[5]

These sliding and slurring effects in Afro-American music, the basic "aberrant" quality of a blues scale, are, of course, called "blueing" the notes. But why not of "scalar value?" It is my idea that this is a different scale.

Sidney Finkelstein, in *Jazz: A People's Music*: ". . . these deviations from the pitch familiar to concert music are not, of course, the result of an inability to sing or play in tune. They mean that the blues are a non-diatonic music. . . . Many books on jazz . . . generally describe the blues as a sequence of chords, such as the tonic, subdominant and dominant seventh. Such a definition, however, is like putting the cart before the horse. There are definite patterns of chords which have been evolved to support the blues, but these do not define the blues, and the blues can exist as a melody perfectly recognizable as the blues without them. Neither are the blues simply a use of the major scale with the 'third' and 'seventh' slightly blued or flattened. The fact is that both this explanation, and the chord explanation, are attempts to explain one musical system in terms of another; to describe a non-diatonic music in diatonic terms."[6]

The most apparent survivals of African music in Afro-American music are its rhythms: not only the seeming emphasis in the African music on rhythmic, rather than melodic or harmonic, qualities, but also the use of polyphonic, or contrapuntal, rhythmic effects. Because of this seeming neglect of harmony and melody, Westerners thought the music "primitive." It did not occur to them that Africans might have looked askance at a music as vapid rhythmically as the West's.

The reason for the remarkable development of the rhythmic qualities of African music can certainly be traced to the fact that Africans also used drums for communication; and not, as was once thought, merely by using the drums in a kind of primitive Morse code, but by the phonetic reproduction of the words themselves—the result being that Africans developed an extremely fine and extremely complex rhythmic sense, as well as becoming unusually responsive to timbral subtleties. Also, the elaborately developed harmonic system used in the playing of percussion instruments, i.e., the use of drums or other percussion instruments of different timbres to produce harmonic contrasts, was not immediately recognizable to the Western ear; neither was the use of two and three separate rhythmic patterns to underscore the same melody a concept easily recognizable to Westerners used to less subtle musical devices.

Melodic diversity in African music came not only in the actual arrangments of notes (in terms of Western transcription) but in the singer's vocal interpretation. The "tense, slightly hoarse-sounding vocal techniques" of the work songs and the blues stem directly from West African musical tradition. (This kind of singing voice is also common to much other non-Western music.) In African languages the meaning of a word can be changed simply by altering the pitch of the word, or changing its stress—basically, the way one can change the word yeh from simple response to stern challenge simply by moving the tongue slightly. Philologists call this "significant tone," the "combination of pitch and timbre" used to produce changes of meaning in words. This was basic to the speech and music of West Africans, and was definitely passed on to the Negroes of the New World.

Another important aspect of African music found very readily in the American Negro's music is the antiphonal singing technique. A leader sings a theme and a chorus answers him. These answers are usually comments on the leader's theme or comments on the answers themselves in improvised verses. The amount of improvisation depends on how long the chorus wishes to continue. And improvisation, another major facet of African music, is certainly one of the strongest survivals in American Negro music. The very character of the first work songs suggests that they were largely improvised. And, of course, the very structure of jazz is the melodic statement with an arbitrary number of improvised answers or comments on the initial theme.

Just as some of the African customs survived in America in their totality, although usually given just a thin veneer of Euro-American camouflage, so pure African songs, dances, and instruments showed up on this side of the water. However, I consider this less significant because it seems to me much more important, if we speak of music, that features such as basic rhythmic, harmonic, and melodic devices were transplanted almost intact rather than isolated songs, dances, or instruments.

The very nature of slavery in America dictated the way in which African culture could be adapted. Thus, a Dahomey river god ceremony had no chance of survival in this country at all unless it was incorporated into an analogous rite that was present in the new culture — which is what happened. The Christians of the New World called it baptism. Just as the African songs of recrimination survive as a highly competitive game called "the dozens." (As any young Harlemite can tell you, if someone says to you, "Your father's a woman," you must say, as a minimal comeback, "Your mother likes it," or a similar putdown.) And in music: where the use of the African drum was strictly forbidden, other percussive devices had to be found, like the empty oil drums that led to the development of the West Indian steel bands. Or the metal wash basin turned upside down and floated in another basin that sounds, when beaten, like an African hollow-log drum. The Negro's way in this part of the Western world was adaptation and reinterpretation. The banjo (an African word) is an African instrument, and the xylophone, used now in all Western concert orchestras, was also brought over by the Africans. But the survival of the system of African music is much more significant than the existence of a few isolated and finally superfluous features. The notable fact is that the only so-called popular music in this country of any real value is of African derivation.

Another important aspect of African music was the use of folk tales in song lyrics, riddles, proverbs, etc., which, even when not accompanied by music, were the African's chief method of education, the way the wisdom of the elders was passed down to the young. The use of these folk stories and legends in the songs of the American Negro was quite common, although it was not as common as the proportion of "Americanized" or American material grew. There are however, definite survivals not only in the animal tales which have become part of this country's tradition (the Uncle Remus/Br'er Rabbit tales, for example) but in the lyrics of work songs and even later blues forms.

And just as the lyrics of the African songs were usually as important or more important than the music, the lyrics of the work songs and the later blues were equally important to the Negro's concept of music. In fact the "shouts" and "field hollers" were little more than highly rhythmical lyrics. Even the purely instrumental music of the

American Negro contains constant reference to vocal music. Blues-playing is the closest imitation of the human voice of any music I've heard; the vocal effects that jazz musicians have delighted in from Bunk Johnson to Ornette Coleman are evidence of this. (And it seems right to conclude that the African and blues scales proceed from this concept of vocal music, which produces note values that are almost impossible to reproduce on the fixed Western tempered scale, but can nevertheless be played on Western instruments.)

If we think of African music as regards its intent, we must see that it differed from Western music in that it was a purely *functional* music. Borneman lists some basic types of songs common to West African cultures: songs used by young men to influence young women (courtship, challenge, scorn); songs used by workers to make their tasks easier; songs used by older men to prepare the adolescent boys for manhood, and so on. "Serious" Western music, except for early religious music, has been strictly an "art" music. One would not think of any particular *use* for Haydn's symphonies, except perhaps the "cultivation of the soul." "Serious music" (a term that could only have extra-religious meaning in the West) has never been an integral part of the Westerner's life; no art has been since the Renaissance. Of course, before the Renaissance, art could find its way into the lives of almost all the people because all art issued from the Church, and the Church was at the very center of Western man's life. But the discarding of the religious attitude for the "enlightened" concepts of the Renaissance also created the schism between what was art and what was life. It was, and is, inconceivable in the African culture to make a separation between music, dancing, song, the artifact, and a man's life or his worship of his gods. *Expression* issued from life, and *was* beauty. But in the West, the "triumph of the economic mind over the imaginative," as Brooks Adams said, made possible this dreadful split between life and art. Hence, a music that is an "art" music as distinguished from something someone would whistle while tilling a field.

There are still relatively cultivated Westerners who believe that before Giotto no one *could* reproduce the human figure well, or that the Egyptians painted their figures in profile because they *could not* do it any other way. The idea of progress, as it has infected all other areas of Western thought, is thus carried over into the arts as well. And so a Western listener will criticize the tonal and timbral qualities of an African or American Negro singer whose singing has a completely alien *end* as the "standard of excellence." The "hoarse, shrill" quality of African singers or of their cultural progeny, the blues singers, is thus atributed to their lack of proper vocal training, instead of to a conscious desire dictated by their own cultures to produce a prescribed and certainly calculated effect. A blues singer and, say, a Wagnerian tenor cannot be compared to one another in any way. They issue from cultures that have almost nothing in common, and the musics they make are equally alien. The Western concept of "beauty" cannot be reconciled to African or Afro-American music (except perhaps now in the twentieth century, Afro-American music has enough of a Euro-American tradition to make it seem possible to judge it by purely Western standards. This is not quite true.) For a Westerner to say that the Wagnerian tenor's voice is "better" than the African singer's or the blues singer's is analogous to a non-Westerner disparaging Beethoven's Ninth Symphony because it wasn't improvised.

The Western concept of the cultivation of the voice is foreign to African or Afro-American music. In the West, only the artifact can be beautiful, mere expression cannot be thought to be. It is only in the twentieth century that Western art has moved away from this concept and toward the non-Western modes of art-making, but the principle of the beautiful thing as opposed to the natural thing still makes itself felt. The tendency of white jazz musicians to play "softer" or with "cleaner, rounder tones" than their Negro counterparts is, I think, an insistence on the same Western artifact. Thus an alto saxophonist like Paul Desmond, who is white, produces a sound on his instrument that can almost be called legitimate, or classical, and the finest Negro alto saxophonist, Charlie Parker, produced a sound on the same instrument that was called by some "raucous and uncultivated." But Parker's sound was *meant* to be both those adjectives. Again, reference determines value. Parker also would literally imitate the human voice with his cries, swoops, squawks, and slurs, while Desmond always insists he is playing an instrument, that it is an artifact separate from himself. Parker did not admit that there was any separation between himself and the agent he had chosen as his means of self-expression.

By way of further illustration of this, another quote from Mr. Borneman:

"While the whole European tradition strives for regularity—of pitch, of time, of timbre and of vibrato—the African tradition strives precisely for the negation of these elements. In language, the African tradition aims at circumlocution rather than at exact definition. The direct statement is considered crude and unimaginative; the veiling of all contents in ever-changing paraphrases is considered the criterion of intelligence and personality. In music, the same tendency towards obliquity and ellipsis is noticeable: no note is attacked straight; the voice or instrument always approaches it from above or below, plays around the implied pitch without ever remaining any length of time, and departs from it without ever having committed itself to a single meaning. The timbre is veiled and paraphrased by constantly changing vibrato, tremolo and overtone effects. The timing and accentuation, finally, are not *stated*, but *implied* or *suggested*. The denying or withholding of all signposts."[7]

NOTES

1. H. E. Krehbiel, *Afro-American Folksongs* (New York, G. Schirmer, 1914), p. 73.
2. *Ibid.*, p. 80.
3. From Maud Cuney-Hare, *Negro Musicians and Their Music* (Washington, D.C., Associated Publishers, 1936), p. 27.
4. *Ibid.*, p. 73.
5. "The Roots of Jazz," in Nat Hentoff and Albert J. McCarthy, eds., *Jazz* (New York, Rinehart, 1959) p. 13.
6. *Jazz: A People's Music* (New York, Citadel, 1948), p. 68.
7. Hentoff and McCarthy, *Jazz*, pp. 23–24.

Swing—From Verb to Noun

The blues was conceived by freedmen and ex-slaves—if not as the result of a personal or intellectual experience, at least as an emotional confirmation of, and reaction to, the way in which most Negroes were still forced to exist in the United States. The blues impulse was a psychological correlative that obscured the most extreme ideas of *assimilation* for most Negroes, and made any notion of the complete abandonment of the traditional black culture an unrealizable possibility. In a sense, the middle-class spirit could not take root among most Negroes because they sensed the final fantasy involved. Besides, the pay check, which was the aspect of American society that created a modern black middle class, was, as I mentioned before, also available to what some of my mother's friends would refer to as "low-type coons." And these "coons" would always be unavailable both socially and culturally to any talk of assimilation from white man or black. The Negro middle class, always an exaggeration of its white model, could include the professional men and educators, but after the move north it also included men who worked in stores and as an added dig, "sportsmen," i.e., gamblers and numbers people. The idea of Negro "society," as E. Franklin Frazier pointed out, is based only on acquisition, which, as it turns out, makes the formation of a completely parochial meta-society impossible. Numbers bankers often make as much money as doctors and thereby are part of Negro "society." And even if the more formal ("socially responsible") Negro middle class wanted to become simply white Americans, they were during the late twenties and thirties merely a swelling minority.

The two secularities I spoke of are simply the ways in which the blues was beginning to be redistributed in black America through these years. The people who were beginning to move toward what they could think of as citizenship also moved away from the older blues. The unregenerate Northerners already had a music, the thin-willed "society" bands of Jim Europe, and the circus as well as white rag had influenced the "non-blues" bands of Will Marion Cook and Wilbur Sweatman that existed before the migration. But the huge impact the Southerners made upon the North changed that. When the city blues began to be powerful, the larger Negro dance bands hired some of the emigrants as soloists, and to some degree the blues began to be heard in most of the black cabarets, "dance schools," and theaters. The true jazz sound had moved north, and even the blackest blues could be heard in the house parties of Chicago and New York. But for most of America by the twenties, jazz (or *jass*, the noun, not the verb) meant the Original Dixieland Jazz Band (to the hip) and Paul Whiteman (to the square). Whiteman got rich; the O.D.J.B. never did.

The O.D.J.B. was a group of young white men who had been deeply influenced by the King Oliver band in New Orleans; they moved north, and became the first jazz band to record. They had a profound influence upon America, and because they, rather than the actual black innovators, were heard by the great majority of Americans *first*, the cultural lag had won again.

A Negro jazz band, Freddie Keppard's Original Creoles, turned down an invitation to record a few months before the O.D.J.B.; Keppard (myth says) didn't accept the offer because he thought such a project would merely invite imitation of his style! That is probably true, but it is doubtful that Keppard's band would have caught as much national attention as the smoother O.D.J.B. anyway, for the same reason the O.D.J.B. could never have made as much money as Whiteman.

It is significant that by 1924, when Bessie Smith was still causing riots in Chicago and when young Louis Armstrong was on his way to New York to join the Fletcher Henderson band — and by so doing, to create the first really swinging big jazz band, the biggest names in "jazz" were Whiteman and the Mound City Blue Blowers, another white group. Radio had come into its own by 1920, and the irony is that most Negroes probably thought of jazz, based on what they had heard, as being a white dilution of older blues forms! It was only after there had been a few recordings sufficiently distributed through the black Northern and urban Southern neighborhoods, made by Negro bands like King Oliver's (Oliver was then in Chicago with his historic Creole Jazz Band, which featured Louis Armstrong, second cornet), Fletcher Henderson's, and two Kansas City bands — Bennie Moten's and Clarence Williams', that the masses of Negroes became familiar with jazz. At Chicago's Lincoln Gardens Cafe, Oliver first set the Northern Negro neighborhoods on fire, and then bands like Moten's and Williams' in the various clubs around Kansas City; but Henderson reached his Negro audience mostly via records because even when he got his best band together (with Coleman Hawkins, Louis Armstrong, Don Redman, etc.) he was still playing at Roseland, which was a white club.

The earliest jazz bands, like Buddy Bolden's, were usually small groups. Bolden's instrumentation was supposed to have been cornet, clarinet, trombone, violin, guitar, bass (which was one of the first instrumental innovations for that particular group since most bands of that period and well after used the tuba) and drums. These groups were usually made up of musicians who had other jobs (like pre-classic blues singers) since there was really no steady work for them. And they played most of the music of the time: quadrilles, schottisches, polkas, ragtime tunes, like many of the other "cleaner" groups around New Orleans. But the difference with the Bolden band was the blues quality, the Uptown flavor, of all their music. But this music still had the flavor of the brass marching bands. Most of the musicians of that period had come through those bands; in fact, probably still marched with them when there was a significant funeral. Another quality that must have distinguished the Bolden band was the improvisational character of a good deal of their music. Charles Edward Smith remarks that "the art of group improvisation — like the blues, the life blood of jazz — was associated with this uptown section of New Orleans in particular. As in folk music, two creative forces were involved, that of the group and that of the gifted individual."[1]

Most of the Uptown bands were noted for their "sloppy ensemble styles." The Bolden band and the other early jazz groups must have sounded even sloppier. The music was a raw mixture of march, dance, blues, and early rag rhythm, with all the players improvising simultaneously. It is a wonderful concept, taking the unison tradition of European march music, but infesting it with teeming improvisations, catcalls, hollers, and the murky rhythms of the ex-slaves. The Creoles must have hated that music more than anything in life.

But by the time the music came upriver along with the fleeing masses, it had changed a great deal. Oliver's Creole Band, the first really influential Negro jazz band in the North, had a much smoother ensemble style than the Bolden band: the guitar and violin had disappeared, and a piano had been added. In New Orleans, pianists had been largely soloists in the various bawdy houses and brothels of Storyville. In fact, pianists were the only Negro musicians who worked steadily and needed no other jobs. But the early New Orleans jazz groups usually did not have pianos. Jelly Roll Morton, one of the first jazz pianists, was heavily influenced by the ragtime style, though his own rags were even more heavily influenced by blues and that rougher rag style called "barrelhouse." As

Bunk Johnson is quoted as saying, Jelly played music "the whores liked." And played in a whorehouse, it is easy to undersand how functional that music must have been. But the piano as part of a jazz ensemble was something not indigenous to earlier New Orleans music. The smoother and more clearly polyphonic style of Oliver's band, as opposed to what must have been a veritable heterophony of earlier bands like Bolden's—Kid Ory's Sunshine Orchestra, the first black jazz band to record (Los Angeles, 1921), gives us some indication—showed a discipline and formality that must certainly have been imposed to a large degree by ragtime and the more precise pianistic techniques that went with it.

Oliver's band caused a sensation with audiences and musicians alike and brought the authentic accent of jazz into the North. Garvin Bushell remembers: "We went on the road with Mamie Smith in 1921. When we got to Chicago, Bubber Miley and I went to hearing Oliver at the Dreamland every night. [This was before Armstrong joined the band and they moved to Lincoln Gardens.] It was the first time I'd heard New Orleans jazz to any advantage and I studied them every night for the entire week we were in town. I was very much impressed with their blues and their sound. The trumpets and clarinets in the East had a better 'legitimate' quality, but their [Oliver's band's] sound touched you more. It was less cultivated but more expressive of how the people felt. Bubber and I sat there with our mouths open."[2]

Louis Armstrong's arrival at twenty-two with Oliver's band had an even more electrifying effect on these Northern audiences, which many times included white jazz musicians. Hoagy Carmichael went to the Lincoln Gardens with Bix Beiderbecke in 1923 to hear that band:

"The King featured two trumpets, a piano, a bass fiddle and a clarinet . . . a big black fellow . . . slashed into *Bugle Call Rag*.

"I dropped my cigarette and gulped my drink. Bix was on his feet, his eyes popping. For taking the first chorus was that second trumpet, Louis Armstrong.

"Louis was taking it fast. Bob Gillette slid off his chair and under the table.

"Every note Louis hit was perfection."[3]

This might seem amusing if it is noted that the first and deepest influences on most white Northern and Midwestern jazz musicians were necessarily the recordings of the O.D.J.B., who were imitating the earlier New Orleans styles, and Oliver, who had brought that style to its apex. Thus, this first hearing of the genuine article by these white musicians must have been much like tasting real eggs after having been brought up on the powdered variety. (Though, to be sure, there's no certainty that a person will like the original if he has developed a taste for the other. So it is that Carmichael can write that he still preferred Beiderbecke to Armstrong, saying, "Bix's breaks were not as wild as Armstrong's but they were hot and he selected each note with musical care." [4])

Blues as an autonomous music had been in a sense inviolable. There was no clear way into it, i.e., its production, not its appreciation, except as concomitant with what seems to me to be the peculiar social, cultural, economic, and emotional experience of a black man in America. The idea of a white blues singer seems an even more violent contradiction of terms than the idea of a middle-class blues singer. The materials of blues were not available to the white American, even though some strange circumstance might prompt him to look for them. It was as if these materials were secret and obscure, and blues a kind of ethno-historic rite as basic as blood.

The classic singers brought this music as close to white America as it could ever get and still survive. W. C. Handy, with the publication of his various "blues compositions," *invented* it for a great many Americans and also showed that there was some money to be made from it. Whiteman, Wilbur Sweatman, Jim Europe, all played Handy's compositions with success. There was even what could be called a "blues craze" (of which Handy's compositions were an important part) just after the ragtime craze went on the skids. But the music that resulted from the craze had little, if anything, to do with legitimate blues. That could not be got to, except as the casual expression of a whole culture. And for this reason, blues remained, and remains in its most moving manifestations, obscure to the mainstream of American culture.

Jazz made it possible for the first time for something of the legitimate feeling of Afro-American music to be imitated successfully. (Ragtime had moved so quickly away from any pure reflection of Negro life that by the time it became popular, there was no more original source to imitate. It was, in a sense, a premature attempt at the socio-cultural merger that later produced jazz.) Or rather, jazz enabled separate and *valid* emotional expressions to be made that were based on older traditions of Afro-American music that were clearly not a part of it. The Negro middle class would not have a music if it were not for jazz. The white man would have no access to blues.

It was a music capable of reflecting not only the Negro and a black America but a white America as well.

During the twenties, serious young white musicians were quick to pick up more or less authentic jazz accents as soon as they had some contact with the music. The O.D.J.B., who came out of a parallel tradition of white New Orleans marching bands, whizzed off to Chicago and stunned white musicians everywhere as well as many Negro musicians in the North who had not heard the new music before. Young white boys, like Beiderbecke, in the North and Midwest were already forming styles of their own based on the O.D.J.B.'s records and the playing of another white group, the New Orleans Rhythm Kings, before Joe Oliver's band got to Chicago. And the music these boys were making, or trying to make, had very little to do with Paul Whiteman. They had caught the accent, understood the more generalized emotional statements, and genuinely moved, set out to involve themselves in this music as completely as possible. They hung around the Negro clubs, listening to the newly employed New Orleans musicians, and went home and tried to play their tunes.

The result of this cultural "breakdown" was not always mere imitation. As I have said, jazz had a broadness of emotional meaning that allowed of many separate ways into it, not all of them dependent on the "blood ritual" of blues. Bix Beiderbecke, as a mature musician, was even an innovator. But the real point of this breakdown was that it reflected not so much the white American's increased understanding of the Negro, but rather the fact that the Negro had created a music that offered such a profound reflection of America that it could attract white Americans to want to play it or listen to it for exactly that reason. The white jazz musician was even a new *class* of white American. Unlike the earlier blackface acts and the minstrels who sought to burlesque certain facets of Negro life (and, superficially, the music associated with it), there were now growing ranks of white jazz musicians who wanted to play the music because they thought it emotionally and intellectually fulfilling. It made a common cultural ground where black and white America seemed only day and night in the same city and at their most disparate, proved only to result in different *styles*, a phenomenon I have always taken to be the whole point (and value) of divergent cultures.

It is interesting that most of these young white musicians who emerged during the early twenties were from the middle class and from the Middle West. Beiderbecke was born in Davenport, Iowa;

that town, however, at the turn of the century was a river port, and many of the riverboats docked there—riverboats whose staffs sometimes included bands like Fate Marable's, Dewey Jackson's, and Albert Wynn's, and musicians like Jelly Roll Morton and Louis Armstrong. Beiderbecke's first group, the Wolverines, played almost exclusively at roadhouses and colleges in the Midwest, most notably at Indiana University.

A few years after the Wolverines had made their reputation as what George Hoefer calls "the first white band to play the genuine Negro style of jazz," another group of young white musicians began to play jazz "their own way." They were also from the Midwest, but from Chicago. Eddie Condon, Jimmy McPartland, Bud Freeman, PeeWee Russell, Dave Tough, and some others, all went to Austin High School and became associated with a style of playing known as "Chicago jazz," which took its impetus from the records of the O.D.J.B. and the New Orleans Rhythm Kings dates on the North Side of Chicago.

Chicago and nearby parts of the Midwest were logically the first places where jazz could take root in the North (although there were some parallel developments in New York). In a sense Chicago was, and to a certain extent is now, a kind of frontier town. It sits at the end of the riverboat runs, and it was the kind of industrial city that the first black emigrants were drawn to. It had many of the heavy industries that would employ Negroes, whereas New York's heaviest industry is paperwork. And in Chicago, during what was called the "Jazz Age," there was an easiness of communication on some levels between black and white that was not duplicated in New York until some time later. Chicago at this time was something like the musical capital of America, encompassing within it black emigrants, white emigrants, country blues people, classic stylists, city house-party grinders, New Orleans musicians, and young Negro musicians and younger white musicians listening and reacting to this crush of cultures that so clearly typified America's rush into the twentieth century.

The reaction of young white musicians to jazz was not always connected directly to any "understanding of the Negro." In many cases, the most profound influence on young white musicians was the music of other white musicians. Certainly this is true with people like Beiderbecke and most of the Chicago-style players. But the entrance of the white man into jazz at this level of sincerity and emotional legitimacy did at least bring him, by implication, much closer to the Negro; that is, even if a white trumpet player were to learn to play "jazz" by listening to Nick LaRocca and had his style set (as was Beiderbecke's case) *before* he ever heard black musicians, surely the musical debt to Negro music (and to the black culture from which it issued) had to be understood. As in the case of LaRocca's style, it is certainly an appropriation of black New Orleans brass style, most notably King Oliver's; though the legitimacy of its deviation can in no way be questioned, the fact that it is a deviation must be acknowledged. The serious white musician was in a position to do this. And this acknowledgment, whether overt or tacit, served to place the Negro's culture and Negro society in a position of intelligent regard it had never enjoyed before.

This acknowledgment of a developed and empirical profundity to the Negro's culture (and as the result of its separation from the mainstream of American culture) also caused the people who had to make it to be separated from this mainstream themselves. Any blackness admitted within the mainstream existed only as it could be shaped by the grimness of American sociological (and political) thought. There was no life to Negroes in America that could be understood by America, except negatively or with the hopeless idealism of impossible causes. During the Black Renaissance the white liberal and sensual dilettante "understood" the Negro. During the Depression, so did the Communist Party. The young white jazz musicians at least had to face the black American head-on and with only a very literal drum to beat. And they could not help but do this with some sense of rebellion or separateness from the rest of white America, since white America could have no understanding of what they were doing, except perhaps in the terms that Whiteman and the others succeeded in doing it, which was not at all—that is, explaining a bird by comparing it with an airplane.

"Unlike New Orleans style, the style of these musicians—often and confusingly labeled 'Chicago'—sacrificed ease and relaxation for tension and drive, perhaps because they were mastering a new idiom in a more hectic environment. They had read some of the literature of the 20s, drummer Dave Tough loved Mencken and the *American Mercury*, and their revolt against their own middle-class background tended to be conscious. The role of the improvising—and usually non-reading—musician became almost heroic."[5]

Music, as paradoxical as it might seem, is the result of thought. It is the result of thought perfected at its most empirical, i.e., as *attitude*, or *stance*. Thought is largely conditioned by reference; it is the result of consideration or speculation against reference, which is largely arbitrary.

There is no *one* way of thinking, since reference (hence value) is as scattered and dissimilar as men themselves. If Negro music can be seen to be the result of certain attitudes, certain specific ways of thinking about the world (and only ultimately about the *ways* in which music can be made), then the basic hypothesis of this book is understood. The Negro's music changed as he changed, reflecting shifting attitudes or (and this is equally important) *consistent attitudes within changed contexts*. And it is *why* the music changed that seems most important to me.

When jazz first began to appear during the twenties on the American scene, in one form or another, it was introduced in a great many instances into that scene by white Americans. Jazz as it was originally conceived and in most instances of its most vital development was the result of certain attitudes, or empirical ideas, attributable to the Afro-American culture. Jazz as played by white musicians was not the same as that played by black musicians, nor was there any reason for it to be. The music of the white jazz musician did not issue from the same cultural circumstance; it was, at its most profound instance, a learned art. The blues, for example, which I take to be an autonomous black music, had very little weight at all in pre-jazz white American culture. But blues is an extremely important part of jazz. However, the way in which jazz utilizes the blues "attitude" provided a musical analogy the white musician could understand and thus utilize in his music to arrive at a style of jazz music. The white musician understood the blues first as music, but seldom as an attitude, since the attitude, or world-view, the white musician was responsible to was necessarily quite a different one. And in many cases, this attitude, or world-view, was one that was not consistent with the making of jazz.

There should be no cause for wonder that the trumpets of Bix Beiderbecke and Louis Armstrong were so dissimilar. The white middle-class boy from Iowa was the product of a culture which could *place* Louis Armstrong, but could never understand him. Beiderbecke was also the product of a subculture that most nearly emulates the "official" or formal culture of North America. He was an instinctive intellectual who had a musical taste that included Stravinsky, Schoenberg, and Debussy, and had an emotional life that, as it turned out, was based on his conscious or unconscious disapproval of most of the sacraments of his culture. On the other hand, Armstrong was, in terms of emotional archetypes, an honored priest of his culture, one of the most impressive products of his society. Armstrong was not *rebelling* against anything with his music.

In fact, his music was one of the most beautiful refinements of Afro-American musical tradition, and it was immediately recognized as such by those Negroes who were not busy trying to pretend that they had issued from Beiderbecke's culture. The incredible irony of the situation was that both stood in similar places in the superstructure of American society: Beiderbecke, because of the isolation any deviation from mass culture imposed upon its bearer; and Armstrong, because of the socio-historical estrangement of the Negro from the rest of America. Nevertheless, the music the two made was as dissimilar as is possible within jazz. Beiderbecke's slight, reflective tone and impressionistic lyricism was the most impressive example of "the artifact given expression" in jazz. He played "white jazz" in the sense I am trying to convey, that is, as a music that is the product of attitudes expressive of a peculiar culture. Armstrong, of course, played jazz that was securely within the traditions of Afro-American music. His tone was brassy, broad, and aggressively dramatic. He also relied heavily on the vocal blues tradition in his playing to amplify the expressiveness of his instrumental technique.

I am using these two men as examples because they were two early masters of a developing *American* music, though they expressed almost antithetical versions of it. The point is that Afro-American music did not become a completely American expression until the white man could play it! Bix Beiderbecke, more than any of the early white jazzmen, signified this development because he was the first white jazz musician, the first white musician who brought to the jazz he created any of the *ultimate concern* Negro musicians brought to it as a casual attitude of their culture. This development signified also that jazz would someday have to contend with the idea of its being an art (since that was the white man's only way into it). The emergence of the white player meant that Afro-American culture had already become the expression of a particular kind of American experience, and what is most important, that this experience was available intellectually, that it could be learned.

Louis Armstrong's departure from the Oliver Creole Jazz Band is more than an historical event; given further consideration, it may be seen as a musical and socio-cultural event of the highest significance. First, Armstrong's departure from Chicago (as well as Beiderbecke's three years later, in 1927, to join the Goldkette band and then Paul Whiteman's enterprise) was, in a sense, symbolic of the fact that the most fertile period for jazz in Chicago was finished and that the jazz capital was moving to New York. It also meant that

Louis felt mature enough musically to venture out on his own without the presence of his mentor Joe Oliver. But most important, Armstrong in his tenure with Fletcher Henderson's Roseland band was not only responsible to a great degree for giving impetus to the first big jazz band, but in his capacity as one of the hot soloists in a big dance (later, jazz) band, he moved jazz into another era: the ascendancy of the soloist began.

Primitive jazz, like most Afro-American music that preceded it, was a communal, collective music. The famous primitive ensemble styles of earlier jazz allowed only of "breaks," or small solo-like statements by individual players, but the form and intent of these breaks were still dominated by the form and intent of the ensemble. They were usually just quasi-melodic punctuations at the end of the ensemble chorus. Jazz, even at the time of Oliver's Creole Band, was still a matter of *collective improvisation*, though the Creole Band did bring a smoother and more complex polyphonic technique to the ensemble style. As Larry Gushee remarked in a review of a recent LP of the Creole Band (Riverside 12-122) ". . . the Creole Jazz Band . . . sets the standard (possibly, who knows, only because of an historical accident) for all kinds of jazz that do not base their excellence on individual expressiveness, but on form and *shape* achieved through control and balance."[6]

The emergence of this "individual expressiveness" in jazz was signaled impressively by Armstrong's recordings with a small group known as the Hot Five. The musicians on these recordings, made in 1925 and 1926, were Kid Ory, trombone; Johnny Dodds, clarinet and *alto saxophone*; Lil Hardin, now Mrs. Armstrong, piano; and Johnny St. Cyr, banjo. On these sides, Armstrong clearly dominates the group, not so much because he is the superior instrumentalist, but because rhythmically and harmonically the rest of the musicians followed where Louis led, sometimes without a really clear knowledge of where that would be. The music made by the Hot Five is Louis Armstrong music: it has little to do with collective improvisation.

"The 1926 Hot Five's playing is much less purely collective than King Oliver's. In a sense, the improvised ensembles are cornet solos accompanied by *impromptu countermelodies* [my italics], rather than true collective improvisation. This judgment is based on the very essence of the works, and not merely on the cornet's closeness to the microphone. Listen to them carefully. Isn't it obvious that Armstrong's personality absorbs the others? Isn't your attention spontaneously concentrated on Louis? With King Oliver, you listen to the band, here, you listen first to Louis."[7]

The development of the soloist is probably connected to the fact that about this time in the development of jazz, many of the "hot" musicians had to seek employment with larger dance bands of usually dubious quality. The communal, collective improvisatory style of early jazz was impossible in this context, though later the important big jazz bands and big "blues bands" of the Southwest solved this problem by "uniting on a higher level the individual contribution with the entire group."[8]

The isolation that had nurtured Afro-American musical tradition before the coming of jazz had largely disappeared by the mid-twenties, and many foreign, even debilitating, elements drifted into this broader instrumental music. The instrumentation of the Henderson Roseland band was not chosen initially for its jazz possibilities, but in order to imitate the popular white dance bands of the day. The Henderson band became a jazz band because of the collective personality of the individual instrumentalists in the band, who were stronger than any superficial forms that might be imposed upon them. The saxophone trio, which was a clichéd novelty in the large white dance bands, became something of remarkable beauty when transformed by Henderson's three reeds, Buster Bailey, Don Redman, and Coleman Hawkins. And just as earlier those singular hollers must have pierced lonely Southern nights after the communal aspect of the slave society had broken down and had been replaced by a pseudoautonomous existence on many tiny Southern plots (which represented, however absurd it might seem, the widest breadth of this country for those Negroes, and their most exalted position in it), so the changed society in which the large Negro dance bands existed represented, in a sense, another post-communal black society. The move north, for instance, had broken down the old communities (the house parties were one manifestation of a regrouping of the newer communities: the Harlems and South Chicagos). Classic blues, the public face of a changed Afro-American culture, was the solo. The blues that developed at the house parties was the collective, communal music. So the jam sessions of the late twenties and thirties became the musicians' collective communal expression, and the solo in the large dance bands, that expression as it had to exist to remain vital outside its communal origins. The dance bands or society orchestras of the North replaced the plot of land, for they were the musician's only means of existence, and the solo, like the holler, was the only link with an earlier, more intense sense of the self in its most vital relationship to the world. The solo spoke singly of a collective music, and because of the emergence of the great soloists (Armstrong, Hawkins, Hines, Harrison), even forced the great bands (Henderson's, Ellington's, and later Basie's) into wonderfully extended versions of that communal expression.

The transformation of the large dance bands into jazz bands was in good measure the work of the Fletcher Henderson orchestra, aided largely by the arrangements of Don Redman, especially his writing for the reed section which gave the saxophones in the Henderson band a fluency that was never heard before. The reeds became the fiery harmonic and melodic imagination of the big jazz bands. And it was the growing prominence of the saxophone in the big band and the later elevation of that instrument to its fullest expressiveness by Coleman Hawkins that planted the seed for the kind of jazz that is played even today. However, it was not until the emergence of Lester Young that jazz became a saxophone or reed music, as opposed to the brass music it had been since the early half-march, half-blues bands of New Orleans.

Louis Armstrong had brought *brass jazz* to its fullest flowering and influenced every major innovation in jazz right up until the forties, and behop. Earl Hines, whose innovations as a pianist began a new, single-note line approach to the jazz piano, was merely utilizing Armstrong's trumpet style on a different instrument, thereby breaking out of the ragtime-boogie-stride approach to piano that had been predominant since that instrument was first used in jazz bands. Coleman Hawkins' saxophone style is still close to the Armstrong-perfected brass style, and of course, all Hawkins' imitators reflect that style as well. Jimmy Harrison, the greatest innovator on the trombone, was also profoundly influenced by Armstrong's brass style.

With the emergence of many good "hot" musicians from all over the country during the mid-twenties, the big jazz bands continued to develop. By the late twenties there were quite a few very good jazz bands all over the country. And competent musicians "appeared from everywhere, from 1920 on; by 1930 every city outside the Deep South with a Negro population (1920 census) above sixty thousand except Philadelphia had produced an important band: Washington, Duke Ellington; Baltimore, Chick Webb; Memphis, Jimmy Lunceford; St. Louis, the Missourians; Chicago, Luis Russell and Armstrong; New York, Henderson, Charlie Johnson, and half a dozen more."[9]

So an important evolution in Afro-American musical form had occurred again and in much the same manner that characterized the many other changes within the tradition of Negro music. The form can be called basically a Euro-American one—the large (sweet) dance band, changed by the contact with Afro-American musical tradition into another vehicle for that tradition. Just as the Euro-American religious song and ballad had been used, so with the transformation of the large dance band into the jazz band and the adaptation of the thirty-two-bar popular song to jazz purposes, the music itself was broadened and extended even further, and even more complex expressions of older musical traditions were made possible.

By the late twenties a great many more Negroes were going to high school and college, and the experience of an American "liberal" education was bound to leave traces. The most expressive big bands of the late twenties and thirties were largely middle-class Negro enterprises. The world of the professional man had opened up, and many scions of the new Negro middle class who had not gotten through professional school went into jazz "to make money." Men like Fletcher Henderson (who had a chemistry degree), Benny Carter, Duke Ellington, Coleman Hawkins, Jimmie Lunceford, Sy Oliver, and Don Redman, for example, all went to college: "They were a remarkable group of men. Between 1925 and 1935 they created, in competition, a musical tradition that required fine technique and musicianship (several of them were among the earliest virtuosi in jazz); they began to change the basis of the jazz repertory from blues to the wider harmonic possibilities of the thirty-two-bar popular song; they created and perfected the new ensemble-style big-band jazz; they kept their groups together for years, working until they achieved a real unity. They showed that jazz could absorb new, foreign elements without losing its identity, that it was in fact capable of evolution."[10]

These men were all "citizens" and they had all, to a great extent, moved away from the older *lowdown* forms of blues. Blues was not so *direct* to them, it had to be utilized in other contexts. Big show-band jazz was a music of their own, a music that still relied on older Afro-American musical tradition, but one that had begun to utilize still greater amounts of popular American music as well as certain formal European traditions. Also, the concept of making music as a means of making a living that had developed with the coming of classic blues singers was now thoroughly a part of the constantly evolving Afro-American culture. One did not expect to hear Bessie

Smith at a rent party, one went to the theater to hear her. She was, at all levels, a *performer*. The young middle-class Negroes who came into jazz during the development of the show bands and dance bands all thought of themselves as performers as well. No matter how deeply the music they played was felt, they still thought of it as a public expression.

"If so many musicians came to jazz after training in one of the professions, it was because jazz was both more profitable and safer for a Negro in the 1920's; it was a survival of this attitude that decided Ellington to keep his son out of M.I.T. and aeronautical engineering in the 1930's."[11]

Just as Bessie Smith perfected vocal blues style almost as a Western artifact, and Louis Armstrong perfected the blues-influenced brass style in jazz (which was a great influence on all kinds of instrumental jazz for more than two decades), so Duke Ellington perfected the big jazz band, transforming it into a highly expressive instrument. Ellington, after the Depresson had killed off the big theater-band "show-biz" style of the large jazz bands, began to create a personal style of jazz expression as impressive as Armstrong's innovation as a soloist (if not more so). Ellington replaced a "spontaneous collective music by a worked-out orchestral language."[12]

Ellington's music (even the "jungle" bits of his twenties show-band period, which were utilized in those uptown "black and tan" clubs that catered largely to sensual white liberals) was a thoroughly American music. It was the product of a native American mind, but more than that, it was a music that *could* for the first time exist within the formal boundaries of American culture. A freedman could not have created it, just as Duke could never have played like Peatie Wheatstraw. Ellington began in much the same way as a great many of the significant Northern Negro musicians of the era had begun, by playing in the ragtime, show-business style that was so prevalent. But under the influence of the Southern styles of jazz and with the growth of Duke as an orchestra leader, composer, and musician, the music he came to make was as "moving" in terms of the older Afro-American musical tradition as it was a completely American expression. Duke's sophistication was to a great extent the very quality that enabled him to integrate so perfectly the older blues traditions with the "whiter" styles of big-band music. But Ellington was a "citizen," and his music, as Vic Bellerby has suggested, was "the detached impressionism of a sophisticated Negro city dweller."

Even though many of Ellington's compositions were "hailed as uninhibited jungle music," the very fact that the music was so much an American music made it cause the stir it did: "Ellington used musical materials that were familiar to concert-trained ears, making jazz music more listenable to them. These, however, do not account for his real quality. . . . In his work all the elements of the old music may be found, but each completely changed because it had to be changed. . . . Ellington's accomplishment was to solve the problem of form and content for the large band. He did it not by trying to play pure New Orleans blues and stomp music rearranged for large bands, as Henderson did, but by re-creating all the elements of New Orleans music in new instrumental and harmonic terms. What emerged was a music that could be traced back to the old roots and yet sounded fresh and new."[13]

For these reasons, by the thirties the "race" category could be dropped from Ellington's records. Though he would quite often go into his jungle things, faking the resurrection of "African music," the extreme irony here is that Ellington was making "African sounds," but as a sophisticated American. The "African" music he made had much less to do with Africa than his best music, which, in the sense I have used throughout this book, can be seen as a truly Afro-American music, though understandable only in the context of a completely American experience. This music could, and did, find a place within the main culture. Jazz became more "popular" than ever. The big colored dance bands of the thirties were a national entertainment and played in many white night clubs as well as the black clubs that had been set up especially for white Americans. These bands were also the strongest influence on American popular music and entertainment for twenty years.

The path of jazz and the further development of the Afro-American musical tradition paradoxically had been taken over at this level to a remarkable degree by elements of the Negro middle class. Jazz was their remaining connection with blues; a connection they could make, at many points, within the mainstream of American life.

The music had moved so far into the mainstream that soon white "swing" bands developed that could play with some of the authentic accent of the great Negro bands, though the deciding factor here was the fact that there were never enough good white jazz musicians to go around in those big bands, and most of the bands then were packed with a great many studio and section men, and perhaps one or two "hot" soloists. By the thirties quite a few white bands had mastered the swing idiom of big-band jazz with varying degrees of authenticity. One of the most successful of these bands, the Benny

Goodman orchestra, even began to buy arrangements from Negro arrangers so that it would have more of an authentic tone. The arranger became one of the most important men in big-band jazz, demonstrating how far jazz had gotten from earlier Afro-American musical tradition. (Fletcher Henderson, however, was paid only $37.50 per arrangement by Goodman before Goodman actually hired him as the band's chief arranger.)

The prominence of radio had also created a new medium for this new music, and the growing numbers of white swing bands automatically qualified for these fairly well-paying jobs: "The studio work was monopolized by a small group of musicians who turn up on hundreds of records by orchestras of every kind. One of the least admirable characteristics of the entire arrangement was that it was almost completely restricted to white musicians and it was the men from the white orchestras who were getting the work. The Negro musicians complained bitterly about the discrimination, but the white musicians never attempted to help them, and the contractors hired the men they wanted. At the Nest Club or the Lenox Club the musicians were on close terms, but the relationship ended when the white musicians went back to their Times Square hotels. A few of them, notably Goodman, were to use a few of the Harlem musicians, but in the first Depression years the studio orchestras were white."[14]

So the widespread development of the swing style produced yet another irony when the "obscurity" of the Negro's music was lessened with the coming of arranged big-band jazz, and the music, in effect, did pass into the mainstream of American culture, in fact, could be seen as an integral part of that culture, it not only ceased to have meaning for a great many Negroes but also those Negroes who were most closely involved with the music were not even allowed to play it at the highest salaries that could be gotten. The spectacle of Benny Goodman hiring Teddy Wilson and later Lionel Hampton, Charlie Christian, and Cootie Williams into his outrageously popular bands and thereby making them "big names" in the swing world seems to me as fantastically amusing as the fact that in the jazz polls during the late thirties and early forties run by popular jazz magazines, almost no Negro musicians won. Swing music, which was the result of arranged big-band jazz, as it developed to a music that had almost nothing to do with blues, had very little to do with black America, though that is certainly where it had come from. But there were now more and more Negroes like that, too.

NOTES

1. "New Orleans and Traditions in Jazz," in *Jazz*, p. 39.
2. "Garvin Bushell and New York Jazz in the 1920's," in *Jazz Review* (February 1959), p. 9.
3. Hoagy Carmichael, *The Stardust Road* (New York, Rinehart, 1946), p. 53.
4. As quoted in Marshall Stearns, *The Story of Jazz* (New York, Oxford University Press, 1956), p. 128.
5. *The Story of Jazz*, p. 129.
6. *Jazz Review* (November 1958), p. 37.
7. André Hodeir, *Jazz: Its Evolution and Essence* (New York, Grove Press, 1956), pp. 50–51.
8. Sidney Finkelstein, *Jazz: A People's Music* (New York, Citadel, 1948), p. 206.
9. Hsio Wen Shih, "The Spread of Jazz and the Big Bands," in *Jazz*, p. 161.
10. *Ibid.*, p. 164.
11. *Ibid.*, p. 164.
12. *Jazz: Its Evolution and Essence*, p. 33.
13. *Jazz: A People's Music*, p. 192.
14. Samuel Charters and Leonard Kunstadt, *Jazz: A History of the New York Scene* (New York, Doubleday, 1962), p. 262.

From *The Dead Lecturer*

▌▌▌▌▌▌▌▌

**A contract.   (for the destruction and
rebuilding of Paterson**

Flesh, and cars, tar, dug holes beneath stone
a rude hierarchy of money, band saws cross out
music, feeling. Even speech, corrodes.
                                        I came here
from where I sat boiling in my veins, cold fear
at the death of men, the death of learning, in
cold fear, at my own. Romantic vests of same death
blank at the corner, blank when they raise their fingers

Criss the hearts, in dark flesh staggered so marvelous
are their lies. So complete, their mastery, of these
stupid niggers. Loud spics kill each other, and will not

make the simple trip to Tiffany's. Will not smash their stainless
heads, against the simpler effrontery of so callous a code as gain.

You are no brothers, dirty woogies, dying under dried rinds, in
    massa's
droopy tuxedos. Cab Calloways of the soul, at the soul's
    juncture, a
music, they think will save them from our eyes. (In back of the
    terminal

where the circus will not go. At the backs of crowds, stooped
    and vulgar
breathing hate syllables, unintelligible rapes of all that linger in
our new world. Killed in white fedora hats, they stand so mute
    at what

whiter slaves did to my fathers. They muster silence. They pray
    at the

steps of abstract prisons, to be kings, when all is silence, when
    all
is stone. When even the stupid fruit of their loins is gold, or
    something
else they cannot eat.

An Agony. As Now.

two selves?

    — self of white world

I am inside someone
who hates me. I look
out from his eyes. Smell
what fouled tunes come in
to his breath. Love his
wretched women.

    two selves fractured self

Slits in the metal, for sun. Where
my eyes sit turning, at the cool air
the glance of light, or hard flesh
rubbed against me, a woman, a man,
without shadow, or voice, or meaning.

This is the enclosure (flesh,
where innocence is a weapon. An
abstraction. Touch. (Not mine.
Or yours, if you are the soul I had
and abandoned when I was blind and had
my enemies carry me as a dead man
(if he is beautiful, or pitied.

    emprisonment

It can be pain. (As now, as all his
flesh hurts me.) It can be that. Or
pain. As when she ran from me into
that forest.
        Or pain, the mind
silver spiraled whirled against the
sun, higher than even old men thought
God would be. Or pain. And the other. The
yes. (Inside his books, his fingers. They
are withered yellow flowers and were never

    pain

beautiful.) The yes. You will, lost soul, say
'beauty.' Beauty, practiced, as the tree. The
slow river. A white sun in its wet sentences.

Or, the cold men in their gale. Ecstasy. Flesh
or soul. The yes. (Their robes blown. Their bowls
empty. They chant at my heels, not at yours.) Flesh
or soul, as corrupt. Where the answer moves too quickly.
Where the God is a self, after all.)

Cold air blown through narrow blind eyes. Flesh,
white hot metal. Glows as the day with its sun.
It is a human love, I live inside. A bony skeleton
you recognize as words or simple feeling.

But it has no feeling. As the metal, is hot, it is not,
given to love.

It burns the thing
inside it. And that thing
screams.

A Poem For Willie Best

*Willie Best was a Negro character actor whose Hollywood
name was Sleep'n'eat.*

—A.B.

I

The face sings, alone
at the top
            of the body. All
flesh, all song, aligned. For hell
is silent, at those cracked lips
flakes of skin and mind
twist and whistle softly
as they fall.
            It was your own death
you saw. Your own face, stiff

and raw. This
without sound, or
movement. Sweet afton, the
dead beggar bleeds
yet. His blood, for a time
alive, and huddled in a door
way, struggling to sing. Rain
washes it into cracks. Pits
whose bottoms are famous. Whose sides
are innocent broadcasts
of another life.

II

At this point, neither
front nor back. A point, the
dimensionless line. The top
of a head, seen from Christ's
heaven, stripped of history
or desire.
       Fixed perpendicular
to shadow. (even speech, vertical,
leaves no trace. Born in to death
held fast to it, where
the lover spreads his arms, the line
he makes to threaten Gods with history.
The fingers stretch to emptiness. At
each point, after flesh, even light
is speculation. But an end, his end,
failing a beginning.

2

A cross. The gesture, symbol, line
arms held stiff, nailed stiff, with
no sign, of what gave them strength.
The point, become a line, a cross, or
the man, and his material, driven in
the ground. If the head rolls back
and the mouth opens, screamed into
existence, there will be perhaps
only the slightest hint of movement —

a smear; no help will come. No one
will turn to that station again.

III

At a cross roads, sits the
player. No drum, no umbrella, even
though it's raining. Again, and we
are some how less miserable because
here is a hero, used to being wet.
One road is where you are standing now
(reading this, the other, crosses then
rushes into a wood.

     5 lbs neckbones.
     5 lbs hog innards.
     10 bottles cheap wine.
             (The contents

of a paper bag, also shoes, with holes
for the big toe, and several rusted
knives. This is a literature, of
symbols. And it is his gift, as the
bag is.
   (The contents
again, holy saviours,

      300 men on horseback
      75 bibles
      the quietness

of a field. A rich
man, though wet through
by the rain.
    I said,
      47 howitzers
      7 polished horses jaws
      a few trees being waved

softly back under
the black night
     All This should be
invested.

IV

Where
ever,
        he has gone. Who ever
mourns
or sits silent
to remember

There is nothing of pity
here. Nothing
of sympathy.

V

This is the dance of the raised
leg. Of the hand on the knee
quickly.
        As a dance it punishes
speech. 'The house burned. The
old man killed.'
        As a dance it
is obscure.

VI

This is the song
of the highest C.
        The falsetto. An elegance
that punishes silence. This is the song
of the toes pointed inward, the arms swung, the
hips, moved, for fucking, slow, from side
to side. He is quoted
saying, "My father was
never a jockey,
        but
        he did teach me
        how to ride."

VII

The balance.
        (Rushed in, swarmed of dark, cloaks,

and only red lights pushed a message
to the street. Rub.

           This is the lady,
I saw you with.
This is your mother.
This is the lady I wanted
some how to sleep with.

              As a dance, or
our elegant song. Sun red and grown
from trees, fences, mud roads in dried out
river beds. This is for me, with no God
but what is given. Give me.

                    Something more
than what is here. I must tell you
my body hurts.

The balance.

              Can you hear? Here
I am again. Your boy, dynamite. Can
you hear? My soul is moved. The soul
you gave me. I say, my soul, and it
is moved. That soul
you gave me.

           Yes, I'm sure
this is the lady. You
slept with her. Witness, your boy,
here, dynamite. Hear?

                  I mean
can you?

The balance.

              He was tired of losing. (And
his walking buddies tired
of walking.

           Bent slightly,
at the waist. Left hand low, to flick
quick showy jabs ala Sugar. The right
cocked, to complete,

              any combination.

                  He was
tired of losing, but he was fighting
a big dumb "farmer."

Such a blue bright
afternoon, and only a few hundred yards
from the beach. He said, I'm tired
of losing.
"I got ta cut 'cha."

VIII

A renegade
behind the mask. And even
the mask, a renegade
disguise. Black skin
and hanging lip.

        Lazy
        Frightened
        Thieving
        Very potent sexually
        Scars
        Generally inferior
             (but natural

rhythms.

His head is
at the window. The only
part
    that sings.

(The word he used
        (we are passing St. Mark's place
        and those crazy jews who fuck)
                to provoke

in neon, still useful
in the rain,
      to provoke
some meaning, where before
these was only hell. I said
silence, at his huddled blood.

        It is an obscene invention.
        A white sticky discharge.
        "Jism," in white chalk
        on the back of Angel's garage.
        Red jackets with the head of

Hobbes staring into space. "Jasm"
the name the leader took, had it
stenciled on his chest.

And he sits
wet at the crossroads, remembering distinctly
each weightless face that eases by. (Sun at
the back door, and that hideous mindless grin.

(Hear?

SHORT SPEECH TO MY FRIENDS

A political art, let it be
tenderness, low strings the fingers
touch, or the width of autumn
climbing wider avenues, among the virtue
and dignity of knowing what city
you're in, who to talk to, what clothes
—even what buttons—to wear. I address

/ the society
the image, of
common utopia.

/ The perversity
of separation, isolation,
after so many years of trying to enter their kingdoms,
now they suffer in tears, these others, saxophones whining
through the wooden doors of their less than gracious homes.
The poor have become our creators. The black. The thoroughly
ignorant.

Let the combination of morality
and inhumanity
begin.

2

Is power, the enemy? (Destroyer
of dawns, cool flesh of valentines, among
the radios, pauses, drunks
of the 19th century. I see it,

as any man's single history. All the possible heroes
dead from heat exhaustion
>> at the beach,
>> or hiding for years from cameras
only to die cheaply in the pages
of our daily lie.
>> One hero
has pretensions toward literature
one toward the cultivation of errors, arrogance,
and constantly changing disguises, as trucker, boxer,
valet, barkeep, in the aging taverns of memory. Making love
to those speedy heroines of masturbation. Or kicking literal evil
continually down filmy public stairs.

A compromise
would be silence. To shut up, even such risk
as the proper placement
of verbs and nouns. To freeze the spit
in mid-air, as it aims itself
at some valiant intellectual's face.

There would be someone
who would understand, for whatever
fancy reason. Dead, lying, Roi, as your children
came up, would also rise. As George Armstrong Custer
these 100 years, has never made
a mistake.

The politics of rich painters

>> is something like the rest
>> of our doubt, whatever slow thought
>> comes to rest, beneath the silence
>> of starving talk.
>> >> Just their fingers' prints
>> staining the cold glass, is sufficient
>> for commerce, and a proper ruling on
>> humanity. You know the pity
>> of democracy, that we must sit here

and listen to how he made his money.
Tho the catalogue of his possible ignorance
roars and extends through the room
like fire. "Love," becomes the pass,
the word taken intimately to combat
all the uses of language. So that learning
itself falls into disrepute.

2

What they have gathered into themselves
in that short mean trip from mother's iron tit
to those faggot handmaidens of the french whore
who wades slowly in the narrows, waving her burnt out
torch. There are movies, and we have opinions. There are
regions of compromise so attractive, we daily long
to filthy our minds with their fame. And all the songs
of our handsome generation fall clanging like stones
in the empty darkness of their heads.

                             Couples, so beautiful
in the newspapers, marauders of cheap sentiment. So much *taste*,
so little understanding, except some up and coming queer
    explaining
cinema and politics while drowning a cigarette.

3

They are more ignorant than the poor
tho they pride themselves with that accent. And
move easily in fake robes of egalitarianism. Meaning,
I will fuck you even if you don't like art. And are wounded
that you call their italian memories petit bourgeois.

                                    Whose death
will be Malraux's? Or the names Senghor, Price, Baldwin
whispered across the same dramatic pancakes, to let each eyelash
    flutter
at the news of their horrible deaths. It is a cheap game
to patronize the dead, unless their deaths be accountable
to your own understanding. Which be nothing nothing
if not bank statements and serene trips to our ominous
    countryside.
Nothing, if not whining talk about handsome white men.

Nothing
if not false glamourous and static. Except, I admit, your lives
are hideously real.

4

The source of their art crumbles into legitimate history.
The whimpering pigment of a decadent economy, slashed into
    life
as Yeats' mad girl plummeting over the nut house wall, her
    broken
knee caps rattling in the weather, reminding us of lands
our antennae do not reach.

And there are people in these savage geographies
use your name in other contexts
think, perhaps, the title of your latest painting
another name for liar.

Rhythm & Blues (I

(for Robert Williams, in exile)

The symbols hang limply
in the street. A forest of objects,
motives,

> black steaming christ
> meat wood and cars
> flesh light and stars
> scream each new dawn for

whatever leaves pushed from gentle lips
fire shouted from the loins of history
immense dream of each silence grown to punctuation
against the grey flowers of the world.

I live against them, and hear them, and move
the way they move. Hanged against the night, so many
leaves, not even moving. The women scream tombs

and give the nights a dignity. For his heels
dragged in the brush. For his lips dry as brown wood. As
the simple motion of flesh whipping the air.

An incorrigible motive.
An action so secret it creates.
Men dancing on a beach.
Disappeared laughter erupting as the sea
erupts.
Controlled eyes seeing now all
there is
Ears that have grown
to hold their new maps
Enemies that grow
in silence
Empty white fingers
against the keys (a drunken foolish stupor
to kill these men
and scream "Economics," my God, "Economics"
for all the screaming women drunker still, laid out to rest
under the tables of nightclubs
under the thin trees of expensive forests
informed of nothing save the stink of their failure
the peacock insolence of zombie regimes
the diaphanous silence of empty churches
the mock solitude of a spastic's art.

                            "Love." My God, (after they
scream "Economics," these shabby personalities
the pederast anarchist chants against millions of
Elk-sundays in towns quieter than his. Lunches. Smells
the sidewalk invents, and the crystal music even dumb niggers
hate. They scream it down. They will not hear your jazz. Or
let me tell of the delicate colors of the flag, the graphic blouse
of the beautfiul italian maiden. Afternoon spas
with telephone booths, Butterfingers, grayhaired anonymous
     trustees
dying with the afternoon. The people of my life
caressed with a silence that only they understand. Let their sons
make wild sounds of their mothers for your pleasure. Or
drive deep wedges in flesh / screaming birds of morning, at
their own. The invisible mountains of New Jersey, linger
where I was born. And the wind on that stone.

2)

Street of tinsel, and the jeweled dancers
of Belmont. Stone royalty they tear down
for new buildings where fags invent jellies.

A tub, a slick head, and the pink houses waving
at the night as it approaches. A dead fish truck
full of porters I ran track with, effeminate blues singers, the
    wealth
of the nation transposed into the ring of my flesh's image. Grand
    dancers
spray noise and disorder in these old tombs. Liverwurst
    sandwiches dry
on brown fenced-in lawns, unfinished cathedrals tremble with
    our screams.
Of the dozens, the razor, the cloth, the sheen, all speed adven-
    ture locked
in my eyes. I give you now, to love me, if I spare what flesh of
    yours
is left. If I see past what I feel, and call music simply "Art" and
    will
not take it to its logical end. For the death by hanging, for
the death by the hooded political murderer, for the old man dead
    in his
tired factory; election machines chime quietly his fraudulent
    faith.

For the well that marks the burned stores. For the deadly idiot of
    compromise
who shrieks compassion, and bids me love my neighbor. Even
    beyond the meaning
of such act as would give all my father's dead ash to fertilize
    their bilious
land. Such act as would give me legend, "This is the man who
    saved us
Spared us from the disappearance of the sixteenth note, the
    destruction
of the scale. This is the man who against the black pits of
    despairing genius
cried, "Save the Popular Song." For them who pat me in the
    huddle and do not

argue at the plays. For them who finish second and are happy
     they are Chinese,
and need not run those 13 blocks.

I am moved. I will not move to save them. There is no
"melody." Only the foot stomped, the roaring harmonies of need.
     The
hand banged on the table, waved in the air. The teeth pushed
     against
the lip. The face and fingers sweating. "Let me alone," is praise
     enough
for these musicians.

3)

My own mode of conscience. And guilt, always the obvious
     connection.
They spread you in the sun, and leave you there, one of a kind,
     who
has no sons to tell this to. The mind so bloated at its own
     judgment. The
railing consequence of energy given in silence. Ideas whose sole
     place
is where they form. The language less than the act. The act so far
     beyond
itself, meaning all forms, all modes, all voices, chanting for
     safety.

I am deaf and blind and lost and will not again sing your quiet
     verse. I have lost
even the act of poetry, and writhe now for cool horizonless
     dawn.
     The
shake and chant, bulled electric motion, figure of what there will
     be
as it sits beside me waiting to live past my own meekness. My
     own
light skin. Bull of yellow perfection, imperfectly made,
     imperfectly
understood, except as it rises against the mountains, like sun
but brighter, like flame but hotter. There will be those
who will tell you it will be beautiful.

Crow Jane

*"Crow Jane, Crow Jane, don't hold your head so high,
You realize, baby, you got to lay down and die."*

—MISSISSIPPI JOE WILLIAMS

For Crow Jane
        Mama Death.

For dawn, wind
off the river. Wind
and light, from
the lady's hand. Cold
stuff, placed against
strong man's lips. Young gigolo's
of the 3rd estate. Young ruffians
without no homes. The wealth
is translated, corrected, a
dark process, like thought, tho
it provide a landscpae
with golden domes.
                'Your people
without love.' And life
rots them. Makes a silence
blankness in every space
flesh thought to be. (First light,
is dawn. Cold stuff
to tempt a lover. Old lady
of flaking eyes. Moon lady
of useless thighs.

Crow Jane's Manner.

                Is some pilgrimage
to thought. Where she goes, in fairness,
"nobody knows." And then, without love,
returns to those wrinkled stomachs

ragged bellies / of young ladies
gone with seed. Crow
will not have. Dead virgin
of the mind's echo. Dead lady
of thinking, back now, without
the creak of memory.

                              Field is yellow. Fils dead
(Me, the last . . . black lip hung
in dawn's gray wind. The last,
for love, a taker, took my kin.

Crow. Crow. Where
you leave my
other boys?

Crow Jane In High Society.

                              (Wipes
her nose
on the draperies. Spills drinks
fondles another man's
life. She is looking
for alternatives. Openings
where she can lay all
this greasy talk
on somebody. Me, once. Now
I am her teller.

                    (And I tell
her symbols, as the grey movement
of clouds. Leave
grey movements
of clouds. Leave, always,
more.

Where is she? That she
moves without light. Even
in our halls. Even with
our laughter, lies, dead drunk

in a slouch hat famous king.

Where?

To come on so.

Crow Jane The Crook.

Of the night
of the rain, she
reigned, reined, her
fat whores and horse.

(A cloud burst,
and wet us. The mountain
split, and burned us. We thought
we were done.

Jane.
Wet lady of no image. We
thought, you had left us. Dark
lady, of constant promise. We
thought
you had gone.

2

My heart is cast in bitter
metal. Condiments, spices
all the frustration of earth,
that has so much more desire

than resolution. Want than pleasure.
Oh, Jane. (Her boat bumps at the
ragged
shore. Soul of the ocean, go out,
return.
Oh, Jane, we thought you had gone.

The dead lady canonized.

               (A thread
of meaning. Meaning light. The quick
response. To breath, or the virgins
sick odor against the night.

               (A trail
of objects. Dead nouns, rotted faces
propose the night's image. Erect
for that lady, a grave of her own.

               (The stem
of the morning, sets itself, on
each window (of thought, where it
goes. The lady is dead, may the Gods,

               (those others
get our forgiveness. And Damballah, kind father,
sew up
her bleeding hole.

I Substitute for the Dead Lecturer

      What is most precious, because
        it is lost. What is lost,
           because it is most
               precious.

They have turned, and say that I am dying. That
I have thrown
my life
away. They
have left me alone, where
there is no one, nothing
save who I am. Not a note
nor a word.

Cold air batters
the poor (and their minds
turn open
like sores). What kindness
What wealth
can I offer? Except
what is, for me
ugliest. What is
for me, shadows, shrieking
phantoms. Except
they have need
of life. Flesh
at least,
should be theirs.

The Lord has saved me
to do this. The Lord
has made me strong. I
am as I must have
myself. Against all
thought, all music, all
my soft loves.

For all these wan roads
I am pushed to follow, are
my own conceit. A simple muttering
elegance, slipped in my head
pressed on my soul, is my heart's
worth. And I am frightened
that the flame of my sickness
will burn off my face. And leave
the bones, my stewed black skull,
an empty cage of failure.

BLACK DADA NIHILISMUS

Against   what   light

is false what breath
sucked, for deadness.
          Murder, the cleansed

purpose, frail, against
God, if they bring him
          bleeding, I would not

forgive, or even call him
black dada nihilismus.

The protestant love, wide windows,
color blocked to Mondrian, and the
ugly silent deaths of jews under
the surgeon's knife. (To awake on
69th street with money and a hip
nose. Black dada nihilismus, for

the umbrella'd jesus. Trilby intrigue
movie house presidents sticky the floor.
B.D.N., for the secret men, Hermes, the

blacker art. Thievery (ahh, they return
those secret gold killers. Inquisitors
of the cocktail hour. Trismegistus, have

them, in their transmutation, from stone
to bleeding pearl, from lead to burning
looting, dead Moctezuma, find the West

a grey hideous space.

                    *   *   *   *

From Sartre, a white man, it gave
the last breath. And we beg him die,
before he is killed. Plastique, we

do not have, only thin heroic blades.
The razor. Our flail against them, why
you carry knives? Or brutaled lumps of

heart? Why you stay, where they can
reach? Why you sit, or stand, or walk
in this place, a window on a dark

warehouse. Where the minds packed in
straw. New homes, these towers, for those
lacking money or art. A cult of death,

need of the simple striking arm under
the streetlamp. The cutters, from under
their rented earth. Come up, black dada

nihilismus. Rape the white girls. Rape
their fathers. Cut the mothers' throats.
Black dada nihilismus, choke my friends

in their bedrooms with their drinks spilling
and restless for tilting hips or dark liver
lips sucking splinters from the master's thigh.

Black scream
and chant, scream,
and dull, un
earthly
hollering. Dada, bilious
what ugliness, learned
in the dome, colored holy
shit (i call them sinned

or lost
        burned masters
                of the lost
                        nihil German killers
                                all our
                                        learned

art, 'member
what you said

money, God, power,
a moral code, so cruel
it destroyed Byzantium, Tenochtitlan, Commanch

                                            (got it, *Baby!*
For tambo, willie best, dubois, patrice, mantan, the
bronze buckaroos.

            For Jack Johnson, asbestos, tonto, buckwheat,
            billie holiday.

            For tom russ, l'overture, vesey, beau jack,

(may a lost god damballah, rest or save us
against the murders we intend
against his lost white children
black dada nihilismus

Political Poem

(for Basil)

            Luxury, then, is a way of
            being ignorant, comfortably
            An approach to the open market
            of least information. Where theories
            can thrive, under heavy tarpaulins
            without being cracked by ideas.

            (I have not seen the earth for years
            and think now possibly "dirt" is
            negative, positive, but clearly
            social. I cannot plant a seed, cannot
            recognize the root with clearer dent
            than indifference. Though I eat
            and shit as a natural man. (Getting up
            from the desk to secure a turkey sandwich
            and answer the phone: the poem undone
            undone by my station, by my station,
            and the bad words of Newark.) Raised up

to the breech, we seek to fill for this
crumbling century. The darkness of love,
in whose sweating memory all error is forced.

Undone by the logic of any specific death. (Old gentlemen
who still follow fires, tho are quieter
and less punctual. It is a polite truth
we are left with. Who are you? What are you
saying? Something to be dealt with, as easily.
The noxious game of reason, saying, "No, No,
you cannot feel," like my dead lecturer
lamenting thru gipsies his fast suicide.

The Liar

What I thought was love
in me, I find a thousand instances
as fear. (Of the tree's shadow
winding around the chair, a distant music
of frozen birds rattling
in the cold.
        Where ever I go to claim
my flesh, there are entrances
of spirit. And even its comforts
are hideous uses I strain
to understand.
        Though I am a man
who is loud
on the birth
of his ways. Publicly redefining
each change in my soul, as if I had predicted
them,
        and profited, biblically, even tho
        their chanting weight,
                erased familiarity
                from my face.
                      A question I think,
an answer; whatever sits
counting the minutes

till you die.
                When they say, "It is Roi
                who is dead?" I wonder
                who will they mean?

Dutchman

DUTCHMAN was first presented at The Cherry Lane Theatre, New York City on March 24, 1964.

Original Cast: Jennifer West, Robert Hooks

Produced by Theater 1964
(Richard Barr, Clinton Wilder, Edward Albee)
Directed by Edward Parone

Characters

CLAY, twenty-year-old Negro

LULA, thirty-year-old white woman

RIDERS OF COACH, white and black

YOUNG NEGRO

CONDUCTOR

In the flying underbelly of the city. Steaming hot, and summer on top, outside. Underground. The subway heaped in modern myth.

Opening scene is a man sitting in a subway seat, holding a magazine but looking vacantly just above its wilting pages. Occasionally he looks blankly toward the window on his right. Dim lights and darkness whistling by against the glass. (Or paste the lights, as admitted props, right on the subway windows. Have them move, even dim and flicker. But give the sense of speed. Also stations, whether the train is stopped or the glitter and activity of these stations merely flashes by the windows.)

The man is sitting alone. That is, only his seat is visible, though the rest of the car is outfitted as a complete subway car. But only his seat is shown. There might be, for a time, as the play begins, a loud scream of the actual train. And it can recur throughout the play, or continue on a lower key once the dialogue starts.

The train slows after a time, pulling to a brief stop at one of the stations. The man looks idly up, until he sees a woman's face staring at him through the window; when it realizes that the man has noticed the face, it begins very premeditatedly to smile. The man smiles too, for a moment, without a trace of self-consciousness. Almost an instinctive though undesirable response. Then a kind of awkwardness or embarrassment sets in, and the man makes to look away, is further embarrassed, so he brings back his eyes to where the face was, but by now the train is moving again, and the face would seem to be left behind by the way the man turns his head to look back through the other windows at the slowly fading platform. He smiles then; more comfortably confident, hoping perhaps that his memory of this brief encounter will be pleasant. And then he is idle again.

Scene I

Train roars. Lights flash outside the windows.

LULA enters from the rear of the car in bright, skimpy summer clothes and sandals. She carries a net bag full of paper books, fruit, and other anonymous articles. She is wearing sunglasses, which she pushes up on her forehead from time to time. LULA is a tall, slender, beautiful woman with long red hair hanging straight down her back, wearing only loud lipstick in somebody's good taste. She is eating an apple, very daintily. Coming down the car toward CLAY.

She stops beside CLAY's seat and hangs languidly from the strap, still managing to eat the apple. It is apparent that she is going to sit in the seat next to CLAY, and that she is only waiting for him to notice her before she sits.

CLAY sits as before, looking just beyond his magazine, now and again pulling the magazine slowly back and forth in front of his face in a hopeless effort to fan himself. Then he sees the woman hanging there beside him and he looks up into her face, smiling quizzically.

LULA. Hello.

CLAY. Uh, hi're you?

LULA. I'm going to sit down. . . . O.K.?

CLAY. Sure.

LULA. [*Swings down onto the seat, pushing her legs straight out as if she is very weary*] Oooof! Too much weight.

CLAY. Ha, doesn't look like much to me. [*Leaning back against the window, a little surprised and maybe stiff*]

LULA. It's so anyway. [*And she moves her toes in the sandals, then pulls her right leg up on the left knee, better to inspect the bottoms of the sandals and the back of her heel. She appears for a second not to notice that CLAY is sitting next to her or that she has spoken to him just a second before. CLAY looks at the magazine, then out the black window. As he does this, she turns very quickly toward him*] Weren't you staring at me through the window?

CLAY. [*Wheeling around and very much stiffened*] What?

LULA. Weren't you staring at me through the window? At the last stop?

CLAY. Staring at you? What do you mean?

LULA. Don't you know what staring means?

CLAY. I saw you through the window . . . if that's what it means. I don't know if I was staring. Seems to me you were staring through the window at me.

LULA. I was. But only after I'd turned around and saw you staring through that window down in the vicinity of my ass and legs.

CLAY. Really?

LULA. Really. I guess you were just taking those idle potshots. Nothing else to do. Run your mind over people's flesh.

CLAY. Oh boy. Wow, now I admit I was looking in your direction. But the rest of that weight is yours.

LULA. I suppose.

CLAY. Staring through train windows is weird business. Much weirder than staring very sedately at abstract asses.

LULA. That's why I came looking through the window . . . so you'd have more than that to go on. I even smiled at you.

CLAY. That's right.

LULA. I even got into this train, going some other way than mine. Walked down the aisle . . . searching you out.

CLAY. Really? That's pretty funny.

LULA. That's pretty funny. . . . God, you're dull.

CLAY. Well, I'm sorry, lady, but I really wasn't prepared for party talk.

LULA. No, you're not. What are you prepared for? [*Wrapping the apple core in a Kleenex and dropping it on the floor*]

CLAY. [*Takes her conversation as pure sex talk. He turns to confront her squarely with this idea*] I'm prepared for anything. How about you?

LULA. [*Laughing loudly and cutting it off abruptly*] What do you think you're doing?

CLAY. What?

LULA. You think I want to pick you up, get you to take me somewhere and screw me, huh?

CLAY. Is that the way I look?

LULA. You look like you been trying to grow a beard. That's exactly what you look like. You look like you live in New Jersey with your parents and are trying to grow a beard. That's what. You look like you've been reading Chinese poetry and drinking lukewarm sugarless tea. [*Laughs, uncrossing and recrossing her legs*] You look like death eating a soda cracker.

CLAY. [*Cocking his head from one side to the other, embarrassed and trying to make some comeback, but also intrigued by what the woman is saying . . . even the sharp city coarseness of her voice, which is still a kind of gentle sidewalk throb*] Really? I look like all that?

LULA. Not all of it. [*She feints a seriousness to cover an actual somber tone*] I lie a lot. [*Smiling*] It helps me control the world.

CLAY. [*Relieved and laughing louder than the humor*] Yeah, I bet.

LULA. But it's true, most of it, right? Jersey? Your bumpy neck?

CLAY. How'd you know all that? Huh? Really, I mean about Jersey . . . and even the beard. I met you before? You know Warren Enright?

LULA. You tried to make it with your sister when you were ten.

[*CLAY leans back hard against the back of the seat, his eyes opening now, still trying to look amused*]

LULA. But I succeeded a few weeks ago. [*She starts to laugh again*]

CLAY. What're you talking about? Warren tell you that? You're a friend of Georgia's?

LULA. I told you I lie. I don't know your sister. I don't know Warren Enright.

CLAY. You mean you're just picking these things out of the air?

LULA. Is Warren Enright a tall skinny black black boy with a phony English accent?

CLAY. I figured you knew him.

LULA. But I don't. I just figured you would know somebody like that. [*Laughs*]

CLAY. Yeah, yeah.

LULA. You're probably on your way to his house now.

CLAY. That's right.

LULA. [*Putting her hand on Clay's closest knee, drawing it from the knee up to the thigh's hinge, then removing it, watching his face very closely, and continuing to laugh, perhaps more gently than before*] Dull, dull, dull. I bet you think I'm exciting.

CLAY. You're O.K.

LULA. Am I exciting you now?

CLAY. Right. That's not what's supposed to happen?

LULA. How do I know? [*She returns her hand, without moving it, then takes it away and plunges it in her bag to draw out an apple*] You want this?

CLAY. Sure.

LULA. [*She gets one out of the bag for herself*] Eating apples together is always the first step. Or walking up uninhabited Seventh Avenue in the twenties on weekends. [*Bites and giggles, glancing at Clay and speaking in loose singsong*] Can get you involved . . . boy! Get us involved. Um-huh. [*Mock seriousness*] Would you like to get involved with me, Mister Man?

CLAY. [*Trying to be as flippant as Lula, whacking happily at the apple*] Sure. Why not? A beautiful woman like you. Huh, I'd be a fool not to.

LULA. And I bet you're sure you know what you're talking about. [*Taking him a little roughly by the wrist, so he cannot eat the apple, then shaking the wrist*] I bet you're sure of almost everything anybody ever asked you about . . . right? [*Shakes his wrist harder*] Right?

CLAY. Yeah, right. . . . Wow, you're pretty strong, you know? Whatta you, a lady wrestler or something?

LULA. What's wrong with lady wrestlers? And don't answer because you never knew any. Huh. [*Cynically*] That's for sure. They don't have any lady wrestlers in that part of Jersey. That's for sure.

CLAY. Hey, you still haven't told me how you know so much about me.

LULA. I told you I didn't know anything about *you* . . . you're a well-known type.

CLAY. Really?

LULA. Or at least I know the type very well. And your skinny English friend too.

CLAY. Anonymously?

LULA. [*Settles back in seat, single-mindedly finishing her apple and humming snatches of rhythm and blues song*] What?

CLAY. Without knowing us specifically?

LULA. Oh boy. [*Looking quickly at Clay*] What a face. You know, you could be a handsome man.

CLAY. I can't argue with you.

LULA. [*Vague, off-center response*] What?

CLAY. [*Raising his voice, thinking the train noise has drowned part of his sentence*] I can't argue with you.

LULA. My hair is turning gray. A gray hair for each year and type I've come through.

CLAY. Why do you want to sound so old?

LULA. But it's always gentle when it starts. [*Attention drifting*] Hugged against tenements, day or night.

CLAY. What?

LULA. [*Refocusing*] Hey, why don't you take me to that party you're going to?

CLAY. You must be a friend of Warren's to know about the party.

LULA. Wouldn't you like to take me to the party? [*Imitates clinging vine*] Oh, come on, ask me to your party.

CLAY. Of course I'll ask you to come with me to the party. And I'll bet you're a friend of Warren's.

LULA. Why not be a friend of Warren's? Why not? [*Taking his arm*] Have you asked me yet?

CLAY. How can I ask you when I don't know your name?

LULA. Are you talking to my name?

CLAY. What is it, a secret?

LULA. I'm Lena the Hyena.

CLAY. The famous woman poet?

LULA. Poetess! The same!

CLAY. Well, you know so much about me . . . what's my name?

LULA. Morris the Hyena.

CLAY. The famous woman poet?

LULA. The same. [*Laughing and going into her bag*] You want another apple?

CLAY. Can't make it, lady. I only have to keep one doctor away a day.

LULA. I bet your name is . . . something like . . . uh, Gerald or Walter. Huh?

CLAY. God, no.

LULA. Lloyd, Norman? One of those hopeless colored names creeping out of New Jersey. Leonard? Gag. . . .

CLAY. Like Warren?

LULA. Definitely. Just exactly like Warren. Or Everett.

CLAY. Gag. . . .

LULA. Well, for sure, it's not Willie.

CLAY. It's Clay.

LULA. Clay? Really? Clay what?

CLAY. Take your pick. Jackson, Johnson, or Williams.

LULA. Oh, really? Good for you. But it's got to be Williams. You're too pretentious to be a Jackson or Johnson.

CLAY. Thass right.

LULA. But Clay's O.K.

CLAY. So's Lena.

LULA. It's Lula.

CLAY. Oh?

LULA. Lula the Hyena.

CLAY. Very good.

LULA. [Starts laughing again] Now you say to me, "Lula, Lula, why don't you go to this party with me tonight?" It's your turn, and let those be your lines.

CLAY. Lula, why don't you go to this party with me tonight. Huh?

LULA. Say my name twice before you ask, and no huh's.

CLAY. Lula, Lula, why don't you go to this party with me tonight?

LULA. I'd like to go, Clay, but how can you ask me to go when you barely know me?

CLAY. That is strange, isn't it?

LULA. What kind of reaction is that? You're supposed to say, "Aw, come on, we'll get to know each other better at the party."

CLAY. That's pretty corny.

LULA. What are you into anyway? [*Looking at him half sullenly but still amused*] What thing are you playing at, Mister? Mister Clay Williams? [*Grabs his thigh, up near the crotch*] What are *you* thinking about?

CLAY. Watch it now, you're gonna excite me for real.

LULA. [*Taking her hand away and throwing her apple core through the window*] I bet. [*She slumps in the seat and is heavily silent*]

CLAY. I thought you knew everything about me? What happened?

[*LULA looks at him, then looks slowly away, then over where the other aisle would be. Noise of the train. She reaches in her bag and pulls out one of the paper books. She puts it on her leg and thumbs the pages listlessly. CLAY cocks his head to see the title of the book. Noise of the train. LULA flips pages and her eyes drift. Both remain silent*]

CLAY. Are you going to the party with me, Lula?

LULA. [*Bored and not even looking*] I don't even know you.

CLAY. You said you know my type.

LULA. [*Strangely irritated*] Don't get smart with me, Buster. I know you like the palm of my hand.

CLAY. The one you eat the apples with?

LULA. Yeh. And the one I open doors late Saturday evening with. That's my door. Up at the top of the stairs. Five flights. Above a lot of Italians and lying Americans. And scrape carrots with. Also . . . [*Looks at him*] the same hand I unbutton my dress with, or let my skirt fall down. Same hand. Lover.

CLAY. Are you angry about anything? Did I say something wrong?

LULA. Everything you say is wrong. [*Mock smile*] That's what makes you so attractive. Ha. In that funnybook jacket with all the buttons. [*More animate, taking hold of his jacket*] What've you got that jacket and tie on in all this heat for? And why're you wearing a jacket and tie like that? Did your people ever burn witches or start revolutions over the price of tea? Boy, those narrow-shoulder clothes come from a tradition you ought to feel oppressed by. A three-button suit. What right do you have to be wearing a three-button suit and striped tie? Your grandfather was a slave, he didn't go to Harvard.

CLAY. My grandfather was a night watchman.

LULA. And you went to a colored college where everybody thought they were Averell Harriman.

CLAY. All except me.

LULA. And who did you think you were? Who do you think you are now?

CLAY. [*Laughs as if to make light of the whole trend of the conversation*] Well, in college I thought I was Baudelaire. But I've slowed down since.

LULA. I bet you never once thought you were a black nigger.

[*Mock serious, then she howls with laughter. CLAY is stunned but after initial reaction, he quickly tries to appreciate the humor. LULA almost shrieks*]

LULA. A black Baudelaire.

CLAY. That's right.

LULA. Boy, are you corny. I take back what I said before. Everything you say is not wrong. It's perfect. You should be on television.

CLAY. You act like you're on television already.

LULA. That's because I'm an actress.

CLAY. I thought so.

LULA. Well, you're wrong. I'm no actress. I told you I always lie.
I'm nothing, honey, and don't you ever forget it. [*Lighter*] Although my mother was a Communist. The only person in my family ever to amount to anything.

CLAY. My mother was a Republican.

LULA. And your father voted for the man rather than the party.

CLAY. Right!

LULA. Yea for him. Yea, yea for him.

CLAY. Yea!

LULA. And yea for America where he is free to vote for the mediocrity of his choice! Yea!

CLAY. Yea!

LULA. And yea for both your parents who even though they differ
about so crucial a matter as the body politic still forged a union
of love and sacrifice that was destined to flower at the birth of the
noble Clay . . . what's your middle name?

CLAY. Clay.

LULA. A union of love and sacrifice that was destined to flower at
the birth of the noble Clay Clay Williams. Yea! And most of all yea
yea for you, Clay Clay. The Black Baudelaire. Yes! [*And with
knifelike cynicism*] My Christ. My Christ.

CLAY. Thank you, ma'am.

LULA. May the people accept you as a ghost of the future. And love
you, that you might not kill them when you can.

CLAY. What?

LULA. You're a murderer, Clay, and you know it. [*Her voice darkening with significance*] You know goddamn well what I mean.

CLAY. I do?

LULA. So we'll pretend the air is light and full of perfume.

CLAY. [*Sniffing at her blouse*] It is.

LULA. And we'll pretend the people cannot see you. That is, the citizens. And that you are free of your own history. And I am free of my history. We'll pretend that we are both anonymous beauties smashing along through the city's entrails. [*She yells as loud as she can*] GROOVE!

Black

Scene II

Scene is the same as before, though now there are other seats visible in the car. And throughout the scene other people get on the subway. There are maybe one or two seated in the car as the scene opens, though neither CLAY *nor* LULA *notices them.* CLAY's *tie is open.* LULA *is hugging his arm.*

CLAY. The party!

LULA. I know it'll be something good. You can come in with me, looking casual and significant. I'll be strange, haughty, and silent, and walk with long slow strides.

CLAY. Right.

LULA. When you get drunk, pat me once, very lovingly on the flanks, and I'll look at you cryptically, licking my lips.

CLAY. It sounds like something we can do.

LULA. You'll go around talking to young men about your mind, and to old men about your plans. If you meet a very close friend who is also with someone like me, we can stand together, sipping our drinks and exchanging codes of lust. The atmosphere will be slithering in love and half-love and very open moral decision.

CLAY. Great. Great.

LULA. And everyone will pretend they don't know your name, and then . . . [*She pauses heavily*] later, when they have to, they'll claim a friendship that denies your sterling character.

CLAY. [*Kissing her neck and fingers*] And then what?

LULA. Then? Well, then we'll go down the street, late night, eating apples and winding very deliberately toward my house.

CLAY. Deliberately?

LULA. I mean, we'll look in all the shopwindows, and make fun of the queers. Maybe we'll meet a Jewish Buddhist and flatten his conceits over some very pretentious coffee.

CLAY. In honor of whose God?

LULA. Mine.

CLAY. Who is . . . ?

LULA. Me . . . and you?

CLAY. A corporate Godhead.

LULA. Exactly. Exactly. [*Notices one of the other people entering*]

CLAY. Go on with the chronicle. Then what happens to us?

LULA. [*A mild depression, but she still makes her description triumphant and increasingly direct*] To my house, of course.

CLAY. Of course.

LULA. And up the narrow steps of the tenement.

CLAY. You live in a tenement?

LULA. Wouldn't live anywhere else. Reminds me specifically of my novel form of insanity.

CLAY. Up the tenement stairs.

LULA. And with my apple-eating hand I push open the door and lead you, my tender big-eyed prey, into my . . . God, what can I call it . . . into my hovel.

CLAY. Then what happens?

LULA. After the dancing and games, after the long drinks and long walks, the real fun begins.

CLAY. Ah, the real fun. [*Embarrassed, in spite of himself*] Which is . . . ?

LULA. [*Laughs at him*] Real fun in the dark house. Hah! Real fun in the dark house, high up above the street and the ignorant cowboys. I lead you in, holding your wet hand gently in my hand . . .

CLAY. Which is not wet?

LULA. Which is dry as ashes.

CLAY. And cold?

LULA. Don't think you'll get out of your responsibility that way. It's not cold at all. You Fascist! Into my dark living room. Where we'll sit and talk endlessly, endlessly.

CLAY. About what?

LULA. About what? About your manhood, what do you think? What do you think we've been talking about all this time?

CLAY. Well, I didn't know it was that. That's for sure. Every other thing in the world but that. [*Notices another person entering, looks quickly, almost involuntarily up and down the car, seeing the other people in the car*] Hey, I didn't even notice when those people got on.

LULA. Yeah, I know.

CLAY. Man, this subway is slow.

LULA. Yeah, I know.

CLAY. Well, go on. We were talking about my manhood.

LULA. We still are. All the time.

CLAY. We were in your living room.

LULA. My dark living room. Talking endlessly.

CLAY. About my manhood.

LULA. I'll make you a map of it. Just as soon as we get to my house.

CLAY. Well, that's great.

LULA. One of the things we do while we talk. And screw.

CLAY. [*Trying to make his smile broader and less shaky*] We finally
got there.

LULA. And you'll call my rooms black as a grave. You'll say, "This
place is like Juliet's tomb."

CLAY. [*Laughs*] I might.

LULA. I know. You've probably said it before.

CLAY. And is that all? The whole grand tour?

LULA. Not all. You'll say to me very close to my face, many, many
times, you'll say, even whisper, that you love me.

CLAY. Maybe I will.

LULA. And you'll be lying.

CLAY. I wouldn't lie about something like that.

LULA. Hah. It's the only kind of thing you will lie about. Especially if you think it'll keep me alive.

CLAY. Keep you alive? I don't understand.

LULA. [*Bursting out laughing, but too shrilly*] Don't understand? Well, don't look at me. It's the path I take, that's all. Where both feet take me when I set them down. One in front of the other.

CLAY. Morbid. Morbid. You sure you're not an actress? All that self-aggrandizement.

LULA. Well, I told you I wasn't an actress . . . but I also told you I lie all the time. Draw your own conclusions.

CLAY. Morbid. Morbid. You sure you're not an actress? All scribed? There's no more?

LULA. I've told you all I know. Or almost all.

CLAY. There's no funny parts?

LULA. I thought it was all funny.

CLAY. But you mean peculiar, not ha-ha.

LULA. You don't know what I mean.

CLAY. Well, tell me the almost part then. You said almost all. What else? I want the whole story.

LULA. [*Searching aimlessly through her bag. She begins to talk breathlessly, with a light and silly tone*] All stories are whole stories. All of 'em. Our whole story . . . nothing but change. How could things go on like that forever? Huh? [*Slaps him on the shoulder, begins finding things in her bag, taking them out and throwing them over her shoulder into the aisle*] Except I do go on as I do. Apples and long walks with deathless intelligent lovers. But you mix it up. Look out the window, all the time. Turning pages. Change change change. Till, shit, I don't know you. Wouldn't, for that matter. You're too serious. I bet you're even too serious to be psychoanalyzed. Like all those Jewish poets from

Yonkers, who leave their mothers looking for other mothers, or others' mothers, on whose baggy tits they lay their fumbling heads. Their poems are always funny, and all about sex.

CLAY. They sound great. Like movies.

LULA. But you change. [*Blankly*] And things work on you till you hate them.

[*More people come into the train. They come closer to the couple, some of them not sitting, but swinging drearily on the straps, staring at the two with uncertain interest*]

CLAY. Wow. All these people, so suddenly. They must all come from the same place.

LULA. Right. That they do.

CLAY. Oh? You know about them too?

LULA. Oh yeah. About them more than I know about you. Do they frighten you?

CLAY. Frighten me? Why should they frighten me?

LULA. 'Cause you're an escaped nigger.

CLAY. Yeah?

LULA. 'Cause you crawled through the wire and made tracks to my side.

CLAY. Wire?

LULA. Don't they have wire around plantations?

CLAY. You must be Jewish. All you can think about is wire. Plantations didn't have any wire. Plantations were big open whitewashed places like heaven, and everybody on 'em was grooved to be there. Just strummin' and hummin' all day.

LULA. Yes, yes.

CLAY. And that's how the blues was born.

LULA. Yes, yes. And that's how the blues was born.

[LULA *begins to make up a song that becomes quickly hysterical.
As she sings she rises from her seat, still throwing things out of
her bag into the aisle, beginning a rhythmical shudder and twist-
like wiggle, which she continues up and down the aisle, bumping
into many of the standing people and tripping over the feet of
those sitting. Each time she runs into a person she lets out a very
vicious piece of profanity, wiggling and stepping all the time*]

LULA. And that's how the blues was born. Yes. Yes. Son of a bitch,
get out of the way. Yes. Quack. Yes. Yes. And that's how the blues
was born. Ten little niggers sitting on a limb, but none of them
ever looked like him. [*Points to* CLAY, *returns toward the seat,
with her hands extended for him to rise and dance with her*] And
that's how blues was born. Yes. Come on, Clay. Let's do the nasty.
Rub bellies. Rub bellies.

CLAY. [*Waves his hands to refuse. He is embarrassed, but determined to get a kick out of the proceedings*] Hey, what was in those
apples? Mirror, mirror on the wall, who's the fairest one of all?
Snow White, baby, and don't you forget it.

LULA. [*Grabbing for his hands, which he draws away*] Come on,
Clay. Let's rub bellies on the train. The nasty. The nasty. Do the
gritty grind, like your ol' rag-head mammy. Grind till you lose
your mind. Shake it, shake it, shake it, shake it. OOOOweeee!
Come on, Clay. Let's do the choo-choo train shuffle, the navel
scratcher.

CLAY. Hey, you coming on like the lady who smoked up her grass
skirt.

LULA. [*Becoming annoyed that he will not dance, and becoming
more animated as if to embarrass him still further*] Come on,
Clay . . . let's do the thing. Uhh! Uhh! Clay! Clay! You middle-
class black bastard. Forget your social-working mother for a few
seconds and let's knock stomachs. Clay, you liver-lipped white
man. You would-be Christian. You ain't no nigger, you're just a
dirty white man. Get up, Clay. Dance with me, Clay.

CLAY. Lula! Sit down, now. Be cool.

LULA. [*Mocking him, in wild dance*] Be cool. Be cool. That's all you
know . . . shaking that wildroot cream-oil on your knotty head,
jackets buttoning up to your chin, so full of white man's words.
Christ. God. Get up and scream at these people. Like scream
meaningless shit in these hopeless faces. [*She screams at people
in train, still dancing*] Red trains cough Jewish underwear for
keeps! Expanding smells of silence. Gravy snot whistling like sea
birds. Clay. Clay, you got to break out. Don't sit there dying the
way they want you to die. Get up.

CLAY. Oh, sit the fuck down. [*He moves to restrain her*] Sit down,
goddamn it.

LULA. [*Twisting out of his reach*] Screw yourself, Uncle Tom.
Thomas Woolly-head. [*Begins to dance a kind of jig, mocking
Clay with loud forced humor*] There is Uncle Tom . . . I mean,
Uncle Thomas Woolly-Head. With old white matted mane. He
hobbles on his wooden cane. Old Tom. Old Tom. Let the white
man hump his ol' mama, and he jes' shuffle off in the woods and
hide his gentle gray head. Ol' Thomas Woolly-Head.

[*Some of the other riders are laughing now. A drunk gets up and
joins* LULA *in her dance, singing, as best he can, her "song."* CLAY
*gets up out of his seat and visibly scans the faces of the other
riders*]

CLAY. Lula! Lula!

[*She is dancing and turning, still shouting as loud as she can. The
drunk too is shouting, and waving his hands wildly*]

CLAY. Lula . . . you dumb bitch. Why don't you stop it? [*He
rushes half stumbling from his seat, and grabs one of her flailing
arms*]

LULA. Let me go! You black son of bitch. [*She struggles against
him*] Let me go! Help!

[CLAY *is dragging her towards her seat, and the drunk seeks to interfere. He grabs* CLAY *around the shoulders and begins wrestling
with him.* CLAY *clubs the drunk to the floor without releasing*

LULA, *who is still screaming.* CLAY *finally gets her to the seat and throws her into it]*

CLAY. Now you shut the hell up. [*Grabbing her shoulders*] Just shut up. You don't know what you're talking about. You don't know anything. So just keep your stupid mouth closed.

LULA. You're afraid of white people. And your father was. Uncle Tom Big Lip!

[CLAY *slaps her as hard as he can, across the mouth.* LULA's *head bangs against the back of the seat. When she raises it again,* CLAY *slaps her again*]

CLAY. Now shut up and let me talk.

[*He turns toward the other riders, some of whom are sitting on the edge of their seats. The drunk is on one knee, rubbing his head, and singing softly the same song. He shuts up too when he sees* CLAY *watching him. The others go back to newspapers or stare out the windows*]

CLAY. Shit, you don't have any sense, Lula, nor feelings either. I could murder you now. Such a tiny ugly throat. I could squeeze it flat, and watch you turn blue, on a humble. For dull kicks. And all these weak-faced ofays squatting around here, staring over their papers at me. Murder them too. Even if they expected it. That man there . . . [*Points to well-dressed man*] I could rip that *Times* right out of his hand, as skinny and middle-classed as I am, I could rip that paper out of his hand and just as easily rip out his throat. It takes no great effort. For what? To kill you soft idiots? You don't understand anything but luxury.

LULA. You fool!

CLAY. [*Pushing her against the seat*] I'm not telling you again, Tallulah Bankhead! Luxury. In your face and your fingers. You telling me what I ought to do. [*Sudden scream frightening the whole coach*] Well, don't! Don't you tell me anything! If I'm a middle-class fake white man . . . let me be. And let me be in the way I want. [*Through his teeth*] I'll rip your lousy breasts off! Let me be who I feel like being. Uncle Tom. Thomas. Whoever. It's none of your business. You don't know anything except what's there for you to see. An act. Lies. Device. Not the pure heart, the pumping black heart. You don't ever know that. And I sit here, in this buttoned-up suit, to keep myself from cutting all your throats. I mean wantonly. You great liberated whore! You fuck some black man, and right away you're an expert on black people. What a lotta shit that is. The only thing you know is that you come if he bangs you hard enough. And that's all. The belly rub? You wanted to do the belly rub? Shit, you don't even know how. You don't know how. That ol' dipty-dip shit you do, rolling your ass like an elephant. That's not my kind of belly rub. Belly rub is not Queens. Belly rub is dark places, with big hats and overcoats held up with one arm. Belly rub hates you. Old bald-headed four-eyed ofays popping their fingers . . . and don't know yet what they're doing. They say, "I love Bessie Smith." And don't even understand that Bessie Smith is saying, "Kiss my ass, kiss my black unruly ass." Before love, suffering, desire, anything you can explain, she's saying, and very plainly, "Kiss my black ass." And if you don't know that, it's you that's doing the kissing.

Charlie Parker? Charlie Parker. All the hip white boys scream for Bird. And Bird saying, "Up your ass, feeble-minded ofay! Up your ass." And they sit there talking about the tortured genius of Charlie Parker. Bird would've played not a note of music if he just walked up to East Sixty-seventh Street and killed the first ten white people he saw. Not a note! And I'm the great would-be poet. Yes, that's right. Poet. Some kind of bastard literature . . . all it needs is a simple knife thrust. Just let me bleed you, you loud whore, and one poem vanished. A whole people of neurotics, struggling to keep from being sane. And the only thing that would cure the neurosis would be your murder. Simple as that. I mean if I murdered you, then other white people would begin to understand me. You understand? No. I guess not. If Bessie Smith had killed some white people she wouldn't have needed that music. She could have talked very straight and plain about the world. No metaphors. No grunts. No wiggles in the dark of her soul. Just straight two and two are four. Money. Power. Luxury. Like that. All of them. Crazy niggers turning their backs on sanity. When all it needs is that simple act. Murder. Just murder! Would make us all sane. [*Suddenly weary*] Ahhh. Shit. But who needs it? I'd rather be a fool. Insane. Safe with my words, and no deaths, and clean, hard thoughts, urging me to new conquests. My people's madness. Hah! That's a laugh. My people. They don't need me to claim them. They got legs and arms of their own. Personal insanities. Mirrors. They don't need all those words. They don't need any defense. But listen, though, one more thing. And you tell this to your father, who's probably the kind of man who needs to know at once. So he can plan ahead. Tell him not to preach so much rationalism and cold logic to these niggers. Let them alone. Let them sing curses at you in code and see your filth as simple lack of style. Don't make the mistake, through some irresponsible surge of Christian charity, of talking too much about the advantages of Western rationalism, or the great intellectual legacy of the white man, or maybe they'll begin to listen. And then, maybe one day, you'll find they actually do understand exactly what you are talking about, all these fantasy people. All these blues people. And on that day, as sure as shit, when you really believe you can "accept" them into your fold, as half-white trusties late of the subject peoples. With no more blues, except the very old ones, and not a watermelon in sight, the great missionary heart will have triumphed, and all of those ex-coons will be stand-up Western men, with eyes for clean hard useful lives, sober, pious and sane, and they'll murder you. They'll murder you, and have very rational explanations. Very much like your own. They'll cut your throats, and drag you out to the edge of your cities so the flesh can fall away from your bones, in sanitary isolation.

LULA. [Her voice takes on a different, more businesslike quality] I've heard enough.

CLAY. [Reaching for his books] I bet you have. I guess I better collect my stuff and get off this train. Looks like we won't be acting out that little pageant you outlined before.

LULA. No. We won't. You're right about that, at least. [She turns to look quickly around the rest of the car] All right!

[The others respond]

CLAY. [Bending across the girl to retrieve his belongings] Sorry, baby, I don't think we could make it.

[As he is bending over her, the girl brings up a small knife and plunges it into CLAY's chest. Twice. He slumps across her knees, his mouth working stupidly]

LULA. Sorry is right. [Turning to the others in the car who have already gotten up from their seats] Sorry is the rightest thing you've said. Get this man off me! Hurry, now!

[*The others come and drag* CLAY's *body down the aisle*]

LULA. Open the door and throw his body out.

[*They throw him off*]

LULA. And all of you get off at the next stop.

[LULA *busies herself straightening her things. Getting everything in order. She takes out a notebook and makes a quick scribbling note. Drops it in her bag. The train apparently stops and all the others get off, leaving her alone in the coach.*

Very soon a young Negro of about twenty comes into the coach, with a couple of books under his arm. He sits a few seats in back of LULA. *When he is seated she turns and gives him a long slow look. He looks up from his book and drops the book on his lap. Then an old Negro conductor comes into the car, doing a sort of restrained soft shoe, and half mumbling the words of some song. He looks at the young man, briefly, with a quick greeting*]

CONDUCTOR. Hey, brother!

YOUNG MAN. Hey.

[*The conductor continues down the aisle with his little dance and the mumbled song.* LULA *turns to stare at him and follows his movements down the aisle. The conductor tips his hat when he reaches her seat, and continues out the car*]

Curtain

From *The System of Dante's Hell*

The System of Dante's Hell is Baraka's only novel. With some modification, the modernist racial hell he depicts is patterned after the structure of the *Inferno*, providing modern equivalences to Dante's circles, or levels, of Hell. Unlike Dante, however, he places the heretics, that is, those who betray their origins, on the lowest level. The first sections of the book are free-associational, stream-of-consciousness prose poems, but it concludes with the brilliant and self-contained section "The Heretics," which lyrically deals with the issue of divided racial consciousness.

—wjh

The Heretics

"The whole of lower Hell is surrounded by a great wall, which is defended by rebel angels and immediately within which are punished the arch-heretics and their followers."
                                        And then,
the city of Dis, "the stronghold of Satan, named after him, . . . the deeper Hell of willful sin."

Blonde summer in our south. Always it floats down & hooks in the broad leaves of those unnamed sinister southern trees. Blonde. Yellow, a narrow sluggish water full of lives. Desires. The crimson heavy blood of a race, concealed in those absolute black nights. As if, each tiny tragedy had its own universe / or God to strike it down.

• •

Faceless slow movement. It was warm & this other guy had his sleeves rolled up. (You cd go to jail for that without any trouble. But we were loose, & maybe drunk. And I turned away & doubled up like rubber or black figure sliding at the bottom of any ocean. Thomas, Joyce, Eliot, Pound, all gone by & I thot agony at how beautiful I was. And sat sad many times in latrines fingering my joint.

But it was dusty. And time sat where it could, covered me dead, like under a stone for years, and my life was already over. A dead man stretched & a rock rolled over . . . till a light struck me straight on & I entered some madness, some hideous elegance . . . "A Patrician I wrote to him. Am I a Patrician?"

• •

We both wore wings. My hat dipped & shoes maybe shined. This other guy was what cd happen in this country. Black & his silver wings & tilted blue cap made up for his mother's hundred bogus kids. Lynchings. And he waved his own flag in this mosquito air, and walked straight & beauty was fine, and so easy.

He didn't know who I was, or even what. The light, then (what george spoke of in his letters . . . "a soft intense light") was spread thin over the whole element of my world.

Two flyers, is what we thot people had to say. (I was a gunner, the other guy, some kind of airborne medic.) The bright wings & starched uniform. Plus, 24 dollars in my wallet.

That air rides you down, gets inside & leaves you weightless, sweating & longing for cool evening. The smells there wide & blue like eyes. And like kids, or the radio calling saturdays of the world of simple adventure. Made me weep with excitement. Heart pumping: not at all towards where we were. But the general sweep of my blood brought whole existences fresh and tingling into those images of romance had trapped me years ago.

• •

The place used me. Its softness, and in a way, indirect warmth, coming from the same twisting streets we walked. (After the bus, into the main fashion of the city: Shreveport, Louisiana. And it all erected itself for whoever . . . me, I supposed then, "it's here, and of course, the air, for my own weakness. Books fell by. But open yr eyes, nose, speak to whom you want to. Are you contemporary?")

And it seemed a world for aztecs lost on the bone side of mountains. A world, even strange, sat in that leavening light & we had come in raw from the elements. From the cardboard moonless world of ourselves . . . to whatever. To grasp at straws. (If indeed we wd confront us with those wiser selves . . . But that was blocked. The weather held. No rain. That smell wrapped me up finally & sent me off to seek its source. And men stopped us. Split our melting fingers. The sun moved till it stopped at the edge of the

city. The south stretched past any eye. Outside any peculiar thot. Itself, whatever it becomes, is lost to what formal selves we have.
Lust, a condition of the weather. The air, lascivious. Men die from
anything . . . and this portion of my life was carefully examining
the rules. How to die? How to die?

•

The place, they told us, we'd have to go to "ball" was called by them
Bottom. The Bottom; where the colored lived. There, in whatever
wordless energies your lives cd be taken up. Step back: to the edge,
soothed the wind drops. Fingers are cool. Air sweeps. Trees one
hundred feet down, smoothed over, the wind sways.

And
they tell me there is one place/

> for me to be. Where
> it all
>   comes down. &
> you take up
> your sorrowful
>   life. There/
> with us all. To
> whatever death

•

The Bottom lay like a man under a huge mountain. You cd see it
slow in some mist, miles off. On the bus, the other guy craned &
pulled my arm from the backseats at the mile descent we'd make to
get the juice. The night had it. Air like mild seasons and come. That
simple elegance of semen on the single buds of air. As if the night
were feathers . . . and they settled solid on my speech . . . and
preached sinister love for the sun.

The day . . .
where had it gone? It had moved away as we wound down into the
mass of trees and broken lives.

The bus stopped
finally a third of the way down the slope. The last whites had gotten
off a mile back & 6 or seven negroes and we two flyers had the bus.
The driver smiled his considerate paternal smile in the mirror at our
heads as we popped off. Whole civilization considered, considered.
"They live in blackness. No thought runs out. They kill each other
& hate the sun. They have no God save who they are. Their black
selves. Their lust. Their insensible animal eyes."

"Hey, son, 'dyou pay for him?" He asked me because I hopped off last. He meant not my friend, the other pilot, but some slick head coon in yellow pants cooling it at top speed into the grass. & knowing no bus driver was running in after no 8 cents.

> "Man, the knives
> flash. Souls
> are spittle
> on black earth. Metal
> dug in flesh chipping
> at the bone."

I turned completely around to look at the bus driver. I saw a knife in him hacking chunks of bone. He stared, & smiled at the thin mob rolling down the hill. Friday night. Nigguhs is Nigguhs. I agreed. & smiled, he liked the wings, had a son who flew. "You gon pay for that ol coon?"

> "No, " I said, "No. Fuck, man, I hate coons." He
laughed. I saw the night around his head warped with blood. The bus, moon & trees floated heavily in blood. It washed down the side of the hill & the negroes ran from it.

I turned towards my friend who was loping down the hill shouting at me & ran towards him & what we saw at the foot of the hill. The man backed the bus up & turned around / pretending he was a mystic.

• • •

I caught Don (?) and walked beside him laughing. And the trees passed & some lights and houses sat just in front of us. We trailed the rest of the crowd & they spread out soon & disappeared into their lives.

The Bottom was like Spruce & Belmont (the ward) in Nwk. A culture of violence and foodsmells. There, for me. Again. And it stood strange when I thot finally how much irony. I had gotten so elegant (that was college / a new order of foppery). But then the army came & I was dragged into a kind of stillness. Everything I learned stacked up and the bones of love shattered in my face. And I never smiled again at anything. Everything casual in my life (except that life itself) was gone. Those naked shadows of men against the ruined walls. Penis, testicles. All there (and I sat burned like wire, w/ farmers, thinking of what I had myself. When I peed I thot that. "Look. Look what you're using to do this. A dick. And two balls, one a little lower than the other. The first thing warped & crooked when it hardened." But it meant nothing. The books meant noth-

ing. My idea was to be loved. What I accused John of. And it meant
going into that huge city melting. And the first face I saw I went
to and we went home and he shoved his old empty sack of self
against my frozen skin.

• •

Shadows, phantoms, recalled by that night. Its heavy moon. A
turning slow and dug in the flesh and wet spots grew under my
khaki arms. Alive to mystery. And the horror in my eyes made them
large and the moon came in. The moon and the quiet southern night.

• •

We passed white shut houses. It seemed misty or smoky. Things
settled dumbly in the fog and we passed, our lives spinning off in
simple anonymous laughter.

We were walking single file because of
the dirt road. Not wanting to get in the road where drunk niggers
roared by in dead autos stabbing each others' laughter in some grey
abandon of suffering. That they suffered and cdn't know it. Knew
that somehow, forever. Each dead nigger stinking his same suffering thru us. Each word of blues some dead face melting. Some life
drained off in silence. Under some grey night of smoke. They roared
thru this night screaming. Heritage of hysteria and madness, the old
meat smells and silent grey sidewalks of the North. Each father,
smiling mother, walked thru these nights frightened of their children. Of the white sun scalding their nights. Of each hollow loud
footstep in whatever abstruse hall.

• • •

The Joint

(a letter was broken and I
can't remember. The other guy laughed, at the name. And patted
his. I took it literal and looked thru my wallet as not to get inflamed
and sink on that man screaming of my new loves. My cold sin in the
cities. My fear of my own death's insanity, and an actual longing for

men that brooded in each finger of my memory.

He laughed at the sign. And we stood, for the moment (he made me warm with his laughing), huge white men who knew the world (our wings) and would give it to whoever showed as beautiful or in our sad lone smiles, at least willing to love us.

He pointed, like Odysseus wd. Like Virgil, the weary shade, at some circle. For Dante, me, the yng wild virgin of the universe to look. To see what terror. What illusion. What sudden shame, the world is made. Of what death and lust I fondled and thot to make beautiful or escape, at least, into some other light, where each death was abstract & intimate.

● ● ● ●

There were, I think, 4 women standing across the street. The neon winked, and the place seemed mad to be squatted in this actual wilderness. "For Madmen Only." Mozart's Ornithology and yellow greasy fags moaning german jazz. Already, outside. The passage, I sensed in those women. And black space yawned. Damned and burning souls. What has been your sin? Your ugliness?

And they waved. Calling us natural names. "Hey, ol bigeye sweet nigger . . com'ere." "Littl ol' skeeter dick . . . don't you want none?" And to each other giggling at their centuries, "Um, that big nigger look sweet" . . . "Yeh, that little one look sweet too." The four walls of some awesome city. Once past you knew that your life had ended. That roads took up the other side, and wound into thicker dusk. Darker, more insane, nights.

And Don shouted back, convinced of his hugeness, his grace . . . my wisdom. I shuddered at their eyes and tried to draw back into the shadows. He grabbed my arm, and laughed at my dry lips.

Of the 4, the pretty one was Della and the fat one, Peaches. 17 year old whores strapped to negro weekends. To the black thick earth and smoke it made to hide their maudlin sins. I stared and was silent and they, the girls and Don, the white man, laughed at my whispering and sudden midnight world.

Frightened of myself, of the night's talk, and not of them. Of myself.

The other two girls fell away hissing at their poverty. And the two who had caught us exchanged strange jokes. Told us of themselves thru the other's mouth. Don already clutching the thin beautiful Della. A small tender flower she seemed. Covered with the pollen of desire. Ignorance. Fear of what she was. At her 17th birthday she had told us she wept, in the department store, at her death. That the years wd make her old and her dresses wd get bigger. She laughed and felt my arm, and laughed, Don pulling her closer. And ugly negroes passed close to us frowning at the uniforms and my shy clipped speech which they called "norf."

So Peaches was mine. Fat with short baked hair split at the ends. Pregnant empty stomach. Thin shrieky voice like knives against a blackboard. Speeded up records. Big feet in white, shiny polished shoes. Fat tiny hands full of rings. A purple dress with wrinkles across the stomach. And perspiring flesh that made my khakis wet.

The four of us went in the joint and the girls made noise to show this world their craft. The two rich boys from the castle. (Don looked at me to know how much cash I had and shouted and shook his head and called "18, man," patting his ass.)

The place was filled with shades. Ghosts. And the huge ugly hands of actual spooks. Standing around the bar, spilling wine on greasy shirts. Yelling at a fat yellow spliv who talked about all their mothers, pulling out their drinks. Laughing with wet cigarettes and the paper stuck to fat lips. Crazy as anything in the world, and sad because of it. Yelling as not to hear the sad breathing world. Turning all music up. Screaming all lyrics. Tough black men . . . weak black men. Filthy drunk women whose perfume was cheap unnatural flowers. Quiet thin ladies whose lives had ended and whose teeth hung stupidly in their silent mouths . . rotted by thousands of nickel wines. A smell of despair and drunkenness. Silence and laughter, and the sounds of their movement under it. Their frightening lives.

• •

Of course the men didn't dig the two imitation white boys come in on their leisure. And when I spoke someone wd turn and stare, or laugh, and point me out. The quick new jersey speech, full of italian idiom, and the invention of the jews. Quick to describe. Quicker to condemn. And when we finally got a seat in the back of the place, where the dance floor was, the whole place had turned a little to look. And the girls ate it all up, laughing as loud as their vanity permitted. Other whores grimaced and talked almost as loud . . . putting us all down.

10 feet up on the wall, in a kind of bal-

cony, a jew sat, with thick glasses and a cap, in front of a table. He had checks and money at the table & where the winding steps went up to him a line of shouting woogies waved their pay & waited for that bogus christ to give them the currency of that place. Two tremendous muthafuckers with stale white teeth grinned in back of the jew and sat with baseball bats to protect the western world.

On the dance floor people hung on each other. Clutched their separate flesh and thought, my god, their separate thots. They stunk. They screamed. They moved hard against each other. They pushed. And wiggled to keep the music on. Two juke boxes blasting from each corner, and four guys on a bandstand who had taken off their stocking caps and come to the place with guitars. One with a saxophone. All that screaming came together with the smells and the music, the people bumped their asses and squeezed their eyes shut.

Don ordered a bottle of schenley's which cost 6 dollars for a pint after hours. And Peaches grabbed my arm and led me to the floor.

The dancing like a rite no one knew, or had use for outside their secret lives. The flesh they felt when they moved, or I felt all their flesh and was happy and drunk and looked at the black faces knowing all the world thot they were my own, and lusted at that anonymous America I broke out of, and long for it now, where I am.

We danced, this face and I, close so I had her sweat in my mouth, her flesh the only sound my brain could use. Stinking, and the music over us like a sky, choked any other movement off. I danced. And my history was there, had passed no further. Where it ended, here, the light white talking jig, died in the arms of some sentry of Africa. Some short-haired witch out of my mother's most hideous dreams. I was nobody now, mama. Nobody. Another secret nigger. No one the white world wanted or would look at. (My mother shot herself. My father killed by a white tree fell on him. The sun, now, smothered. Dead.

• • •

Don and his property had gone when we finished. 3 or 4 dances later. My uniform dripping and soggy on my skin. My hands wet. My eyes turned up to darkness. Only my nerves sat naked and my ears were stuffed with gleaming horns. No one face sat alone, just that image of myself, forever screaming. Chiding me. And the girl, peaches, laughed louder than the crowd. And wearily I pushed her hand from my fly and looked for a chair.

We sat at the table and I looked around the room for my brother, and only shapes of black men moved by. Their noise and smell. Their narrow paths to death. I wanted to panic, but the dancing and gin had me calm, almost cruel in what I saw.

Peaches talked. She talked at what she thought she saw. I slumped on the table and we emptied another pint. My stomach turning rapidly and the room moved without me. And I slapped my hands on the table laughing at myself. Peaches laughed, peed, thinking me crazy, returned, laughed again. I was silent now, and felt the drunk and knew I'd go out soon. I got up feeling my legs, staring at the fat guard with me, and made to leave. I mumbled at her. Somthing ugly. She laughed and held me up. Holding me from the door. I smiled casual, said, "Well, honey, I gotta split . . I'm fucked up." She grinned the same casual, said, "You can't go now, big eye, we jist gittin into sumpum."

"Yeh, yeh, I know . . . but I can't make it." My head was shaking on my chest, fingers stabbed in my pockets. I staggered like an acrobat towards the stars and trees I saw at one end of the hall. "UhUh . . . baby where you goin?"

"Gotta split, gotta split . . . really, baby, I'm fucked . . up." And I twisted my arm away, moving faster as I knew I should towards the vague smell of air. Peaches was laughing and tugging a little at my sleeve. She came around and rubbed my tiny pecker with her fingers. And still I moved away. She had my elbow when I reached the road, head still slumped, and feet pushing for a space to go down solid on. When I got outside she moved in front of me. Her other girls had moved in too, to see what was going on. Why Peaches had to relinquish her share so soon. I saw the look she gave me and wanted somehow to protest, say, "I'm sorry. I fucked up. My mind, is screwy, I don't know why. I can't think. I'm sick. I've been fucked in the ass. I love books and smells and my own voice. You don't want me. Please, Please, don't want me."

But she didn't see. She heard, I guess, her own blood. Her own whore's bones telling her what to do. And I twisted away from her, headed across the road and into the dark. Out of, I hoped, Bottom, towards what I thot was light. And I could hear the girls laughing at me, at Peaches, at whatever thing I'd brought to them to see.

So the fat bitch grabbed my hat. A blue "overseas cap" they called it in the service. A cunt cap the white boys called it. Peaches had it and was laughing like kids in the playground doing the same thing to some unfortunate fag. I knew the second she got it, and stared crazily at her, and my look softened to fear and I grinned,

I think. "You ain't going back without dis cap, big eye nigger," toss-ing it over my arms to her screaming friends. They tossed it back to her. I stood in the center staring at the lights. Listening to my own head. The things I wanted. Who I thot I was. What was it? Why was this going on? Who was involved? I screamed for the hat. And they shot up the street, 4 whores, Peaches last in her fat, shout-ing at them to throw the hat to her. I stood for awhile and then tried to run after them. I cdn't go back to my base without that cap. Go to jail, drunken nigger! Throw him in the stockade! You're out of uniform, shine! When I got close to them, the other three ran off, and only Peaches stood at the top of the hill waving the hat at me, cackling at her wealth. And she screamed at the world, that she'd won some small niche in it. And did a dance, throwing her big hips at me, cursing and spitting . . . laughing at the drunk who had sat down on the curb and started to weep and plead at her for some cheap piece of cloth.

And I was mumbling under the tears. "My hat, please, my hat. I gotta get back, please." But she came over to me and leaned on my shoulder, brushing the cap in my face. "You gonna buy me another drink . . . just one more?"

● ● ●

She'd put the cap in her brassiere, and told me about the Cotton Club. Another place at the outskirts of Bottom. And we went there, she was bouncing and had my hand, like a limp cloth. She talked of her life. Her husband, in the service too. Her family. Her friends. And predicted I would be a lawyer or something else rich.

The Cotton Club, was in a kind of ditch. Or valley. Or three flights down. Or someplace removed from where we stood. Like movies, or things you think up abstractly. Poles, where the moon was. Signs, for streets, beers, pancakes. Out front. No one moved out-side, it was too late. Only whores and ignorant punks were out.

The place when we got in was all light. A bar. Smaller than the joint, with less people and quieter. Tables were strewn around and there was a bar with a fat white man sitting on a stool behind it. His elbows rested on the bar and he chewed a cigar spitting the flakes on the floor. He smiled at Peaches, knowing her, leaning from his talk. Four or five stood at the bar. White and black, moaning and drunk. And I wondered how it was they got in. The both colors? And I saw a white stripe up the center of the floor, and taped to the bar, going clear up, over the counter. And the black man who talked, stood at one side, the left, of the tape, furtherest from the door. And the white man, on the right, closest to the door. They talked, and were old friends, touching each other, and screaming with laughter at what they said.

We got vodka. And my head slumped, but I looked around to see, what place this was. Why they moved. Who was dead. What faces came. What moved. And they sat in their various skins and stared at me.

Empty man. Walk thru shadows. All lives the same. They give you wishes. The old people at the window. Dead man. Rised, come gory to their side. Wish to be lovely, to be some other self. Even here, without you. Some other soul, than the filth I feel. Have in me. Guilt, like something of God's. Some separate suffering self.

Locked in a lightless shaft. Light at the top, pure white sun. And shadows twist my voice. Iron clothes to suffer. To pull down, what had grown so huge. My life wrested away. The old wood. Eyes of the damned uncomprehending. Who it was. Old slack nigger. Drunk punk. Fag. Get up. Where's your home? Your mother. Rich nigger. Porch sitter. It comes down. So cute, huh? Yellow thing. Think you cute.

And suffer so slight, in the world. The world? Literate? Brown skinned. Stuck in the ass. Suffering from what? Can you read? Who is T. S. Eliot? So what? A cross. You've got to like girls. Weirdo. Break, Roi, break. Now come back, do it again. Get down, hard. Come up. Keep your legs high, crouch hard when you get the ball . . . churn, churn, churn. A blue jacket, and alone. Where? A chinese restaurant. Talk to me. Goddamnit. Say something. You never talk, just sit there, impossible to love. Say something. Alone, there, under those buildings. Your shadows. Your selfish tongue. Move. Frightened bastard. Frightened scared sissy motherfucker.

•   •   •

I felt my head go down. And I moved my hand to keep it up. Peaches laughed again. The white man turned and clicked his tongue at her wagging his hand. I sucked my thin mustache, scratched my chest, held my sore head dreamily. Peaches laughed. 2 bottles more of vodka she drank (half pints at 3.00 each) & led me out the back thru some dark alley down steps and thru a dark low hall to where she lived.

She was dragging me, I tried to walk and couldn't and stuck my hands in my pockets to keep them out of her way. Her house, a room painted blue and pink with Rheingold women glued to the wall. Calendars. The Rotogravure. The picture of her husband? Who she thot was some officer, and he was grinning like watermelon photos with a big white apron on and uncle jemima white hat and should've had a skillet. I slumped on the bed, and she made me get up and sit in a chair and she took my hat out of her clothes and threw it across the room. Coffee, she said, you want coffee. She brought it anyway, and I got some in my mouth. Like winter inside me. I coughed and she laughed. I turned my head away from the bare bulb. And she went in a closet and got out a thin yellow cardboard shade and struck it on the light trying to push the burned part away from the huge white bulb.

Willful sin. In your toilets jerking off. You refused God. All frauds, the cold mosques glitter winters. "Morsh-Americans." Infidels fat niggers at the gates. What you want. What you are now. Liar. All sins, against your God. Your own flesh. TALK. TALK.

And I still slumped and she pushed my head back against the greasy seat and sat on my lap grinning in my ear, asking me to say words that made her laugh. Orange. Probably. Girl. Newark. Peaches. Talk like a white man, she laughed. From up north (she made the "th" an "f").

And sleep seemed good to me. Something my mother would say. My grandmother, all those heads of heaven. To get me in. Roi, go to sleep, You need sleep, and eat more. You're too skinny. But this fat bitch pinched my neck and my eyes would shoot open and my hands dropped touching the linoleum and I watched roaches, trying to count them getting up to 5, and slumped again. She pinched me. And I made some move and pushed myself up standing and went to the sink and stuck my head in cold water an inch above the pile of stale egg dishes floating in brown she used to wash the eggs off.

I shook my head. Took out my handkerchief to dry my hands, leaving my face wet and cold, for a few seconds. But the heat came back, and I kept pulling my shirt away from my body and smelled under my arms, trying to laugh with Peaches, who was laughing again.

I wanted to talk now. What to say. About my life. My thots. What I'd found out, and tried to use. Who I was. For her. This lady, with me.

She pushed me backwards on the bed and said you're sleepy I'll get in with you. And I rolled on my side trying to push up on the bed and couldn't, and she pulled one of my shoes off and put it in her closet. I turned on my back and groaned at my head told her again I had to go. I was awol or something. I had to explain awol and she knew what it meant when I finished. Everybody that she knew was that. She was laughing again. O, God, I wanted to shout and it was groaned. Oh, God.

She had my pants in her fingers pulling them over my one shoe. I was going to pull them back up and they slipped from my hands and I tried to raise up and she pushed me back. "Look, Ol nigger, I ain't even gonna charge you. I like you." And my head was turning, flopping straight back on the chenille, and the white ladies on the wall did tricks and grinned and pissed on the floor. "Baby, look, Baby," I was sad because I fell. From where it was I'd come to. My silence. The streets I used for books. All come in. Lost. Burned. And soothing she rubbed her hard hair on my stomach and I meant to look to see if grease was there it was something funny I meant to say, but my head twisted to the side and I bit the chenille and figured there would be a war or the walls would collapse and I would have to take the black girl out, a hero. And my mother would grin and tell her friends and my father would call me "mcgee" and want me to tell about it.

When I had only my shorts on she pulled her purple dress over her head. It was all she had, except a grey brassiere with black wet moons where her arms went down. She kept it on.

Some light got in from a window. And one white shadow sat on a half-naked woman on the wall. Nothing else moved. I drew my legs up tight & shivered. Her hands pulled me to her.

•

It was Chicago. The fags & winter. Sick thin boy, come out of those els. Ask about the books. Thin mathematics and soup. Not the black Beverly, but here for the first time I'd seen it. Been pushed in. What was flesh I hadn't used till then. To go back. To sit lonely. Need to be used, touched, and see for the first time how it moved.

Why the world moved on it. Not a childish sun. A secret fruit. But hard things between their legs. And lives governed under it. So here, it can sit now, as evil. As demanding, for me, to have come thru and found it again. I hate it. I hate to touch you. To feel myself go soft and want some person not myself. And here, it had moved outside. Left my wet fingers and was not something I fixed. But dropped on me and sucked me inside. That I walked the streets hunting for warmth. To be pushed under a quilt, and call it love. To shit water for days and say I've been loved. Been warm. A real thing in the world. See my shadow. My reflection. I'm here, alive. Touch me. Please. Please, touch me.

• • •

She rolled on me and after my pants were off pulled me on her thick stomach. I dropped between her legs and she felt between my cheeks to touch my balls. Her fingers were warm and she grabbed everything in her palm and wanted them harder. She pulled to get them harder and it hurt me. My head hurt me. My life. And she pulled, breathing spit on my chest. "Comeon, Baby, Comeon . . . Get hard." It was like being slapped. And she did it that way, trying to laugh. "Get hard . . . Get hard." And nothing happened or the light changed and I couldn't see the paper woman.

And she slapped me now, with her hand. A short hard punch and my head spun. She cursed. & she pulled as hard as she could. I was going to be silent but she punched again and I wanted to laugh . . . it was another groan. "Young peachtree," she had her mouth at my ear lobe. "You don't like women, huh?" No wonder you so pretty . . . ol bigeye faggot." My head was turned from that side to the other side turned to the other side turned again and had things in it bouncing.

"How'd you ever get in them airplanes, peaches (her name she called me)? Why they let fairies in there now? (She was pulling too hard now & I thot everything would give and a hole in my stomach would let out words and tears). Goddam punk, you gonna fuck me tonight or I'm gonna pull your fuckin dick aloose."

How to be in this world. How to be here, not a shadow, but thick bone and meat. Real flesh under real sun. And real tears falling on black sweet earth.

I was crying now. Hot hot tears and trying to sing. Or say to Peaches. "Please, you don't know me. Not what's in my head. I'm beautiful.

Stephen Dedalus. A mind, here where there is only steel. Nothing else. Young pharaoh under trees. Young pharaoh, romantic, liar. Feel my face, how tender. My eyes. My soul is white, pure white, and soars. Is the God himself. This world and all others.

And I thot of a black man under the el who took me home in the cold. And I remembered telling him all these things. And how he listened and showed me his new suit. And I crawled out of bed morning and walked thru the park for my train. Loved. Afraid. Huger than any world. And the hot tears wet Peaches and her bed and she slapped me for pissing.

I rolled hard on her and stuck my soft self between her thighs. And ground until I felt it slip into her stomach. And it got harder in her spreading the meat. Her arms around my hips pulled down hard and legs locked me and she started yelling. Faggot. Faggot. Sissy Motherfucker. And I pumped myself. Straining. Threw my hips at her. And she yelled, for me to fuck her. Fuck her. Fuck me, you lousy fag. And I twisted, spitting tears, and hitting my hips on hers, pounding flesh in her, hearing myself weep.

• • • • • • • •

Later, I slipped out into Bottom. Without my hat or tie, shoes loose and pants wrinkled and filthy. No one was on the streets now. Not even the whores. I walked not knowing where I was or was headed for. I wanted to get out. To see my parents, or to be silent for the rest of my life. Huge moon was my light. Black straight trees the moon showed. And the dirt roads and scattered wreck houses. I still had money and I.D., and a pack of cigarettes. I trotted, then stopped, then trotted, and talked outloud to myself. And laughed a few times. The place was so still, so black and full of violence. I felt myself.

At one road, there were several houses. Larger than alot of them. Porches, yards. All of them sat on cinder blocks so the vermin would have trouble getting in. Someone called to me. I thought it was in my head and kept moving, but slower. They called again. "Hey, psst. Hey comere." A whisper, but loud. "Comere, baby." All the sides of the houses were lit up but underneath, the space the cinder blocks made was black. And the moon made a head shadow on the ground, and I could see an arm in the same light. Someone kneeling under one of the houses, or an arm and the shadow of a head. I stood straight, and stiff, and tried to see right thru the dark.

The voice came back, chiding like. Something you want. Whoever wants. That we do and I wondered who it was kneeling in the dark, at the end of the world, and I heard breathing when I did move, hard and closed.

I bent towards the space to see who it was. Why they had called. And I saw it was a man. Round red-rimmed eyes, sand-colored jew hair, and teeth for a face. He had been completely under the house but when I came he crawled out and I saw his dripping smile and yellow soggy skin full of red freckles. He said, "Come on here. Comere a second." I moved to turn away. The face like a dull engine. Eyes blinking. When I turned he reached for my arm grazing my shirt and the voice could be flushed down a toilet. He grinned and wanted to panic seeing me move. "Lemme suck yo dick, honey. Huh?" I was backing away like from the hyena cage to see the rest of them. Baboons? Or stop at the hotdog stand and read a comic book. He came up off all fours and sat on his knees and toes, shaking his head and hips. "Comeon baby, comeon now." As I moved back he began to scream at me. All lust, all panic, all silence and sorrow, and finally when I had moved and was trotting down the road, I looked around and he was standing up with his hands cupped to his mouth yelling into the darkness in complete hatred of what was only some wraith. Irreligious spirit pushing thru shadows, frustrating and confusing the flesh. He screamed behind me and when the moon sunk for minutes behind the clouds or trees his scream was like some animal's, some hurt ugly thing dying alone.

● ● ● ●

It was good to run. I would jump every few steps like hurdling, and shoot my arm out straight to take it right, landing on my right heel, snapping the left leg turned and flat, bent for the next piece. 3 steps between 180 yard lows, 7 or 9 between the 220's. The 180's I thought the most beautiful. After the first one, hard on the heel and springing up. Like music; a scale. Hit, 1-23. UP (straight right leg, down low just above the wood. Left turned at the ankle, flat, tucked. Head low to the knee, arms reaching for the right toe, pulling the left leg to snap it down. HIT (right foot). Snap left HIT (left). Stride. The big one. 1-23. UP. STRETCH. My stride was long enough for the 3 step move. Stretching and hopping almost but in perfect scale. And I moved ahead of Wang and held it, the jew boy pooping at the last wood. I hit hard and threw my chest out, pulling the knees high, under my chin. Arms pushing. The last ten yards I picked up 3 and won by that, head back wrong (Nap said) and galloping like a horse (wrong again Nap said) but winning in new time and leaping in the air like I saw heroes do in flicks.

• • • •

I got back to where I thought the Joint would be, and there were city-like houses and it was there somewhere. From there, I thought I could walk out, get back to the world. It was getting blue again. Sky lightening blue and grey trees and buildings black against it. And a few lights going on in some wood houses. A few going off. There were alleys now. And high wood fences with slats missing. Dogs walked across the road. Cats sat on the fences watching. Dead cars sulked. Old newspapers torn in half pushed against fire hydrants or stoops and made tiny noises flapping if the wind came up.

I had my hands in my pockets, relaxed. The anonymous seer again. Looking slowly at things. Touching wood rails so years later I would remember I had touched wood rails in Louisiana when no one watched. Swinging my leg at cans, talking to the cats, doing made up dance steps or shadow boxing. And I came to a corner & saw some big black soldier stretched in the road with blood falling out of his head and stomach. I thot first it was Don. But this guy was too big and was in the infantry. I saw a paratrooper patch on his cap which was an inch away from his chopped up face, but the blue and silver badge had been taken off his shirt.

He was groaning quiet, talking to himself. Not dead, but almost. And I bent over him to ask what happened. He couldn't open his eyes and didn't hear me anyway. Just moaned and moaned losing his life on the ground. I stood up and wondered what to do. And looked at the guy and saw myself and looked over my shoulder when I heard someone move behind me. A tall black skinny woman hustled out of the shadows and looking back at me disappeared into a hallway. I shouted after her. And stepped in the street to see the door she'd gone in.

I turned to go back to the soldier and there was a car pulling up the road. A red swiveling light on top and cops inside. One had his head hung out the window and yelled towards me. "Hey, you, Nigger, What's going on?" That would be it. AWOL. Out of uniform (with a norfern accent). Now murder too. "30 days for nigger killing." I spun and moved. Down the road & they started to turn. I hit the fence, swinging up and dove into the black yard beyond. Fell on my hands and knees & staggered, got up, tripped on garbage, got up, swinging my hands, head down and charged off in the darkness.

The crackers were yelling on the other side of the fence and I could hear one trying to scale it. There was another fence beyond, and I took it the same as the first. Swinging down into another yard. And turned right and went over another fence, ripping my shirt. Huge cats leaped out of my path and lights went on in some houses. I saw the old woman who'd been hiding near the soldier just as I got to the top of one fence. She was standing in a hallway that led out in that yard, and she ducked back laughing when she saw me. I started to go after her, but I just heaved a big rock in her direction and hit another fence.

I got back to where the city houses left off, and there were the porches and cinder blocks again. I wondered if "sweet peter eater" would show up. (He'd told me his name.) And I ran up the roads hoping it wdn't get light until I found Peaches again.

At the Cotton Club I went down the steps, thru the alley, rested in the black hall, and tapped on Peaches' door. I bounced against it with my ass, resting between bumps, and fell backwards when she opened the door to shove her greasy eyes in the hall.

"You back again? What you want, honey? Know you don't want no pussy. Doyuh?"

I told her I had to stay there. That I wanted to stay there, with her. That I'd come back and wanted to sleep. And if she wanted money I'd give her some. And she grabbed my wrist and pulled me in, still bare-assed except for the filthy brassiere.

She loved me, she said. Or liked me alot. She wanted me to stay, with her. We could live together and she would show me how to fuck. How to do it good. And we could start as soon as she took a pee. And to undress, and get in bed and wait for her, unless I wanted some coffee, which she brought back anyway and sat on the edge of the bed reading a book about Linda Darnell.

"Oh, we can have some good times baby. Movies, all them juke joints. You live here with me and I'll be good to you. Wallace (her husband) ain't due back in two years. We can raise hell waiting for him." She put the book down and scratched the inside of her thighs, then under one arm. Her hair was standing up and she went to a round mirror over the sink and brushed it. And turned around and shook her big hips at me, then pumped the air to suggest our mission. She came back and we talked about our lives: then she pushed back the sheets, helped me undress again, got me hard and pulled me into her. I came too quick and she had to twist her hips a few minutes longer to come herself. "Uhauh, good even on a sof. But I still got to teach you."

• • • • • •

I woke up about 1 the next afternoon. The sun, thru that one window, full in my face. Hot, dust in it. But the smell was good. A daytime smell. And I heard daytime voices thru the window up and fat with optimism. I pulled my hands under my head and looked for Peaches, who was out of bed. She was at the kitchen end of the room cutting open a watermelon. She had on a slip, and no shoes, but her hair was down flat and greased so it made a thousand slippery waves ending in slick feathers at the top of her ears.

"Hello, sweet," she turned and had a huge slice of melon on a plate for me. It was bright in the room now & she'd swept and straightened most of the shabby furniture in her tiny room. And the door sat open so more light, and air could come in. And her radio up on a shelf above the bed was on low with heavy blues and twangy guitar. She sat the melon on the "end table" and moved it near the bed. She had another large piece, dark red and spilling seeds in her hand and had already started. "This is good. Watermelon's a good breakfast. Peps you up."

And I felt myself smiling, and it seemed that things had come to an order. Peaches sitting on the edge of the bed, just beginning to perspire around her forehead, eating the melon in both hands, and mine on a plate, with a fork (since I was "smart" and could be a lawyer, maybe). It seemed settled. That she was to talk softly in her vague american, and I was to listen and nod, or remark on the heat or the sweetness of the melon. And that the sun was to be hot on our faces and the day smell come in with dry smells of knuckles or greens or peas cooking somewhere. Things moving naturally for us. At what bliss we took. At our words. And slumped together in anonymous houses I thought of black men sitting on their beds this saturday of my life listening quietly to their wives' soft talk. And felt the world grow together as I hadn't known it. All lies before, I thought. All fraud and sickness. This was the world. It leaned under its own suns, and people moved on it. A real world of flesh, of smells, of soft black harmonies and color. The dead maelstrom of my head, a sickness. The sun so warm and lovely on my face, the melon sweet going down. Peaches' music and her radio's. I cursed chicago, and softened at the world. "You look so sweet," she was saying. "Like you're real rested."

· · · · ·

I dozed again even before I finished the melon and Peaches had taken it and put it in the icebox when I woke up. The greens were cooking in our house now. The knuckles on top simmering. And biscuits were cooking, and chicken. "How you feel, baby," she watched me stretch. I yawned loud and scratched my back getting up to look at what the stove was doing. "We gonna eat a good lunch before we go to the movies. You so skinny, you could use a good meal. Don't you eat nuthin?" And she put down her cooking fork and hugged me to her, the smell of her, heavy, traditional, secret.

"Now you get dressed, and go get me some tomatoes . . . so we can eat." And it was good that there was something I could do for her. And go out into that world too. Now I knew it was there. And flesh.

I put on the stained khakis & she gave me my hat. "You'll get picked up without yo cap. We have to get you some clothes so you can throw that stuff away. The army don't need you no way." She laughed. "Leastways not as much as I does. Old Henry at the joint'll give you a job. You kin count money as good as that ol' jew I bet."

And I put the tie on, making some joke, and went out shopping for my wife.

· · · · · · ·

Into that sun. The day was bright and people walked by me smiling. And waved "Hey" (a greeting) and they all knew I was Peaches' man.

I got to the store and stood talking to the man about the weather about airplanes and a little bit about new jersey. He waved at me when I left "O.K. . . . you take it easy now." "O.K., I'll see you," I said. I had the tomatoes and some plums and peaches I bought too. I took a tomato out of the bag and bit the sweet flesh. Pushed my hat on the back of my head and strutted up the road towards the house.

It was a cloud I think came up. Something touched me. "That color which cowardice brought out in me." Fire burns around the tombs. Closed from the earth. A despair came down. Alien grace. Lost to myself, I'd come back. To that ugliness sat inside me waiting. And the mere sky greying could do it. Sky spread thin out away from this place. Over other heads. Beautiful unknowns. And my marriage a heavy iron to this tomb. "Show us your countenance." Your light.

It was a light clap of thunder. No lightning. And the sky greyed. Introitus. That word came in. And the yellow light burning in my rooms. To come to see the world, and yet lose it. And find sweet grace alone.

It was this or what I thought, made me turn and drop the tomatoes on Peaches' porch. Her window was open and I wondered what she was thinking. How my face looked in her head. I turned and looked at the sad bag of tomatoes. The peaches, some rolling down one stair. And a light rain came down. I walked away from the house. Up the road, to go out of Bottom.

●   ●   ●   ●

The rain wet my face and I wanted to cry because I thot of the huge black girl watching her biscuits get cold. And her radio playing without me. The rain was hard for a second, drenching me. And then it stopped, and just as quick the sun came out. Heavy bright hot. I trotted for awhile then walked slow, measuring my steps. I stank of sweat and the uniform was a joke.

I asked some people how to get out and they pointed up the road where 10 minutes walking had me at the bottom of the hill the bus came down. A wet wind blew up soft full of sun and I began to calm. To see what had happened. Who I was and what I thought my life should be. What people called "experience." Young male. My hands in my pockets, and the grimy silver wings still hanging gravely on my filthy shirt. The feeling in my legs was to run up the rest of the hill but I just took long strides and stretched myself and wondered if I'd have K.P. or some army chastisement for being 2 days gone.

3 tall guys were coming down the hill I didn't see until they got close enough to speak to me. One laughed (at the way I looked). Tall strong black boys with plenty of teeth and pegged rayon pants. I just looked and nodded and kept on. One guy, with an imitation tattersall vest with

no shirt, told the others I was in the Joint last night "playin cool." Slick city nigger, one said. I was going to pass close to them and the guy with the vest put up his hand and asked me where I was coming from. One with suspenders and a belt asked me what the wings stood for. I told him something. The third fellow just grinned. I moved to walk around them and the fellow with the vest asked could he borrow fifty cents. I only had a dollar in my pocket and told him that. There was no place to get change. He said to give him the dollar. I couldnt do that and get back to my base I told him and wanted to walk away. And one of the guys had gotten around in back of me and kneeled down and the guy with the vest pushed me backwards so I fell over the other's back. I fell backwards into the dust, and my hat fell off, and I didn't think I was mad but I still said something stupid like "What'd you do that for."

"I wanna borrow a dollar, Mr. Half-white muthafucka. And that's that." I sidestepped the one with the vest and took a running step but the grinning one tripped me, and I fell tumbling head forward back in the dust. This time when they laughed I got up and spun around and hit the guy who tripped me in the face. His nose was bleeding and he was cursing while the guy with the suspenders grabbed my shoulders and held me so the hurt one could punch me back. The guy with the vest punched too. And I got in one good kick into his groin, and stomped hard on one of their feet. The tears were coming again and I was cursing, now when they hit me, completely crazy. The dark one with the suspenders punched me in my stomach and I felt sick and the guy with the vest, the last one I saw, kicked me in my hip. The guy still held on for awhile then he pushed me at one of the others and they hit me as I fell. I got picked up and was screaming at them to let me go. "Bastards, you filthy stupid bastards, let me go." Crazy out of my head. Stars were out. And there were no fists just dull distant jolts that spun my head. It was in a cave this went on. With music and whores danced on the tables. I sat reading from a book aloud and they danced to my reading. When I finished reading I got up from the table and for some reason, fell forward weeping on the floor. The negroes danced around my body and spilled whisky on my clothes. I woke up 2 days later, with white men, screaming for God to help me.

The Black Nationalist Period (1965–1974)

We also charge that so-called allegations of "outside force" are just racist propaganda. The white man has never been able to understand that black people can think for themselves. So that even now, faced with the murders of our children and our women, they still think that we have to be egged on by outside agitators. You understand this? We declare now that this is a lie. . . . What is responsible for this violence, for this rebellion, is the inability of the city government to feel, as human beings, the plight of the majority of people in this city. And *that* is the cause of this violence.

We also say this: That as long as these unfeeling, illiterate swine continue to dominate our lives, there will *be* violence and there will *be* rebellion.

> —LeRoi Jones, press conference, Newark, New Jersey, with Ron Karenga, H. Rap Brown, Floyd McKissick, and Larry Neal, speaking in the wake of civil disturbance in Newark. Broadcast on 22 July 1967

* * *

The problem with many of us is [that] for too long we have been used to dealing in Western politics so that we feel that if we lose a vote that we must be permanently enemies. African consensus says that we have to stay until we agree, until we come to some kind of consensus. We have already moved on that motion and it has [been] passed and adopted by this convention. But on the other hand, in the interests of the integrity of this body, we still would like to hear those minority positions, even though this has been adopted, and then move the rest of this agenda. Can we do that please? Will please everybody, will please everybody sit down and calm down before we go on? Nothing will be solved by emotionalism without substance. Now let's get back. Let's get back to it. . . .

—From *Nationtime: Gary*, a documentary by William Greaves about the National Black Politican Convention, 1972

* * *

. . . When I die, the consciousness I carry I will to black people. May they pick me apart and take the useful parts, the sweet meat of my feelings. And leave the bitter bullshit rotten white parts alone.

—From "leroy," a poem from the collection *Black Magic*, 1969

Home is a collection of Baraka's early black nationalist essays, which trace his spiritual and political journey back to the black world, back to his black self—literally, back home. (In the course of writing the essays in this book Baraka moved from Greenwich Village to Harlem, and then back home to Newark, New Jersey.) In the preface he notes: "These essays are placed chronologically (from 1960 to 1965) to show just how my mind and my place in America have changed since the 'Cuba Libre' essay." The works reprinted here should suggest the transformations in Baraka's thought over this five-year period.

—wjh

Cuba Libre

Preface

If we live all our lives under lies, it becomes difficult to see *anything* if it does not have anything to do with these lies. If it is, for example, true or, say, honest. The idea that things of this nature continue to exist is not ever brought forward in our minds. If they do, they seem, at their most sympathetic excursion, monstrous untruths. Bigger lies than our own. I am sorry. There are things, elements in the world, that continue to exist, for whatever time, completely liberated from our delusion. They press us also, and we, of course, if we are to preserve the sullen but comfortable vacuum we inhabit, must deny that anyone else could possibly tolerate what we all agree is a hellish world. And for me to point out, assuming I am intrepid enough, or, all right, naïve enough to do so, i.e., that perhaps it is just this miserable subjection to the fantastic (in whatever fashion, sphere, or presence it persists) that makes your/our worlds so hellish, is, I admit, presumption bordering on insanity. But it is certainly true . . . whether I persist or no . . . or whether you believe (at least the words) or continue to stare off into space. It's a bad scene either way.

(What I Brought to the Revolution)

A man called me on a Saturday afternoon some months ago and asked if I wanted to go to Cuba with some other Negroes, some of whom were also writers. I had a house full of people that afternoon and since we had all been drinking, it seemed pretty silly for me to suddenly drop the receiver and say, "I'm going to Cuba," so I hesitated for a minute, asking the man just why would we (what seemed to me to be just "a bunch of Negroes") be going. For what purpose? He said, "Oh, I thought that since you were a poet you might like to know what's *really* going on down there." I had never really thought of anything in that particular light. Being an American poet, I suppose, I thought my function was simply to talk about everything as if I knew . . . it had never entered my mind that I might really like to find out for once what was actually happening someplace else in the world.

There were twelve of us scheduled to go to Habana, July 20. Twelve did go, but most were last-minute replacements for those originally named. James Baldwin, John Killens, Alice Childress, Langston Hughes, were four who were replaced. The only other "professional" writer on this trip was Julian Mayfield, the novelist, who went down before the main body with his wife.

At Idlewild Airport, the 20th, we straggled in from our various lives, assembling at last at 3 P.M. We met each other, and I suppose, took stock of each other. I know I took stock of them, and was disappointed. First, because there were no other, what I considered, "important" Negro writers. The other reasons were accreted as the trip went on. But what I could get at that initial meeting was: One embarrassingly dull (white) communist, his professional Negro (i.e., unstraightened hair, 1930s bohemian peasant blouses, etc., militant integrationist, etc.) wife who wrote embarrassingly inept social comment-type poems, usually about one or sometimes a group of Negroes being mistreated or suffering in general (usually in Alabama, etc.). Two middle-class young Negro ladies from Philadelphia who wrote poems, the nature of which I left largely undetermined. One 1920s "New Negro" type African scholar (one of those terrible examples of what the "Harlem Renaissance" was at its worst). One 1930s type Negro "essayist" who turned out to be marvelously un-lied to. One strange tall man in a straw hat and feathery beard (whom I later go to know as Robert Williams and who later figured very largely in the trip, certainly in my impressions of it). The first Negro to work for the *Philadelphia Inquirer*—I think probably this job has deranged him permanently, because it has made him begin to believe that this (the job) means that white America (i.e., at large) loves him . . . and it is only those "other" kinds of Negroes that they despise and sometimes even lynch. Two (white) secretaries for an organization called The Fair Play For Cuba Committee, who I suppose are as dedicated (to whatever it is they are dedicated to) as they are unattractive. One tall skinny black charming fashion model, who wore some kind of Dior slacks up into the Sierra Maestra mountains (she so reminded me of my sister, with her various younger-generation liberated-type Negro comments, that it made any kind of adulterous behavior on my part impossible). One young Negro abstract expressionist painter, Edward Clarke, whom I had known vaguely before, and grew to know and like very much during this, as he called it, "wild scene." Also at the terminal, but not traveling with us, a tall light-skinned young, as white liberals like to say, "Negro intellectual." It was he, Richard Gibson, who had called me initially and who had pretty much arranged the whole trip. (I understand now that he has just recently been fired from his job at CBS because of his "Cuban activities.")

We didn't get to leave the 20th. Something very strange happened. First, the airline people at the desk (Cubana Airlines) said they had no knowledge of any group excursion of the kind Gibson thought he had arranged. Of course, it was found out that he, Gibson, had letters from various officials, not only verifying the trip, but assuring him that passage, etc., had been arranged and that we only need appear, at 3 P.M., the 20th, and board the plane. After this problem was more or less resolved, these same airline people (ticket sellers, etc.) said that none of our tickets had been paid for, or at least, that the man who must sign for the free tickets had not done so. This man who was supposed to sign the free passes to make them valid was the manager of Cubana Airlines, New York, who, it turned out, was nowhere to be found. Gibson raged and fumed, but nothing happened.

Then, a Señor Molario, the head of the July 26th movement in New York City appeared (he was supposed to accompany us to Habana), and the problem took on new dimensions. "Of course," Señor Molario said, "there are tickets. I have a letter here signed by the Minister of Tourism himself authorizing this trip. The passes need only be signed by the manager of the New York office of Cubana."

Gibson and the airline people told Molario about the manager's inconvenient disappearance. Molario fumed. Gibson and Molario telephoned frantically, but the manager did not appear. (His secretary said she had "no idea" where he was.) Finally, when it was ascertained that the manager had no intention of showing up by plane time, Señor Molario offered to pay for all our tickets out of his own pocket. Then the other dimension appeared. The two men behind the desk talked to each other and then they said, "I'm very sorry, but the plane is all filled up." Molario and Gibson were struck dumb. The rest of us milled around uncertainly. At 4:30 P.M., the plane took off without us. Five hours later, I suppose, it landed in Habana. We found out soon after it took off that there were thirteen empty seats.

The communist and his wife were convinced that the incident represented an attempt by the U.S. government to discourage us from going to Cuba at all. It seemed a rational enough idea to me.

There was no trouble at all with our tickets, etc., the next day. We took off, as scheduled, at 4:30 P.M. and landed at Jose Martí airport five hours later (8:30 P.M. because of the one-hour time difference). At the airport we were met in the terminal by a costumed Calypso band and a smiling bartender who began to pass out daiquiris behind a quickly set up "Bacardi bar" at an alarming rate. There were also crowds of people standing outside the customs office, regular citizens they looked to be, waving and calling to us through the glass. Between daiquiris, we managed to meet our official interpreter, a small pretty Cuban girl named Olga Finlay. She spoke, of course, better English than most of my companions. (I found out later that she had lived in New York about ten years and that she was the niece of some high official in the revolutionary government.) We also met some people from Casa De Las Americas, the sponsoring organization, as well as its sub-director, a young architect named Alberto Robaina. I met two young Cuban poets, Pablo Armando Fernandez, who had translated one of my poems for *Lunes de Revolución*, the literary supplement of the official newspaper of the revolution, and Guillermo Cabrera Infante, the editor of the supplement.

From the very outset of the trip I was determined not to be "taken." I had cautioned myself against any undue romantic persuasion and had vowed to set myself up as a completely "objective" observer. I wanted nothing to do with the official type tours, etc., I knew would be waiting for us and I had even figured out several ways to get around the country by myself in the event that the official tours got to be too much. Casa De Las Americas, the government, was paying all our bills and I was certain that they would want to make very sure that we saw everything they wanted us to see. I wanted no part of it. I speak Spanish fairly well, can't be mistaken for a "gringo yanqui" under any circumstances, and with the beard and without the seersucker suit I was wearing, I was pretty sure I'd be relatively free to tramp around where I wanted to. So of course with these cloak-and-dagger ideas and amidst all the backslapping, happy crowds (crowds in the U.S. are never "happy". . . . hysterical, murderous, duped, etc., viz. Nathanael West, yes, but under no circumstances "happy." A happy crowd *is* suspect), government-supplied daiquiris, Calypsos, and so forth, I got extremely paranoid. I felt immediately sure that the make was on.

In New York we were told that we would probably be staying at the Hotel Riviera, one of the largest luxury hotels in Habana. However, the cars took us to another hotel, the Hotel Presidente. The Presidente is hardly what could be called a luxury hotel, although I'm sure it was one of the great *tourista* places during the 1930s. Now, in contrast to the thirty-story Hilton and the other newer "jeweled pads" of Habana, the Presidente looked much like the 23rd Street YMCA. It had become, after the advent of the skyscraper hotels, more or less a family residence with about 35 permanent guests.

When we got out of the cars and realized that by no stretch of the imagination could we be said to be in a luxury hotel, there was an almost audible souring throughout the little band. The place was fronted, and surrounded, by a wide, raised awning-covered tile terrace. There were rattan chairs and tables scattered all over it. At the top of the stairs, as we entered, a small glass-enclosed sign with movie schedules, menus for the dining room, and pictures of the entertainers who worked (only weekends now) in the hotel bar. There was one working elevator run by a smiling, one-armed, American slang-speaking operator. The sign-in desk was exactly the way they are in movies and I was startled for a moment by the desk clerk, who in his slightly green tinted glasses and thin eyes looked exactly like pictures of Fulgencio Batista.

To further sour our little group, the men were billeted two in a room. Clarke and I managed to get into a room with a connecting door to another room. As soon as we got into our room, the other door opened and the model came through smiling and mildly complaining. She definitely missed the Riviera. However, the three of us established an immediate rapport and I called room service and ordered two bottles before we even took off our jackets.

The liquor was brought upstairs and when I opened the door to let the bellhop in, the essayist and the tall bearded man were standing outside the door also. We invited them in and everyone re-introduced himself. As the evening moved on, and more liquor was consumed, we talked more and more about ourselves. I was most interested in the tall man. His name, Robert Williams, was vaguely familiar. I remembered just where it was, and in what context, I had seen Williams' name. He was the president of the Monroe, North Carolina, branch of the NAACP. He was also the man who had stated publicly that he didn't hold too much with "passive resistance," especially as championed by Rev. Martin Luther King, and he had advocated that the Southern Negro meet violence with violence. He had been immediately suspended by the home office, but the people in his branch had told the New York wheels that if Williams was out so were they. He had been reinstated, but very, very reluctantly. Williams had gone on, as he told us in some detail later, to establish a kind of pocket militia among the Negroes of Monroe, and had managed to so terrorize the white population of the town that he could with some finality ban any further meetings of the local Ku Klux Klan. The consensus among the white population was that "Williams was trying to provoke them and they weren't going to be provoked."

Somehow, people in Cuba heard about Williams' one-man war in Monroe and invited him to see for himself what was happening in Cuba. Apparently, when the people who were in charge of trying to attract U.S. Negro tourists to Cuba found out that they drew blanks in their dealings with NAACP people and other "official" Negroes, viz. the tragedy of Joe Louis, they thought Williams would be a good risk. He was. He came down to Habana with Richard Gibson and toured the entire country at government expense, meeting Fidel Castro as well as most of the other important men in the revolutionary government. There were many pictures of Williams in most Cuban newspapers, many interviews given to newspapers and over the various television networks. In most of the interviews Williams put down the present administration of the U.S. very violently for its aberrant foreign policy and its hypocritical attitude on what is called "The Negro Question." He impressed almost all of Cuba with the force of his own personality and the patent hopelessness of official Uncle Sham.

On his return to the States, Williams, of course, was castigated by whatever portion of the American press that would even bother to report that there had been an American Negro "leader" who had actually gone down to Cuba and had, moreover, heartily approved of what he had seen. The NAACP people in New York called Williams in and said he was wasting his talent down in that small town and offered him a good job at the home office in New York. When he was offered a return trip to Cuba, Williams jumped at the chance.

Later in the evening, the two middle-class ladies from Philadelphia turned up, drawn I suppose by all the noise that must have been coming out of our room. The one pretty middle-class lady talked for awhile about not being at the Riviera, and what people in Philadelphia had said when she told them she was going to Cuba. I was pretty surprised, in one sense, at her relation of those comments, because the comments themselves, which I suppose must have come from people pretty much like herself, i.e., middle-class, middle-brow young Negroes living in Philadelphia, were almost exactly the same as the comments that had been tossed my way from the various beats, bohemians and intellectuals in Greenwich Village, New York City (of course, given that proper knowing cynicism that is fashionable among my contemporaries). It made me shudder. I mean to find how homogenous most thinking in the U.S. has become, even among the real and/or *soi disant* intellectual. A New York taxicab driver taking me out to Idlewild says ". . . Those rotten commies. You'd better watch yourself, mister, that you don't get shot or something. Those guys are mean." And from a close friend of mine, a young New York poet, "I don't trust guys in uniforms." The latter, of course, being more reprehensible because he is supposed to come up with thought that is alien to the cliché, completely foreign to the well-digested particle of moral engagement. But this is probably the biggest symptom of our moral disintegration (call it, as everyone else is wont, complacency), this so-called rebellion against what is most crass and ugly in our society, but without the slightest thought of, say, any kind of direction or purpose. Certainly, without any knowledge of what could be put up as alternatives. To fight against one kind of dullness with an even more subtle dullness is, I suppose, the highwater mark of social degeneracy. Worse than mere lying.

In 1955, on leave from an airbase in Puerto Rico, I came into Habana for three days. I suppose, then, probably next to Tangiers, Habana was the vice capital of the world. I remember coming out of my hotel and being propositioned by three different people on my way to a bus stop. The first guy, a boy around fifteen, wanted to sell me his sister. The second guy, also around fifteen, had a lot of women he wanted to sell. Probably not all of them were his sisters. The third guy had those wild comic books and promises of blue movies. The town was quieter in the daytime; then it was only an occasional offer to buy narcotics. No one even came out on the streets except billions of beggars and, of course, the Americans, until the sun went down . . . then it was business as usual. The best liberty town in the world. I remember also blowing one hundred bucks in the casino and having some beautiful red-haired woman give it back to me to play again. She was the wife of a bigtime British film maker who said she was in love with Africans. She was extremely dragged when she found out I was just an American G.I. without even money enough to buy a box of prophylactics.

(What I Brought Back Here)

The next morning I was awakened by the phone on the night table next to my head. It was the historian, who had assumed the role of official spokesman, etc., and, I suppose, co-ordinator of the group. He said that the group was waiting for Clarke and me to come down, hadn't we been advised as to what time to meet in the lobby, etc.

Our official guides and interpreters were waiting, Olga Finlay and the architect, Robaina. Robaina, about 28-years old and blond, wore a fairly expensive Italian suit and was driving a white Jaguar. He spoke almost no English, though he understood it perfectly, but had to go along with us because he was sub-director of the sponsoring organization.

That was our first stop, Casa De Las Americas. It was housed in a large white building about three blocks from the Presidente. The organization itself is responsible for disseminating and promoting Cuban culture throughout the Americas. It is also responsible for such things as intercultural exchanges between Cuba and other countries: traveling art shows, arranging visits to Cuba by American (North and South) persons from all the arts, setting up writers conferences (such as the one that included Simone de Beauvoir and Jean-Paul Sartre), running an adult education center, discussion groups, lecture series, and hundreds of other things. They've had a few North Americans down to lecture and perform: William Warfield gave several concerts all over the country, Waldo Frank lectured, and Maya Deren, the experimental film maker, was down in May, showing her films and lecturing. Many more North American artists, etc., have been invited to come down just to see what's going on in the country, but most have refused or been very busy.

The adult school, which is run very much like the New School for Social Research, specializes in what's known as "Cultura Para El Pueblo" (Culture For The People). The courses of study are French, English, Portuguese, American History, Cuban History, Cuban Literature, Political Geography, Latin-American Literature, Music, North American Literature, and one in Film. The library, which specializes in "Asuntos Americanos," has about 25,000 volumes, including literary magazines from all over the Americas.

La Casa also maintains a record library of Latin-American music, classical as well as folk. They also serve as a publishing house for Latin-American authors, having just conducted this spring an inter–Latin-American competition for the best new books, poetry, drama, short stories, a novel, and a collection of essays. The prizes were $1,000 and publication of the work. Two Argentines, a Cuban, a Guatemalan and an Ecuadorian won the first prizes.

The place is a jumble of activity. Even early in the morning when we got there, there were secretaries running through the various offices speaking Spanish, Portuguese, English and French. We were introduced to the director of La Casa, Señora Haydee Santamaria, a blonde buxom woman of about forty. The first thing she told us, through Olga, was that although special tours had been arranged for our party, we were free to go anywhere we could. This brought a low roar of approval from the group, although the communist and his wife said they hoped the official tour would include at least one peasant's home and a typical Cuban Negro family. Señora Santamaria said that if the tours did not already include these things, she would make sure they were added. She talked to us briefly about La Casa's functions and had small pamphlets passed around which went into these functions in detail. We were also given copies of the five prize-winning books I mentioned before, even though the only members of our party who could read or speak Spanish were the essayist and myself.

The small demitasse cups of Cuban coffee were served and we asked Señora Santamaria questions as well as the other employees of La Casa who were present for just that purpose. Robaina was standing next to me so I began to ask him about Cuban poets. Were there any literary magazines in Cuba? What were the young poets like? What was Cuban painting like? Would I get a chance to meet Nicolas Guillen (the best known Cuban poet—he and Neruda are considered the best living Latin-American poets). Robaina's English conversation was mostly Spanish, but we got on very well. He answered almost all of my questions energetically and even offered to take me around to see some of the young Cuban painters and poets.

We hung around La Casa another hour then went downstairs to the production offices of *Arma Nueva*, the organ of La Comisión Nacional De Alfabetización, the organization in charge of elementary adult education. This organization is attempting to educate the great masses of illiterate Cubans concentrated mostly in rural areas. They number more than two million throughout the country. *Arma Neuva* is "a review for rebel soldiers, workers, and farmers." Most of the articles in the magazine deal with popular heroes, current events and sports and are written the way a child's primer is. In the edition I received, there were articles on Great Cuban Women, Great Cuban Sports Figures, The Seas Around Cuba, What Is a Biography?, The Life of Camilo Cienfuegos, The Agrarian Reform, A History of Cuba in 10 Paragraphs, The Battle of "El Uvero," What Is a Cooperative, The Rebel Army, and many features like crossword puzzles, double crostics, etc. Each article, as well as giving basic information, attempts to point out the great changes in Cuba since the revolution. Each article is, of course, trying to do two things at once, educate as well as proselytize. For example, one of the word games went: "Who is the chief of the Cuban revolution? — FIDEL." "What is the principal product of Cuban economy? — SUGAR." "What is the hope of all the people? — LIBERTY."

These offices were small and in the basement of La Casa. There were about five young men busily stapling mimeographed announcements inside the current issue of *Arma Nueva*. They all got up to shake our hands and greet us when we came in. The only young woman in the office gave us a brief talk about the magazine, and the adult education program in Cuba. Most of the people in the office seemed to recognize Robert Williams immediately, and after the young woman's talk, some of the young men left their stapling to ask Robert about the U.S. and why he thought U.S. newspapers told so many lies. One of them asked, "Are they paid to lie? Don't they ever tell the truth about what's happening down here? That man in the *Times* (Tad Szulc) is a filthy liar. He should be kicked out of the country and an honest man brought down." Robert thought this was funny and so did I, but I could see the possible headlines in the *New York Times* if said Szulc were to have overheard this exchange. CUBAN EXTREMISTS ADVOCATE EXPULSION OF U.S. NEWSMEN.

We drank some more Cuban coffee and hit the road again.

At the Ministry of Education, a prewar, Spanish style office building in old Habana, we met the assistant minister (or sub-secretary) of education, Doctor Jose Aguilera. The minister, a short dark man in his forties, talked about an hour, with frequent interruptions, about the educational situation in Cuba. He compared the status of the Cuban educational system as of January 1, 1959, with the system as it stood now; outlining the many changes the revolutionary government has brought about. The statistics were staggering. In their excellent book *Cuba: Anatomy of a Revolution*, Leo Huberman and Paul M. Sweezy give exact facts and figures, comparisons outlining precisely how far, not just the educational system has come since the first days of the revolutionary government, but just how much extreme progress has been made in all areas of economic, social and cultural adjustment. It would seem to me that since the *New York Times* is usually so fond of facts and statistics, it would reprint a few of the innumerable graphs, charts and tables in this book instead of printing long, tiresomely untrue "reports" by middle-class Americans suffering from that uniquely American sickness called "identification." This is a disease wherein the victim somehow thinks that he receives monies or other fringe benefits from Standard Oil, Coca-Cola, Dupont, U.S. Steel, etc., and feels genuinely hurt if some of "their properties" are expropriated. "They're taking our oil and our Coca-Cola."

Dr. Aguilera talked softly and convincingly, smoking constantly. The Cuban coffee came in, and he had some pamphlets passed around the table, as well as a few examples of new Cuban schoolbooks. (This had been a country of notoriously few schoolbooks.) He gave us copies of what had been the first first-aid book printed in Cuba for general use, then went on calmly and confidently citing statistics as only a government official can. "In the last seven-year period," he said, "a total of only 400 classrooms were created. The revolutionary government by September 1960 will have created almost 10,000. As Fidel said, we're changing every former Batista military fortification into a school. School cities we call them. You'll probably get a chance to visit a few before you leave. [We did the next day.] To show you the amount of blatant corruption that infested this country before the revolution, the educational budget during the years 1907–08, the beginning of the republic, was $4,208,368. The index of illiterates then was 31.47 percent. Fifty years later, in 1958–59, the budget was $88,389,450, 22 times larger, but the index of illiterates remained the same. Only about 8.9 percent of people between the ages of twelve and nineteen (secondary school age) received any schooling at all. That meant only about nine out of 100 young people were receiving any secondary schooling at all."

Most of the ladies in our group gasped politely, genuinely impressed. The minister went on: "Another very, very amusing fact about the Cuban education system is that in 1959, just before the revolutionary government took over, there were 24,011 teachers in Cuba, but 1,514 of them were school inspectors." The minister briefly turned the pages of one of the pamphlets he had given us and then with a broad smile resumed his statistics. "Yes, 1,514 inspectors in this little country. Do you know that in the countries of Belgium and France combined they have only 760 inspectors." Everybody in the office broke up. "Well, we've reduced the number of inspectors to around 400, which still means we've got about eighty more than France, a country whose population is eight times larger than ours."

Robert Williams poked me in the side. "Ol' Fulgencio must have had a bunch of relatives."

The group then began to ask questions of the minister. He answered most of them very thoroughly, sometimes asking the opinions of some of his aides who were in the room. More statistics were cited, photographs of old, now demolished school buildings were shown, photos of the new school city in Oriente, "Camilo Cienfuegos," other new school cities just being built. Then the communist's wife wanted to know if in the new schoolbooks that were being manufactured, little Negro children were portrayed as well as white. The minister did not understand at first, or rather, his interpreter did not. The wife said, "I mean, to show the little Negro children that they are not inferior, I think you should have little colored boys and girls in schoolbooks as well as little white boys and girls." I began to laugh very impolitely, and the woman silenced me with a cold look of dignity. When the interpreter got through explaining to the minister again, the puzzled look did not leave his face, but he picked up a few new geography books and thumbed quickly through them. When he reached the page he wanted, he pressed it down and handed it to the woman. She smiled ecstatically and showed the book to her husband. The minister handed her a newly printed notebook for elementary schools; on the cover were five children at a blackboard, two of them black. The woman almost swooned. The minister laughed and shook his head.

We scrambled into waiting cabs and Olga told us our next stop was The National Agrarian Reform Institute (INRA). The Agrarian

Reform Law is the basic law passed by the revolutionary government. And it is the application of this law, and its subsequent repercussions that have been largely responsible for the shaping of public opinion (i.e., opinions of specific governments and their subsequent popularization throughout the populations controlled by these governments) about the new Cuban government, whether pro of con. The Agrarian Reform Law *is* radical social legislation. As Fidel Castro himself admitted. "I *am* a radical," he said, "a very radical young man. But I am right."

The INRA is responsible for seeing that the statutes of the Agrarian Reform Law are carried out. The head of the institute, Dr. Antonio Nuñez Jiménez, is responsible only to Fidel Castro. Once one is in Cuba it becomes more than vaguely apparent that the Agrarian Reform and its continued fulfillment by the new government is the key to their success, and that as long as this law is upheld, the majority of the Cuban people will love Fidel Castro even if it were proven that he was Lucifer himself.

We left old Habana and passed the huge white monument to Jose Martí, the father of the Cuban republic. The institute is a massive white building still in the last stages of completion. It was begun by Batista for some now obscure purpose, but after the revolution the INRA offices were moved in immediately.

The entire front walk of the glass and stone building was covered with milling crows. Mostly the crowd was made up of rebel soldiers and *campesinos* (peasant farmers). The *campesinos* had probably come from one of the many rural areas of the country to settle some business affair at the institute. They wear the traditional big straw hats with the front brim turned up and all carry the also traditional machete. As we got out of the cabs, a small unit of *miliciana* marched by. The *miliciana* are the female contingent of the home guard that has been formed all over the island. The various units are usually made up of particular age groups. Some, like the one that was passing us, were made up of teen-age girls, others include older women, some even younger girls. This unit wore dark skirts, maroon shirts, and dark berets. They moved by in perfect step; a pretty young red-haired girl stepping beside the main body called out cadence loud and clear.

There were two soldiers sitting just inside the glass doors. They smiled at us as we went by, one pointing over his shoulder toward an information desk. Another soldier sat behind the information desk reading a newspaper, beside him one of the young girl *miliciana*. Olga spoke to the soldier briefly and he waved us on.

The elevators were so crowded we had to go up in smaller groups. Everywhere in the building there were young soldiers, many of them bearded, all of them carrying some sort of firearm. There were also hundreds of farmers walking around, some even with their wives, children, and huge lunch pails. The noise in the lobbies was unbelievable.

We went into a quiet air-conditioned office with great windows looking out at the sea. A speaker on one of the walls kept up a steady hum of music as well as news broadcasts and announcements. A very dark Negro welcomed us in Cuban English as did a tall blond man who sounded like an Irishman. We were given chairs, and the Irishman, after talking to Olga, dragged out a huge wooden map of Cuba. Another man came out of an inner office, very tall and thin with a neat Latin mustache. He greeted everyone in the office very warmly. He was about thirty, and wore a loose-fitting Brooks Bros. type suit, with an open collared button-down shirt. He was one of the directors of one agency of the institute. He spoke very bookish English, but seemed to become embarrassed when he couldn't find proper adjectives so he asked Olga to interpret.

Using the huge map, which showed how the country was divided into provinces, he began to outline INRA's responsibilities and the different problems that confronted it. He too began citing reams of statistics, and the Irish-sounding man joined in. Soon, we were having a joint lecture, neither of the men seeming to get in the other's way. "The reason Cuban economy and thereby most of the people were in such bad shape," said the Irishman, "is that before the revolution we were a monoculture, most of the cultivated land being given over to the growing of sugar cane. Do you know we even imported rice from the United States. Somebody was paying off. Most of the land was owned by large corporations that employed the Cuban labor force for only three months a year, leaving them to starve in the off season. And most of the people did starve. The average per capita income in 1950–54 was about $312.00 per year. Small farms under 25 acres made up only about 3.3 percent of total land holdings. They were almost nonexistent. The majority of farms in the country were being planted and worked by people who did not own the land: sharecroppers. We were a nation of sharecroppers and squatters. Most of the workable land was in the hands of absentee landlords, in some cases foreign corporations."

The tall man butted in "That's why The Agrarian Reform Law was so important. That's also why it was so controversial." He went to a desk and picked up copies of a mimeographed booklet, and beckoned for one of the uniformed young men to pass them around to us. "The first article of the law is the basis for our revolution. It is the only thing that makes us a sovereign country." He read it to us. "Article One. Latifundium (uneconomic and extensive production of large land holdings) is hereby proscribed. The maximum area of land that may be possessed by a natural or juridical person shall be thirty *caballerias* (about 1,000 acres). The lands belonging to a natural or juridical person that exceed that limit will be expropriated for distribution among the peasants and agricultural workers who have no land."

This meant of course that United Fruit, American Sugar, etc., got burnt immediately. The tall man went on, "And of course, the direct complement to this basic tenet of the reform law is Article Sixteen. It says that an area of two *caballerias* (about 66 acres) of fertile land, without irrigation and distant from urban centers, is established as the "vital minimum" for a peasant family of five persons engaged in crops of medium economic yield."

"That *is* communism," one of the ladies next to me said half-jokingly.

"Is it wrong?" the tall man wanted to know. The woman agreed that it was not.

After more questions, a soldier came into the office and said a few words to Olga. She stood up and our interview with these young men was over. "We're in luck," she said. "We're going to be able to get in to see Antonio Nuñez Jiménez, the executive director of INRA, for about ten minutes." We all got up, finished our coffee, and began shaking hands with everyone in the office.

Nuñez Jiménez' office was directly across the hall from the office we were leaving. In the outer office, a large, smoothfaced Negro soldier sat at a desk typing. He had a huge pearl-handled .45 strapped to his hip and faultlessly polished boots. When we came in, he spun around in his secretary's chair and let us have all 32 teeth. He recognized Robert Williams immediately and shook his hand vigorously. While we sat in the outer office waiting for our interview, Williams enthralled him, at his request, with unbelievable tales about separate toilets and chromatic buses. The soldier was obviously too intelligent to believe all of the stories. He kept saying, "Ah, mon, go on!"

Finally, another soldier, this one carrying what Williams described to me as "a new Belgian automatic rifle," came out of the inner offices and beckoned to Olga. There were two more offices inside the one we had waited in. They were filled with clerical workers and soldiers. The door to Nuñez Jiménez' office was standing open and we all crowded in. There were two other soldiers in the office besides the executive director, both with .45s. There were also two young Negroes in civilian clothes talking to each other very animatedly. When we came through the door, Dr. Jiménez wheeled away from his conversation and made a polite Latin bow with both hands extended in greeting. Everyone shook his hand. After the many handshakes he began talking pleasantly to our interpreter. She conveyed his greetings to the group and then began to laugh as she continued to translate the Captain's words. "Dr. Nuñez says that he is glad there are still Americans who want to see Cuba even though the travel agencies no longer think of it as the paradise just five hours from Manhattan. From a paradise to a hell in little over a year . . . we're making progress no matter how you look at it."

While we laughed, one of the soldiers passed out cigars to the men from a box that was on Dr. Nuñez' desk. Some of the group began to ask questions. The Captain did his best to answer all of them. While he was doing this, the model leaned over to me and whispered, "God, he's beautiful! Why're all these guys so good-looking?" And she was right, he was beautiful. A tall, scholarly-looking man with black hair and full black beard, he talked deliberately but brightly about everything, now and then emphasizing a point by bringing his hands together and wringing them in slow motion, something like college English professors. He wore the uniform of the rebel army with the black and red shoulder insignia of a captain. A black beret was tucked neatly in one of his epaulets. He also carried a big square-handled .45.

Finally one of the secretaries asked, "Dr. Jiménez, why is it everyone, even high-ranking officials like yourself, still carry weapons?" There were embarrassed titters from other people in the group, but I thought it the highwater mark of most of the questioning so far.

The Captain smiled cheerfully and ran the fingers of one hand from his mustache to the tip of his beard with that gesture characteristic of most men with beards, "Well, señorita, we are still a revolutionary government and as such we are still liable to attack by our enemies. Actual physical attack, not just terrible speeches a thousand miles away. We have to be ready for such developments, and we have to let our enemies know that we're ready."

"But don't you think there's been enough killing," the woman continued.

Nuñez Jiménez stopped smiling for a second and looked down at his shiny-handled weapon. "I've never killed anyone in my life. I was a professor at the University. But it is just because I feel that there's been enough killing that I and the other members of the revolutionary government carry these weapons. We have to carry them until we are strong enough to defend ourselves diplomatically. There are people all over the world who would like for us never to become that strong."

After he had stopped answering questions, the captain passed out copies of a book he had written that had just been published called *La Liberación De Las Islas*. Most of the group had him autograph their copies; when I filed past I took the book, tucked it under my arm and shook the minister's hand. He said, "No autograph?" I answered in Spanish, telling him that I thought the speech and handshake were fine enough souvenirs. He asked was I an American? and I told him that I was an American poet, which meant that I wasn't a real American like Señor Nixon or Arthur Godfrey but that I had certainly been born in that country. He slapped his sides laughing and shouted my answer to his aides.

The last stop was the Ministry of Housing. We were talked to there by a young man of about 27 in a tattersall vest and desert boots. He was one of the sub-directors of the ministry. He used charts, pamphlets, and scale models of new housing to illustrate his points. He talked earnestly and excitedly for an hour and then we left for the hotel. As we were leaving I didn't see Ed Clarke, so I thought he had gotten separated from the party. I went back upstairs with Robaina, the architect, to try and locate him. We met the sub-director in the elevator and after he had helped us look vainly around the now empty halls for Clarke (he had left earlier), we began to talk about the States where, it turned out, he had lived for about six or seven years. One thing he was extremely interested in was whether Miles Davis, the trumpet player, was playing again and healthy after the terrible beating a policeman had given him outside of a nightclub where Miles was working. I told him that Miles was fine and playing as well as ever. "Wow," the sub-director of housing said, "that place is turning into a real police state."

After dinner, Clarke, the essayist and I went into Old Habana to look around. We walked down almost every narrow street and back alley in that section of the city, peering into cafés, ogling the women, talking to bus drivers, thinking we looked pretty Cuban. The essayist and I spoke Spanish, and Clarke is the kind of light-skinned, straight-haired Negro that looks very Latin. Finally we stopped in one particularly grubby bar in the real 42nd Street part of town.

We went in and I said to the bartender, "Tres cervezas, por favor." The bartender said, "Que clase?"

I looked at Ed and said, "Hey, what kind of beer you want?" He told me and the bartender whipped around and got them.

We had barely begun to sip the beer when a large stocky man across the bar, who was drunker than he should have been, raised his head, probably for the first time in three hours and stared across the bar at us. Then he growled very drunkenly, "Abajo imperialismo Yanqui! Viva Cuba Libre!" Then his head slumped again unwillingly. The three of us on the other side of the bar looked at each other with whatever expression comes into people's faces in that kind of situation and tried to continue sipping calmly. The man raised his head again, "Abajo imperialismo Yanqui! Viva Fidel! Viva Cuba Libre!" His head slumped. Clarke nudged me. The essayist made a face. I looked at my foot. "Cuba Si, Yanqui No! Cuba Si, Yanqui No! Venceremos!" (We will win.) The head was up again.

Other people in the bar began to look up at us and smile or happily nudge their friends. This time the essayist called across to the man in Spanish. "Look, friend," he said firmly, "if you're talking to us, there's no need to, we readily agree with you. Down with Yankee imperialism. Cuba Yes, Yankee No! It's true." I tried to find my cigarettes.

The man seemed to gather strength from my companion's intrusion and began to shout even louder, then he began to come around the bar toward us. The essayist repeated what the man had just said and Clarke put the newspaper he'd been carrying on the bar. I turned to face the man, hoping I was smiling. But the man sidestepped me and walked around to the essayist and began to talk very loudly, waving his newspaper, instructing my friend on the spot in the virtues of the Cuban revolution and the evils of American imperialism. The essayist agreed and agreed. Clarke and I were agreeing also, but the man never turned to face us. He went on and on. Finally, the bartender came over and told him to be quiet. He lowered his voice one-half decibel and continued his seemingly endless tirade. I thought the only sensible thing was to get out of the place, so I dumped the rest of the beer down my throat, pointed at Clarke's and tried to step between the loud man and his prey. The prey resisted, shaking his finger in the man's face, stopping only long enough to tell me that he was trying to tell this fellow that not all Americans were John Foster Dulles, and that there were still some intelligent people left in the country. That seemed like a pretty farfetched idea to try to convince a Cuban of, so I ordered another beer and tried to relax. The two men wailed on and on.

Presently a shabbily dressed Negro, who was obviously a drifter, came in the bar with a sketchbook under his arm. He came over to where the discussion was raging, stood for a second, then looked over at Clarke and me. Finally he said to me, "Hey man, you American?" I nodded resignedly. "Yeh, yeh, no kidding?"

"That's right," I mumbled, "but only if you don't want to argue."

"Argue?" he pulled up a stool and sat in front of us. "No, man, I don't argue. You my brother." He pointed at his dark arm and then my own. "I just want you to tell me about Harlem. Tell me about Harlem, man."

This was the wildest thing I'd heard all night. I almost fell off the stool laughing. "What's the matter, didn't you read Jimmy Baldwin's article in *Esquire*?"

"What?" He looked at me quizzically. "Que dice?"

"Oh, forget it." I then proceeded to tell him about Harlem as best I could, not even leaving out Hulan Jack and Adam Clayton Powell. While I told him about Harlem, he drew an awful little sketch of me on the back of a matchbook cover which he titled "The Comic." I also bought him two beers and promised to show him around Harlem if he ever got to the States.

When we got to leave the bar around four in the morning, the essayist and his assailant were still agreeing violently. When we left the bar, the man followed us all the way to the bus stop, promising to show us Habana.

The next day toward afternoon, we drove out first to a beach club called El Obrero Circulo, one of the hundreds of formerly privately owned beach clubs that have since been expropriated and turned into public resorts. "La Playa es por El Pueblo," a big sign outside the beach house said. (The beach is for the people.) It was a marvelous white beach with unbelievably blue water and hundreds of beautiful women, but true to my American heritage, I sat in the bar and drank daiquiris till it was time to leave.

When we got back to the hotel bar, Ed Clarke between sips of beer asked me, "Hey, have you seen any old people? There's nothing but young people running this country. What is Fidel, 33? Ché, Nuñez Jiménez, both in their early thirties. Raul's not even that old. What'd they do to all those old people?"

I laughed. "They must all be in Miami." But it was true, the wild impression one gets from the country, is that it is being run by a group of young radical intellectuals, and the young men of Latin America are radical. Whether Marxist or not, it is a social radicalism that they want. No one speaks of compromise. The idea has never occurred to them. The many so-called friends of Castro who have run out since the revolution were in most cases people who were prepared to compromise. People who knew that Fidel's radicalism would make him dangerous to the "free world." That free world of bankers, political pawns, grasping industrialists and liars. The free world that cited the inhumanity of the government of Fulgencio Batista an "internal problem," just as they now condone the hateful willfulness of Generalissimo Trujillo (whose picture, until a few months ago, was plastered up all over Cooper Square in New York City).

The weird stupidity of this situation is that in most cases the so-called American intellectual is not even aware of what is happening any place in the world. Not any place where it serves the interests of the various trusts and gangsters that situations be obfuscated. The intelligent American reads an "account" of what is happening someplace in the world, say in the New York Times. He is certainly aware to a certain extent that some of what is being "accounted" is slanted in the general direction of American "well-meaningness." The most severe condemnation of American leaders by the American intellectual is that they are "bumblers," unintelligent but well-meaning clowns. But we do not realize how much of the horrible residue of these paid liars is left in our heads. Who is it in the U.S. that is not afraid of China? Who is it that does not believe that there is such a things as "the free world"? That West Germany is "freer" than East Germany? That there are communist influences in the Cuban government? We reject the blatant, less dangerous lie in favor of the subtle subliminal lie, which is more dangerous because we feel we are taking an intelligent stance, not being had. What do we know about China? Who told you about the communist influences in the Cuban government? How do you know the Indian people love Nehru? We go to Mexico for a vacation. The place is a haven for bearded young men of my generation to go and make their "scene," but not one in a hundred will come back realizing that there are students there getting murdered and beaten because they are protesting against the fraudulent one-party regime that controls the country, which is backed to the hilt by our "well-meaning" government.

It is sad, and there is nothing I can even suggest as an alternative. We've gone too far. There is a certain hopelessness about our attitude that can even be condoned. The environment sickens. The young intellectual living in the United States inhabits an ugly void. He cannot use what is around him, neither can he revolt against it. Revolt against whom? Revolution in this country of "due processes of law" would be literally impossible. Whose side would you be on? The void of being killed by what is in this country and not knowing what is outside of it. Don't tell me about the dead minds of Europe. They stink worse than our own.

It was late at night, and still Habana had not settled down to its usual quiet. Crowds of people were squatting around bus stops, walking down the streets in groups headed for bus stops. Truckloads of militia were headed out of the city. Young men and women with rucksacks and canteens were piling into buses, trucks, and private cars all over the city. There were huge signs all over Habana reading "A La Sierra Con Fidel . . . Julio 26." Thousands of people were leaving Habana for the July 26th celebration at Sierra Maestra all the way at the other end of the island in Oriente province. The celebration was in honor of Fidel Castro's first onslaught against Moncada barracks, July 26, 1953, which marked the beginning of his drive against the Batista government. Whole families were packing up, trying to get to Oriente the best way they could. It was still three days before the celebration and people clogged the roads from Habana all the way to the Eastern province.

The night of our departure for Oriente we arrived at the train station in Habana about 6 P.M. It was almost impossible to move around in the station. *Campesinos*, businessmen, soldiers, *milicianas*, tourists — all were thrashing around trying to make sure they had seats in the various trains. As we came into the station, most of the delegates of a Latin-American Youth Congress were coming in also. There were about nine hundred of them, representing students from almost every country in Latin America. Mexicans, Colombians, Argentines, Venezuelans, Puerto Ricans (with signs reading "For the Liberation of Puerto Rico"), all carrying flags, banners, and wearing the large, ragged straw hat of the *campesino*. We were to go in the same train as the delegates.

As we moved through the crowds toward our train, the students began chanting: "Cuba, Si, Yanqui No . . . Cuba Si, Yanqui No . . . Cuba Si, Yanqui No." The crowds in the terminal joined in, soon there was a deafening crazy scream that seemed to burst the roof off the terminal. Cuba Si, Yanqui No! We raced for the trains. Once inside the train, a long modern semi–air-conditioned "Silver Meteor," we quickly settled down and I began scribbling illegibly in my notebook. But the Latin Americans came scrambling into the train still chanting furiously and someone handed me a drink of rum. They were yelling "Venceremos, Venceremos, Venceremos, Venceremos." Crowds of soldiers and militia on the platform outside joined in. Everyone was screaming as the train began to pull away.

The young militia people soon came trotting through the coaches asking everyone to sit down for a few seconds so they could be counted. The delegates got to their seats and in my coach everyone began to sing a song like "two, four, six, eight, who do we appreciate . . . Fidel, Fidel, Fidel!!" Then they did Ché (Guevara), Raul, President Dorticos, etc. It was about 1,000 kilometers to Oriente and we had just started.

Young soldiers passed out ham sandwiches and Maltina, a thick syrupy sweet beverage that only made me thirstier. Everyone in the train seemed to be talking excitedly and having a wild time. We were about an hour outside Habana and I was alternating between taking notes and reading about ancient Mexican religion when Olga Finlay came up to my seat accompanied by a young woman. "I told her you were an American poet," Olga said, "and she wanted to meet you." I rose quickly and extended my hand, for some reason embarrassed as hell. Olga said, "Señora Betancourt, Señor LeRoi Jones." She was very short, very blonde and very pretty, and had a weird accent that never ceased to fascinate me. For about thirty minutes we stood in the middle aisle talking to each other. She was a Mexican delegate to the Youth Congress, a graduate student in Economics at one of the universities, the wife of an economist, and a mother. Finally, I offered her the seat next to mine at the window. She sat, and we talked almost continuously throughout the fourteen-hour ride.

She questioned me endlessly about American life, American politics, American youth—although I was jokingly cautioned against using the word *American* to mean the U.S. or North America. "Everyone in this car is American," she said. "You from the North, we from the South." I explained as best I could about the Eisenhowers, the Nixons, the DuPonts, but she made even my condemnations seem mild. "Everyone in the world," she said, with her finger, "has to be communist or anti-communist. And if they're anti-communist, no matter what kind of foul person they are, you people accept them as your allies. Do you really think that hopeless little island in the middle of the sea is China? That is irrational. You people are irrational!"

I tried to defend myself, "Look, why jump on me? I understand what you're saying. I'm in complete agreement with you. I'm a poet . . . what can I do? I write, that's all, I'm not even interested in politics."

She jumped on me with both feet as did a group of Mexican poets later in Habana. She called me a "cowardly bourgeois individualist." The poets, or at least one young wild-eyed Mexican poet, Jaime Shelley, almost left me in tears, stomping his foot on the floor, screaming: "You want to cultivate your soul? In that ugliness you live in, you want to cultivate your soul? Well, we've got millions of starving people to feed, and that moves me enough to make poems out of."

Around 10 P.M. the train pulled into the town of Matanzas. We had our blinds drawn, but the militia came running through the car telling us to raise them. When I raised the blind I was almost startled out of my wits. There were about 1,500 people in the train station and surrounding it, yelling their lungs out. We pulled up the windows. People were all over. They ran back and forth along the train screaming at us. The Mexicans in the train had a big sign painted on a bedspread that read "Mexico is with Fidel. Venceremos." When they raised it to the windows young men leaped in the air, and women blew kisses. There was a uniformed marching band trying to be heard above the crowd, but I could barely hear them. When I poked my head out of the window to wave at the crowds, two young Negro women giggled violently at first, then one of them ran over to the train and kissed me as hard as she could manage. The only thing to do I could think of was to say "Thank you." She danced up and down and clapped her hands and shouted to her friend, "Un americano, un americano." I bowed my head graciously.

What was it, a circus? That wild mad crowd. Social ideas? Could there be that much excitement generated through all the people? Damn, that people still *can* move. Not us, but people. It's gone out of us forever. "Cuba Si, Yanqui No," I called at the girls as the train edged away.

We stopped later in the town of Colon. There again the same mobs of cheering people. Camaguey. Santa Clara. At each town, the chanting crowds. The unbelievable joy and excitement. The same idea, and people made beautiful because of it. People moving, being moved. I was ecstatic and frightened. Something I had never seen before, exploding all around me.

The train rocked wildly across and into the interior. The delegates were singing a "cha cha" with words changed to something like "Fidel, Fidel, cha cha cha, Ché Ché, cha cha cha, Abajo Imperialismo Yanqui, cha cha cha." Some American students whom I hadn't seen earlier ran back and forth in the coaches singing "We cannot be moved." The young folk-song politicians in blue jeans and pigtails.

About two o'clock in the morning they shut the lights off in most of the coaches, and everybody went to sleep. I slept for only an hour or so and woke up just in time to see the red sun come up and the first early people come out of their small grass-roofed shacks beside the railroad tracks, and wave sleepily at the speeding train. I pressed my face against the window and waved back.

The folk singing and war cries had just begun again in earnest when we reached the town of Yara, a small town in Oriente province, the last stop on the line. At once we unloaded from the train, leaving most luggage and whatever was considered superfluous. The dirt streets of the town were jammed with people. Probably everyone in town had come to meet the train. The entire town was decorated with some kind of silver Christmas tree tinsel and streamers. Trees, bushes, houses, children, all draped in the same silver holiday tinsel. Tiny girls in brown uniforms and red berets greeted us with armfuls of flowers. Photographers were running amok through the crowd, including an American newsreel cameraman who kept following Robert Williams. I told Robert that he ought to put his big straw hat in front of his face American gangster style.

From the high hill of the train station it was possible to see a road running right through Yara. Every conceivable kind of bus, truck, car, and scooter was being pushed toward the Sierra, which was now plainly visible in the distance. Some of the *campesinos* were on horses, dodging in and out of the sluggish traffic, screaming at the top of their lungs.

The sun had already gotten straight up over our heads and was burning down viciously. The big straw *campesino* hats helped a little but I could tell that it was going to be an obscenely hot day. We stood around for a while until everyone had gotten off our train, and then some of the militia people waved at us to follow them. We walked completely out of the town of Yara in about two minutes. We walked until we came to more railroad tracks; a short spur leading off in the direction of Sierra Maestra. Sitting on the tracks were about ten empty open cattle cars. There were audible groans from the American contingent. The cars themselves looked like movable jails. Huge thick bars around the sides. We joked about the American cameraman taking a picture of them with us behind the bars and using it as a *Life* magazine cover. They would caption it "Americans in Cuba."

At a word from the militia we scrambled up through the bars, into the scalding cars. The metal parts of the car were burning hot, probably from sitting out in the sun all day. It was weird seeing hundreds of people up and down the tracks climbing up into the cattle cars by whatever method they could manage. We had been told in Habana that this was going to be a rough trip and that we ought to dress accordingly. Heavy shoes, old clothes, a minimum of equipment. The women were told specifically to wear slacks and flat shoes because it would be difficult to walk up a mountain in a sheath dress and heels. However, one of the American women, the pretty young middle-class lady from Philadelphia, showed up in a flare skirt and "Cuban" heels. Two of the Cubans had to pull and tug to get her into the car, which still definitely had the smell of cows. She slumped in a corner and began furiously mopping her brow.

I sat down on the floor and tried to scribble in my notebook, but it was difficult because everyone was jammed in very tight. Finally, the train jerked to a start, and everyone in all the cars let out a wild yell. The delegates began chanting again. Waving at all the people along the road, and all the dark barefoot families standing in front of their grass-topped huts calling to us. The road which ran along parallel to the train was packed full of traffic, barely moving. Men sat on the running boards of their cars when the traffic came to a complete halt, and drank water from their canteens. The train was going about five miles an hour and the *campesinos* raced by on their plow horses jeering, swinging their big hats. The sun and the hot metal car were almost unbearable. The delegates shouted at the trucks, "Cuba Si, Yanqui No," and then began their "Viva" shouts. After one of the "Vivas," I yelled, "Viva Calle Cuaranta y dos" (42nd Street), "Viva Symphony Sid," "Viva Cinco Punto" (Five Spot), "Viva Turhan Bey." I guess it was the heat. It was a long slow ride in the boiling cars.

The cattle cars stopped after an hour or so at some kind of junction. All kinds of other coaches were pulled up and resting on various spurs. People milled about everywhere. But it was the end of any tracks going further toward Sierra. We stood around and drank warm water too fast.

Now we got into trucks. Some with nailed-in bus seats, some with straw roofs, others with just plain truck floors. It was a wild scramble for seats. The militia people and the soldiers did their best to indicate which trucks were for whom, but people staggered into the closest vehicle at hand. Ed Clarke and I ran and leaped up into a truck with leather bus seats in the back. The leather was too hot to sit on for a while so I put my handkerchief on the seat and sat forward. A woman was trying to get up into the truck, but not very successfully, so I leaned over the rail and pulled her up and in. The face was recognizable immediately, but I had to sit back on the hot seat before I remembered it was Françoise Sagan. I turned to say something to her, but some men were already helping her back down to the ground. She rode up front in the truck's cab with a young lady companion, and her manager on the running board, clinging to the door.

The trucks reared out onto the already heavily traveled road. It was an unbelievable scene. Not only all the weird trucks and buses but thousands of people walking along the road. Some had walked from places as far away as Matanzas. Whole detachments of militia were marching, route step, but carrying rifles or .45s. Women carrying children on their shoulders. One group of militia with blue shirts, green pants, pistols and knives, was carrying paper fans, which they ripped back and forth almost in unison with their step. There were huge trucks full of oranges parked along the road with lines of people circling them. People were sitting along the edge of the road eating their lunches. Everyone going *a la* Sierra.

Our trucks sped along on the outside of the main body of traffic, still having to stop occasionally when there was some hopeless roadblock. The sun, for all our hats, was baking our heads. Sweat poured in my dry mouth. None of us Americans had brought canteens and there was no water to be had while we were racing along the road. I tried several times to get some oranges, but never managed. The truck would always start up again when we came close to an orange vendor.

There was a sign on one of the wood shack "stores" we passed that read "Niños No Gustan Los Chicle Ni Los Cigarros Americanos Ni El Rocan Rool." It was signed "Fondin." The traffic bogged down right in front of the store so several French photographers leaped off the truck and raced for the orange stand. Only one fellow managed to make it back to our truck with a hat full of oranges. The others had to turn and run back empty handed as the truck pulled away. Sagan's manager, who had strapped himself on the running board with a leather belt, almost broke his head when the truck hit a bump and the belt snapped and sent him sprawling into the road. Another one of the correspondents suddenly became violently ill and tried to shove his head between the rough wooden slats at the side of the truck; he didn't quite make it, and everyone in the truck suffered.

After two hours we reached a wide, slow, muddy river. There was only one narrow cement bridge crossing it, so the trucks had to wait until they could ease back into the regular line of traffic. There were hundreds of people wading across the river. A woman splashed in with her child on her shoulders, hanging around her neck, her lunch pail in one hand, a pair of blue canvas sneakers in the other. One group of militia marched right into the brown water, holding their rifles high above their heads. When our truck got on the bridge directly over the water, one of the Cuban newspapermen leaped out of the truck down ten feet into the water. People in the trucks would jump right over the side, sometimes pausing to take off their shoes. Most went in shoes and all.

Now we began to wind up the narrow mountain road for the first time. All our progress since Yara had been upgrade, but this was the first time it was clearly discernible that we were going up a mountain. It took another hour to reach the top. It was afternoon now and already long lines of people were headed back down the mountain. But it was a narrow line compared to the thousands of people who were scrambling up just behind us. From one point where we stopped just before reaching the top it was possible to look down the side of the long hill and see swarms of people all the way down past the river seeming now to inch along in effortless pantomime.

The trucks stopped among a jumble of rocks and sand not quite at the top of the last grade. (For the last twenty minutes of our climb we actually had to wind in and out among groups of people. The only people who seemed to race along without any thought of the traffic were the *campesinos* on their broken-down mounts.) Now everyone began jumping down off the trucks and trying to re-form into their respective groups. It seemed almost impossible. Detachments of *campesino* militia (work shirts, blue jeans, straw hats and machetes) marched up behind us. *Milicianas* of about twelve and thirteen separated our contingent, then herds of uniformed, trotting boys of about seven. "Hup, hup, hup, hup," one little boy was calling in vain as he ran behind the rest of his group. One of the girls called out "Hup, hup, hup, hup," keeping her group more orderly.

Rebel soldiers wandered around everywhere, some with long, full beards, others with long, wavy black hair pulled under their blue berets or square-topped khaki caps, most of them young men in their twenties or teen-agers. An old man with a full gray beard covering most of his face, except his sparkling blue eyes and the heavy black cigar stuck out of the side of his mouth, directed the comings and goings up and down this side of the mountain. He wore a huge red-and black-handled revolver and had a hunting knife sewn to his boot. Suddenly it seemed that I was lost in a sea of uniforms, and I couldn't see anyone I had come up the mountain with. I sat down on a rock until most of the uniforms passed. Then I could see Olga about fifty yards away waving her arms at her lost charges.

There was a public address system booming full blast from what seemed the top of the hill. The voice (Celia Sanchez, Fidel's secretary) was announcing various groups that were passing in review. When we got to the top of the rise, we could see a large, austere platform covered with all kinds of people, and at the front of the platform a raised section with a dais where the speakers were. Señora Sanchez was announcing one corps of militia and they marched out of the crowd and stopped before the platform. The crowd cheered and cheered. The militia was commended from the platform and then they marched off into the crowd at the other side. Other groups marched past. Young women, teen-age girls, elderly *campesinos*, each with their own militia detachment, each to be commended. This had been going on since morning. Hundreds of commendations, thousands of people to be commended. Also, since morning, the officials had been reading off lists of names of *campesinos* who were to receive land under the Agrarian Reform Law. When they read the name of some farmer close enough to the mountain to hear it, he would leap straight up in the air and, no matter how far away from the platform he was, would go barreling and leaping toward the speaker. The crowd delighted in this and would begin chanting "Viva Fidel, Viva Fidel, Viva Reforma Agraria." All this had been going on since morning and it was now late afternoon.

After we walked past the dais, introduced to the screaming crowd as "intellectual North American visitors," we doubled back and went up onto the platform itself. It was even hotter up there. By now all I could think about was the sun; it was burning straight down and had been since early morning. I tugged the straw hat down over my eyes and trudged up onto the platform. The platform itself in back of the dais was almost overflowing, mostly with rebel soldiers and young militia troops. But there were all kinds of visitors also, the Latin-American delegates, newsmen, European writers, American intellectuals, as well as Cuban officials. When we got up on the platform, Olga led us immediately over to the speakers' dais and the little group of seats around it. We were going to be introduced to all the major speakers.

The first person to turn around and greet us was a tall, thin, bearded Negro in a rebel uniform bearing the shoulder markings of a *Commandante*. I recognized his face from the papers as that of Juan Almeida, chief of the rebel army, a man almost unknown in the United States. He grinned and shook our hands and talked in a swift combination of Spanish and English, joking constantly about conditions in the United States. In the middle of one of his jokes he leaned backward, leaning over one man to tap another taller man on the shoulder. Fidel Castro leaned back in his seat, then got up smiling and came over to where we were standing. He began shaking hands with everybody in the group, as well as the many other visitors who moved in at the opportunity. There were so many people on the platform in what seemed like complete disorder that I wondered how wise it was as far as security was concerned. It seemed awfully dangerous for the Prime Minister to be walking around so casually, almost having to thread his way through the surging crowd. Almost immediately, I shoved my hand toward his face and then grasped his hand. He greeted me warmly, asking through the interpreter where I was from and what I did. When I told him I was a New York poet, he seemed extremely amused and asked me what the government thought about my trip. I shrugged my shoulders and asked him what did he intend to do with this revolution.

We both laughed at the question because it was almost like a reflex action on my part: something that came out so quick that I was almost unaware of it. He twisted the cigar in his mouth and grinned, smoothing the strangely grown beard on his cheeks. "That *is* a poet's question," he said, "and the only poet's answer I can give you is that I will do what I think is right, what I think the people want. That's the best I can hope for, don't you think?"

I nodded, already about to shoot out another question, I didn't know how long I'd have. Certainly this was the most animated I'd been during the entire trip. "Uh—" I tried to smile—"what do you think the United States will do about Cuba ultimately?" The question seemed weird and out of place because everyone else was just trying to shake his hand.

"Ha, well, that's extremely difficult to say, your government is getting famous for its improvisation in foreign affairs. I suppose it depends on who is running the government. If the Democrats win it may get better. More Republicans . . . I suppose more trouble. I cannot say, except that I really do not care what they do as long as they do not try to interfere with the running of this country."

Suddenly the idea of a security lapse didn't seem so pressing. I had turned my head at a weird angle and looked up at the top of the platform. There was a soldier at each side of the back wall of the platform, about ten feet off the ground, each one with a machine gun on a tripod. I asked another question. "What about communism? How big a part does that play in the government?"

"I've said a hundred times that I'm not a communist. But I am certainly not an anti-communist. The United States likes anti-communists, especially so close to their mainland. I said also a hundred times that I consider myself a humanist. A radical humanist. The only way that anything can ever be accomplished in a country like Cuba is radically. The old has been here so long that the new must make radical changes in order to function at all."

So many people had crowded around us now that it became almost impossible to hear what Fidel was saying. I had shouted the last question. The young fashion model brushed by me and said how much she had enjoyed her stay in Cuba. Fidel touched his hand to the wide *campesino* hat he was wearing, then pumped her hand up and down. One of the Latin-American girls leaned forward suddenly and kissed him on the cheek. Everyone milled around the tall young Cuban, asking questions, shaking his hand, taking pictures, getting autographs (an American girl with pigtails and blue jeans) and, I suppose, committing everything he said to memory. The crowd was getting too large, I touched his arm, waved, and walked toward the back of the platform.

I hadn't had any water since early morning, and the heat and the excitement made my mouth dry and hard. There were no water fountains in sight. Most of the masses of Cubans had canteens or vacuum bottles, but someone had forgotten to tell the Americans (North and South) that there'd be no water. Also, there was no shade at all on the platform. I walked around behind it and squatted in a small booth with a tiny tin roof. It had formerly been a soda stand, but because the soda was free, the supply had given out rapidly and the stand had closed. I sat in the few inches of shade with my head in my hands, trying to cool off. Some Venezuelans came by and asked to sit in the shade next to me. I said it was all right and they offered me the first cup of water I'd had in about five hours. They had a whole chicken also, but I didn't think I'd be able to stand the luxury.

There were more speakers, including a little boy from one of the youngest militia units, but I heard them all over the public address system. I was too beat and thirsty to move. Later Ed Clarke and I went around hunting for water and finally managed to find a small brown stream where the soldiers were filling up their canteens. I drank two Coca-Cola bottles full, and when I got back to Habana came down with a fearful case of dysentery.

Suddenly there was an insane, deafening roar from the crowd. I met the girl economist as I dragged out of the booth and she tried to get me to go back on the front platform. Fidel was about to speak. I left her and jumped off the platform and trotted up a small rise to the left. The roar lasted about ten minutes, and as I got settled on the side of the hill Fidel began to speak.

He is an amazing speaker, knowing probably instinctively all the laws of dynamics and elocution. The speech began slowly and halt-ingly, each syllable being pronounced and with equal stress, as if he were reading a poem. He was standing with the *campesino* hat pushed back slightly off his forehead, both hands on the lectern. As he made his points, one of the hands would slide off the lectern and drop to his side, his voice becoming tighter and less warm. When the speech was really on its way, he dropped both hands from the lectern, putting one behind his back like a church usher, gesturing with the other. By now he would be rocking from side to side, point-ing his finger at the crowd, at the sky, at his own chest. Sometimes he seemed to lean to the side and talk to his own ministers there on the platform with him and then wheel toward the crowd calling for them to support him. At one point in the speech the crowd inter-rupted for about twenty minutes, crying, "Venceremos, vencere-mos, venceremos, venceremos, venceremos, venceremos, vencere-mos, venceremos." The entire crowd, 60 or 70,000 people all chanting in unison. Fidel stepped away from the lectern grinning, talking to his aides. He quieted the crowd with a wave of his arms and began again. At first softly, with the syllables drawn out and precisely enunciated, then tightening his voice and going into an al-most musical rearrangement of his speech. He condemned Eisen-hower, Nixon, the South, the Monroe Doctrine, the Platt Amend-ment, and Fulgencio Batista in one long, unbelievable sentece. The crowd interrupted again, "Fidel, Fidel, Fidel, Fidel, Fidel, Fidel, Fidel, Fidel, Fidel, Fidel, Fidel, Fidel." He leaned away from the lectern, grinning at the chief of the army. The speech lasted almost two and a half hours, being interrupted time and again by the exultant crowd and once by five minutes of rain. When it began to rain, Almeida draped a rain jacket around Fidel's shoulders, and he re-lit his cigar. When the speech ended, the crowd went out of its head, roaring for almost 45 minutes.

When the speech was over, I made a fast move for the platform. Almost a thousand other people had the same idea. I managed to shout something to Castro as he was being whizzed to the back of the platform and into a car. I shouted, "A fine speech, a tremendous speech."

He shouted back, "I hope you take it home with you," and disappeared in a host of bearded uniforms.

We were told at first that we would be able to leave the mountain in about three hours. But it had gotten dark already, and I didn't really fancy shooting down that mountain road with the same exuberance with which we came . . . not in the dark. Clarke and I went out looking for more water and walked almost a mile before we came to a big pavilion where soft drinks and sandwiches were being served. The soft drinks were hot and the sandwiches took too long to get. We came back and lay down at the top of a hill in back of the speakers' platform. It drizzled a little bit and the ground was patently uncomfortable. I tried to go to sleep but was awakened in a few minutes by explosions. The whole sky was lit up. Green, red, bright orange: the soldiers were shooting off fireworks. The platform was bathed in the light from the explosions and, suddenly, floodlights from the rear. The public address system announced that we were going to have a show.

The show was a strange mixture of pop culture and mainstream highbrow *haute culture*. There was a choral group singing a mildly atonal tone poem, a Jerome Robbinsesque ballet about Hollywood, Calypso dancers, and Mexican singers and dancers. The last act was the best, a Mardi Gras scene involving about a hundred West Indian singers and dancers, complete with floats, huge papier-mâché figures, drummers, and masks. The West Indians walked through the audience shouting and dancing, their many torches shooting shadows against the mountains. When they danced off and out of the amphitheatre area up toward a group of unfinished school buildings, except for the huge floodlights on stage, the whole area was dark.

Now there was great confusion in the audience. Most Cubans were still going to try to get home that night, so they were getting themselves together, rounding up wives and children, trying to find some kind of transportation off the mountain. There were still whole units of militia piling into trucks or walking off down the hill in the dark. The delegates, our group and a couple more thousand people who didn't feel like charging off into the dark were left. Olga got all the Americans together and we lined up for what was really our first meal of the day: beans, rice, pork, and a small can of fruit juice. At that time, we still had some hopes of leaving that night, but soon word was passed around that we weren't leaving, and it was best that we slept where we were. "Sleep wherever you want," was what Olga said. That meant the ground, or maybe cement sidewalks around the unfinished school buildings and dormitories of the new "school city." Some of the Americans started grumbling, but there was nothing that could be done. Two of our number were missing because of the day's festivities: the young lady from Philadelphia had to be driven back to Habana in a station wagon because she had come down with diarrhea and a fever, and the model had walked around without her hat too often and had gotten a slight case of sun-stroke. She was resting up in the medical shack now, and I began to envy her her small canvas cot.

It was a very strange scene, about three or four thousand people wandering around in semi-darkness among a group of unfinished buildings, looking for places to sleep. The whole top of the mountain alive with flashlights, cigarette lighters, and small torches. Little groups of people huddled together against the sides of buildings or stretched out under new "street lamps" in temporary plazas. Some people managed to climb through the windows of the new buildings and sleep on dirt floors, some slept under long aluminum trucks used for hauling stage equipment and some, like myself and the young female economist, sat up all night under dim lights, finally talking ourselves excitedly to sleep in the cool gray of early morning. I lay straight back on the cement "sidewalk" and slept without moving, until the sun began to burn my face.

We had been told the night before to be ready by 6 A.M. to pull out, but when morning came we loitered around again till about eight o'clock, when we had to line up for a breakfast of hot milk and French bread. It was served by young militia women, one of whom wore a big sidearm in a shoulder holster. By now, the dysentery was beginning to play havoc with my stomach, and the only toilet was a heavy thicket out behind the amphitheatre. I made it once, having to destroy a copy of a newspaper with my picture in it.

By nine no trucks had arrived, and with the sun now beginning to move heavily over us, the crowds shifted into the few shady areas remaining. It looked almost as if there were as many people still up on the mountain as there had been when we first arrived. Most of the Cubans, aside from the soldiers, stood in front of the pavilion and drank lukewarm Maltina or pineapple soda. The delegates and the other visitors squatted against buildings, talking and smoking. A French correspondent made a bad joke about Mussolini keeping the trains running on time, and a young Chinese student asked him why he wasn't in Algeria killing rebels.

The trucks did arrive, but there were only enough of them to take the women out. In a few minutes the sides of the trucks were almost bursting, so many females had stuffed inside. And they looked terribly uncomfortable, especially the ones stuck in the center who couldn't move an inch either way. An American newspaperman with our group who was just about to overstay his company-sanctioned leave began to panic, saying that the trucks wouldn't be back until the next day. But only a half-hour after the ladies pulled out, more trucks came and began taking the men out. Clarke, Williams, another member of our group, and I sat under the tin roof of an unfinished school building drinking warm soda, waiting until the last truck came, hoping it would be the least crowded. When we did climb up into one of the trucks it was jammed anyway, but we felt it was time to move.

This time we all had to stand up, except for a young *miliciano* who was squatting on a case of warm soda. I was in the center of the crowd and had nothing to hold on to but my companions. Every time the truck would stop short, which it did every few yards we traveled, everyone in the truck was slung against everyone else. When the truck did move, however, it literally zoomed down the side of the mountain. But then we would stop again, and all of us felt we would suffocate being mashed so tightly together, and from all the dust the trucks in front of us kicked up. The road now seemed like The Exodus. Exactly the same as the day before, only headed the opposite way. The trucks, the people on foot, the families, the militias, the *campesinos*, all headed down the mountain.

The truck sat one place twenty minutes without moving, and then when it did move it only edged up a few yards. Finally the driver pulled out of the main body of traffic and honking his horn continuously, drove down the opposite side of the road. When the soldiers directing traffic managed to flag him down, he told them that we were important visitors who had to make a train in Yara. The truck zoomed off again, rocking back and forth and up and down, throwing its riders at times almost out the back gate.

After a couple of miles, about five Mexicans got off the truck and got into another truck headed for Santiago. This made the rest of the ride easier. The *miliciano* began opening the soda and passing it around. We were really living it up. The delegates' spirits came back and they started their chanting and waving. When we got to the train junction, the cattle cars were sitting, but completely filled with soldiers and farmers. We didn't even stop, the driver gunned the thing as fast as it would go and we sailed by the shouting soldiers. We had only a few more stops before we got to Yara, jumped down in the soft sand, and ran for the big silver train marked "CUBA" that had been waiting for us since we left. When we got inside the train we discovered that the women still hadn't gotten back, so we sat quietly in the luxurious leather seats slowly sipping rum. The women arrived an hour later.

While we were waiting in Yara, soldiers and units of militia began to arrive in the small town and squat all around the four or five sets of trucks waiting for their own trains. Most of them went back in boxcars, while we visitors had the luxury of the semi-air-conditioned coach.

The ride back was even longer than the fourteen hours it took us before. Once when we stopped for water, we sat about two hours. Later, we stopped to pick up lunches. The atmosphere in the train was much the same as before, especially the Mexican delegates who whooped it up constantly. They even made a conga line up and down the whole length of the train. The young Mexican woman and I did a repeat performance also and talked most of the fifteen or sixteen hours it took us to get back to Habana. She was gentler with me this time, calling me "Yanqui imperialist" only a few times.

Everyone in the train was dirty, thirsty, and tired when it arrived in Habana. I had been wearing the same clothes for three days and hadn't even once taken off my shoes. The women were in misery. I hadn't seen a pocket mirror since the cattle cars.

The terminal looked like a rear outpost of some battlefield. So many people in filthy wrinkled clothes scrambling wearily out of trains. But even as tired as I was I felt excited at the prospect of being back in the big city for five more days. I was even more excited by the amount of thinking the trip to the Sierra was forcing me to. The "new" ideas that were being shoved at me, some of which I knew would be painful when I eventually got to New York.

The idea of "a revolution" had been foreign to me. It was one of those inconceivably "romantic" and/or hopeless ideas that we Norteamericanos have been taught since public school to hold up to the cold light of "reason." That reason being whatever repugnant lie our usurious "ruling class" had paid their journalists to disseminate. The reason that allows that voting, in a country where the parties are exactly the same, can be made to assume the gravity of actual moral engagement. The reason that permits a young intellectual to believe he has said something profound when he says, "I don't trust men in uniforms." The residue had settled on all our lives, and no one can function comfortably in this country without it. That thin crust of lie we cannot even detect in our own thinking. That rotting of the mind which had enabled us to think about Hiroshima as if someone else had done it, or to believe vaguely that the "counter-revolution" in Guatemala was an "internal" affair.

The rebels among us have become merely people like myself who grow beards and will not participate in politics. Drugs, juvenile delinquency, complete isolation from the vapid mores of the country, a few current ways out. But name an alternative here. Something not inextricably bound up in a lie. Something not part of liberal stupidity or the actual filth of vested interest. There is none. It's much too late. We are an *old* people already. Even the vitality of our art is like bright flowers growing up through a rotting carcass.

But the Cubans, and the other *new* peoples (in Asia, Africa, South America) don't need us, and we had better stay out of their way.

I came out of the terminal into the street and stopped at a newsstand to buy a paper. The headlines of one Miami paper read, "CUBAN CELEBRATION RAINED OUT." I walked away from the stand as fast as I could.

1960

The Legacy of Malcolm X, and the Coming of the Black Nation

I

The reason Malik was killed (the reasons) is because he was thought dangerous by enough people to allow and sanction it. Black People and white people.

Malcolm X was killed because he was dangerous to America. He had made too great a leap, in his sudden awareness of *direction* and the possibilities he had for influencing people, anywhere.

Malcolm was killed because he wanted to become official, as, say, a statesman. Malcolm wanted an effective form in which to enrage the white man, a practical form. And he had begun to find it.

For one thing, he'd learned that Black Conquest will be a *deal*. That is, it will be achieved through deals as well as violence. (He was beginning through his African statesmanship to make deals with other nations, as statesman from a *nation*. An oppressed Black Nation "laying" in the Western Hemisphere.)

This is one reason he could use the "universal" Islam—to be at peace with all dealers. The idea was to broaden, formalize, and elevate the will of the Black Nation so that it would be able to move a great many people and resources in a direction necessary to *spring* the Black Man.

"The Arabs must send us guns or we will accuse them of having sold us into slavery!" is international, and opens Black America's ports to all comers. When the ports are open, there is an instant *brotherhood of purpose* formed with most of the world.

Malcolm's legacy was his life. What he rose to be and through what channels, e.g., Elijah Muhammad and the Nation of Islam, as separate experiences. Malcolm changed as a minister of Islam: under Elijah's tutelage, he was a different man—the difference being, between a man who is preaching Elijah Muhammad and a man who is preaching political engagement and finally, national sovereignty. (Elijah Muhammad is now the second man, too.)

The point is that Malcolm had begun to call for Black National Consciousness. And moved this consciousness into the broadest possible arena, operating with it as of now. We do not want a Nation, we are a Nation. We must strengthen and formalize, and play the world's game with what we have, from where we are, as a *truly* separate people. America can give us nothing; all bargaining must be done by mutual agreement. But finally, terms must be given by Black Men *from their own shores*—which is where they live, where we all are, now. The land is literally ours. And we must begin to act like it.

The landscape should belong to the people who see it all the time.

We begin by being Nationalists. But a nation is land, and wars are fought over land. The sovereignty of nations, the sovereignty of culture, the sovereignty of race, the sovereignty of ideas and ways "into" the world.

The world in the twentieth century, and for some centuries before, is, literally, backward. The world can be understood through any idea. And the purely *social* condition of the world in this millennium, as, say, "compared" to other millennia, might show a far greater loss than gain, if this were not balanced by concepts and natural forces. That is, we think ourselves into the balance and ideas are necessarily "advanced" of what is simply here (*what's going on*, so to speak). And there are rockets and super cars. But, again, the loss? What might it have been if my people were turning the switches? I mean, these have been our White Ages, and all learning has suffered.

And so Nationalist concept is the arrival of conceptual and environmental strength, or the realization of it in its totality by the Black Man in the West, i.e., that he is not of the West, but even so, like the scattered Indians after movie cavalry attacks, must regroup, and return that force on a fat, ignorant, degenerate enemy.

We are a people. We are unconscious captives unless we realize this—that we have always been separate, except in our tranced desire to be the thing that oppressed us, after some generations of having been "programmed" (a word suggested to me by Jim Campbell and Norbert Wieners) into believing that our greatest destiny was to become white people!

2

Malcolm X's greatest contribution, other than to propose a path to internationalism and hence, the entrance of the American Black Man into a world-wide allegiance against the white man (in most recent times he proposed to do it using a certain kind of white liberal as a lever), was to preach Black Consciousness to the Black Man. As a minister for the Nation of Islam, Malcolm talked about a black consciousness that took its form from religion. In his last days he talked of another black consciousness that proposed politics as its moving energy.

But one very important aspect of Malcolm's earlier counsels was his explicit call for a National Consciousness among Black People. And this aspect of Malcolm's philosophy certainly did abide throughout his days. The feeling that somehow the Black Man was different, as being, as a being, and finally, in our own time, as judge. And Malcolm propounded these differences as life anecdote and religious (political) truth and made the consideration of Nationalist ideas significant and powerful in our day.

Another very important aspect of Malcolm's earlier (or the Honorable Elijah Muhammad's) philosophy was the whole concept of land and land-control as central to any talk of "freedom" or "independence." The Muslim tack of asking for land within the continental United States in which Black People could set up their own nation, was given a special appeal by Malcolm, even though the request was seen by most people outside the movement as "just talk" or the amusing howls of a gadfly.

But the whole importance of this insistence on land is just now beginning to be understood. Malcolm said many times that when you speak about revolution you're talking about land—changing the ownership or usership of some specific land which you think is yours. But any talk of Nationalism also must take this concept of land and its primary importance into consideration because, finally, any Nationalism which is not intent on restoring or securing autonomous space for a people, i.e., a nation, is at the very least shortsighted.

Elijah Muhammad has said, "We want our people in America, whose parents or grandparents were descendants from slaves, to be allowed to establish a separate state or territory of their own—either on this continent or elsewhere. We believe that our former slavemasters are obligated to provide such land and that the area must be fertile and minerally rich." And the Black Muslims seem separate from most Black People because the Muslims have a national consciousness based on their aspirations for land. Most of the Nationalist movements in this country advocate that that land is in Africa, and Black People should return there, or they propose nothing about land at all. It is impossible to be a Nationalist without talking about land. Otherwise your Nationalism is a misnamed kind of "difficult" opposition to what the white man has done, rather than the advocation of another people becoming the rulers of themselves, and sooner or later the rest of the world.

The Muslims moved from the Back-to-Africa concept of Marcus Garvey (the first large movement by Black People back to a National

Consciousness, which was, finally, only viable when the Black Man focused on Africa as literally "back home") to the concept of a Black National Consciousness existing in this land the Black captives had begun to identify as home. (Even in Garvey's time, there was not a very large percentage of Black People who really wanted to leave. Certainly, the newly emerging Black bourgeoisie would have nothing to do with "returning" to Africa. They were already created in the image of white people, as they still are, and wanted nothing to do with Black.)

What the Muslims wanted was a profound change. The National Consciousness focused on actual (nonabstract) land, identifying a people, in a land where they lived. Garvey wanted to go back to Jordan. A real one. The Nation of Islam wanted Jordan closer. Before these two thrusts, the Black Man in America, as he was Christianized, believed Jordan was in the sky, like pie, and absolutely supernatural.

Malcolm, then, wanted to give the National Consciousness its political embodiment, and send it out to influence the newly forming third world, in which this consciousness was to be included. The concept of Blackness, the concept of the National Consciousness, the proposal of a political (and diplomatic) form for this aggregate of Black spirit, these are the things given to us by Garvey, through Elijah Muhammad and finally given motion into still another area of Black response by Malcolm X.

Malcolm's legacy to Black People is what he moved toward, as the accretion of his own spiritual learning and the movement of Black People in general, through the natural hope, a rise to social understanding within the new context of the white nation and its decline under hypocrisy and natural "oppositeness" which has pushed all of us toward "new" ideas. We are all the products of national spirit and worldview. We are drawn by the vibrations of the entire nation. If there were no bourgeois Negroes, none of us would be drawn to that image. They, bourgeois Negroes, were shaped through the purposive actions of a national attitude, and finally, by the demands of a particular culture.

At which point we must consider what cultural attitudes are, what culture is, and what National Consciousness has to do with these, i.e., if we want to understand what Malcolm was pointing toward, and why the Black Man now must move in that direction since the world will not let him move any other way. The Black Man is possessed by the energies of historic necessity and the bursting into flower of a National Black Cultural Consciousness, and with that, in a living future, the shouldering to power of Black culture and, finally, Black Men . . . and then, Black ideals, which are different descriptions of a God. A righteous sanctity, out of which worlds are built.

3

What the Black Man must do now is look down at the ground upon which he stands, and claim it as his own. It is not abstract. Look down! Pick up the earth, or jab your fingernails into the concrete. It is real and it is yours, if you want it.

But to want it, as our own, is the present direction. To want what we are and where we are, but rearranged by our own consciousness. That is why it was necessary first to recrystallize national aspirations behind a Garvey. The Africans who first came here were replaced by Americans, or people responding to Western stimuli and then Americans. In order for the Americans to find out that they had come from another place, were, hence, alien, the Garvey times had to come. Elijah said we must have a place, to be, ourselves. Malcolm made it contemporarily secular.

So that now we must find the flesh of our spiritual creation. We must be *conscious*. And to be conscious is to be *cultured*, processed in specific virtues and genius. We must respond to this National Consciousness with our souls, and use the correspondence to come into our own.

The Black Man will always be frustrated until he has land (A Land!) of his own. All the thought processes and emotional orientation of "national liberation movements"—from slave uprisings onward—have always given motion to a Black National (and Cultural) Consciousness. These movements proposed that judgments were being made by Black sensibility, and that these judgments were *necessarily* different from those of the white sensibility—different, and after all is said and done, inimical.

Men are what their culture predicts (enforces). Culture is, simply, the way men live. How they have come to live. What they are formed by. Their total experience, and its implications and theories. Its paths.

The Black Man's paths are alien to the white man. Black Culture is alien to the white man. Art and religion are the results and idealized supernumeraries of culture. Culture in this sense, as Sapir said, is "The National Genius," whether it be a way of fixing rice or killing a man.

I said in *Blues People*: "Culture is simply how one lives and is connected to history by habit." God is man idealized (humanist definition). Religion is the aspiration of man toward an idealized existence. An existence in which the functions of God and man are harmonious, even identical. Art is the movement forward, the understanding progress of man. It is feeling and making. A nation (social order) is made the way people *feel* it should be made. A face is too. Politics is man's aspiration toward an order. Religion is too. Art is an ordering as well. And all these categories are spiritual, but are also the result of the body, at one point, serving as a container of feeling. The soul is no less sensitive.

Nations are races. (In America, white people have become a nation, an identity, a race.) Political integration in America will not work because the Black Man is played on by special forces. His life, from his organs, i.e., the life of the body, what it needs, what it wants, to become, is different—and for this reason racial is biological, finally. We are a different *species*. A species that is evolving to world power and philosophical domination of the world. The world will move the way Black People move!

If we take the teachings of Garvey, Elijah Muhammad and Malcolm X (as well as Frazier, Du Bois and Fanon), we know for certain that the solution of the Black Man's problems will come only through Black National Consciousness. We also know that the focus of change will be racial. (If we *feel* differently, we have different *ideas*. Race is feeling. Where the body, and the organs come in. Culture is the preservation of these feelings in superrational to rational form. Art is one method of expressing these feelings and identifying the form, as an emotional phenomenon.) In order for the Black Man in the West to absolutely know himself, it is necessary for him to see himself first as culturally separate from the white man. That is, to be conscious of this separation and use the strength it proposes.

Western Culture (the way white people live and think) is passing. If the Black Man cannot identify himself as separate, and understand what this means, he will perish along with Western Culture and the white man.

What a culture produces, is, and refers to, is an image—a picture of a process, since it is a form of a process: movement seen. The changing of images, of references, is the Black Man's way back to the racial integrity of the captured African, which is where we must take ourselves, in feeling, to be truly the warriors we propose to be. To form an absolutely rational attitude toward West man, and West thought. Which is what is needed. To see the white man as separate and as enemy. To make a fight according to the absolute realities of the world as it is.

Good–Bad, Beautiful–Ugly, are all formed as the result of image. The mores, customs, of a place are the result of experience, and a common reference for defining it—common images. The three white men in the film *Gunga Din* who kill off hundreds of Indians, Greek hero–style, are part of an image of white men. The various black porters, gigglers, ghostchumps and punkish Indians, etc., that inhabit the public image the white man has fashioned to characterize Black Men are references by Black Men to the identity of Black Men in the West, since that's what is run on them each day by white magic, i.e., television, movies, radio, etc.—the Mass Media (the *Daily News* does it with flicks and adjectives).

The song title "A White Man's Heaven Is a Black Man's Hell" describes how complete an image reversal is necessary in the West. Because for many Black People, the white man has succeeded in making this hell seem like heaven. But Black youth are much better off in this regard than their parents. They are the ones who need the least image reversal.

The Black artist, in this context, is desperately needed to change the images his people identify with, by asserting Black feeling, Black mind, Black judgment. The Black intellectual, in this same context, is needed to change the interpretation of facts toward the Black Man's best interests, instead of merely tagging along reciting white judgments of the world.

Art, Religion, and Politics are impressive vectors of a culture. Art describes a culture. Black artists must have an image of what the Black sensibility is in this land. Religion elevates a culture. The Black Man must aspire to Blackness. God is man idealized. The Black Man must idealize himself as Black. And idealize and aspire to that. Politics gives a social order to the culture, i.e., makes relationships within the culture definable for the functioning organism. The Black man must seek a Black politics, an ordering of the world that is beneficial to his culture, to his interiorization and judgment of the world. This is strength. And we are hordes.

4

Black People are a race, a culture, a Nation. The legacy of Malcolm X is that we know we can move from where we are. Our land is where we live. (Even the Muslims have made this statement about Harlem.) If we are a separate Nation, we must make that separateness where we are. There are Black cities all over this white nation. Nations within nations. In order for the Black Man to survive he must not only identify himself as a unique being, but take steps to insure that this being has what the Germans call *Lebensraum* ("living room"), literally, space in which to exist and develop.

The concepts of National Consciousness and the Black Nation, after the death of Malik, have moved to the point where now some Black People are demanding national sovereignty as well as National (and Cultural) Consciousness. In Harlem, for instance, as director of the Black Arts Repertory Theater-School, I have issued a call for a Black Nation. In Harlem, where 600,000 Black People reside.

The first act must be the nationalization of all properties and resources belonging to the white people, within the boundaries of the Black Nation. (All the large concentrations of Black People in the West are already nations. All that is missing is the consciousness of this state of affairs. All that is missing is that the Black Man take control. As Margaret Walker said in her poem "For My People": *A race of men must rise, and take control.*)

Nationalization means that all properties and resources must be harnessed to the needs of the Nation. In the case of the coming Black Nation, all these materials must be harnessed to the needs of Black People. In Harlem, it is almost common knowledge that the Jews, etc., will go the next time there's a large "disturbance," like they say. But there must be machinery set up to transfer the power potential of these retail businesses, small industries, etc., so that they may benefit Black People.

Along with nationalization of foreign-owned businesses (which includes Italian underworld businesses, some of which, like the policy racket, can be transformed into a national lottery, with the monies staying with Black People, or as in the case of heroin-selling, completely abolished) must come the nationalization of all political voices setting up to function within the community/Nation.

No white politicians can be allowed to function within the Nation. Black politicians doing funny servant business for whites, must be eliminated. Black people must have absolute political and economic control. In other words they must have absolute control over their lives and destinies.

These moves are toward the working form of any autonomous nation. And it is this that the Black Man must have. An autonomous Nation. His own forms: treaties, agreements, laws.

These are moves that the conscious Black Man (artist, intellectual,

Nationalist, religious thinker, dude with "common sense") must prepare the people for. And the people must be prepared for moves they themselves are already making. And moves they have already made must be explained and analyzed. They, the people, are the bodies. . . . Where are the heads?

And it is the heads that are needed for the next move Black People will make. The move to Nationhood. The exact method of transformation is simple logistics.

What we are speaking about again is sovereignty. Sovereignty and independence. And when we speak of these things, we can understand just how far Malik went. The point now is to take ourselves the rest of the way.

Only a united Black Consciousness can save Black People from annihilation at the white man's hands. And no other nation on earth is safe, unless the Black Man in America is safe. Not even the Chinese can be absolutely certain of their continued sovereignty as long as the white man is alive. And there is only one people on the planet who can slay the white man. The people who know him best. His ex-slaves.

1965

State/meant

The Black Artist's role in America is to aid in the destruction of America as he knows it. His role is to report and reflect so precisely the nature of the society, and of himself in that society, that other men will be moved by the exactness of his rendering and, if they are black men, grow strong through this moving, having seen their own strength, and weakness; and if they are white men, tremble, curse, and go mad, because they will be drenched with the filth of their evil.

The Black Artist must draw out of his soul the correct image of the world. He must use this image to band his brothers and sisters together in common understanding of the nature of the world (and the nature of America) and the nature of the human soul.

The Black Artist must demonstrate sweet life, how it differs from the deathly grip of the White Eyes. The Black Artist must teach the

White Eyes their deaths, and teach the black man how to bring these
deaths about.

> We are unfair, and unfair.
> We are black magicians, black art
> s we make in black labs of the heart.
>
> The fair are
> fair, and death
> ly white.
>
> The day will not save them
> and we own
> the night.

                                        1965

From *Tales*

Tales is Baraka's only collection of short stories. These autobiographical, experimental stories document Baraka's
movement toward a blacker self in prose. "The Screamers"
pays tribute to the revolutionary potential of black music;
"Words" shows the author's alienation from the black community. This collection along with the novel *The System of
Dante's Hell*, put Baraka in the forefront of contemporary
black avant-garde fiction writers.

—wjh

The Screamers

Lynn Hope adjusts his turban under the swishing red green yellow
shadow lights. Dots. Suede heaven raining, windows yawning cool
summer air, and his musicians watch him grinning, quietly, or high
with wine blotches on four-dollar shirts. A yellow girl will not
dance with me, nor will Teddy's people, in line to the left of the
stage, readying their *Routines*. Haroldeen, the most beautiful, in her
pitiful dead sweater. Make it yellow, wish it whole. Lights. Teddy,
Sonny Boy, Kenny & Calvin, Scram, a few of Nat's boys jamming
long washed handkerchiefs in breast pockets, pushing shirts into
homemade cummerbunds, shuffling lightly for any audience.
                                                    "The Cross-Over,"
Deen laughing at us all. And they perform in solemn unison a social
tract of love. (With no music till Lynn finishes "macking" with any
biglipped Esther screws across the stage. White and green plaid
jackets his men wear, and that twisted badge, black turban/on red
string conked hair. (OPPRESSORS!) A greasy hip-ness, down-ness,
nobody in our camp believed (having social-worker mothers and
postman fathers; or living squeezed in lightskinned projects with
adulterers and proud skinny ladies with soft voices). The theory, the
spectrum, this sound baked inside their heads, and still rub sweaty
against those lesser lights. Those niggers. Laundromat workers,
beauticians, pregnant short-haired jail bait separated all ways from
"us," but in this vat we sweated gladly for each other. And rubbed.
And Lynn could be a common hero, from whatever side we saw

him. Knowing that energy, and its response. That drained silence we had to make with our hands, leaving actual love to Nat or Al or Scram.

He stomped his foot, and waved one hand. The other hung loosely on his horn. And their turbans wove in among those shadows. Lynn's tighter, neater, and bright gorgeous yellow stuck with a green stone. Also, those green sparkling cubes dancing off his pinkies. A-boomp bahba bahba, A-boomp bahba bahba, A-boomp bahba bahba, A-boomp bahba bahba, the turbans sway behind him. And he grins before he lifts the horn, at Deen or drunk Becky, and we search the dark for girls.

Who would I get? (Not anyone who would understand this.) Some light girl who had fallen into bad times and ill-repute for dating Bubbles. And he fixed her later with his child, now she walks Orange St. wiping chocolate from its face. A disgraced white girl who learned to calypso in vocational school. Hence, behind halting speech, a humanity as paltry as her cotton dress. (And the big hats made a line behind her, stroking their erections, hoping for photographs to take down south.) Lynn would oblige. He would make the most perverted hopes sensual and possible. Chanting at that dark crowd. Or some girl, a wino's daughter, with carefully vaselined bow legs would drape her filthy angora against the cardboard corinthian, eying past greediness a white man knows, my soft tyrolean hat, pressed corduroy suit, and "B" sweater. Whatever they meant, finally, to her, valuable shadows barely visible.

Some stuck-up boy with "good" hair. And as a naked display of America, for I meant to her that same oppression. A stunted head of greased glass feathers, orange lips, brown pasted edge to the collar of her dying blouse. The secret perfume of poverty and ignorant desire. Arrogant too, at my disorder, which calls her smile mysterious. Turning to be eaten by the crowd. That mingled foliage of sweat and shadows: Night Train was what they swayed to. And smelled each other in The Grind, The Rub, The Slow Drag. From side to side, slow or jerked staccato as their wedding dictated. Big hats bent tight skirts, and some light girls' hair swept the resin on the floor. Respectable ladies put stiff arms on your waist to keep some light between, looking nervously at an ugly friend forever at the music's edge.

I wanted girls like Erselle, whose father sang on television, but my hair was not straight enough, and my father never learned how to drink. Our house sat lonely and large on a half-Italian street, filled with important Negroes. (Though it is rumored they had a son, thin with big eyes, they killed because he was crazy.) Surrounded by the haughty daughters of depressed economic groups. They plotted in their projects for mediocrity, and the neighborhood smelled of their despair. And only the wild or the very poor thrived in Graham's or could be roused by Lynn histories and rhythms. America had choked the rest, who could sit still for hours under popular songs, or be readied for citizenship by slightly bohemian social workers. They rivaled pure emotion with wind-up record players that pumped Jo Stafford into Home Economics rooms. And these carefully scrubbed children of my parents' friends fattened on their rhythms until they could join the Urban League or Household Finance and hound the poor for their honesty.

I was too quiet to become a murderer, and too used to extravagance for their skinny lyrics. They mentioned neither cocaine nor Bach, which was my reading, and the flaw of that society. I disappeared into the slums, and fell in love with violence, and invented for myself a mysterious economy of need. Hence, I shambled anonymously thru Lloyd's, The Nitecap, The Hi-Spot, and Graham's desiring everything I felt. In a new English overcoat and green hat, scouring that town for my peers. And they were old pinch-faced whores full of snuff and weak dope, celebrity fags with radio programs, mute bass players who loved me, and built the myth of my intelligence. You see, I left America on the first fast boat.

This was Sunday night, and the Baptists were still praying in their "faboulous" churches. Though my father sat listening to the radio, or reading pulp cowboy magazines, which I take in part to be the truest legacy of my spirit. God never had a chance. And I would be walking slowly toward The Graham, not even knowing how to smoke. Willing for any experience, any image, any further separation from where my good grades were sure to lead. Frightened of post offices, lawyer's offices, doctor's cars, the deaths of clean politicians. Or of the imaginary fat man, advertising cemeteries to his "good colored friends." Lynn's screams erased them all, and I thought myself intrepid white commando from the West. Plunged into noise and flesh, and their form become an ethic.

Now Lynn wheeled and hunched himself for another tune. Fast dancers fanned themselves. Couples who practiced during the week talked over their steps. Deen and her dancing clubs readied *avant-garde* routines. Now it was *Harlem Nocturne*, which I whistled loudly one Saturday in a laundromat, and the girl who stuffed in my khakis and stiff underwear asked was I a musician. I met her at Graham's that night and we waved, and I suppose she knew I loved her.

Nocturne was slow and heavy and the serious dancers loosened their ties. The slowly twisting lights made specks of human shadows, the darkness seemed to float around the hall. Any meat you clung to was yours those few minutes without interruption. The length of the music was the only form. And the idea was to press against each other hard, to rub, to shove the hips tight, and gasp at whatever passion. Professionals wore jocks against embarrassment. Amateurs, like myself, after the music stopped, put our hands quickly into our pockets, and retreated into the shadows. It was as meaningful as anything else we knew.

All extremes were popular with that crowd. The singers shouted, the musicians stomped and howled. The dancers ground each other past passion or moved so fast it blurred intelligence. We hated the popular song, and any freedman could tell you if you asked that white people danced jerkily, and were slower than our champions. One style, which developed as Italians showed up with pegs, and our own grace moved toward bellbottom pants to further complicate the cipher, was the honk. The repeated rhythmic figure, a screamed riff, pushed in its insistence past music. It was hatred and frustration, secrecy and despair. It spurted out of the diphthong culture, and reinforced the black cults of emotion. There was no compromise, no dreary sophistication, only the elegance of something that is too ugly to be described, and is diluted only at the agent's peril. All the saxophonists of that world were honkers, Illinois, Gator, Big Jay, Jug, the great sounds of our day. Ethnic historians, actors, priests of the unconscious. That stance spread like fire thru the cabarets and joints of the black cities, so that the sound itself became a basis for thought, and the innovators searched for uglier modes. Illinois would leap and twist his head, scream when he wasn't playing. Gator would strut up and down the stage, dancing for emphasis, shaking his long gassed hair in his face and coolly mopping it back. Jug, the beautiful horn, would wave back and forth so high we all envied him his connection, or he'd stomp softly to the edge of the stage whispering those raucous threats. Jay first turned the mark around, opened the way further for the completely nihilistic act. McNeely, the first Dada coon of the age, jumped and stomped and yowled and finally sensed the only other space that form allowed. He fell first on his knees, never releasing the horn, and walked that way across the stage. We hunched together drowning any sound, relying on Jay's contorted face for evidence that there was still music, though none of us needed it now. And then he fell backwards, flat on his back, with both feet stuck up high in the air, and he kicked and thrashed and the horn spat enraged sociologies.

That was the night Hip Charlie, the Baxter Terrace Romeo, got wasted right in front of the place. Snake and four friends mashed him up and left him for the ofays to identify. Also the night I had the grey bells and sat in the Chinese restaurant all night to show them off. Jay had set a social form for the poor, just as Bird and Dizzy proposed it for the middle class. On his back screaming was the Mona Lisa with the mustache, as crude and simple. Jo Stafford could not do it. Bird took the language, and we woke up one Saturday whispering *Ornithology*. Blank verse.

And Newark always had a bad reputation, I mean, everybody could pop their fingers. Was hip. Had walks. Knew all about The Apple. So I suppose when the word got to Lynn what Big Jay had done, he knew all the little down cats were waiting to see him in this town. He knew he had to cook. And he blasted all night, crawled and leaped, then stood at the side of the stand, and watched us while he fixed his sky, wiped his face. Watched us to see how far he'd gone, but he was tired and we weren't, which was not where it was. The girls rocked slowly against the silence of the horns, and big hats pushed each other or made plans for murder. We had not completely come. All sufficiently eaten by Jay's memory, "on his back, kicking his feet in the air, Go-ud Damn!" So he moved cautiously to the edge of the stage, and the gritty Muslims he played with gathered close. It was some mean honking blues, and he made no attempt to hide his intentions. He was breaking bad. "Okay, baby," we all thought. "Go for yourself." I was standing at the back of the hall with one arm behind my back, so the overcoat could hang over in that casual gesture of fashion. Lynn was moving, and the camel walkers were moving in the corners. The fast dancers and practicers making the whole hall dangerous. "Off my suedes, motherfucker." Lynn was trying to move us, and even I did the one step I knew, safe at the back of the hall. The hippies ran for girls. Ugly girls danced with each other. Skippy, who ran the lights, made them move faster in that circle on the ceiling, and darkness raced around the hall. Then Lynn got his riff, that rhythmic figure we knew he would repeat, the honked note that would be his personal evaluation of the world. And he screamed it so the veins in his face stood out like neon. "Uhh, yeh, Uhh, yeh, Uhh, yeh," we all screamed to push him further. So he opened his eyes for a second, and really made his move. He looked over his shoulder at the other turbans, then marched in time with his riff, on his toes across the stage. They followed; he marched across to the other side, repeated, then finally he descended, still screaming, into the crowd, and as the sidemen followed, we made a path for them around the hall. They were strutting, and all their horns held very high, and they were only playing that one scary note. They moved near the back of the hall, chanting and swaying, and passed right in front of me. I had a little cup full of wine a murderer friend of mine made me drink, so I drank it and tossed the cup in the air, then fell in line behind the last wild horn man, strutting like the rest of them. Bubbles and Rogie followed me, and four-eyed Moselle Boyd. And we strutted back and forth pumping our arms, repeating with Lynn Hope, "Yeh, Uhh, Yeh, Uhh." Then everybody fell in behind us, yelling still. There was confusion and stumbling, but there were no real fights. The thing they wanted was right there and easily accessible. No one could stop you from getting in that line. "It's too crowded. It's too many people on that line!" some people yelled. So Lynn thought further, and made to destroy the ghetto. We went out into the lobby and in perfect rhythm down the marble steps. Some musicians laughed, but Lynn and some others kept the note, till the others fell back in. Five or six hundred hopped-up woogies tumbled out into Belmont Avenue. Lynn marched right in the center of the street. Sunday night traffic stopped, and honked. Big Red yelled at a bus driver, "Hey, baby, honk that horn in time or shut it off!" The bus driver cooled it. We screamed and screamed at the clear image of ourselves as we should always be. Ecstatic, completed, involved in a secret communal expression. It would be the form of the sweetest revolution, to huckle-buck into the fallen capital, and let the oppressors lindy hop out. We marched all the way to Spruce, weaving among the stalled cars, laughing at the dazed white men who sat behind the wheels. Then Lynn turned and we strutted back toward the hall. The late show at the National was turning out, and all the big hats there jumped right in our line.

Then the Nabs came, and with them, the fire engines. What was it, a labor riot? Anarchists? A nigger strike? The paddy wagons and cruisers pulled in from both sides, and sticks and billies started flying, heavy streams of water splattering the marchers up and down the street. America's responsible immigrants were doing her light work again. The knives came out, the razors, all the Biggers who would not be bent, counterattacked or came up behind the civil servants smashing at them with coke bottles and aerials. Belmont writhed under the dead economy and splivs floated in the gutter, disappearing under cars. But for a while, before the war had reached its peak, Lynn and his musicians, a few other fools, and I, still marched, screaming thru the maddened crowd. Onto the sidewalk, into the lobby, halfway up the stairs, then we all broke our different ways, to save whatever it was each of us thought we loved.

Words

Now that the old world has crashed around me, and it's raining in early summer. I live in Harlem with a baby shrew and suffer for my decadence which kept me away so long. When I walk in the streets, the streets don't yet claim me, and people look at me, knowing the strangeness of my manner, and the objective stance from which I attempt to "love" them. It was always predicted this way. This is what my body told me always. When the child leaves, and the window goes on looking out on empty walls, you will sit and dream of old things, and things that could never happen. You will be alone, and ponder on your learning. You will think of old facts, and sudden seeings which made you more than you had bargained for, yet a coward on the earth, unless you claim it, unless you step upon it with your heavy feet, and feel actual hardness.

Last night in a bar a plump black girl sd, "O.K., be intellectual, go write some more of them jivey books," and it could have been anywhere, a thousand years ago, she sd "Why're you so cold," and I wasn't even thinking coldness. Just tired and a little weary of myself. Not even wanting to hear me thinking up things to say.

But the attention. To be always looking, and thinking. To be always under so many things' gaze, the pressure of such attention. I wanted something, want it now. But don't know what it is, except words. I cd say anything. But what would be left, what would I have made? Who would love me for it? Nothing. No one. Alone, I will sit and watch the sun die, the moon fly out in space, the earth wither, and dead men stand in line, to rot away and never exist.

Finally, to have passed away, and be an old hermit in love with silence. To have the thing I left, and found. To be older than I am, and with the young animals marching through the trees. To want what is natural, and strong.

Today is more of the same. In the closed circle I have fashioned. In the alien language of another tribe. I make these documents for some heart who will recognize me truthfully. Who will know what I am and what I wanted beneath the maze of meanings and attitudes that shape the reality of everything. Beneath the necessity of talking or the necessity for being angry or beneath the actual core of life we make reference to digging deep into some young woman, and listening to her come.

Selves fly away in madness. Liquid self shoots out of the joint. Lives which are salty and sticky. Why does everyone live in a closet, and hope no one will understand how badly they need to grow? How many errors they canonize or justify, or kill behind? I need to be an old monk and not feel sorry or happy for people. I need to be a billion years old with a white beard and all of ASIA to walk around.

The purpose of myself, has not yet been fulfilled. Perhaps it will never be. Just these stammerings and poses. Just this need to reach into myself, and feel something wince and love to be touched.

The dialogue exists. Magic and ghosts are a dialogue, and the body bodies of material, invisible sound vibrations, humming in emptyness, and ideas less than humming, humming, images collide in empty ness, and we build our emotions into blank invisible structures which never exist, and are not there, and are illusion and pain and madness. Dead whiteness.

> We turn white when we are afraid.
> We are going to try to be happy.
> We do not need to be fucked with.
> We can be quiet and think and love the silence.
> We need to look at trees more closely.
> We need to listen.

Harlem 1965

From *Black Music*

Black Music features fugitive music reviews and articles (originally published between 1959 and 1967) and is Baraka's black-nationalist meditation on Afro-American music. It includes pieces on such artists as Billie Holiday, Sonny Rollins, Archie Shepp, and John Coltrane. For Baraka, Coltrane is the great black-nationalist artist-hero. He declares: "Trane is a mature swan whose wing span was a whole world. But he also shows us to murder the popular song. To do away with weak Western forms. He is a beautiful philosopher." Baraka wants the black artist to emulate Coltrane by creating art that will destroy Western forms.

—wjh

Jazz and the White Critic

Most jazz critics have been white Americans, but most important jazz musicians have not been. This might seem a simple enough reality to most people, or at least a reality which can be readily explained in terms of the social and cultural history of American society. And it is obvious why there are only two or three fingers' worth of Negro critics or writers on jazz, say, if one understands that until relatively recently those Negroes who *could* become critics, who would largely have to come from the black middle class, have simply not been interested in the music. Or at least jazz, for the black middle class, has only comparatively recently lost some of its stigma (though by no means is it yet as popular among them as any vapid musical product that comes sanctioned by the taste of the white majority). Jazz was collected among the numerous skeletons the middle-class black man kept locked in the closet of his psyche, along with watermelons and gin, and whose rattling caused him no end of misery and self-hatred. As one Howard University philosophy professor said to me when I was an undergraduate, "It's fantastic how much bad taste the blues contain!" But it is just this "bad taste" that this Uncle spoke of that has been the one factor that has kept the best of Negro music from slipping sterilely into the echo chambers of middle-brow American culture. And to a great extent such "bad taste" was kept extant in the music, blues or jazz because the Negroes who were responsible for the best of the music, were always aware of their identities as black Americans and really did not, themselves, desire to become vague, featureless, Americans as is usually the case with the Negro middle class. (This is certainly not to say that there have not been very important Negro musicians from the middle class. Since the Henderson era, their number has increased enormously in jazz.)

Negroes played jazz as they had sung blues or, even earlier, as they had shouted and hollered in those anonymous fields, because it was one of the few areas of human expression available to them. Negroes who felt the blues, later jazz, impulse, as a specific means of expression, went naturally into the music itself. There were fewer social or extra-expressive considerations that could possibly disqualify any prospective Negro jazz musician than existed, say, for a Negro who thought he might like to become a writer (or even an elevator operator, for that matter). Any Negro who had some ambition towards literature, in the earlier part of this century, was likely to have developed so powerful an allegiance to the sacraments of middle-class American culture that he would be horrified by the very idea of writing about jazz.

There were few "jazz critics" in America at all until the '30s and then they were influenced to a large extent by what Richard Hadlock has called "the carefully documented gee-whiz attitude" of the first serious European jazz critics. They were also, as a matter of course, influenced more deeply by the social and cultural mores of their own society. And it is only natural that their criticism, whatever its intention, should be a product of that society, or should reflect at least some of the attitudes and thinking of that society, even if not directly related to the subject they were writing about, Negro music.

Jazz, as a Negro music, existed, up until the time of the big bands, on the same socio-cultural level as the sub-culture from which it was issued. The music and its sources were *secret* as far as the rest of America was concerned, in much the same sense that the actual life of the black man in America was secret to the white American. The first white critics were men who sought, whether consciously or not, to understand this secret, just as the first serious white jazz musicians (Original Dixieland Jazz Band, Bix, etc.) sought not only to understand the phenomenon of Negro music but to appropriate it as a means of expression which they themselves might utilize. The success of this "appropriation" signaled the existence of an American music, where before there was a Negro music. But the white jazz musician had an advantage the white critic seldom had. The white musician's commitment to jazz, the *ultimate concern*, proposed that the sub-cultural attitudes that produced the music as a profound expression of human feelings, could be *learned* and need not be passed on as a secret blood rite. And Negro music is essentially the expression of an attitude, or a collection of attitudes, about the world, and only secondarily an attitude about the way music is made. The white jazz musician came to understand this attitude as a way of making music, and the intensity of his understanding produced the "great" white jazz musicians, and is producing them now.

Usually the critic's commitment was first to his *appreciation* of the music rather than to his understanding of the attitude which produced it. This difference meant that the potential critic of jazz had only to appreciate the music, or what he thought was the music, and that he did not need to understand or even be concerned with the attitudes that produced it, excepts perhaps as a purely sociological consideration. This last idea is certainly what produced the reverse patronization that is known as Crow Jim. The disparaging "all you folks got rhythm" is no less a stereotype, simply because it is proposed as a positive trait. But this Crow Jim attitude has not been as menacing or as evident a flaw in critical writing about jazz as has another manifestation of the white critic's failure to concentrate on the blues and jazz attitude rather than his conditioned appreciation of the music. The major flaw in this approach to Negro music is that it strips the music too ingenuously of its social and cultural intent. It seeks to define jazz as an art (or a folk art) that has come out of no intelligent body of socio-cultural philosophy.

We take for granted the social and cultural milieu and philosophy that produced Mozart. As western people, the socio-cultural thinking of eighteenth-century Europe comes to us as a history legacy that is a continuous and organic part of the twentieth-century West. The socio-cultural philosophy of the Negro in America (as a continuous historical phenomenon) is no less specific and no less important for any intelligent critical speculation about the music that came out of it. And again, this is not a plea for narrow sociological analysis of jazz, but rather that this music cannot be completely understood (in critical terms) without some attention to the attitudes which produced it. It is the philosophy of Negro music that is most important, and this philosophy is only partially the result of the sociological disposition of Negroes in America. There is, of course, much more to it than that.

Strict musicological analysis of jazz, which has come into favor recently, is also as limited as a means of jazz criticism as a strict sociological approach. The notator of any jazz solo, or blues, has no chance of capturing what in effect are the most important elements of the music. (Most transcriptions of blues lyrics are just as frustrating.) A printed musical example of an Armstrong solo, or of a Thelonious Monk solo, tells us almost nothing except the futility of formal musicology when dealing with jazz. Not only are the various jazz effects almost impossible to notate, but each note *means something* quite in adjunct to musical notation. The notes of a jazz solo exist in a notation strictly for musical reasons. The notes of a jazz solo, as they are coming into existence, exist as they do for reasons that are only concomitantly musical. Coltrane's cries are not "musical," but they *are* music and quite moving music. Ornette Coleman's screams and rants are only musical once one understands the music his emotional attitude seeks to create. This attitude is real, and perhaps the most singularly important aspect of his music. Mississippi Joe Williams, Snooks Eaglin, Lightnin' Hopkins have different emotional attitudes than Ornette Coleman, but all of these attitudes are continuous parts of the historical and cultural biography of the Negro as it has existed and developed since there was a Negro in America, and a music that could be associated with him that did not exist anywhere else in the world. The notes *mean something*; and the something is, regardless of its stylistic considerations, part of the black psyche as it dictates the various forms of Negro culture.

Another hopeless flaw in a great deal of the writing about jazz that has been done over the years is that in most cases the writers, the jazz critics, have been anything but intellectuals (in the most complete sense of that word). Most jazz critics began as hobbyists or boyishly brash members of the American petit bourgeoisie, whose only claim to any understanding about the music was that they knew it was *different*; or else they had once been brave enough to make a trip into a Negro slum to hear their favorite instrumentalist defame Western musical tradition. Most jazz critics were (and are) not only white middle-class Americans, but middle-brows as well. The irony here is that because the majority of jazz critics are white middle-brows, most jazz criticism tends to enforce white middle-brow standards of excellence as criteria for performance of a music that in its most profound manifestations is completely antithetical to such standards; in fact, quite often is in direct reaction against them. (As an analogy, suppose the great majority of the critics of Western formal music were poor, "uneducated" Negroes?) A man can speak of the "heresy of bebop" for instance, only if he is completely unaware of the psychological catalysts that made that music the exact registration of the social and cultural thinking of a whole generation of black Americans. The blues and jazz aesthetic, to be fully understood, must be seen in as nearly its complete human context as possible. People made bebop. The question the critic must ask is: *why?* But it is just this *why* of Negro music that has been consistently ignored or misunderstood; and it is a question that cannot be adequately answered without first understanding the necessity of asking it. Contemporary jazz during the last few years has begun to take on again some of the anarchy and excitement of the bebop years. The cool and hard bop/funk movements since the '40s seem pitifully tame, even decadent, when compared to the music men like Ornette Coleman, Sonny Rollins, John Coltrane, Cecil Taylor and some others have been making recently. And of the bop pioneers, only Thelonious Monk has managed to maintain without question the vicious creativity with which he first entered the jazz scene back in the '40s. The music has changed again, for many of the same basic reasons it changed twenty years ago. Bop was, at a certain level of consideration, a reaction by young musicians against the sterility and formality of Swing as it moved to become a formal part of the mainstream American culture. The New Thing, as recent jazz has been called, is, to a large degree, a reaction to the hard bop-funk-groove-soul camp, which itself seemed to come into being in protest against the squelching of most of the blues elements in cool and progressive jazz. Funk (groove, soul) has become as formal and clichéd as cool or swing, and opportunities for imaginative expression within that form have dwindled almost to nothing.

The attitudes and emotional philosophy contained in "the new music" must be isolated and understood by critics before any consideration of the *worth* of the music can be legitimately broached. Later on, of course, it becomes relatively easy to characterize the emotional penchants that informed earlier aesthetic statements. After the fact, is a much simpler way to work and think. For example, a writer who wrote liner notes for a John Coltrane record mentioned how difficult it had been for him to appreciate Coltrane earlier, just as it had been difficult for him to appreciate Charlie Parker when he first appeared. To quote: "I wish I were one of those sages who can say, 'Man, I dug Bird the first time I heard him.' I didn't. The first time I heard Charlie Parker, I thought he was ridiculous . . ." Well, that's a noble confession and all, but the responsibility is still the writer's and in no way involves Charlie Parker or what he was trying to do. When that writer first heard Parker he simply did not understand *why* Bird should play the way he did, nor could it have been very important to him. But now, of course, it becomes almost a form of reverse snobbery to say that one did not think Parker's music was worth much at first hearing, etc. etc. The point is, it seems to me, that if the music is worth something now, it must have been worth something then. Critics are supposed to be people in a position to tell what is of value and what is not, and, hopefully, at the time it first appears. If they are consistently mistaken, what is their value?

Jazz criticism, certainly as it has existed in the United States, has served in a great many instances merely to obfuscate what has actually been happening with the music itself—the pitiful harangues that raged during the '40s between two "schools" of critics as to which was the "real jazz," the new or the traditional, provide some very ugly examples. A critic who praises Bunk Johnson at Dizzy Gillespie's expense is no critic at all, but then neither is a man who turns it around and knocks Bunk to swell Dizzy. If such critics would (or could) reorganize their thinking so that they begin their concern for these musicians by trying to understand why each played the way he did, and in terms of the constantly evolving and redefined philosophy which has informed the most profound examples of Negro music throughout its history, then such thinking would be impossible.

It has never ceased to amaze and infuriate me that in the '40s a European critic could be arrogant and unthinking enough to inform serious young American musicians that what they were feeling (a consideration that exists before, and without, the music) was false. What had happened was that even though the white middle-brow critic had known about Negro music for only about three decades, he was already trying to formalize and finally institutionalize it. It is a hideous idea. The music was already in danger of being forced into that junk pile of admirable objects and data the West knows as *culture*.

Recently, the same attitudes have become more apparent in the face of a fresh redefinition of the form and content of Negro music. Such phrases as "anti-jazz" have been used to describe musicians who are making the most exciting music produced in this country. But as critic A. B. Spellman asked, "What does anti-jazz mean and who are these ofays who've appointed themselves guardians of last year's blues?" It is that simple, really. What does anti-jazz mean? And who coined the phrase? What is the definition of jazz? And who was authorized to make one?

Reading a great deal of old jazz criticism is usually like boning up on the social and cultural malaise that characterizes and delineates the bourgeois philistine in America. Even rereading someone as intelligent as Roger Pryor Dodge in the old *Record Changer* ("Jazz: its rise and decline," 1955) usually makes me either very angry or very near hysterical. Here is a sample: ". . . let us say flatly that there is no future in preparation for jazz through Bop . . . ," or "The Boppists, Cools, and Progressives are surely stimulating a dissolution within the vagaries of a non-jazz world. The Revivalists, on the other hand have made a start in the right direction." It sounds almost like political theory. Here is Don C. Haynes in the April 22, 1946 issue of *Down Beat*, reviewing Charlie Parker's "Billie's Bounce" and "Now's The Time": "These two sides are bad taste and ill-advised fanaticism. . . ." and, "This is the sort of stuff that has thrown innumerable impressionable young musicians out of stride, that has harmed many of them irreparably. This can be as harmful to jazz as Sammy Kaye." It makes you blush.

Of course there have been a few very fine writers on jazz, even as there are today. Most of them have been historians. But the majority of popular jazz criticism has been on about the same level as the quoted examples. Nostalgia, lack of understanding or failure to see the validity of redefined emotional statements which reflect the changing psyche of the Negro in opposition to what the critic might think the Negro ought to feel; all these unfortunate failures have been built many times into a kind of critical stance or aesthetic. An aesthetic whose standards and measure are connected irrevocably to the continuous gloss most white Americans have always made over Negro life in America. Failure to understand, for instance, that Paul Desmond and John Coltrane represent not only two very divergent ways of thinking about music, but more importantly two very different ways of viewing the world, is at the seat of most of the established misconceptions that are daily palmed off as intelligent commentary on jazz or jazz criticism. The catalysts and necessity of Coltrane's music must be understood as they exist even before they are expressed as music. The music is the result of the attitude, the stance. Just as Negroes made blues and other people did not because of the Negro's peculiar way of looking at the world. Once this attitude is delineated as a continuous though constantly evolving social philosophy directly attributable to the way the Negro responds to the psychological landscape that is his Western environment, criticism of Negro music will move closer to developing as consistent and valid an aesthetic as criticism in other fields of Western art.

There have been so far only two American playwrights, Eugene O'Neill and Tennessee Williams who are as profound or as important to the history of ideas as Louis Armstrong, Bessie Smith, Duke Ellington, Charlie Parker or Ornette Coleman, yet there is a more valid and consistent body of dramatic criticism written in America than there is a body of criticism about Negro music. And this is simply because there is an intelligent tradition and body of dramatic criticism, though it has largely come from Europe, that any intelligent American drama critic can draw on. In jazz criticism, no reliance on European tradition or theory will help at all. Negro music, like the Negro himself, is strictly an American phenomenon, and we have got to set up standards of judgment and aesthetic excellence that depend on our native knowlege and understanding of the underlying philosophies and local cultural references that produced blues and jazz in order to produce valid critical writing or commentary about it. It might be that there is still time to start.

1963

The Changing Same (R&B and New Black Music)

The blues impulse transferred . . . containing a race, and its expression. *Primal* (mixtures . . . transfers and imitations). Through its many changes, it remained the exact replication of The Black Man In The West.

An expression of the culture at its most unself- (therefore showing the larger consciousness of a *one self*, immune to bullshit) conscious. The direct expression of a place . . . jazz seeks another place as it weakens, a middle-class place. Except the consciously separate from those aspirations. Hence the so-called avant-garde or new music, the new Black Music, is separate because it seeks to be equally separate, equally unself-conscious . . . meaning more conscious of the real weights of existence as the straightest R&B. There are simply more temptations for the middle-class Negro because he can make believe in America more, cop out easier, become whiter and slighter with less trouble, than most R&B people. Simply because he is closer to begin with.

Jazz, too often, becomes a music of special, not necessarily emotional, occasion. But R&B now, with the same help from white

America in its exploitation of energy for profit, the same as if it was a gold mine, strings that music out along a similar weakening line. Beginning with their own vacuous "understanding" of what Black music is, or how it acts upon you, they believe, from the Beatles on down, that it is about white life.

The Blues, its "kinds" and diversity, its identifying parent styles. The phenomenon of jazz is another way of specifying cultural influences. The jazz that is most European, popular or avant, or the jazz that is Blackest, still makes reference to a central body of cultural experience. The impulse, the force that pushes you to sing . . . all up in there . . . is one thing . . . what it produces is another. It can be expressive of the entire force, or make it the occasion of some special pleading. Or it is all equal . . . we simply identify the part of the world in which we are most responsive. It is all there. We are exact (even in our lies). The elements that turn our singing into direct reflections of our selves are heavy and palpable as weather.

We are moved and directed by our total response to the possibility of all effects.

We are bodies responding differently, a (total) force, like against you. You react to push it, re-create it, resist it. It is the opposite pressure producing (in this case) the sound, the music.

The City Blues tradition is called that by me only to recognize different elements active in its creation. The slick city people we become after the exodus, the unleashing of an energy into the Northern urban situation. Wholesale.

The line we could trace, as musical "tradition," is what we as a people dig and pass on, as best we can. The call and response form of Africa (lead and chorus) has never left us, as a mode of (musical) expression. It has come down both as vocal and instrumental form.

The rhythm quartet of the last thirty years is a very obvious continuation of Black vocal tradition, and a condensation in the form from the larger tribal singing units . . . through the form of the large religious choirs (chorus) which were initially *dancers and singers*, of religious and/or ritual purpose.

Indeed, to go back in any historical (or emotional) line of ascent in Black music leads us inevitably to religion, i.e., spirit worship. This phenomenon is always at the root in Black art, the worship of spirit—or at least the summoning of or by such force. As even the music itself was that, a reflection of, or the no thing itself.

The slave ship destroyed a great many formal art traditions of the Black man. The white man enforced such cultural rape. A "cultureless" people is a people without a memory. No history. This is the best state for slaves; to be objects, just like the rest of massa's possessions.

The breakdown of Black cultural tradition meant finally the destruction of most formal art and social tradition. Including the breakdown of the Black pre-American religious forms. Forcibly so. Christianity replaced African religions as the outlet for spirit worship. And Christian forms were traded, consciously and unconsciously, for their own. Christian forms were emphasized under threat of death. What resulted were Afro-Christian forms. These are forms which persist today.

The stripping away, gradual erosion, of the pure African form as means of expression by Black people, and the gradual embracing of mixed Afro-Christian, Afro-American forms is an initial reference to the cultural philosophy of Black People, Black Art.

Another such reference, or such stripping, is an American phenomenon, i.e., it is something that affected all of America, in fact the entire West. This, of course, is the loss of religiosity in the West, in general.

Black Music is African in origin. African-American in its totality, and its various forms (especially the vocal) show just how the African impulses were redistributed in its expression, and the expression itself became Christianized and post-Christianized.

Even today a great many of the best-known R&B groups, quartets, etc., have church backgrounds, and the music itself is as churchified as it has ever been . . . in varying degrees of its complete emotional identification with the Black African-American culture (Sam and Dave, etc. at one end . . . Dionne Warwick in the middle . . . Leslie Uggams, the other end . . . and fading).

The church continues, but not the devotion (at no level of its existence is it as large, though in the poorest, most abstractly altruistic levels of churchgoing, the emotion is the devotion, and the God, the God of that feeling and movement, remains as powerful though "redistributed" somewhat).

But the kind of church Black people belonged to usually connected them with the society as a whole . . . identified them, their aspirations, their culture: because the church was one of the few places complete fullness of expression by the Black was not constantly censored by the white man. Even the asking of freedom, though in terms veiled with the biblical references of "The Jews," went down in church.

It was only those arts and cultural practices that were less obviously capable of "alien" social statement that could survive during slavery. (And even today in contemporary America, it is much the same . . . though instead of out and out murder there are hardly more merciful ways of limiting Black protest or simple state-ment . . . in the arts just as in any other aspect of American life.)

Blues (Lyric) its song quality is, it seems, the deepest expression of memory. Experience re/feeling. It is the racial memory. It is the "abstract" design of racial character that is evident, would be evi-dent, in creation carrying the force of that racial memory.

Just as the God spoken about in the Black songs is not the same one in the white songs. Though the words might look the same. (They are not even pronounced alike.) But it is a different quality of energy they summon. It is the simple tone of varying evolution by which we distinguish the races. The peoples. The body is directly figured in it. "The life of the organs."

But evolution is not merely physical: yet if you can understand what the physical alludes to, is reflective of, then it will be under-stood that each process in "life" is duplicated at all levels.

The Blues (impulse) lyric (song) is even descriptive of a plane of evolution, a direction . . . coming and going . . . through whatever worlds. Environment, as the social workers say . . . but Total Environment (including at all levels, the spiritual).

Identification is Sound Identification is Sight Identification is Touch, Feeling, Smell, Movement. (For instance, I can tell, even in the shadows, halfway across the field, whether it is a white man or Black man running. Though Whitney Young would like to see us all run the same.)

For instance, a white man could box like Muhammad Ali, only *af-ter* seeing Muhammad Ali box. He could not initiate that style. It is no description, it *is* the culture. (A.D. 1966)

The Spirituals . . . The Camp Meeting Songs at backwoods churches . . . or Slave Songs talking about deliverance.

The God the slaves worshipped (for the most part, except maybe the "pure white" God of the toms) had to be willing to free them, somehow, someway . . . one sweet day.

The God, the perfection of what the spiritual delivery and world are said to be, is what the worshippers sang. That perfect Black land. The land changed with the God in charge. The churches the slaves and freedmen went to identified these Gods, and their will in heaven, as well as earth.

The closer the church was to Africa, the Blacker the God. (The Blacker the spirit.) The closer to the will (and meaning) of the West, the whiter the God, the whiter the spirit worshipped. The whiter the worshippers. This is still so. And the hard Black core of America is African.

From the different churches, the different Gods, the different versions of Earth. The different weights and "classic" versions of reality. And the different singing. Different expressions (of a whole). A whole people . . . a nation, in captivity.

Rhythm and Blues is part of "the national genius," of the Black man, of the Black nation. It is the direct, no monkey business expression of urban and rural (in its various stylistic variations) Black America.

The hard, driving shouting of James Brown identifies a place and image in America. A people and an energy, harnessed and not harnessed by America. JB is straight out, open, and speaking from the most deeply religious people on this continent.

The energy is harnessed because what JB does has to go down in a system governed by "aliens," and he will probably never become, say, as wealthy, etc., that is he will never reap the *material* benefits that several bunches of white folks will, from his own efforts. But the will of the expression transcends the physical-mental "material," finally alien system-world it has to go through to allow any "benefits" in it. Because the will of the expression is spiritual, and as such it must transcend its mineral, vegetable, animal, environment.

Form and content are both mutually expressive of the whole. And they are both equally expressive . . . each have an identifying motif and function. In Black music, both identify place and direction. We want different contents and different forms because we have different feelings. We are different peoples.

James Brown's form and content identify an entire group of people in America. However these may be transmuted and reused, reappear in other areas, in other musics for different purposes in the society, the initial energy and image are about a specific grouping of people. Black People.

Music makes an image. What image? What environment (in that word's most extended meaning, i.e., total, external and internal, environment)? I mean there is a world powered by that image. The world James Brown's images power is the lowest placement (the most alien) in the white American social order. Therefore, it is the Blackest and potentially the strongest.

It is not simply "the strongest" because of the transmutation and harnessing I spoke of earlier. This is social, but it is total. The world is a total. (And in this sense, the total function of "free music" can be understood. See, especially, H. Dumas' story in *Negro Digest* "Will the Circle Be Unbroken?" and understand the implications of music as an autonomous *judge* of civilizations, etc. Wow!)

By image, I mean that music (art for that matter . . . or anything else if analyzed) summons and describes where its energies were gotten. The blinking lights and shiny heads, or the gray concrete and endless dreams. But the description is of a total environment. The content speaks of this environment, as does the form.

The "whitened" Negro and white man want a different content from the people James Brown "describes." They are different peoples. The softness and so-called "well being" of the white man's environment is described in his music (art) . . . in all expressions of his self. All people's are.

If you play James Brown (say, "Money Won't Change You . . . but time will take you out") in a bank, the total environment is changed. Not only the sardonic comment of the lyrics, but the total emotional placement of the rhythm, instrumentation and sound. An energy is released in the bank, a summoning of images that take the bank, and everybody in it, on a trip. That is, they visit another place. A place where Black People live.

But dig, not only is it a place where Black People live, it is a place, in the spiritual precincts of its emotional telling, where Black People move in almost absolute openness and strength. (For instance, what is a white person who walks into a James Brown or Sam and Dave song? How would he function? What would be the social metaphor for his existence in that world? What would he be doing?)

This is as true, finally, with the John Coltrane world or the Sun-Ra world. In the Albert Ayler world, or Ornette Coleman world, you would say, "well, they might just be playing away furiously at some stringed instrument." You understand?

In the Leslie Uggams world? They would be marrying a half-white singer and directing the show . . . maybe even whispering lyrics and stuff from the wings. You understand? *The song and the people is the same.*

The reaction to any expression moves the deepest part of the psyche and makes its identifications throughout. The middle-class Negro wants a different content (image) from James Brown, because he has come from a different place, and wants a different thing (he thinks). The something you want to hear is the thing you already are or move toward.

We feel. Where is the expression going? What will it lead to?

What does it characterize? What does it make us feel like? What is its image? Jazz content, of course, is as pregnant.

The Implications of Content

The form content of much of what is called New Thing or Avant-Garde or New Music differs (or seems to differ) from Rhythm and Blues, R&B oriented jazz, or what the cat on the block digs. (And here I'm talking about what is essentially *Black Music*. Although, to be sure, too often the "unswinging-ness" of much of the "new" is because of its association, derivation and even straight-out imitation of certain aspects of contemporary European and white Euro-American music . . . whether they are making believe they are Bach or Webern.) Avant-garde, finally, is a bad term because it also means a lot of quacks and quackers, too.

But the significant difference is, again, direction, intent, sense of identification . . . "kind" of consciousness. And that's what it's about; consciousness. What are you *with* (the word Con-With/Scio-Know). The "new" musicians are self-conscious. Just as the boppers were. Extremely conscious of self. They are more conscious of a total self (or *want* to be) than the R&B people who, for the most part, are all-expression. Emotional expression. Many times self-consciousness turns out to be just what it is as a common figure of speech. It produces world-weariness, cynicism, corniness. Even in the name of Art. Or what have you . . . social uplift. "Now we can play good as white folks," or "I went to Juilliard, and this piece exhibits a Bach-like contrapuntal line," and so forth right on out to lunch.

But at its best and most expressive, the New Black Music is expression, and expression of reflection as well. What is presented is a consciously proposed learning experience. It is no wonder that many of the new Black musicians are or say they want to be "Spiritual Men" (Some of the boppers embraced Islam), or else they are interested in the Wisdom Religion itself, i.e., the rise to spirit. It is expanding the consciousness of the given that they are interested in, not merely expressing what is already there, or alluded to. They are interested in the unknown. The mystical.

But it is interpretation. The Miracles are spiritual. They sing (and sing about) feeling. Their content is about feeling . . . the form is to make feeling, etc. The self-conscious (reflective, long-form, New Thing, bop, etc.) Art Musicians cultivate consciousness that wants more feeling, to rise . . . up a scale one measures with one's life.

It is about thought, but thought can kill it. Life is complex in the same simplicity.

R&B is about emotion, issues purely out of emotion. New Black Music is also about emotion, but from a different place, and, finally, towards a different end. What these musicians feel is a more complete existence. That is, the digging of everything. What the wisdom religion preaches.

(But the actual New Black Music will be a larger expression. It will include the pretension of The New Music, as actuality, as summoner of Black Spirit, the evolved music of the then evolved people.)

The differences between rhythm and blues and the so-called new music or art jazz, the different places, are artificial, or they are merely indicative of the different placements of spirit. (Even "purely" social, like what the musicians want, etc.)

For instance, use of Indian music, old spirituals, even heavily rhythmic blues licks (and soon electronic devices) by new music musicians point toward the final close in the spectrum of the sound that will come. A really new, really all inclusive music. The whole people.

Any analysis of the content of R&B, the lyrics, or the total musical will and direction, will give a placement in contrast to analysis of new jazz content. (Even to the analysis of the implied vocalism of the new music: what are its intent and direction, what place it makes, etc., are concerned.) Again even the purely social, as analyzing reference, will give the sense of difference, what directions, what needs are present in the performers, and then, why the music naturally flows out of this.

The songs of R&B, for instance, what are they about? What are the people, for the most part, singing about? Their lives. That's what the New Musicians are playing about, and the projection of forms for those lives. (And I think any analysis will immediately show, as I pointed out in *Blues People*, that the songs, the music, changed, as the people did.) Mainly, I think the songs are about what is known as "love," requited and un. But the most popular songs are always a little sad, in tune with the temper of the people's lives. The extremes. Wild Joy—Deep Hurt.

The songs about unrequited, incompleted, obstructed, etc., love probably outnumber the others very easily. Thinking very quickly of just the songs that come readily to my mind, generally current, and favorites of mine (and on the other *top ten*, which is, you bet, the indication of where the minds, the people, are). "Walk On By"

"Where Did Our Love Go?" "What Becomes of the Broken Hearted?"
"The Tracks of My Tears," high poetry in the final character of their
delivery . . . but to a very large extent, the songs are about love
affairs which do not, did not, come off. For God knows how many
reasons. Infidelity, not enough dough, incredibly "secret" reasons
where the loved and the lover or the lovers are already separated and
longing one for the other, according to who's singing, male or female. And all more precise and specific than the Moynihan Report,
e.g., listen to Jr. Walker's "Road Runner." And this missed love that
runs through these songs is exactly reflective of what is the term of
love and loving in the Black world of America Twentieth Century.

The miss-understanding, nay, gap . . . abyss, that separates
Black man and Black woman is always, over and over, again and
again, told about and cried about. And it's old, in this country, to
us. "Come back baby, Baby, please don't go . . . Cause the way I
love you, Baby, you will never know . . . So come back, Baby,
let's talk it over . . . one more time." A blues which bees older
than Ray Charles or Lightnin' Hopkins, for that matter. "I got to
laugh to keep from cryin'," which The Miracles make, "I got to dance
to keep from cryin'," is not only a song but the culture itself. It is
finally the same cry, the same people. You really got a hold on me.
As old as our breath here.

But there are many songs about love triumphant. "I feel good
. . . I got you . . . Hey!" the score, the together self, at one and
in love and swinging, flying God-like. But a differently realized life-
triumph than in the older more formally religious songs. The Jor-
dans, the Promised Lands, now be cars and women-flesh, and especially dough. (Like *power*) There are many many songs about Money, e.g., Barrett Deems' "Money," J.B.'s "I Got Money . . . now all
I need is love," among so many others. But the songs are dealing
with the everyday, and how to get through it and to the other side
(or maybe not) which for the most part still bees that world, but on
top of it, power full, and beauty full.

The older religiosity falls away from the music, but the deepest
feel of spirit worship always remains, as the music's emotional patterns continue to make reference to. The new jazz people are usually
much more self-consciously concerned about "God" than the R&B
folks. But most of the R&B people were *really* in the church at one
time, and sang there first, only to drift or rush away later.

Even the poorest, Blackest, Black people drifted away from the
church. Away from a church, usually corrupted, Europeanized, or
both, that could no longer provide for their complete vision of what

this world ought to be, or the next. The refuge the church had provided during the early days of the Black man's captivity in America, when it was really the one place he could completely unleash his emotions and hear words of encouragement for his life here on earth. Now the world had opened up, and the church had not. But the emotionalism the church contained, and the spirit it signified, would always demand the animating life of the Black man, and as Frazier says, "The masses of Negroes may increasingly criticize their church and their ministers, but they cannot escape from their heritage. They may develop a more secular outlook on life and complain that the church and the ministers are not sufficiently concerned with the problems of the Negro race, yet they find in their religious heritage an opportunity to satisfy their deepest emotional yearnings." (*The Negro Church in America*, E. Franklin Frazier, Shocken, 1963, p. 73.)

It was the more emotional Blacker churches that the blues people were members of, rather than the usually whiter, more middle-class churches the jazz people went to. The church, as I said, carries directly into the secular music, which is really not secular at all. It's an old cliché that if you just change the lyrics of the spirituals they are R&B songs. That's true by and large, though there are more brazen, even whiter, strings and echo effects the blues people use that most of the spiritual and gospel people don't use. But that's changed and changing, too, and in the straight city jamup gospel, echo chambers, strings, electric guitars, all are in evidence, and Jesus is jamup contemporary, with a process and silk suit too, my man.

But the gospel singers have always had a more direct connection with the blues than the other religious singers. In fact, gospel singing is a city blues phenomenon, and Professor Thomas Dorsey, who is generally credited with popularizing the gospel form back in Chicago in the late twenties and thirties, was once a blues singer–piano player named Georgia Tom, and even worked with Ma Rainey. (He was last known to be arranging for Mahalia Jackson, who with Ray Charles at another much more legitimate and powerful level, were the popularizers of Black church sound in "popular" music during the '50s.) But then so many of them, from G.T., and even before that to J.B., have all come that way.

The meeting of the practical God (i.e., of the existent American idiom) and the mystical (abstract) God is also the meeting of the tones, of the moods, of the knowledge, the different musics and the emergence of the new music, the really new music, the all-inclusive whole. The emergence also of the new people, the Black people conscious of all their strength, in a unified portrait of strength, beauty and contemplation.

The new music began by calling itself "free," and this is social and is in direct commentary on the scene it appears in. Once free, it is spiritual. But it is soulful before, after, any time, anyway. And the spiritual and free and soulful must mingle with the practical, as practical, as existent, anywhere.

The R&B people left the practical God behind to slide into the slicker scene, where the dough was, and the swift folks congregated. The new jazz people never had that practical God, as practical, and seek the mystical God both emotionally and intellectually.

John Coltrane, Albert Ayler, Sun-Ra, Pharoah Sanders, come to mind immediately as God-seekers. In the name of energy sometimes, as with Ayler and drummer Sonny Murray. Since God is, indeed, energy. To play strong forever would be the cry and the worshipful purpose of life.

The titles of Trane's tunes, "A Love Supreme," "Meditations," "Ascension," imply a strong religious will, conscious of the religious evolution the pure mind seeks. The music is a way into God. The absolute open expression of everything.

Albert Ayler uses the older practical religion as key and description of his own quest. Spirits. Ghosts. Spiritual Unity, Angels, etc. And his music shows a graphic connection with an older sense of the self. The music sounds like old timey religious tunes and some kind of spiritual march music, or probably the combination as a religious marching song if you can get to that. (New crusades, so to speak. A recent interview article, with Albert Ayler and his brother, trumpet player Donald Ayler, was titled "The Truth Is Marching In," and this is an excellent metaphor of where Albert and his brother Donald want to move.)

Albert's music, which he characterizes as "spiritual," has much in common with older Black-American religious forms. An openness that characterizes the "shouts" and "hollers." But having the instruments shout and holler, say a saxophone, which was made by a German, and played, as white folks call it, "legitimately" sounds like dead Lily Pons at a funeral, is changed by Ayler, or by members of any Sanctified or Holy Roller church (the blacker churches) into howling spirit summoner tied around the "mad" Black man's neck. The Daddy Grace band on 125th Street and 8th Avenue in Harlem, in the Grace Temple, is a brass band, with somewhat the same instrumentation as a European brass choir, but at the lips of Daddy's summoners, the band is "free" and makes sounds to tear down the walls of anywhere. The instruments shout and holler just like the folks. It is their lives being projected then, and they are different from the lives Telemann, or Vivaldi sought to reanimate with their music.

But James Brown still shouts, and he is as secular as the old shouters, and the new ones. With the instruments, however, many people would like them to be more securely European oriented, playing notes of the European tempered scale. While the Eastern Colored peoples' music demands, at least, that many many half, quarter, etc. tones be sounded, implied, hummed, slurred, that the whole sound of a life get in . . . no matter the "precision" the Europeans claim with their "reasonable" scale which will get only the sounds of an order and reason that patently deny most colored peoples the right to exist. To play their music is to be them and to act out their lives, as if you were them. There is then, a whole world of most intimacy and most expression, which is yours, colored man, but which you will lose playing melancholy baby in B-flat, or the *Emperor Concerto*, for that matter. Music lessons of a dying people.

Albert Ayler has talked about his music as a contemporary form of collective improvisation (Sun-Ra and John Coltrane are working in this area as well). Which is where our music was when we arrived on these shores, a collective expression. And to my mind, the *solo*, in the sense it came to be represented on these Western shores, and as first exemplified by Louis Armstrong, is very plain indication of the changed sensibility the West enforced.

The return to collective improvisations, which finally, the West-oriented, the whitened, says, is chaos, is the *all-force* put together, and is what is wanted. Rather than accompaniment and a solo voice, the miniature "thing" securing its "greatness." Which is where the West is.

The Ornette Coleman *Double Quartet* which was called *Free Jazz* was one breakthrough to open the '60s. (It seems now to me that some of bassist Charlie Mingus' earlier efforts, e.g. *Pithecanthropus Erectus*, provide a still earlier version of this kind of massive orchestral breakthrough. And called rightly, too, I think. *Pithecanthropus Erectus*, the first man to stand. As what we are, a first people, and the first people, the primitives, now evolving, to recivilize the world. And all these and Sun-Ra who seems to me to have made the most moving orchestral statements with the New Music, all seem not so curiously joined to Duke Ellington. Ellington's "KoKo" and "Diminuendo and Crescendo . . ." can provide some immediate reference to freed orchestral form.)

The secular voice seeking clarity, or seeking religion (a spirit worship) compatible with itself. They are both pushed by an emotionalism that seeks freedom. Its answering category, the definition of the freedom sought, is equally descriptive of who is playing what? If we say we want social freedom, i.e., we do not want to be exploited or have our lives obstructed, there are roots now spreading everywhere. People even carry signs, etc. There is also the "freedom" to be a white man, which, for the most part is denied the majority of people on the earth, which includes jazz players, or for that matter, blues people. The freedom to want your own particular hip self is a freedom of a somewhat different and more difficult nature.

Then, there are all kinds of freedom, and even all kinds of spirits. We can use the past as shrines of our suffering, as a poeticizing beyond what we think the present (the "actual") has to offer. But that is true in the sense that any clear present must include as much of the past as it needs to clearly illuminate it.

Archie Shepp is a tenor man of the new jazz, who came out of an American background of Black slums and white palaces. He is a Marxist playwrighting tenor-saxophone player now. His music sounds like a peculiar barrelhouse whore tip. It wavers chunks of vibrato Ben Webster Kansas City style, but turns that character actor wail into a kind of polished cry. Which, finally, if you have ever heard him speak at some public social gathering, is articulate at a very definite place in America.

Archie's is a secular music, that remains, demands secularity, as its insistence. He probably even has theories explaining why there is no God. But he makes obeisances to the spirits of ancient, "traditional," colored people ("Hambone," "The Mac Man," "The Picaninny") and what has happened to them from ancient times, traditionally, here (*Rufus, Swung, his face at last to the wind. Then his neck snapped* or *Malcolm* or *picked clean*).

Archie is the secular demanding clarity of itself. A reordering according to the known ("The Age of Cities"). Modern in this sense. But of "modern" we must begin to ask, "What does Modern Mean?" and "What is The Future?" or "Where Does One Want To Go?" or "What Does One *Want* to Happen?" You hear in Archie's music moans that are pleas for understanding.

Cecil Taylor is also secular. He is very much an *artist*. His references determinedly Western and modern, contemporary in the most Western sense. One hears Europe and the influence of French poets on America and the world of "pure art" in Cecil's total approach to his playing. Cecil's is perhaps the most European sounding of the

New Music, but his music is moving because he is still Black, still has imposed an emotional sensibility on the music that knows of actual beauty beyond "what is given."

Even though Cecil is close to what's been called Third Stream, an "integrated" Western modernism, he is always *hotter, sassier* and newer than that music. But the Black artist is most often always hip to European art, often at his jeopardy.

The most complete change must be a spiritual change. A change of Essences. The secular is not complete enough. It is not the new music, it is a breaking away from old American forms. Toward new American forms. Ornette Coleman is the elemental land change, the migratory earth man, the country blues person of old come in the city with a funkier wilder blues. Such energy forces all kinds of movement. The freshness of this Americana. A bebopier bebop, a funkier funky. But tuxedoes can be planted among such vegetation, strings and cords tied up to send the life stretched out along a very definite path. Like ivy, finally growed up fastened to an academy. No longer wild, no longer funky, but domesticated like common silence.

Ornette, Archie and Cecil. Three versions of a contemporary Black Secularism. Making it in America, from the country, the ghetto, into the gnashing maw of the Western art world. The freedom they, the music, want is *the freedom to exist in this.* (What of the New? Where?) The freedom of the given. The freedom to exist as artists. Freedom would be the change.

But the device of their asking for this freedom remains a device for asking if the actual is not achieved. Literary Negro-ness, the exotic instance of abstract cultural resource, say in one's head, is not the Black Life Force for long if we are isolated from the real force itself, and, in effect, cooled off. Cool Jazz was the abstraction of these life forces. There can be a cool avant, in fact there is, already. The isolation of the Black artist relating to, performing and accommodating his expression for aliens. Where is the returned energy the artist demands to go on? His battery (guns and engines)?

We want to please the people we see (feel with and/or for) all the time, in the respect of actual living with. Our neighbors? Our people? Who are these? Our definitions change. Our speech and projection. Is that a chick or a broad or a woman or a girl or a bird . . . or what is it? Where are you? What is this place that you describe with all your energies? Is it your own face coloring the walls, echoing in the halls, like hip talk by knowledgeable millionaires. What does a millionaire want as he passes through the eye of the needle? Can he really pass?

The New Music (any Black Music) is cooled off when it begins to reflect blank any place "universal" humbug. It is this fag or that kook, and not the hope and promise and need for evolution into a higher species. The artist's resources must be of the strongest, purest possible caliber. They must be truest and straightest and deepest. Where is the deepest feeling in our lives? There is the deepest and most meaningful art and life. Beware "the golden touch," it will kill everything you useta (used to) love.

There are other new musicians, new music, that take freedom as already being. Ornette was a cool breath of open space. Space, to move. So freedom already exists. The change is spiritual. The total. The absolutely new. That is the absolute realization. John Coltrane, who has been an innovator of one period in jazz and a master in another period, is an example of the secular yearning for the complete change, for the religious, the spiritual.

Sun-Ra is spiritually oriented. He understands "the future" as an ever widening comprehension of what space is, even to the "physical" travel between the planets as we do anyway in the long human chain of progress. Sun-Ra's Arkestra sing in one of his songs, "We travel the spaceways, from planet to planet." It is science-fact that Sun-Ra is interested in, not science-fiction. It is evolution itself, and its fruits. God as evolution. The flow of *is*.

So the future revealed is man explained to himself. The travel through inner space as well as outer. Sun-Ra's is a new content for jazz, for Black music, but it is merely, again, the spiritual defining itself. ("Love in Outer Space," "Ankh," "Outer Nothingness," "The Heliocentric World," "When Angels Speak of Love," "Other Worlds," " The Infinity of the Universe," "Of Heavenly Things," etc., etc.) And the mortal seeking, the human knowing spiritual, and willing the evolution. Which is the Wisdom Religion.

But the content of The New Music, or The New Black Music, is toward change. It is change. It wants to change forms. From physical to physical (social to social) or from physical to mental, or from physical-mental to spiritual. Soon essences. Albert Ayler no longer wants notes. He says he wants sound. The total articulation. Ra's music changes places, like Duke's "jungle music." Duke took people to a spiritual past, Ra to a spiritual future (which also contains "Little Sally Walker . . . sitting in a saucer . . . what kind'a saucer? . . . a flying saucer").

African sounds, too: the beginnings of our sensibility. The new, the "primitive," meaning *first*, new. Just as Picasso's borrowings were Western avant-garde and "the new" from centuries ago, and Stravinsky's borrowings were new and "savage," centuries old and brand new.

The Black musicians who know about the European tempered scale (Mind) no longer want it, if only just to be contemporary. That changed. The other Black musicians never wanted it, anyway.

Change

Freedom

and finally Spirit. (But spirit makes the first two possible. A cycle, again?)

What are the qualitative meanings and implications of these words?

There is the freedom to exist (and the change to) in the existing, or to reemerge in a new thing.

Essence

How does this content differ from that of R&B.

Love, for R&B, is an absolute good. There is love but there is little of it, and it is a valuable possession. How Sweet It Is To Be Loved By You. But the practical love, like the practical church the R&B people left, a much more emotional church and spirit worship than most jazz people had, is a day-to-day physical, social, sensual love. Its presence making the other categories of human experience mesh favorably with beautiful conclusions. "Since I Lost My Baby" (or older) "When I Lost My Baby . . . I almost lost my mind." There is the *object* (even, the person). But what is the *object* of John Coltrane's "Love" . . . There is none. It is for the sake of Loving, Trane speaks of. As Ra's "When Angels Speak of Love."

I said before, "the cleansed purpose." The rise, the will *to be* love. The contemplative and the expressive, side by side, feeding each other. Finally, the rhythms carry to the body, the one (R&B) more "quickly," since its form definitely includes the body as a high register of the love one seeks.

The change to Love. The freedom to (of) Love. And in this constant evocation of Love, its need, its demands, its birth, its death, there is a morality that shapes such a sensibility, and a sensibility shaped by such moralizing.

Sometimes through Archie Shepp's wailing comes a dark yowl of desire in the place we are at, and for that place, to love him. And of actual flesh, that also comes through, that it is a man, perhaps crying. But he will reason it (logic as popping fingers, a hip chorus with arcane reference) down to what you hear.

Otis Redding will sing "You Don't Miss Your Water," and it is love asked for. Some warm man begging to be with a woman. Or The Temptations' "If It's Love That You're Running From" . . . there's no hiding place . . . But the cry in Shepp's sound is not for a woman, it is a cry, a wail. But not so freed from the object, the specific, as say Trane's.

Content Analysis, total content, Musical, Poetic, Dramatic, Literary, is the analysis in total, which must come, too. But, briefly, the R&B content is usually about this world in a very practical, where we literally are, approach. Spiritual Concern, in big letters, or "Other World" would be corn or maudlin, would not serve, in most R&B, because to the performers it would mean a formal church thing. But this will change, too. Again, "I got the money, now all I need is love," and that insistence will demand a clearer vision of a *new* spiritual life.

The Black Man in R&B is the Black Man you can readily see. Maybe Sadder or Happier or Swifter or Slower than the actual, as with all poetry, but that average is still where the real is to be seen. (Even the "process" on the hand is practical in a turned around way, to say, "I'monna get me some hair like that . . . blow stuff." Badge of power, etc. The more literary or bourgeois Black man would never wear his badge (of oppression) so openly. His is more hidden (he thinks). He will tell you about Mozart and Kafka, or he will tell you about Frank Sinatra and James Michener. It works out the same, to the same obstruction to self. And, finally, the conk is easier to get rid of. If you can dig that.

R&B is straight on and from straight back out of traditional Black spirit feeling. It has the feeling of an actual spontaneity and *happiness*, or at least *mastery*, at the time. Even so, as the arrangements get more complicated in a useless sense, or whitened, this spontaneity and mastery is reduced. The R&B presents expression and spontaneity, but can be taken off by the same subjection to whitening influences. A performer like Dionne Warwick (and The Supremes sometimes as well among others) with something of the light quickness of the "Detroit (Motown) Sound," treads a center line with something like grace. The strings and softness of her arrangements, and of many of her songs, are like white torch singers' delight, but her beat (she used to be a gospel singer in New Jersey) and sound take her most times into a warmth undreamed of by the whites. Though as the $$$ come in, and she leans for a "bigger audience," traveling in them circles, too, etc., then she may get even whiter perhaps. It is a social phenomenon and a spiritual-artistic phenomenon as well.

The New Black Music people, by and large, have been exposed to more white influences than the R&B people. Most of the new musicians have had to break through these whiteners to get at the sound and music they play now. That is, there is more "formal" training among the jazz people. Hence a doctrinaire whitening.

It is easier to whiten a Cecil Taylor form than a James Brown form because the Taylor form proposes to take in more influences in the first place. It sets itself up as more inclusive of what the world is. Many times it is. But this is true with any of the new forms. Finally, it depends on the activating energy and vision, where that is, how it can be got to. The new forms are many times the result of contemplation and reflection. Through these and the natural emotional outline of the performer, the new music hopes to arrive at expression and spontaneity. The R&B begins with expression and spontaneity as its ends. Which are the ends of any Black music. Though this is not to say that this is always the result. Much R&B sounds contrived and simple-minded (much of any form, for sure) because that's what is working with the sounds and forms, but what R&B proposes to be about is more readily available to us from where we are, with just what materials the world immediately has given us. The "widening" and extension, the more intellectual, new music people want many times is just funny-time shit, very very boring. That is, it may *just* be about something intellectual. The R&B might just be about something small and contrived, which is the same thing.

But the new music is consciously said to be about the mind and the spirit, as well as the heart. The beauty of an older hence "simpler" form is that it will be about the mind (and the spirit) if it is *really* about the heart. "Money won't change you . . . but time will take you out." Which can be said some other ways, but then get to them.

And Rhythm and Blues music is "new" as well. It is contemporary and has changed, as jazz has remained the changing same. Fresh Life. R&B has gone through evolution, as its singers have, gotten "modern," taken things from jazz, as jazz has taken things from R&B. New R&B takes things from old blues, gospel, white popular music, instrumentation, harmonies (just as these musics have in turn borrowed) and made these diverse elements its own.

But the Black religious roots are still held on to conspicuously in the most moving of the music. That Black emotionalism which came directly out of, and from as far back as, pre-church religious

gatherings, the music of which might just be preacher to congrega-
tion, in an antiphonal rhythmic chant-poem-moan which is the
form of most of the Black group vocal music that followed: Preacher-
Congregation/Leader-Chorus. It is the oldest and still most common
jazz form as well.

The old collective improvisation that was supposed to come out
of New Orleans, with lead trumpet and clarinet weaving and trombone stunting and signifying and rhythm pounding, this form is as
old as Black religious gatherings in the forests of the West . . . and
connects straight on into Black free-Africa.

But the two Black musics, religious and secular, have always
cross-fertilized each other, because the musicians and singers have
drifted back and forth between the two categories, with whatever
music they finally came to make being largely the result of both influences. During the Depression, a lot of blues people, probably
most of whom had once been in the church, "got religion" and went
back (as I've said, the church was always looked upon by Black People as a Refuge, from the alien white world . . . the less it got to
be a refuge, i.e., the more it got integrated, the less hold it had on
colored people). That was a whole church era in jazz and blues.

In the '50s during the funk-groove-soul revival, the church music,
more specifically, Gospel music, was the strongest and healthiest
influence on jazz, and R&B, too. (Grays even opened a nightclub,
The Sweet Chariot with robed hostesses to make them bux off another people's ultimate concern. But nightclub, or not, they still
managed to take the music off to their own advantage.)

In fact it was the Gospel and soul-funk influence, especially as
sung by Ray Charles and played by people like Horace Silver, that
"rescued" the music from the icebox of cool jazz, which finally
turned out to be a white music for elevators, college students, and
TV backgrounds. (The last mentioned have recently got the rhythm
and blues tint via Rock'n'Roll or "Pop," i.e., the soft white "cool"
forms, versions, of Gospel-derived rhythm and blues music. Which
is the way it goes.)

The cool was a whitened degenerative form of bebop. And when
mainline America was vaguely hipped, the TV people (wizards of
total communication) began to use it to make people buy cigarettes
and deodorants . . . or put life into effeminate dicks (uhh, detec-
tives). Then the white boys slid into all the studio gigs, playing
"their" music, for sure.

So-called "pop," which is a citified version of Rock'n'Roll (just as
the Detroit-Motown Sound is a slick citified version of older R&B-

Gospel influenced forms) also sees to it that those TV jobs, indeed that dollar-popularity, remains white. Not only the Beatles, but any group of Myddle-class white boys who need a haircut and male hormones can be a pop group. That's what pop means. Which is exactly what "cool" was, and even clearer, exactly what Dixieland was, complete with funny hats and funny names . . . white boys, in lieu of the initial passion, will always make it about funny hats . . . which be their constant minstrel need, the derogation of the real, come out again.

Stealing Music . . . stealing energy (lives): with their own concerns and lives finally, making it White Music (like influenzaing a shrill rites group). From anyplace, anytime to "We all live in a yellow submarine," with all their fiends, etc., the exclusive white . . . *exclusive* meaning *isolated* from the rest of humanity . . . in the yellow submarine, which shoots nuclear weapons. (Content analysis . . . lyrics of white music show equally their concerns, lives, places, ways, to death.) In the yellow submarine. Chances are it will never come up.

They steals, minstrelizes (but here a minstrelsy that "hippens" with cats like Stones and Beatles saying: 'Yeh, I got everything I know from Chuck Berry," is a scream dropping the final . . . "But I got all the dough . . .") named Animals, Zombies, in imitation (minstrel-hip) of a life style as names which go to show just what they think we are . . . Animals, Zombies, or where they finally be, trying to be that, i.e., Animals, Zombies, Beatles or Stones or Sam the Sham for that matter, and not ever Ravens, Orioles, Spaniels or the contemporary desired excellence of Supremes, Miracles, Imperials, Impressions, Temptations, etc., . . get to them names.

Actually, the more intelligent the white, , the more the realization he has to steal from niggers. They take from us all the way up the line. Finally, what is the difference between Beatles, Stones, etc., and Minstrelsy. Minstrels never convinced anybody they were Black either.

The more adventurous bohemian white groups sing songs with lyric content into where white bohemian poets moved long ago, as say the so-called psychedelic tunes, which may talk about drugs (LSD, Psylocibin, etc.) experience, and may be also shaped by so-called RagaRock (Indian-influenced) or Folk-Rock (i.e., Rock songs with more socially conscious content). Bob Dylan, Fugs, Blues Project, Mothers, etc. But in awe of the poetic-psychedelic and LSD, the chemical saviour of grays. They hope to evolve (as the rest of us) "thru chemistry," which sounds like Dupont. The "widening of the consciousness" type action into a higher sense of existent life, and thereafter, maybe stop stealing and killing, etc., etc., etc.

The Black tip for them is a super-live thing as well. To "Get more than we got" kind of thing. The music . . . lyrics, with instructions to "tune in, turn on, drop out" and sound an Electronic Indian Raga . . . as a meditative eclipse of present reality, a yoga saddhu pop. But in play will still drop out of their society like new Beat thing. Out of it! Yeh. But what to do about what ain't out of it. Like there are people dying, etc. Bullshit.

But the content of some anti-Viet anti-Bad stuff is a generalizing in passionate luxurious ego demonstration to be good anyway though they exists as super-feelers of their evil cement head brothers, and as flexible copout, to be anything, finally, anything but what they patently are. That is, Fugs, Freaks, Mothers, Dylan, etc. Yet is still bees white kids playing around. Dylan's "Blowin in the Wind," which is abstract and luxury playing around stuff with him, is immediately transformed when Stevie Wonder sings it because it becomes about something that is actual in the world and is substantiated by the life of the man singing it. That is, with Dylan it seems just an idea. A sentiment. But with Wonder (dig the name! and his life-style and singing is, of course, more emotional, too) you dig that it is life meant. In life.

The "new content" of white pop was protest, and with that "widening consciousness" as opposed to jes' love. But it is just this love that the white pop cannot sing about because it is not only sweet, stupid, maudlin, but now, frankly cannot be believed. Nobody can be made to believe they could love anybody. So the move.

The superficial advance. The liberal cool protest. Viet. Oh. Viet-Rock. Yeh. LBJ ain't no good. Yeh. But what, what? will happen $$$$$$ . . . stealin' all from the niggers and they bees starvin' all the time. While crooks is good and hates war, for dough. (Wins either way!)

But the "protest" is not new. Black people's songs have carrried the fire and struggle of their lives since they first opened their mouths in this part of the world. They have always wanted a better day. During the socially-conscious thirties, after the city and the social sophistication of white protest movements was acquired, so-called Folk Music was the most ubiquitous Black or near-Black music in the American mainstream. This is the reason "Folk" has been associated with protest. White people saddled that horse with trade unionism, IWW, Spanish Civil War, in the same way the folk-rockers, etc. do today.

Black religious music has always had an element of protest in it. In the so-called "invisible institution," or pre-church worship of the Black slaves, the songs were about freedom, though most times couched in the metaphorical language of the Bible, substituting Jews, etc. for themselves, to escape massa's understanding.

But with secular music, integration (meaning the harnessing of Black energy for dollars by white folks, in this case in the music biz-ness) spilled the content open to a generalizing that took the bite of specific protest out. ("You know you cain't sell that to white folks.")

Early blues is full of talk about Black people and their exact up-hill lives. In fact you can tell an early blues tune if the word "Black" is even mentioned. Or "white" for that matter. The slickening money process shaved a lot of exactness in one area. They talk of love, and that is exact, but as a preacher said, "Today we're gonna talk about Love. I was gonna talk about Truth, but I figured I might offend somebody. So today we're gonna talk about Love." If you can dig that.

But the cycle will turn round. The more bohemian white people's desire to be at least in a recognizable world of war and stuff will be passed around to Black people, as legitimate part of the music biz-ness. (Just as the quickest way to get Black people to dig Africa, wear African clothes, etc. is to let B. Altman's sell it, it would seem to white people, then watch all the hippies show up like they are wor-shipping some Orisha.)

Stevie Wonder with Dylan's "Blowin in the Wind" is a case in point. Now James Brown with his social consciousness of "Don't Be a Dropout." Specific, but civil-servant stuff, nevertheless. The Im-pressions' "Keep On Pushin" or Martha and The Vandellas' "Dancing in the Street" (especially re: summer riots, i.e. "Summer's here . . .") provided a core of legitimate social feeling, though mainly metaphorical and allegorical for Black people. But it is my thought that soon, with the same cycle of the general "integrated" music biz-ness, the R&B songs will be more socially oriented. (Black and Beau-tiful; Jihad Singers. I'm reminded that a few years ago, Ben E. King and a few others . . . *Spanish Harlem*, etc. . . . had made a spe-cial placement of social music, but that was largely picked up by grays.)

Note: *Let the new people take care of some practical bi-ness and the R&B take care of some new bi-ness and the unity musick, the people-leap, can begin in earnest.*

Social consciousness in jazz is something again because it is largely a purely instrumental music . . . though there have always been musicians who had been deeply conscious of their exact placement in the social world, or at least there was a kind of race pride or consciousness that animated the musicians and their music (again, here, Ellington is a giant. "Black Beauty," "Black, Brown and Beige," "For My People," and so many many others.)

In recent times musicians like Charles Mingus (dig "Fables of Faubus," etc.), Max Roach and some others have been outspoken artists on and off the stage, using their music as eloquent vehicles for a consciousness of self in America. The new musicians have been outspoken about the world through their music and off the stage as well. Archie Shepp has perhaps been the most publicized of the new socially conscious musicians. And some of his music is self-consciously socially responsive, e.g., "Malcolm," but this so-called consciousness is actually just a reflection of what a particular generation is heir to, and their various responses from wherever they (are) find themselves.

Also, of course, the music is finally most musicians' strongest statement re: any placement of themselves socially. And the new music, as I have stated before about Black music, is "radical" within the context of mainstream America. Just as the new music begins by being free. That is, freed of the popular song. Freed of American white cocktail droop, tinkle, etc. The strait jacket of American expression *sans* blackness . . . it wants to be freed of that temper, that scale. That life. It screams. It yearns. It pleads. It breaks out (the best of it). But its practitioners sometimes do not. But then the vibrations of a feeling, of a particular place, a conjunction of world spirit, some of everybody can pick up on. (Even imitate, which is Charlie McCarthy shouting freedom! or white snick workers going back to Jumpoff Manor after giving a few months to "The Problem.") It is an ominous world all right. You can say *spiritual*. You can say *Freedom*. But you do not necessarily have to be either one. If you can dig it. White, is abstract. A theory. A saying. A being . . . the verb . . . the energy itself, is what is beautiful, is what we want, sometimes, are.

Music as the consciousness, the expression of where we are. But then Otis Redding in interviews in *Muhammad Speaks* has said things (or Shakey Jake, for that matter) more "radical." Blacker, than many of the new musicians. James Brown's screams, etc., are more "radical" than most jazz musicians sound, etc. Certainly his sound is "further out" than Ornette's. And that sound has been a part of Black music, even out in them backwoods churches since the year one. It is just that on the white man's instrument it is "new." So, again, it is just life need and interpretation.

Sun-Ra speaks of evolution of the cosmic consciousness; that is future, or as old as *purusa*. Where man will go. "Oh you mean space ships?" Which is like the Zen monk answering the student's question about whether or not dogs have souls . . . i.e., "Well, yes . . . and no."

And the social consciousness displayed in that music. Pharoah Sanders will say OMMMMMMMMMMMMMMMMMMMMMMMMMMM MMMMMMMMMMMMMMMMMMMMMMMMMMMMMMMMMMMMMMMM MMMMMMMMMMMMMMMMMMM. Which is more radical than sit-ins. We get to Feel-ins, Know-ins, Be-ins.

But here is a theory stated just before. That what will come will be a *Unity Music*. The Black Music which is jazz and blues, religious and secular. Which is New Thing and Rhythm and Blues. The consciousness of social reevaluation and rise, a social spiritualism. A mystical walk up the street to a new neighborhood where all the risen live. Indian-African anti-Western–Western (as geography) Nigger-sharp Black and strong.

The separations, artificial oppositions in Black Music resolved, are the ditty strong classic. (Ditty bop.) That is, the New Black Music and R&B are the same family looking at different things. Or looking at things differently. The collection of wills is a simple unity like on the street. A bigger music, and muscle, for the move necessary. The swell of a music, of action and reaction, a seeing, thrown in swift slick tone along the entire muscle of a people. The Rhythm and Blues mind blowing evolution of James-Ra and Sun-Brown. That growth to include all the resources, all the rhythms, all the yells and cries, all that information about the world, the Black om mmmmmmmmmmmmmmm, opening and entering.

1966

From *Black Magic*

Black Magic is Baraka's first black nationalist-inspired collection of poetry. The spirit of the book is suggested by its
cover, which depicts a white, blond-haired, blue-eyed voo-
doo doll riddled with huge hat pins.

—wjh

A POEM SOME PEOPLE
WILL HAVE TO UNDERSTAND

Dull unwashed windows of eyes
and buildings of industry. What
industry do I practice? A slick
colored boy, 12 miles from his
home. I practice no industry.
I am no longer a credit
to my race. I read a little,
scratch against silence slow spring
afternoons.

       I had thought, before, some years ago
that I'd come to the end of my life.

       Watercolor ego. Without the preciseness
a violent man could propose.

       But the wheel, and the wheels,
wont let us alone. All the fantasy
       and justice, and dry charcoal winters
All the pitifully intelligent citizens
       I've forced myself to love.

       We have awaited the coming of a natural
phenomenon. Mystics and romantics, knowledgeable
workers
of the land.

But none has come.
(*Repeat*)
          but none has come.
Will the machinegunners please step forward?

Citizen Cain

In the great northwest, always, my grandfather warned me,
cold,
and nothing but foreigners. Inexperienced dudes on trains,
and their other luxuries
like murder, and de-balling
for the young girls, teaching them mambo-fear
at tender age, for any bucks happen to make
seventeen. We string them up or out. Along
the reef of threatening waters. Call it success,
and sit in a bar under eight layers of disease.
Call it disappearance, that even the "terrorists"
shave their heads and sound like Miles Standish.

Where's it all leave me? A romantic liar, a coward, not even
the courage to kill myself, or drink myself to death. Just
be herded off like a common jew, and roasted in my teary
denunciations. I'll go to jail and become a fag, write
a huge treatise on religion, and never speak another
english word.

2

Roi, finish this poem, someone's about to need you. Roi,
dial the mystic number, ask for holy beads, directions,
plans for the destruction of New York. Work out your problems
like your friends on some nice guy's couch. Get up and hit
someone, like you useta. Don't sit here trembling under the
hammer. Fate like a season of abstract reference. Like an
abstract execution where only ideas are shot full of holes.
Don't sit there drowned in your own bad writing. Get up and
throw that ball. Move your hips, cut, like the white boys,

for ten more yards. Tackle and punch, then sit down grinning
and waiting for some Barrymore to lick you clean. Get up
and get high, so you wont understand what those gentlemen want,
spying for months from the dope factory. Ask the white man
for your passport and quit it, little jesus. Your time is up
in this particular feeling. In this particular throb of meaning.
Roi, baby, you blew the whole thing.

Letter to E. Franklin Frazier

Those days when it was all right
to be a criminal, or die, a postman's son,
full of hallways and garbage, behind the hotdog store
or in the parking lots of the beautiful beer factory.

Those days I rose through the smoke of chilling Saturdays
hiding my eyes from the shine boys, my mouth and my flesh
from their sisters. I walked quickly and always alone
watching the cheap city like I thought it would swell
and explode, and only my crooked breath could put it together
again.

By the projects and small banks of my time. Counting my steps
on tar or new pavement, following the sun like a park. I imagined
a life, that was realer than speech, or the city's anonymous
fish markets. Shuddering at dusk, with a mile or so up the hill

to get home. Who did you love
then, Mussolini? What were you thinking,
Lady Day? A literal riddle of image
was me, and my smell was a continent
of familiar poetry. Walking the long way,
always the long way, and up the steep hill.

Those days like one drawn-out song, monotonously
promising. The quick step, the watchful march march,
All were leading here, to this room, where memory
stifles the present. And the future, my man, is long
time gone.

LEADBELLY GIVES AN AUTOGRAPH

Pat your foot
and turn
        the corner. Nat Turner, dying wood
of the church. Our lot
is vacant. Bring the twisted myth
of speech. The boards brown and falling
away. The metal bannisters cheap
and rattly. Clean new Sundays. We thought
it possible to enter
the way of the strongest.

But it is rite that the world's ills
erupt as our own. Right that we take
our own specific look into the shapely
blood of the heart.
        Looking thru trees
the wicker statues blowing softly against
the dusk.
Looking thru dusk
thru dark-
ness. A clearing of stars
and half-soft mud.

The possibilities of music. First
that it does exist. And that we do,
in that scripture of rhythms. The earth,
I mean the soil, as melody. The fit you need,
the throes. To pick it up and cut
away what does not singularly express.

Need.
Motive.
The delay of language.

A strength to be handled by giants.

The possibilities of statement. I am saying, now,
what my father could not remember
to say. What my grandfather

was killed
for believing.
        Pay me off, savages.
        Build me an equitable human assertion.

One that looks like a jungle, or one that looks like the cities
of the West.   But I provide the stock. The beasts
and myths.
      The City's Rise!
             (And what is history, then? An old deaf lady)
             burned to death
             in South Carolina.

Numbers, Letters

If you're not home, where
are you? Where'd you go? What
were you doing when gone? When
you come back, better make it good.
What was you doing down there, freakin' off
with white women, hangin' out
with Queens, say it straight to be
understood straight, put it flat and real
in the street where the sun comes and the
moon comes and the cold wind in winter
waters your eyes. Say what you mean, dig
it out put it down, and be strong
about it.

I cant say who I am
unless you agree I'm real

I cant be anything I'm not
Except these words pretend
to life not yet explained,
so here's some feeling for you
see how you like it, what it
reveals, and that's me.

Unless you agree I'm real
that I can feel
whatever beats hardest
at our black souls

I am real, and I can't say who
I am. Ask me if I know, I'll say
yes, I might say no. Still, ask.

I'm Everett LeRoi Jones, 30 yrs old.
A black nigger in the universe. A long breath singer,
wouldbe dancer, strong from years of fantasy
and study. All this time then, for what's happening
now. All that spilling of white ether, clocks in ghostheads
lips drying and rewet, eyes opening and shut, mouths churning.

I am a meditative man. And when I say something it's all of me
saying, and all the things that make me, have formed me,
    colored me
this brilliant reddish night. I will say nothing that I feel is
lie, or unproven by the same ghostclocks, by the same riders
always move so fast with the word slung over their backs or
in saddlebags, charging down Chinese roads. I carry some
    words,
some feeling, some life in me. My heart is large as my mind
this is a messenger calling, over here, over here, open your eyes
and your ears and your souls; today is the history we must learn
to desire. There is no guilt in love

Western Front

My intentions are colors, I'm filled with
color, every tint you think of lends to mine
my mind is full of color, hard muscle streaks,
or soft glow round exactness registration. All earth
heaven things, hell things, in colors circulate
a wild blood train, turns litmus like a bible coat,
describes music falling flying, my criminal darkness,
static fingers, call it art, high above the streetwalkers

high above real meaning, floaters prop themselves in pillows
letting soft blondes lick them into serenity. Poems are made
by fools like Allen Ginsberg, who loves God, and went to India
only to see God, finding him walking barefoot in the street,
blood sickness and hysteria, yet only God touched this poet,
who has no use for the world. But only God, who is sole dope
manufacturer of the universe, and is responsible for ease
and logic. Only God, the baldhead faggot, is clearly responsible,
not, for definite, no cats we know.

T. T. Jackson sings

I fucked your mother
on top of a house
when I got through
she thought she was
Mickey Mouse.

I fucked your mother
under a tree
when it was over
she couldn't even pee

I fucked your mother
and she hollered OOOO
she thought I was
fu man chu

I fucked your mother
and she started to grin
then she found out
it wasn't even in.

Return of the Native

Harlem is vicious
modernism. BangClash.
Vicious the way its made.
Can you stand such beauty?
So violent and transforming.
The trees blink naked, being
so few. The women stare
and are in love with them
selves. The sky sits awake
over us. Screaming
at us. No rain.
Sun, hot cleaning sun
drives us under it.

The place, and place
meant of
black people. Their heavy Egypt.
(Weird word!) Their minds, mine,
the black hope mine. In Time.
We slide along in pain or too
happy. So much love
for us. All over, so much of
what we need. Can you sing
yourself, your life, your place
on the warm planet earth.
And look at the stones

the hearts, the gentle hum
of meaning. Each thing, life
we have, or love, is meant
for us in a world like this.
Where we may see ourselves
all the time. And suffer
in joy, that our lives
are so familiar.

A Poem for Black Hearts

For Malcolm's eyes, when they broke
the face of some dumb white man, For
Malcolm's hands raised to bless us
all black and strong in his image
of ourselves, For Malcolm's words
fire darts, the victor's tireless
thrusts, words hung above the world
change as it may, he said it, and
for this he was killed, for saying,
and feeling, and being/ change, all
collected hot in his heart, For Malcolm's
heart, raising us above our filthy cities,
for his stride, and his beat, and his address
to the grey monsters of the world, For Malcolm's
pleas for your dignity, black men, for your life,
black man, for the filling of your minds
with righteousness, For all of him dead and
gone and vanished from us, and all of him which
clings to our speech black god of our time.
For all of him, and all of yourself, look up,
black man, quit stuttering and shuffling, look up,
black man, quit whining and stooping, for all of him,
For Great Malcolm a prince of the earth, let nothing in us rest
until we avenge ourselves for his death, stupid animals
that killed him, let us never breathe a pure breath if
we fail, and white men call us faggots till the end of
the earth.

SOS

Calling black people
Calling all black people, man woman child
Wherever you are, calling you, urgent, come in
Black People, come in, wherever you are, urgent, calling
you, calling all black people
calling all black people, come in, black people, come
on in.

Black Art

Poems are bullshit unless they are
teeth or trees or lemons piled
on a step. Or black ladies dying
of men leaving nickel hearts
beating them down. Fuck poems
and they are useful, wd they shoot
come at you, love what you are,
breathe like wrestlers, or shudder
strangely after pissing. We want live
words of the hip world live flesh &
coursing blood. Hearts Brains
Souls splintering fire. We want poems
like fists beating niggers out of Jocks
or dagger poems in the slimy bellies
of the owner-jews. Black poems to
smear on girdlemamma mulatto bitches
whose brains are red jelly stuck
between 'lizabeth taylor's toes. Stinking
Whores! We want "poems that kill.'
Assassin poems, Poems that shoot
guns. Poems that wrestle cops into alleys
and take their weapons leaving them dead
with tongues pulled out and sent to Ireland. Knockoff
poems for dope selling wops or slick halfwhite
politicians Airplane poems, rrrrrrrrrrrrrrrr
rrrrrrrrrrrrrrr . . . tuhtuhtuhtuhtuhtuhtuhtuhtuh
. . . rrrrrrrrrrrrrrrr . . . Setting fire and death to
whities ass. Look at the Liberal
Spokesman for the jews clutch his throat
& puke himself into eternity . . . rrrrrrrr
There's a negroleader pinned to
a bar stool in Sardi's eyeballs melting
in hot flame Another negroleader
on the steps of the white house one
kneeling between the sheriff's thighs
negotiating cooly for his people.

Agggh . . . stumbles across the room . . .
Put it on him, poem. Strip him naked

to the world! Another bad poem cracking
steel knuckles in a jewlady's mouth
Poem scream poison gas on beasts in green berets
Clean out the world for virtue and love,
Let there be no love poems written
until love can exist freely and
cleanly. Let Black People understand
that they are the lovers and the sons
of lovers and warriors and sons
of warriors Are poems & poets &
all the loveliness here in the world

We want a black poem. And a
Black World.
Let the world be a Black Poem
And Let All Black People Speak This Poem
Silently
or LOUD

Poem for HalfWhite College Students

Who are you, listening to me, who are you
listening to yourself? Are you white or
black, or does that have anything to do
with it? Can you pop your fingers to no
music, except those wild monkies go on
in your head, can you jerk, to no melody,
except finger poppers get it together
when you turn from starchecking to checking
yourself. How do you sound, your words, are they
yours? The ghost you see in the mirror, is it really
you, can you swear you are not an imitation greyboy,
can you look right next to you in that chair, and swear,
that the sister you have your hand on is not really
so full of Elizabeth Taylor, Richard Burton is
coming out of her ears. You may even have to be Richard
with a white shirt and face, and four million negroes
think you cute, you may have to be Elizabeth Taylor, old lady,
if you want to sit up in your crazy spot dreaming about dresses,

and the sway of certain porters' hips. Check yourself, learn who
    it is
speaking, when you make some ultrasophisticated point, check
    yourself,
when you find yourself gesturing like Steve McQueen, check it
    out, ask
in your black heart who it is you are, and is that image black or
    white,

you might be surprised right out the window, whistling dixie on
    the way in.

W. W.

Back home the black women are all beautiful,
and the white ones fall back, cutoff from 1000
years stacked booty, and Charles of the Ritz
where jooshladies turn into billy burke in bluegrass
kicks. With wings, and jingly bew-teeful things.
The black women in Newark are fine. Even with all that grease
in their heads. I mean even the ones where the wigs
slide around, and they coming at you 75degrees off course.
I could talk to them. Bring them around. To something.
Some kind of quick course, on the sidewalk, like Hey baby
why don't you take that thing off yo' haid. You look like
Miss Muffett in a runaway ugly machine. I mean. Like that.

Ka 'Ba

A closed window looks down
on a dirty courtyard, and black people
call across or scream across or walk across
defying physics in the stream of their will

Our world is full of sound
Our world is more lovely than anyone's

tho we suffer, and kill each other
and sometimes fail to walk the air

We are beautiful people
with african imaginations
full of masks and dances and swelling chants
with african eyes, and noses, and arms,
though we sprawl in grey chains in a place
full of winters, when what we want is sun.

We have been captured,
brothers. And we labor
to make our getaway, into
the ancient image, into a new

correspondence with ourselves
and our black family. We need magic
now we need the spells, to raise up
return, destroy, and create. What will be

the sacred words?

The World Is Full of Remarkable Things

(for little Bumi)

Quick Night
easy warmth
The girlmother lies next to me
breathing
coughing
sighing
at my absence. Bird Plane
Flying near Mecca
Sun sight warm air
through
my air foils. Womanchild
turns
lays her head

on my stomach. Night aches
acts
Niggers rage

down the street. (Air
Pocket, sinks
us. She lady
angel brings
her self
to touch me
grains & grass & long
silences, the dark
ness my natural
element, in
warm black skin
I love &
understand
things. Sails
cries these
moans, pushed
from her by my
weight, her legs
spreading wrapping
secure the spirit
in her.
        We begin our
ritual breathing
flex the soul clean
out, her eyes slide
into   dreams

leroy

I wanted to know my mother when she sat
looking sad across the campus in the late 20's
into the future of the soul, there were black angels
straining above her head, carrying life from our ancestors,
and knowledge, and the strong nigger feeling. She sat
(in that photo in the yearbook I showed Vashti) getting into

new blues, from the old ones, the trips and passions
showered on her by her own. Hypnotizing me, from so far
ago, from that vantage of knowledge passed on to her passed on
to me and all the other black people of our time.
When I die, the consciousness I carry I will to
black people. May they pick me apart and take the
useful parts, the sweet meat of my feelings. And leave
the bitter bullshit rotten white parts
alone.

Black People!

What about that bad short you saw last week on
Frelinghuysen, or those stoves and refrigerators, record players
in Sears, Bambergers, Klein's, Hahnes', Chase, and the smaller
joosh enterprises? What about that bad jewelry, on Washington
Street, and those couple of shops on Springfield? You know how
to get it, you can get it, no money down, no money never,
money dont grow on trees no way, only whitey's got it, makes it
with a machine, to control you you cant steal nothin from a
white man, he's already stole it he owes you anything you want,
even his life. All the stores will open if you will say the magic
words. The magic words are: Up against the wall mother fucker
this is a stick up! Or: Smash the window at night (these are
magic actions) smash the windows daytime, anytime, together,
let's smash the window drag the shit from in there. No money
down. No time to pay. Just take what you want. The magic
dance in the street. Run up and down Broad Street niggers take
the shit you want. Take their lives if need be, but get what you
want what you need. Dance up and down the streets, turn all the
music up, run through the streets with music, beautiful radios on
Market Street, they are brought here especially for you. Our
brothers are moving all over, smashing at jellywhite faces. We
must make our own World, man, our own world, and we can not
do this unless the white man is dead. Let's get together and
killhim my man, let's get to gather the fruit of the sun, let's make
a world we want black children to grow and learn in do not let
your children when they grow look in your face and curse you
by pitying your tomish ways.

From *Four Black Revolutionary Plays*

Great Goodness of Life

A COON SHOW

(for my father with love and respect)

GREAT GOODNESS OF LIFE was first performed at Spirit House, Newark, by the Spirit House Movers, in November 1967.

Original Cast: David Shakes, Mubarak Mahmoud, Yusef Iman, Larry Miller, Elaine Jones, Jenga Choma, and Damu

Directed by LeRoi Jones
Lighting design by Aminifu

Characters

VOICE OF THE JUDGE

COURT ROYAL, a middle-aged Negro man; gray-haired, slight

ATTORNEY BRECK, middle-aged Negro man

HOODS 1 & 2, KKK–like figures

YOUNG WOMAN, around twenty-five years old, colored

HOODS 3 & 4, more refined than the first two; wear business suits

Scene

[*Outside an old log cabin, with morning frost letting up a little*]

VOICE. Court.

[*A man,* COURT ROYAL, *comes out, grey but still young-looking. He is around fifty. He walks straight, though he is nervous. He comes uncertainly. Pauses*]

Come on.

[*He walks right up to the center of the lights*]

Come on.

COURT ROYAL. I don't quite understand.

VOICE. Shutup, nigger.

COURT ROYAL. What? [*Meekly, then trying to get some force up*]
Now what's going on? I don't see why I should . . .

VOICE. I told you to
shutup,
nigger.

COURT ROYAL. I don't understand. What's going on?

VOICE. Black lunatic. I
said shutup. I'm
not going to tell
you again!

COURT ROYAL. But . . . Yes.

VOICE. You are Court Royal,
are you not?

COURT ROYAL. Yes, I am. But I don't understand.

VOICE. You are charged
with shielding a
wanted criminal.
A murderer.

COURT ROYAL. What? Now I know you have the wrong man. I've
done no such thing. I work in the Post Office. I'm Court Royal. I've
done nothing wrong. I work in the Post Office and have done
nothing wrong.

VOICE. Shutup.

COURT ROYAL. But I'm Court Royal. Everybody knows me. I've always done everything . . .

> VOICE. Court Royal you are charged with harboring a murderer. How do you plead?

COURT ROYAL. Plead? There's a mistake being made. I've never done anything.

> VOICE. How do you plead?

COURT ROYAL. I'm not a criminal. I've done nothing . . .

> VOICE. Then you plead not guilty?

COURT ROYAL. Of course I'm not guilty. I work in the Post Office. [*Tries to work up a little humor*] You know me, probably. Didn't you ever see me in the Post Office? I'm a supervisor; you know me. I work at the Post Office. I'm no criminal. I've worked at the Post Office for thirty-five years. I'm a supervisor. There must be some mistake. I've worked at the Post Office for thirty-five years.

> VOICE. Do you have an attorney?

COURT ROYAL. Attorney? Look you'd better check you got the right man. You're making a mistake. I'll sue. That's what I'll do.

> VOICE. [*The* VOICE *laughs long and cruelly*]

COURT ROYAL. I'll call my attorney right now. We'll find out just what's going on here.

> VOICE. If you don't have an attorney, the court will assign you one.

COURT ROYAL. Don't bother. I have an attorney. John Breck's my attorney. He'll be down here in a few minutes—the minute I call.

> VOICE. The court will assign you an attorney.

COURT ROYAL. But I have an attorney. John Breck. See, it's on this card.

> VOICE. Will the Legal Aid man please step forward?

COURT ROYAL. No. I have an attorney. If you'll just call, or adjourn the case until my attorney gets here.

> VOICE. We have an attorney for you.
> Where is the Legal Aid man?

COURT ROYAL. But I have an attorney. I want my attorney. I don't need any Legal Aid man. I have money. I have an attorney. I work in the Post Office. I'm a supervisor; here, look at my badge. [*A bald-headed smiling house slave in a wrinkled dirty tuxedo crawls across the stage; he has a wire attached to his back leading offstage. A huge key in the side of his head. We hear the motors "animating" his body groaning like tremendous weights. He grins, and slobbers, turning his head slowly from side to side. He grins. He makes little quivering sounds*]

> VOICE. Your attorney.

COURT ROYAL. What kind of foolishness is this? [*He looks at the man*] What's going on? What's your name? [*His "voice" begins some time after the question: the wheels churn out his answer, and the deliberating motors sound throughout the scene*]

ATTORNEY BRECK. Pul . . . lead . . . errrr . . . [*As if the motors are having trouble starting*] Pul . . . pul . . . lead . . . er . . . err . . . Guilty! [*Motors get it together and move in prop-*

er synchronization] Pul . . . Plead guilty, it's your only chance. Just plead guilty, brother. Just plead guilty. It's your only chance. Your only chance.

COURT ROYAL. Guilty? Of what? What are you talking about? What kind of defense attorney are you? I don't even know what I'm being charged with, and you say plead guilty. What's happening here? [*At* VOICE] Can't I even know the charge?

VOICE. We told you the charge. Harboring a murderer.

COURT ROYAL. But that's an obvious mistake.

ATTORNEY BRECK. There's no mistake. Plead guilty. Get off easy. Otherwise. thrrrrit. [*Makes throat-cutting gesture, then chuckles*] Plead guilty, brother, it's your only chance. [*Laughs*]

VOICE. Plea changed to guilty?

COURT ROYAL. What? No, I'm not pleading guilty. And I want my lawyer.

VOICE. You have yr lawyer.

COURT ROYAL. No, my lawyer is John Breck.

ATTORNEY BRECK. Mr. Royal, look at me. [*Grabs him by the shoulder*] I am John Breck. [*Laughs*] Your attorney and friend. And I say plead guilty.

COURT ROYAL. John Bre . . . what? [*He looks at* ATTORNEY *closely*] Breck. Great God, what's happened to you? Why do you look like this?

ATTORNEY BRECK. Why? Haha. I've always looked like this, Mr. Royal. Always. [*Now another voice, strong, young, begins to shout in the darkness at* COURT]

YOUNG VICTIM. Now will you believe me stupid fool? Will you believe what I tell you or your eyes? Even your eyes. You're here with me, with us, all of us, and you can't understand. Plead guilty you are guilty stupid nigger. You'll die they'll kill you and you don't know why now will you believe me? Believe me, half-white coward. Will you believe reality?

> VOICE. Get that criminal out
> of here. Beat him. Shut him
> up. Get him.

[*Now sounds of scuffling come out of darkness. Screams. Of a group of men subduing another man*]

YOUNG VICTIM. You bastard. And you Court Royal you let them take me. You liar. You weakling, you woman in the face of degenerates. You let me be taken. How can you walk the earttttttt . . . [*He is apparently taken away*]

COURT ROYAL. Who's that? [*Peers into darkness*] Who's that talking to me?

> VOICE. Shutup, Royal.
> Fix your plea. Let's
> get on with it.

COURT ROYAL. That voice sounded very familiar. [*Caught in a thought momentarily*] I almost thought it was . . .

> VOICE. Since you keep
> your plea of not
> guilty you won't need a
> lawyer. We can proceed without
> your services, Counselor.

ATTORNEY BRECK. As you wish, your honor. Goodbye, Mr. Royal. [*He begins to crawl off*] Goodbye, dead sucker! Hahahaha [*Waving hands as he crawls off and laughing*] Hahahaha, ain't I a bitch . . . I mean, ain't I? [*Exits*]

COURT ROYAL. John, John. You're my attorney, you can't leave me here like this. [*Starts after him, shouts*] JOHN! [*A siren begins to scream, like in jailbreak pictures . . . "Arrrrrrrerrrr." The lights beat off, on, in time with the metallic siren shriek.* COURT *is stopped in his tracks, bent in anticipation; the siren continues. Machine guns begin to bang bang as if very close to him, cell doors slamming, whistles, yells: "Break . . . Break!" The machine guns chatter,* COURT *stands frozen, half-bent arms held away from his body, balancing him in his terror. As the noise, din, continues, his eyes grow until he is almost going to faint.*]

Ahhhhhhgggg. Please . . . Please . . . don't kill me. Don't shoot me. I didn't do anything. I'm not trying to escape. Please . . . Please PLEEEEEAS . . .

[*The* VOICE *begins to shriek almost as loud with laughter as all the other sounds and jumping lights stop as* VOICE *starts to laugh. The* VOICE *just laughs and laughs, laughs until you think it will explode or spit up blood; it laughs long and eerily out of the darkness.*

[*Still dazed and staggered, he looks around quickly, trying to get himself together. He speaks now very quietly, and shaken*] Please. Please. [*The other* VOICE *begins to subside, the laughs coming in sharp cut-off bursts of hysteria*]

> VOICE. You donkey. [*Laughs*]
> You piece of wood.
> You shiny shuffling
> piece of black vomit.

[*The laughter quits like the tide rolling softly back to silence. Now there is no sound, except for* COURT ROYAL's *breathing, and shivering clothes. He whispers . . .*]

COURT ROYAL. Please? [*He is completely shaken and defeated, frightened like a small animal, eyes barely rolling*] Please. I won't escape. [*His words sound corny tinny stupid dropped in such silence*] Please I won't try again. Just tell me where I am. [*The silence again. For a while no movement.* COURT *is frozen, stiff, with only eyes sneaking; now they stop, he's frozen, cannot move staring off into the cold darkness*]

[*A chain, slightly, more, now heavier, dragged bent, wiggled slowly, light now heavily in the darkness, from another direction. Chains. They're dragged, like things are pulling them across the earth. The chains. And now low chanting voices, moaning, with* incredible pain and despair, the voices press just *softly* behind the chains, for a few seconds, so very very briefly then gone. And silence]

[COURT *does not move. His eyes roll a little back and around. He bends his knees, dipping his head, bending. He moans*]

COURT ROYAL. Just tell me where I am.

VOICE. HEAVEN.

[*The* VOICE *is cool and businesslike.* COURT's *eyes and head raise an imperceptible trifle. He begins to pull his arms slowly to his sides, and claps them together. The lights dim, and only* COURT *is seen in dimmer illumination. The* VOICE *again. . .*]

VOICE. HEAVEN. [*Pause*] WELCOME.

COURT ROYAL. [*Mumbling*] I never understood . . . these things are so confusing. [*His head jerks like he's suddenly heard Albert Ayler. It raises, his whole body jerks around like suddenly animate ragdoll. He does a weird dance like a marionette jiggling and wiggling*] You'll wonder what the devil-meant. A jiggedy bobbidy fool. You'll wonder what the devil-sent. Diggedy dobbidy cool. Ah man. [*Singing*] Ah man, you'll wonder who the devil-sent. And what was heaven heaven heaven. [*This is like a funny joke-dance, with sudden funniness from* COURT; *then suddenly as before he stops frozen again, eyes rolling, no other sound heard. . . .*]

[*Now a scream, and white hooded men push a greasy-head nigger lady across in front of* COURT. *They are pulling her hair, and feeling her ass. One whispers from time to time in her ear. She screams and bites occasionally, occasionally kicking*]

HOOD 1. [*To the* VOICE] She's drunk. [*Now to* COURT] You want to smell her breath?

COURT ROYAL. [*Frightened, also sickened at the sight, embarrassed*] N-no. I don't want to. I smell it from here. She drinks and stinks and brings our whole race down.

HOOD 2. Ain't it the truth!

VOICE. Grind her into
poison jelly.
Smear it on her
daughter's head.

HOOD 2. Right, yr honor. You got a break, sister. [*They go off*] Hey, uncle, you sure you don't want to smell her breath?

COURT ROYAL. [*Shivers*] No.

VOICE. Royal, you have
concealed a murderer,
and we have your punish-
ment ready for you. Are you
ready?

COURT ROYAL. What? No. I want a trial. Please a trial. I deserve that. I'm a good man.

VOICE. Royal, you're not a
man!

COURT ROYAL. Please . . . [*Voice breaking*] your honor, a trial. A simple one, very quick, nothing fancy . . . I'm very conservative . . . no frills or loud colors, a simple concrete black toilet paper trial.

VOICE. And funeral.

[*Now two men in hoods, white work gloves, business suits, very sporty, come in with a stretcher. A black man is dead on it. There is long very piped applause. "Yea, Yea"*]

HOOD 1. It's the Prince, yr honor. We banged him down.

VOICE. He's dead?

HOOD 2. Yes. A nigger did it for us.

VOICE. Conceal the body
in a stone. And sink the stone
deep under the ocean. Call the
newspapers and give the official history.

Make sure his voice is in that stone too, or . . .
[*Heavy nervous pause*] Just go ahead.

HOOD 1. Of course, your honor. [*Looks to* COURT, *almost as an afterthought*] You want to smell his breath? [*They go out*]

COURT ROYAL. [*Mumbling, still very frightened*] No . . . no . . . I have nothing to do with any of this. I'm a good man. I have a car. A home. [*Running down*] A club. [*Looks up, pleading*] Please, there's some mistake. Isn't there? I've done nothing wrong. I have a family. I work in the Post Office. I'm a supervisor. I've worked for thirty-five years. I've done nothing wrong.

> VOICE. Shutup, whimpering
> pig. Shutup and
> get ready for sen-
> tencing. It'll be hard on
> you, you can bet on that.

COURT ROYAL. [*A little life; he sees he's faced with danger*] But tell me what I've done. I can remember no criminal, no murderer I've housed. I work eight hours, then home, and television, dinner, then bowling. I've harbored no murderers. I don't know any. I'm a good man.

> VOICE. Shutup, liar. Do you know
> this man?

[*An image is flashed on the screen behind him. It is a rapidly shifting series of faces. Malcolm. Patrice. Rev. King. Garvey. Dead nigger kids killed by the police. Medgar Evers*]

COURT ROYAL. What?

> VOICE. I asked you do you know
> this man? I'm asking again,
> for the last time. There's no
> need to lie.

COURT ROYAL. But this is many men, many faces. They shift so fast I cannot tell you who they are . . . or what is meant. It's so confusing.

VOICE. Don't lie, Royal. We know
all about you. You are guilty.
Look at that face. You know this man.

COURT ROYAL. I do? [*In rising terror*] No. No. I don't I never saw
that man, it's so many faces, I've never seen those faces . . .
never . . .

VOICE. Look closer, Royal. You cannot
get away with what you've done. Look
more closely. You recognize
that face . . . don't you? The face
of the murderer you've sheltered all
these years. Look, you liar, look at
that face.

COURT ROYAL. No, no, no . . . I don't know them. I can't be
forced into admitting something I never did. Uhhh . . . I have
worked. My God, I've worked. I've meant to do the right thing, I've
tried to be a . . .

[*The faces shift, a long slow wail, like moan, like secret screaming, has underscored the flashing faces. Now it rises sharply to
screaming point thrusts.* COURT *wheels around to face the image
on the screen, directly. He begins shouting loud as the voices*]

No, I've tried . . . please I never wanted anything but peace
. . . please. I tried to be a man I lost my . . . heart . . .
please, it was so deep. I wanted to do the right thing, just to do
the right thing. I wanted . . . everything to be . . . all right.
Oh, please . . . please.

VOICE. Now tell me, whether you
know that murderer's face or not.
Tell me before you die!

COURT ROYAL. No, no. I don't know him. I don't. I want to do the
right thing. I don't know them. [*Raises his hands in his agony*]
Oh, son . . . son . . . dear God, my flesh, forgive me . . .
[*Begins to weep and shake*] My sons. [*He clutches his body,
shaken throughout by his ugly sobs*]

Dear god . . .

VOICE. Just as we thought. You are the one. And you must be sentenced.

COURT ROYAL. I must be sentenced. I am the one. [*Almost trance-like*] I must be sentenced. With the murderer. I am the one.

VOICE. The murderer is dead. You must be sentenced alone.

COURT ROYAL. [*As first realization*] The murderer . . . is . . . dead?

VOICE. And you must be sentenced. Now. Alone.

COURT ROYAL. [*Voice rising, in panic, but catching it up short*] The murderer . . . is dead.

VOICE. Yes. And your sentence is . . .

COURT ROYAL. I must be sentenced . . . alone. Where is the murderer? Where is his corpse?

VOICE. You will see it presently.

COURT ROYAL. [*Head bowed*] God. And I am now to die like the murderer died?

VOICE. No. [*Long pause*] We have decided to spare you. We admire your spirit. It is a compliment to know you can see the clearness of your fate, and the rightness of it. That you love the beauty of the way of life you've chosen here in the anonymous world. No one beautiful is guilty. So how can you be? All the guilty have been punished. Or are being punished. You are absolved of your crime, at this moment, because of your infinite understanding of the compassionate God Of The Cross. Whose head was cut off for you, to absolve you of your weakness. The murderer is dead. The murderer is dead.

[*Applause from the darkness*]

COURT ROYAL. And I am not guilty now?

> VOICE. No, you are free. Forever.
> It is asked only that you give the final
> instruction.

COURT ROYAL. Final instruction . . . I don't understand . . .

> VOICE. Heroes! bring the last issue in.

[*The last two hooded men,* HOODS 3 *and* 4, *return with a young black man of about twenty. The boy does not look up. He walks stiff-legged to the center in front of* COURT. *He wears a large ankh around his neck. His head comes up slowly. He looks into* COURT's *face*]

YOUNG VICTIM. Peace.

COURT ROYAL. [*Looks at his face, begins to draw back. The hooded man comes and places his arms around* COURT's *shoulders*]

> VOICE. Give him the instruction
> instrument.

[*Hooded man takes a pistol out of his pocket and gives it with great show to* COURT]

HOOD 3. The silver bullet is in the chamber. The gun is made of diamonds and gold.

HOOD 4. You get to keep it after the ceremony.

> VOICE. And now, with the rite of instruction, the
> last bit of guilt falls from you as if it was never
> there, Court Royal. Now, at last, you can go free.
> Perform the rite, Court Royal, the final instruction.

COURT ROYAL. What? No. I don't understand.

> VOICE. The final instruction is the death of
> the murderer. The murderer is dead and must

die, with each gift of our God. This gift is the
cleansing of guilt, and the bestowal of freedom.

COURT ROYAL. But you told me the murderer was dead already.

VOICE. It *is* already. The
murderer has been sentenced. You have
only to carry out the rite.

COURT ROYAL. But you told me the murderer was dead. [*Starts to
back away*] You told me . . . you said I would be sentenced
alone.

VOICE. The murderer *is dead*. This
is his shadow. This one is not real.
This is the myth of the murderer. His last
fleeting astral projection. It is the murderer's
myth that we ask you to instruct. To bind it forever
. . . with death.

COURT ROYAL. I don't . . . Why do . . you said I was not
guilty. That my guilt had fallen away.

VOICE. The rite must be finished. This
ghost must be lost in cold space.
Court Royal, this is your destiny.
This act was done by you a million
years ago. This is only the memory of it.
This is only a rite. You cannot kill a shadow,
a fleeting bit of light and memory. This is only
a rite, to show that you would be guilty but for
the cleansing rite. The shadow is killed in place of the
killer. The shadow for reality. So reality can exist
beautiful like it is. This is your destiny, and your already
lived-out life. Instruct, Court Royal, as the centuries
pass, and bring you back to your natural reality. Without
guilt. Without shame. Pure and blameless, your soul
washed [*Pause*] white as snow.

COURT ROYAL. [*Falling to his knees, arms extended as in loving
prayer, to a bright light falling on him, racing around the space*]

Oh, yes . . . I hear you. And I have waited, for this promise to be fulfilled.

> VOICE. This is the fulfillment. You must, at this moment, enter into the covenant of guiltless silence. Perform the rite, Court Royal.

COURT ROYAL. Oh, yes, yes . . . I want so much to be happy . . . and relaxed.

> VOICE. Then carry out your destiny . . .

COURT ROYAL. Yes, yes . . . I will . . . I will be happy . . . [*He rises, pointing the gun straight up at the young man's face*] I must be . . . fulfilled . . . I will. [*He fires the weapon into the boy's face. One short sound comes from the boy's mouth*]

YOUNG VICTIM. Papa. [*He falls*]

[COURT ROYAL *Stands looking at the dead boy with the gun still up. He is motionless*]

> VOICE. Case dismissed, Court Royal . . . you are free.

COURT ROYAL. [*Now suddenly to life, the lights go up full, he has the gun in his hand. He drops, flings it away from him*] My soul is as white as snow. [*He wanders up to the body*] My soul is as white as snow. [*He starts to wander off the stage*] White as snow. I'm free. I'm free. My life is a beautiful thing.

[*He mopes slowly toward the edge of the stage, then suddenly a brighter mood strikes him. Raising his hand as if calling someone*] Hey, Louise, have you seen my bowling bag? I'm going down to the alley for a minute. [*He is frozen, the lights dim to* BLACK]

> *Curtain*

From *It's Nation Time*

IT'S NATION TIME

Time to get
together
time to be one strong fast black energy space
        one pulsating positive magnetism, rising
time to get up and
be
come
be
come, time to
      be come
      time to
      get up be come
      black genius rise in spirit muscle
      sun man get up rise heart of universes to be
future of the world
the black man is the future of the world
be come
rise up
future of the black genius spirit reality
      move
      from crushed roach back
      from dead snake head
      from wig funeral in slowmotion
      from dancing teeth and coward tip
      from jibberjabber patme boss patme smmich
when the brothers strike niggers come out
come out niggers
when the brothers take over the school
help niggers
come out niggers
all niggers negroes must change up
come together in unity unify
for nation time

it's nation time

                                        Boom
                                        Booom
                                        BOOOM
                                        Boom
                                        Dadadadadadadadadadad
                                        Boom
                                        Boom
                                        Boom
                                        Boom
                                        Dadadadad adadadad
                                                        Hey aheee   (soft)
                                                        Hey ahheee   (loud)
                                        Boom
                                        Boom
                                        Boom
sing a get up time to nationfy
singaa miracle fire light
sing a airplane invisibility for the jesus niggers come from the
    grave
for the jesus niggers dead in the cave, rose up, passt jewjuice
on shadow world
raise up christ nigger
Christ was black
krishna was black shango was black
            black jesus nigger come out and strike
                come out and strike boom boom
                        Heyahheeee come out
                strike close ford
                    close prudential burn the policies
                tear glasses off dead statue puppets even those
                    they imitate life
                Shango budda black
                hermes rasis black
                    moses krishna
                                        black

when the brothers wanna stop animals
come out niggers come out
come out niggers niggers niggers come out
help us stop the devil
help us build a new world

niggers come out, brothers are we
  with you and your sons your daughters are ours
  and we are the same, all the blackness from one black allah
    when the world is clear you'll be with us
      come out niggers come out
      come out niggers come out
It's nation time eye ime
          It's nation ti eye ime
              chant with bells and drum
              it's nation time

It's nation time, get up santa claus   (repeat)
  it's nation time, build it
    get up muffet dragger
      get up rastus for real to be rasta farari
        ras jua
          get up got here bow

            It's Nation
            Time!

AFRIKAN REVOLUTION

This poem was originally published in *Black World* (May 1973). It is a Pan-African work, prefiguring Baraka's developing socialist aesthetic. In his *Selected Poetry* (now out of print), Baraka places it as an individual entity between the Black Nationalist and the Marxist periods. Since it is autonomous in that collection, and as it reflects Baraka's thought of that time, I place it in 1973 instead of 1979, the publication date of the *Selected Poetry*.

—wjh

(Conakry, Guinea, February 4, 1973
after Amilcar Cabral's funeral)

Afrikan People all over the world
Suffering from white domination
Afrikan People all over the world
Trying to liberate their Afrikan nation(s)
Afrikan People all over the world
Under the yoke, the gun, the hammer, the lash
Afrikan People all over the world
being killed & stifled melted down for the Imperialists cash
Afrikan People all over the world
   conscious, unconscious, struggling, sleeping
resisting, tomming, killing the enemy, killing each other
Being hurt, surviving, understanding, held in ignorance
Bursting out of chains, lying for Nixon, drowning colonialists
Being shot down in the street
Afrikan People everywhere
Afrikan People all over the world
Evolving because of & in spite of ourselves
Afrikan People all over the world, trying to make Revolution
The world must be changed, split open & changed
All poverty sickness ignorance racism must be eradicated
Who ever pushes these plagues, them also must be eradicated
All capitalists, racists, liars, Imperialists. All who can not change
they also must be eradicated, their life style, philosophies
habits, flunkies, pleasures, wiped out   eliminated
The world must be changed, split open & changed
Transformed, turned upside down.
No more Poverty!
No more dirty ragged black people, cept from hard work
   to beautify + energize a world we help create

Death to Backward Powers
Death to Bad Dancers
  No more trash piled up in the streets
  No more wind in the bedroom
No more Capitalists in penthouses & colored people in tents
  with no houses
Death to disease & carriers of disease
All disease must be cured!
"Individuals" who love disease must be reeducated
If they resist world unity and the progress of all races
Kill them. Don't hesitate! Kill them. They are the Plague
No more filthy places for us to live and be uneducated
No more aimless black children with nothing to do, but die
Death to the creators of unemployment
What do they do for a living? They are thieves.
Jail them! Nixon is a sick thief why does he
remain alive? Who is in charge of killing him?
Why is it Cabral, Lumumba, Nkrumah, Moumie,
Malcolm, Dr. King, Mondlane, Mark Essex, all can
be killed by criminals, & the criminals are not
hung from bridges? No more unfair societies!
We are for world progress. Be conscious of your
life! We need food. We need homes; good
housing—not shacks. Let only people who want to
live in roach gyms live in roach gyms
We do not want to live with roaches. Let
Nixon live with roaches if he wants to. He
is closer to a roach. What is the difference
between Nixon and a roach?
Death to bad housing
Death to no work
We need work. We need education so
we can build houses and create work for
ourselves. All over the world we Afrikans
need to make progress. Why do Europeans
Why do white people why do ignorant
people of our own race obstruct us.
STOP OBSTRUCTING US EUROPEANS!
STOP OBSTRUCTING US IGNORANT PEOPLE OF
  OUR OWN RACE
  Niggers. NeoColonized Amos + Andies
  Everywhere in the Afrikan World.

No more traitors! Death to traitors
  Dope Pushers should be killed
  Niggers who inform on Revolutionary Movements
  Should be killed
  Assassins masquerading as heroes
  Butlers masquerading as presidents of
      Afrikan & Asian & South American
      Nations. They have made them Dough-Nations
So the superpowers can make they bread.
  Leaders who want dialogue with South Afrika
  Leaders who want to box in South Afrika
  Leaders who want to sing in South Afrika
  Leaders who want to observe South Afrika
These are not Leaders but Pleaders and
they should be beaten till their yoke and
their white are stiff & exposed
No more useless pain
We must refuse to be sold out by anyone
The world can be changed, we do not have to lick
  the pavements
All over the world the world can be changed
No more stupid ugliness everywhere
Death to the vultures of primitive disease +
  ignorance. America must change or be
  destroyed. Europe must change or be
  destroyed. Capitalism must be destroyed.
  Imperialism will die. Empty headed
  mummified niggers who support racist
  rule over black people will be killed too
  Dope peddlers. Pimps. Teachers who teach
  Europe's lies. Doctor's who love money more
  than people, muggers, pretenders of revolution.
  Sterile intellectuals. Soul singers who
  Sold their soul to the soulless,   live people who live
  their lives for the dead   all   change or die!
The world revolution cannot be stopped. Understand the
new criteria of life or forfeit what little life you have.
We will not be poor any longer
We will not be dirty, or ashamed of ourselves
  Racists. Capitalists. Imperialists. Sick People
  Fascists, racist rulers of Black.
  Lovers of disease, change or die

   Oppressed People of the world change
   or die
   Afrikan People all over the world Rise
   & Shine
   Shine
   Shine
Afrikan People all over the world, the future is ours
We will create on our feet not our knees
It is a future of Great works, and Freedom
But we can not crawl through life drunk &
unconscious we cannot dance through life
or read the NYTimes through life, or wear vests
all of our life give our lives to parties, & work with no
reason but life in a prison of white domination.
Be conscious. Black People
   Negroes
   Colored People
   Afro Americans Be
     CONSCIOUS
You know you can run your own life
You can have all the money & food & good life
you need
   Be conscious
   meet once a week
Meet once a week. Talk about how to get
   more money, how to get educated, how
   to have scientists for children rather than
   junkies. How to kill the roaches. How to
   stop the toilet from stinking. How to get a
   better job. Once a week. Start NOW.
   How to dress better. How to read.
   How to live longer. How to be respected.
   Meet once a week. Once a week.

All Over the world. We need to meet once a
   week. All over the world Afrikans, Soul
   Brothers Good Sisters we need to meet.
How to live longer be healthier build houses
run cities understand life be happier
Need to meet once a week
OK All over the world
Once a week

All over the world Afrikans
Sweet Beautiful Afrikans
NewArk Afrikans (Niggers too)
Harlem Afrikans (or Spooks)
Ghana Afrikans (Bloods)
Los Angeles Afrikans (Brothers)
Afrikan Afrikans (Ndugu)
West Indian Afrikans (Hey man)
South American Afrikans (Hermano!)
Francophone Afrikans (Monsieur)
Anglophone Afrikans (Mister Man)
Anywhere Afrikans
Afrikans Afrikans Afrikans
People
Afrikans Afrikans Afrikans
Watu Wazuri
Afrikans all over the world
Moving to the new way
A world of Good people is coming!
We gonna help make that world
We gonna help eliminate the negative
accentuate the positive
yellow folks brown folks red
folks will too
they hurting
I can't speak for white folks, they'll
speak for themselves
But the rest of us, Everybody Everybody
Everybody, let us first deal with us
Afrikans
All over the world. Yes. Everywhere Everywhere
Everywhere, we are Afrikans
& going to make change
Change or die
Afrikans
Change or die
to the Whole world too
we are Afrikans
Love is our passport to the perfectability of humanity
Work & Study
Struggle & Victory

THE THIRD WORLD MARXIST PERIOD
(1974–)

As long it was a bourgeois nationalist, reactionary nationalist kind of trend — a "hate whitey" kind of thing, during that period of the movement, they didn't really have any problem with that. They might get officially excited. . . .

That is, if you say that the enemy is "all whites" without making a class analysis and showing that there's only a handful of super-billionaire vampires that actually control the society, the ruling class. When you do that and start making an analysis with your art in a forceful way, then they don't see that as a charming commodity that they need like they might need some tiger teeth around their neck. . . .

In terms of my change, it's based on being involved in struggle — seeing, for instance, the whole nationalist thing turn into its opposite. A lot of people were talking about black liberation, national liberation, then actually being in charge of the exploitation. . . . But then to see that the majority of black people still don't have any change . . . [it became] clear that skin color was not determinant of political content. . . .

You have to criticize yourself for the errors you've made because that's the only way you can break with them. If you don't thoroughly criticize yourself and identify the ideological and social roots and how you're going to correct that in a true kind of Leninist fashion, you remain connected to those errors and you keep making them. We're still trying to break with a lot our old bourgeois nationalist lines and that whole kind of narrow nationalist outlook, and that's really the period I think we're struggling to come out of now, and make a clean break with all of that. . . .

* * *

If you are a modern artist who's not some kind of cultural nationalist, you understand that you can learn from anything and anybody, see that the whole of world culture is at your disposal, because no one people has created the monuments of art and culture in the world, it's been collective. . . .

American culture is multinational. It's not just white, it's not European (it's definitely not European—it's got some European origins like it's got some African origins) . . . but American culture is multinational. . . .

> —Amiri Baraka, from a radio interview
> with David Barsamian on KGNU,
> Boulder, Colorado. Broadcast on
> 27 July 1984.

When We'll Worship Jesus

We'll worship Jesus
When jesus do
Somethin
When jesus blow up
the white house
or blast nixon down
when jesus turn out congress
or bust general motors to
yard bird motors
jesus we'll worship jesus
when jesus get down
when jesus get out his yellow lincoln
w/the built in cross stain glass
window & box w/black peoples
enemies we'll worship jesus when
he get bad enough to at least scare
somebody—cops not afraid
of jesus
pushers not afraid
of jesus, capitalists racists
imperialists not afraid
of jesus shit they makin money
off jesus
we'll worship jesus when mao
do, when toure does
when the cross replaces Nkrumah's
star
Jesus need to hurt some a our
enemies, then we'll check him
out, all that screaming and hollering
& wallering and moaning talkin bout
jesus, jesus, in a red
check velvet vine + 8 in. heels

jesus pinky finger
got a goose egg ruby
which actual bleeds
jesus at the apollo
doin splits and helpin
nixon trick niggers
jesus w/his one eyed self
tongue kissing johnny carson
up the behind
jesus need to be busted
jesus need to be thrown down and whipped
till something better happen
jesus aint did nothin for us
but kept us turned toward the
sky (him and his boy allah
too, need to be checkd
out!)
we'll worship jesus
when he get a boat load of ak-47s
and some dynamite
and blow up abernathy robotin
for gulf
jesus need to be busted
we ain't gonna worship nobody
but niggers gettin up off
the ground
not gon worship jesus
unless he just a tricked up
nigger somebody named
outside his race
need to worship yo self fo
you worship jesus
need to bust jesus (+ check
out his spooky brother
allah while you heavy
on the case
cause we ain gon worship jesus
we aint gon worship
jesus
we aint gon worship
jesus
not till he do somethin

not till he help us

not till the world get changed

and he ain, jesus ain, he cant change the world

we can change the world

we can struggle against the forces of backwardness, we can
change the world

we can struggle against our selves, our slowness, our connection
with
the oppressor, the very cultural aggression which binds us to
our enemies
as their slaves.

we can change the world

we aint gonna worship jesus cause jesus dont exist

xcept in song and story except in ritual and dance, except in
slum stained

tears or trillion dollar opulence stretching back in history, the
history

of the oppression of the human mind

we worship the strength in us

we worship our selves

we worship the light in us

we worship the warmth in us

we worship the world

we worship the love in us

we worship our selves

we worship nature

we worship ourselves

we worship the life in us, and science, and knowledge, and
transformation

of the visible world

but we aint gonna worship no jesus

we aint gonna legitimize the witches and devils and spooks and
hobgoblins

the sensuous lies of the rulers to keep us chained to fantasy and
illusion

sing about life, not jesus

sing about revolution, not no jesus

stop singing about jesus,

sing about, creation, our creation, the life of the world and
fantastic

nature how we struggle to transform it, but dont victimize our
selves by

distorting the world
stop moanin about jesus, stop sweatin and crying and stompin
   and dyin for jesus
unless thats the name of the army we building to force the land
   finally to
change hands. And lets not call that jesus, get a quick
   consensus, on that,
lets damn sure not call that black fire muscle
   no invisible psychic dungeon
no gentle vision strait jacket, lets call that peoples army, or
   wapenduzi or
     simba
wachanga, but we not gon call it jesus, and not gon worship
   jesus, throw
jesus out yr mind. Build the new world out of reality, and new
   vision
we come to find out what there is of the world
to understand what there is here in the world!
to visualize change, and force it.
we worship revolution

A New Reality Is Better Than a New Movie!

How will it go, crumbling earthquake, towering inferno, jugger-
   naut, volcano, smashup,
in reality, other than the feverish nearreal fantasy of the capitalist
   flunky film hacks
tho they sense its reality breathing a quake inferno scar on their
   throat even snorts of
100% pure cocaine cant cancel the cold cut of impending death
   to this society. On all the
screens of america, the joint blows up every hour and a half for
   two dollars an fifty cents.
They have taken the niggers out to lunch, for a minute, made us
   partners (nigger charlie) or
surrogates (boss nigger) for their horror. But just as superafrikan
   mobutu cannot leop
   ardskinhat his
way out of responsibility for lumumba's death, nor even with his
   incredible billions

rockefeller
cannot even save his pale ho's titties in the crushing weight of
things as they really are.
How will it go, does it reach you, getting up, sitting on the side
of the bed, getting ready to go to work. Hypnotized by the machine, and the cement floor, the jungle treachery of
    trying
to survive with no money in a money world, of making the boss
100,000 for every 200
    dollars
you get, and then having his brother get you for the rent, and if
you want to buy the car
    you
helped build, your downpayment paid for it, the rest goes to buy
his old lady a foam
    rubber
rhinestone set of boobies for special occasions when kissinger
drunkenly fumbles with her blouse, forgetting himself.
If you don't like it, what you gonna do about it. That was the
question we asked each
    other, &
still right regularly need to ask. You don't like it? Whatcha
gonna do, about it??
The real terror of nature is humanity enraged, the true
technicolor spectacle that
    hollywood
cant record. They cant even show you how you look when you
go to work, or when you
    come back.
They cant even show you thinking or demanding the new socialist reality, its the ultimate
    tidal
wave. When all over the planet, men and women, with heat in
their hands, demand that
    society
be planned to include the lives and self determination of all the
people ever to live. That is the scalding scenario with a cast of
just under two billion that they dare not even whisper. Its called,
"We Want It All . . . The Whole World!"

The Dictatorship of the Proletariat

The dictatorship
of the proletariat
      you need to say that
      need to hear that
      not be scared of that
      cause thats gonna save your life
          gonna make your life life
          change from suffering

you hear that, the dictatorship
      of the proletariat, and be scared
      think somebody gonna hold you back
      hold you down, downer than you been held
      which aint even in it, is it, not downer than we
        been held cause
      we been held down, like down, down and dirty
      we been held, way down.

it shows you how powerful, how strong and cruel powerful
these capitalists are, these superbillionaire blood suckers
cause they put words in schools, radios, newspapers, televisions
words coming out of the heroic hero's mouth heroically, the
    happy cop,
the strong sensitive cop, the tall cop, the cop whose father
    wanted him to be a lawyer
and he's gonna make it one day type, the cop with the hip
    mustache, the laughing cop,
the hippy cop, batman and robin cops, nigger cops, negro cops,
    puerto rican patrolmen
all comin at you led by our loving goodguys from swat, just the
    thing for the superfly
all these herolover cops, are these the same which shoot yr little
nephew in the back of the head while he hanging up some crepe
paper for a surprise birthday party down in the
    basement
where they got you living. Are these the same gentle goodguy
heroes who killed the little 14 year old in bed stuy, the 12 year
old in queens, the 18 year old in staten island, the 16 year old in
long branch, the ones that slaughtered the 31 dudes in attica,

and is that the same attica where bald head mel stewart be
sneakin cake to the inmates & they all buddies grinning together
and frankly happy they dont have to be out in the world gettin in
rich peoples way?

Yet when you hear the dictatorship of the proletariat. You don't
know. You aint sure. You heard about hitler, and franco. The
daily star ledger news courier times bulletin tells
　　you dic
tatorship is bad. All but the dictatorship bein run now, the
dictatorship of the minority which is currently bein run, at this
moment crushing yr whole self down, the one mashin on you
right now, is frankly, well listen to buckley, sammy davis,
steinem, woody allen, hip, newspeak for the old freak, the
present "legitimate" blood bath incarceration of labor, truth and
beauty . . . "the dictatorship of money is good, the
　　dictatorship
of the bourgeoisie, this is good, the dictatorship of poverty and
terror, this is good." Thats the lies the rulers' mouthpieces spout.
The cackle slobber screech of madness in power. They preach
that the absolute control of our lives by the owners of the factories, the absolute control of our lives by the owners of money,
the absolute control over our
　　lives
by the owners of the land, that bloody clique of fiends, their
parrot mouthpieces claim is just. But listen, we are the producers
of wealth, the factories land and money are created by the
creators, the workers, the laborers in the mills, on the land, it is
the people who must own what shd be owned. What creates food
and clothing and shelter for the Great Majority must be owned by
that great majority. The Workers must own what is necessary for
the whole of society to live. There is enough wealth for
everybody, the world is literally unimaginably rich, yet the
masses of people are landless paupers with nothing to sell but
the muscle in their arms. We call for the dictatorship of the
producers. The absolute control and ownership by the creators of
value itself. The total control of society by the majority, the
multinational working class. The proletariat in modern dress.
Who must lead the masses of us, with a revolutionary vanguard
party at the helm guided by science, guided by the science, the
science of marxism-leninism-mao tse-tung thought. Ask us what
the party taught? Marxism-Leninism-Mao tse-tung thought.

Speak
of
the dictatorship, until you understand it. Explain the
dictatorship until you're behind it. Fight for the dictatorship
until it is reality. The dictatorship of the proletariat, the absolute
control of the state by the working class, the majority.
You need to say that
You need to hear that
not be scared of that

> the goal of our revolution is so the people can rule
> the goal of the revolution is so the people can rule
> the ultimate goal of socialist revolution is so the great
> majority
>> of the people
>> the masses
>> of people
>> can rule

> This is the dictatorship of the proletariat
> the total domination of society by the working class

> you need to hear that
> you need to talk about that
> you gonna have to fight for that

> the dictatorship of the proletariat
> think about that
> the dictatorship of the proletariat

Das Kapital

Strangling women in the suburban bush
they bodies laid around rotting while martinis are drunk
the commuters looking for their new yorkers feel a draft
& can get even drunker watching the teevee later on the Ford
replay. There will be streams of them coming, getting off
near where the girls got killed. Two of them strangled by
the maniac.
There are maniacs hidden everywhere cant you see? By the

dozens
and double dozens, maniacs by the carload (tho they *are*
a minority). But they terrorize us uniformly, all over the place
we look at the walls of our houses, the garbage cans parked full
strewn around our defaulting cities, and we cd get scared. A rat
eases past us on his way to a banquet, can you hear the cheers
   raised
through the walls, full of rat humor. Blasts of fire, some woman's
   son will stumble
and die with a pool of blood around his head. But it wont be the
   maniac. These old houses
crumble, the unemployed stumble by us straining, ashy fingered,
   harassed. The air is cold
winter heaps above us consolidating itself in degrees. We need a
   aspirin or something, and
pull our jackets close. The baldhead man on the television set
   goes on in a wooden way
his unappetizing ignorance can not be stood, or understood. The
   people turn the channel
looking for Good Times and get a negro with a pulldown hat.
   Flashes of maniac shadows before
bed, before you pull down the shade you can see the leaves
   being blown down the street
too dark now to see the writing on them, the dates, and amounts
   we owe. The streets too
will soon be empty, after the church goers go on home having
   been saved again from the
Maniac . . . except a closeup of the chief mystic's face rolling
   down to his hands will send
shivers through you, looking for traces of the maniacs life. Even
   there among the mythophrenics.

What can you do? It's time finally to go to bed. The shadows
   close around and the room is still
Most of us know there's a maniac loose. Our lives a jumble of
   frustrations and unfilled
capacities. The dead girls, the rats noise, the flashing somber
   lights, the dead voice on
television, was that blood and hair beneath the preacher's
   fingernails? A few other clues

we mull them over as we go to sleep, the skeletons of dollarbills,
traces of dead used up
labor, lead away from the death scene until we remember a quiet
fit that everywhere
is the death scene. Tomorrow you got to hit it sighs through us
like the wind, we got to
hit it, like an old song at radio city, working for the yanqui
dollarrrrr, when we were
children, and then we used to think it was not the wind, but the
maniac scratching against
our windows. Who is the maniac, and why everywhere at the
same time . . .

A Poem for Deep Thinkers

Skymen coming down out the clouds land
and then walking into society try to find out
whats happening—"Whats happening," they be saying
look at it, where they been, dabbling in mist, appearing &
disappearing, now there's a real world breathing—inhaling
exhaling concrete & sand, and they want to know what's
happening. What's happening is life itself "onward & upward,"
the spirals of fireconflict clash of opposing forces, the dialogue of
yes and no, showed itself in stabbed children in the hallways of
schools, old men strangling bankguards, a hard puertorican
inmate's
    tears
exchanging goodbyes in the prison doorway, armies sweeping
wave after wave to contest the ancient rule of the minority. What
draws them down, their blood entangled with
    humans,
their memories, perhaps, of the earth, and what they thought it
could be. But blinded by sun, and their own images of things,
rather than things as they actually are, they wobble, they
stumble, sometimes, and people they be cheering alot, cause
they think the skymen dancing, "Yeh . . . Yeh . . . get on
it. . . . ," people grinning and feeling good cause the
    skymen
dancing, and the skymen stumbling, till they get the sun out
they eyes, and integrate the inhead movie show, with the
material reality that exists with and without them. There are

tragedies, tho, a buncha skies bought the loopdieloop program
from the elegant babble of the ancient minorities. Which is
where they loopdieloop in the sky right on just

loopdieloop

in fantastic meaningless curlicues which delight the thin gallery
owners who wave at them on their way to getting stabbed in the
front seats of their silver alfa romeos by lumpen they have gotten
passionate with. And the loopdieloopers go on, sometimes
spelling out complex primitive slogans and shooting symbolic
smoke out their gills in honor of

something

dead. And then they'll make daring dives right down toward the
earth and skag cocaine

money

whiteout and crunch iced into the statue graveyard where Ralph
Ellison sits biting his

banjo

strings retightening his instrument for the millionth time before
playing the star spangled banjo. Or else loopdieloop loopdieloop
up higher and higher and thinner and thinner and

finer

refiner, sugarladdies in the last days of the locust, sucking they
greek lolliepops.

Such intellectuals as we is baby, we need to deal in the real
world, and be be in the real world. We need to use, to use, all
the all the skills all the spills and thrills that we conjure, that we
construct, that we lay out and put together, to create life as
beautiful as we thought it could be, as we dreamed it could be,
as we desired it to be, as we knew it could be, before we took
off, before we split for the sky side, not to settle for endless
meaningless circles of celebration of this madness, this madness,
not to settle for this madness this madness madness, these yoyos
yoyos of the ancient minorities. Its all for real, everythings for
real, be for real, song of the skytribe walking the earth, faint
smiles to open roars of joy, meet you on the battlefield they say,
they be humming, hop, then stride, faint smile to roars of open
joy, hey my man, what's happening, meet you on the

battlefield

they say, meet you on the battlefield they say, what i guess needs
to be discussed here

tonight

is what side yall gon be on

From *Poetry for the Advanced*

███████████

Pres Spoke in a Language

Pres
    spoke in a language
"of his own." What did he say, between the
horn line
s, pork pie hat
tenor tilted
pres once was a drummer but gave it up cause other dudes
    was getting
the foxes
while he packed his tomtoms
"Ding Dong," pres sd, meaning
like a typewriter, its the end
of this
line. "No Eyes," pres wd say, meaning
I didn't cdn't dig it, and what it was was
lame. Pres
had a language
and a life, like,
all his own,
but in the teeming whole of us he lived
toooting on his sideways horn
translating frankie trumbauer into
Bird's feathers
Tranes sinewy tracks
the slickster walking through the crowd
surviving on a terrifying wit
its the jungle the jungle the jungle
we living in
and cats like pres cd make it because they were clear they, at
    least,
had to,
to do anything else.
Save all that comrades, we need it.

Dope

uuuuuuuuuu
uuuuuuuuuu
uuuuuuuuuu   uuu   ray light morning fire lynch yet
uuuuuuu, yester-pain in dreams
comes again. race-pain, people our people
   our people
everywhere . . . yeh . . . uuuuu, yeh
uuuuu. yeh
our people
yes people
every people
most people
uuuuuu, yeh uuuuu, most people
in pain
yester-pain, and pain today
(Screams) ooowow!   ooowow! It must be
   the devil
(jumps up like a claw stuck him) oooo
   wow! oooowow! (screams)

It must be the devil
It must be the devil
it must be the devil
(shakes like evangelical sanctify
shakes tambourine like evangelical sanctify
   in heat)

ooowow! ooowow! yeh, devil, yeh, devil
   ooowow!

Must be the devil must be the devil
(waves plate like collection) mus is mus is
   mus is
mus is be the devil, cain be rockefeller
   (eyes roll
up batting, and jumping all the way around
   to face the
other direction) caint be him, no lawd
aint be dupont, no lawd, cain be, no lawd,

no way
noway, naw saw, no way jose—cain be
   them rich folks
theys good to us theys good to us theys
   good to us theys
good to us theys good to us, i know, the
   massa tolt me
so, i seed it on channel 7, i seed it on
   channel 9 i seed
it on channel 4 and 2 and 5. Rich folks
   good to us
poor folks aint shit, hallelujah, hallelujah,
   ooowow! oowow!
must be the devil, going to heaven after i
   die, after we die
everything gonna be different, after we die
   we aint gon be
hungry, ain gon be pain, ain gon be sufferin
   wont go thru this
again, after we die, after we die owooo!
   owowoooo!
after we die, its all gonna be good, have all
   the money we
need after we die, have all the food we
   need after we die
have a nice house like the rich folks, after
   we die, after we die, after we
die, we can live like rev ike, after we die,
   hallelujah, hallelujah, must be
the devil, it ain capitalism, it aint capitalism,
   it aint capitalism,
naw it aint that, jimmy carter wdnt lie,
   "lifes unfair" but it aint capitalism
must be the devil, owow! it ain the police,
   jimmy carter wdnt lie, you
know rosalynn wdnt not lillian, his
   drunken racist brother aint no reflection
on jimmy, must be the devil got in im, i tell
   you, the devil killed malcolm
and dr king too, even killed both kennedies,
   and pablo neruda and overthrew
allende's govt. killed lumumba, and is

negotiating with step and fetchit,
sleep n eat and birmingham, over there in
  "Rhodesia", goin' under the name
ian smith, must be the devil, caint be vorster,
  caint be apartheid, caint
be imperialism, jimmy carter wdnt lie, didnt
  you hear him say in his state
of the union message, i swear on rosalynn's
  face-lifted catatonia, i wdnt lie
nixon lied, haldeman lied, dean lied, hoover
  lied hoover sucked (dicks) too
but jimmy dont, jimmy wdnt jimmy aint lying,
  must be the devil, put yr
money on the plate, must be the devil, in
  heaven we'all all be straight.
cain be rockfeller, he gave amos pootbootie a
  scholarship to Behavior
Modification Univ, and Genevieve Almoswhite
  works for his foundation
Must be niggers! Cain be Mellon, he gave
  Winky Suckass, a fellowship in
his bank put him in charge of closing out
  mortgages in the lowlife
Pittsburgh Hill nigger section, caint be him.
      (Goes on babbling, and wailing, jerking
  in pathocrazy grin stupor)
Yessuh, yessuh, yessuh, yessuh, yessuh, yes-
  suh, yessuh, yessuh, yessuh, yessuh,
put yr money in the plate, dont be late, dont
  have to wait, you gonna be in
heaven after you die, you gon get all you need
  once you gone, yessuh, i heard
it on *the jeffersons*, i heard it on *the rookies*,
  I swallowed it
whole on *roots*: wasn't it nice slavery was so
  cool and
all you had to do was wear derbies and vests
  and train chickens and buy your
way free if you had a mind to, must be the
  devil, wasnt no *white* folks,
lazy niggers chained theyselves and threw
  they own black asses in the bottom

of the boats, [(well now that you mention it King
Assblackuwasi helped throw yr ass in
the bottom of the boat, yo mamma, wife, and
    you never seed em no more)]] must
a been the devil, gimme your money put your
    money in this plate, heaven be here soon,
just got to die, just got to stop living, close yr
    eyes stop
breathin and bammm-O heaven be here, you
    have all a what you need, Bam-O
all a sudden, heaven be here, you have all you
    need, that assembly line
you work on will dissolve in thin air owowoo!
    owowoo! Just gotta die
just gotta die, this ol world aint nuthin, must be
    the devil got you
thinkin so, it cain be rockefeller, it cain be mor-
    gan, it caint be capitalism
it caint be national oppression owow! No Way!
    Now go back to work and cool
it, go back to work and lay back, just a little
    while longer till you pass
its all gonna be alright once you gone. gimme
    that last bitta silver you got
stashed there sister, gimme that dust now broth-
    er man, itll be ok on the
other side, yo soul be clean be washed pure
    white. yes. yes. yes. owow.
now go back to work, go to sleep, yes, go to
    sleep, go back to work, yes
owow. owow. uuuuuuuuuu, uuuuuuuuuuu,
    uuuuuuuuuuu. yes, uuuuuuu. yes.
    uuuuuuuuuu.
a men

AM/TRAK

1

Trane.
Trane.
History Love Scream Oh
Trane, Oh
Trane, Oh
Scream History Love
Trane

2

Begin on by a Philly night club
or the basement of a cullut chuhch
walk the bars my man for pay
honk the night lust of money
oh
blow-
scream history love

Rabbit, Cleanhead, Diz
Big Maybelle. Trees in the shining night forest

Oh
blow
love, history

Alcohol we submit to thee
3x's consume our lives
our livers quiver under yr poison hits
eyes roll back in stupidness
The navy, the lord, niggers,
the streets
all converge a shitty symphony
of screams
  to come
  dazzled invective
Honk Honk Honk, "I am here

to love
it." Let me be fire-mystery
air feeder beauty."

Honk
Oh
scream—Miles
comes.

3

Hip band alright
sum up life in the slick
street part of the
world, oh,
blow,
if you cd
nigger
man

Miles wd stand back and negative check
oh, he dug him—Trane
But Trane clawed at the limits of cool
slandered sanity
with his tryin to be born
raging
shit
    Oh
    blow,
yeh go do it
honk, scream
uhuh yeh—history
        love
        blue clipped moments
        of intense feeling.
"Trane you blows too long."
Screaming niggers drop out yr solos
Bohemian nights, the "heavyweight champ"
smacked him
in the face
his eyes sagged like a spent

dick, hot vowels escaped the metal clone of his soul
fucking saxophone
tell us shit tell us tell us!

4

There was nothing left to do but
be where monk cd find him
that crazy
mother fucker
      duh duh-duh duh-duh duh
      duh duh
      duh duh-duh duh-duh duh
      duh duh
      duh duh-duh duh-duh duh
      duh duh
      duh Duuuuuuuuuhhhhhh
Can you play this shit? (Life asks
Come by and listen

& at the 5 Spot Bach, Mulatto ass Beethoven
& even Duke, who has given America its hip tongue
checked
checked
Trane stood and dug
Crazy monk's shit
Street gospel intellectual mystical survival codes
Intellectual street gospel funk modes
Tink a ling put downs of dumb shit
pink pink a cool bam groove note air breath
a why I'm here
a why I aint
 & who is you-ha-you-ha-you-ha
Monk's shit
Blue Cooper 5 Spot
was the world busting
on piano bass drums & tenor

This was Coltrane's College. A Ph motherfuckin d
sitting at the feet, elbows
& funny grin

Of Master T Sphere
too cool to be a genius
he was instead
Thelonious
with Comrades Shadow
on tubs, lyric Wilbur
who hipped us to electric futures
& the monster with the horn.

5

From the endless sessions
money lord hovers oer us
capitalism beats our ass
dope & juice wont change it
Trane, blow, oh scream
yeh, anyway.

There then came down in the ugly streets of us
inside the head & tongue
of us
a man
black blower of the now
The vectors from all sources — slavery, renaissance
bop charlie parker,
nigger absolute super-sane screams against reality
course through him
AS SOUND!
"Yes, it says
this is now in you screaming
recognize the truth
recognize reality
& even check me (Trane)
who blows it
Yes it says
Yes &
Yes again   Convulsive multi orgasmic
              Art
              Protest

& finally, brother, you took you were

(are we gathered to dig this?
electric wind find us finally
on red records of the history of ourselves)

The cadre came together
the inimitable 4 who blew the pulse of then, exact
The flame the confusion the love of
whatever the fuck there was
   to love
Yes it says
blow, oh honk-scream (bahhhhhhh - wheeeeeeee)

(If Don Lee thinks I am imitating him in this poem,
this is only payback for his imitating me — we
are brothers, even if he is a backward cultural nationalist
motherfucker — Hey man only socialism brought by revolution
can win)
              Trane was the spirit of the 60's
              He was Malcolm X in New Super Bop Fire
              Baaahhhhh
              Wheeeeeee . . . Black Art!!!
Love
History
   On The Bar Tops of Philly
in the Monkish College of *Express*
in the cool Grottoes of Miles Davis Funnytimery
Be
Be
Be reality
Be reality alive in motion in flame to change (You Knew It!)
                        to change!!
            (All you reactionaries listening
            Fuck you, Kill you
           · get outta here!!!)
Jimmy Garrison, bass, McCoy Tyner, piano, Captain Marvel Elvin
on drums, the number itself — the precise saying
all of it in it afire aflame talking saying being doing meaning

Meditations
Expressions
A Love Supreme
(I lay in solitary confinement, July 67

Tanks rolling thru Newark
& whistled all I knew of Trane
my knowledge heartbeat
& he was *dead*
they
said.

And yet last night I played *Meditations*
& it told me what to do
Live you crazy mother
fucker!
Live!
  & organize
  yr shit
  as rightly
  burning!

What Was the Relationship of the Lone Ranger to the Means of Production?

A PLAY IN ONE ACT

WHAT WAS THE RELATIONSHIP OF THE LONE RANGER TO THE MEANS OF PRODUCTION was first performed at the Yenan Theatre Workshop of the Anti-Imperialist Union, New York City, in June 1979.

Original Cast: Taylor Mead, Ngoma

Directed by Amiri Baraka

Characters

DONNA, worker in Colonel Motors

REG, worker in Colonel Motors

CLARK, worker in Colonel Motors

TUFFY, labor bureaucrat in union in Colonel Motors

MM, a person who is at first unknown

FELIPE, a worker in Colonel Motors

WORKERS in Colonel Motors

POLICE

REG. Hey, [*To his* CO-WORKERS] there's a man with a mask walking towards us!

CLARK. What the fuck is that . . . is he, at? Maaaaan . . . way out.

DONNA. Yow, it's the lone frigging ranger or who else that hip???

REG. Hip? maybee, you betta check him. Ras say they don't let yr ass in the country wit no mask.

DONNA. Naw, you probably be in there already . . .

[*All laugh. The* MASKED MAN *walks slowly directly towards them.* HE *clean, with a blue pinstriped, chalk and red stripes, suit. A cigar,* HE *smoke when he want to, a cane and homburg held in one hand.* HE *is not smiling. Remember. It is a grimace of the explorer walked here to your house through miles of shit, and things* HE *killed. Bats, toads, monkeys, shit* HE *ate to, like, survive, a grimace*]

MASKED MAN. [*Calling as* HE *walks*] Yoo! Yoo! Friends. Americans. Co Workers. Co Woikers. Co Blowed Minds.

CLARK. Co Stompers. Co Whompers. Co Parachuters. Naw. Co Beboppers! Co Freakers! Co Hustlers. [*Does a step*]

MASKED MAN. Co Cos [*Laughs*] yeh, uh, yes, CoCos Co Co-Co's. I'm approaching in the new age. Post strike post strife, post worker post revolutionary post angry post nastyshit . . . I'm approaching [*A brief stop, turn, quickly makes a humping prayer motion*] Thank you Marcuse, CPUSA, Jesse Jackson, NAACP, all who urge righteous moderation!

REG. [*Assembly line begins whizzing by*] Hey the break's over, the line's moving. I didn't hear no bell. Everybody else still out on break too!

CLARK. Wasn't no bell. These motherfuckers brains witherin up.

MASKED MAN. Don't fret. There wasn't any bell because we know you sense when the line's moving. We've inter-rhythmed! We've cofucked, y'all [*A drawled implication*]

DONNA. What? [*Checking him*] Damn!

MASKED MAN. I said. We know the connection is complete. The final interbleeding interfeeling interknowing between us. [*Like dirty sex proposition*] That we are one. Y'all and I or You all and us. [*Shows pictures of other masked men*] These are my bros and sistoos. We together. [*Snaps fingers*]

DONNA. The shit you talk—Together.

REG. Well come on—together-ness—the line's moving. [WORKERS *at it*] If you together, wherever your spot is, you betta start humpin sho nuff. This line moving faster than before.

DONNA. They gonna work us to death now they fired that buncha people last week.

CLARK. Times hard. You oughta be glad you got yr gig.

MASKED MAN. [*All the time line's moving* HE *posturing, like* HE *going to work, but* HE *actually turns it into a dance*] Ah, yes bright youth. Yout! [*Smiles*] You got it [*Whirls. Japanese accent*] iss true. All kinds cheap steel get in country. [*Changes*] Kraut cars. Japmobiles. Lucky. Lucky. Lucky!!! [*Bounces*] Lucky Lucky Lucky you are is to have has a job gig slave.

DONNA. What're you sposed to be Mr? I don't see Assbreath the super over here whining, so you must be part of the accepted ass environment.

REG. In a top hat and mask? The union send you?

CLARK. Advertising for the union picnic? Tryin to scare us into payin dues? Is that Bath Tub Tuffy the union rep in that get up? [*Checks*] Looks like it . . . uh not really.

REG. Mr. Tuffy—on the floor?

DONNA. Huh. Tuffy wdnt set foot near work of any kind. He claims it's unprincipled.

MASKED MAN. Just think about me as yr friend and guardian. As for Tuffy he is yr friend and guardian? That's two! I am yr friend and Guardian One. Capeesh?

DONNA. And a who are is am a you?

MASKED MAN. Public Relations!

CLARK. Public Relations?

DONNA. How's that?

MASKED MAN. Uh, better. Company-Employee relations.

REG. Why the get-up?

MASKED MAN. [*Grinning but slightly annoyed*] It's no get-up—uh, lads. It's my road uniform [*Dry laugh*] Ha Ha! At home I've a different set of threads. [*Blanches*] But wait this is home, a part of it, the workshop. There used to be a time when there was more contrast between Home and away.

[WORKERS *busy on line*]

DONNA. Mad stuff! Hey man're you for real? Company-Employee Relations?

MASKED MAN. Yes I'm here to help.

REG. The best way you could help wd be to get on this line.

DONNA. [*Looking at him closely*] A masked man? Where's Tonto?

MASKED MAN. [*Looking suddenly rather sheepish*] Ton-to? [*Looks off feigning sadness*] Yes, Tonto. Yes.

[WORKERS *looking at each other*]

CLARK. [*Aside*] What's with this dude.

MASKED MAN. I can explain about Tonto. You see hostile Indians killed him. You know the kind . . . Geronimo, Crazy Horse and that Bunch. I had a deep love for Tonto . . . he was my main negotiator . . . and friend. He helped me cool out more bad scenes . . . really. [HE *looks like* HE *could cry if* HE *knew how*]

REG. You mean Tonto is dead?

MASKED MAN. [*Head hung sad-like*] Yes . . . Tonto was a very advanced Indian you know. He could explain about the reservations so thoroughly. We've got a few boys now who can run it about the African problem. Various up and coming chiefs. The blacks have a few trouble makers too ya know.

DONNA. Who are you, mister?

MASKED MAN. You can call me MM.

REG. MM . . . what's that stand for?

MASKED MAN. It could be Masked Man . . .

CLARK. This guy talks wacky. . . . [*Looking around*] Why don't Tuffy show.

DONNA. The guy is from management, in that get-up. He's an owner. MM stands for masked man, alright.

MASKED MAN. It could, but my friends call me mmmmm, for sweet.

REG. Who are you, mister, you must be with management otherwise they'd toss you out. No visitors or strangers on the plant floor.

MASKED MAN. My real name is Money's Master.

DONNA. Of course, and Masked Man too, and mmmm because we in the united snakes and bourgeois ideology dressed up sweetlike.

MASKED MAN. [*At mention of bourgeois,* MASKED MAN *turns suddenly*] Bourgeois? What? How dare you? Do you know who I am?

CLARK. Tell us . . . I don't understand why the foreman or union rep don't come over here and look you up and down.

REG. He wd be management straight out just come from a late/early banquet except for the mask . . .

DONNA. He's trying to tell us something . . .

CLARK. Like what?

DONNA. That we can see their real Face and not be put off by illusions [*To* MASKED MAN] Money's Master. An owner. Not a slave.

MASKED MAN. An owner . . . [*Puffing slightly over the "bourgeois"*] . . . yes even bourgeois . . . young lady I don't mind the name, I know the game, whatever you call me it's still the same . . . MM is me. I.

REG. This a publicity stunt?

MASKED MAN. No, the young lady's right . . . I'm an owner, *the* owner. I'm a collective spirit.

DONNA. Collective . . . ? A class spirit. This is your factory?

MASKED MAN. Of course, but forgive me, you wanted to know about the mask.

DONNA. I got it figured. You're trying to tell us something. Robbers wear masks, the inquisition, the klan . . .

MASKED MAN. Also superheroes, my good woman. [*To the* GROUP] By the way, don't slow down. I'm here to relax you, to give you something . . . gifts, tokens, badges of honor, gold booty for you . . . [*Loud*] You're American workers! American Workers. [*Draws it out*] And I am your leader, your guide, your spiritual father. I wear the mask for the same reason Batman, Robin, Captain America, Spider Man and so many other superheroes wear the mask, to hide my identity from evil doers.

REG. Hey what's with this dude?

CLARK. Sound like he got a warped gourd. Head screwed on backwards, like in the Omen.

MASKED MAN. You liked the Omen?

CLARK. It was alright.

DONNA. [*Holding her nose*] Metaphysical claptrap. Bloody religious spook story. Economic crisis in the U.S. now the rulers want to send us off into thinking about monsters and goblins. Sex, police, money, metaphysics and nostalgia. Anything but how to change things.

MASKED MAN. A great flick. Did you like Jaws 1 and 2, Omen 2, all Clint Eastwood films, Deathwish . . . great films. I helped make those great pictures. If you look carefully in almost all scenes my initials are spelled out in the speeches, on the furniture, slobber coming out of the dead people's mouth. M-M.

REG. What is this an in-plant gig to get our minds off our wage demands. Where's the whiskey, and dope?

MASKED MAN. [*Oblivious to them*] You see, Tonto left me . . . but I cd replace him easy . . . but he was bright . . . He cd have been the first colored UN ambassador from this country . . . before Amos' walking buddy in there now.

DONNA. Oh, man . . .

CLARK. The dude looks crazy . . . He says he owns this factory . . . and he walking around like a circus reject, crazy as a bedbug.

DONNA. Bedbugs suck blood.

CLARK. Can't no crazy people run no big factories like this.

REG. Man, look around you, that's exactly who's running it, this death hole. No safety, speedups all the time, layoffs.

DONNA. Yeh, but don't go for the crazy bit . . . crazy in the sense that what they're doing is gonna fail . . . exploiting all these people . . .

MASKED MAN. [*Wheels around*] Ex-ploiting . . . now wait just a minute . . . [*Remembers his goodwill mission*] ahh . . . ahhh now, yes, just a minute . . . you see you misunderstand us Money Masters. You have a job because of us, MM and his class mates. It is the MM's of the world and there's not a hell of a lot of us . . . who create the jobs for people like you. [*Brightens*] But we love it . . . love to do it . . . love to help you.

REG. Well then help us, we've laughed a bunch now help us. First thing I want, first help I want's a raise? Can you deal with it?

MASKED MAN. I thought you'd never ask . . . that's what I'm about . . . that's exactly why I'm here, to give you, you all, a much needed raise!

CLARK. So we don't have to strike huh?

MASKED MAN. Strike? That doesn't solve anything.

REG. Talk on the raise mister . . . what're yall talking about?

DONNA. Raise? I gotta hear this.

MASKED MAN. And well you should. I have come to show you how to be raised, to give you a raise in spirit.

REG. What?

DONNA. [Laughing] Yeh . . .

CLARK. Man, what the fuck, scuse the expression, you talking about. A raise in spirit. Whatta you Rev. Ike or somebody like that?

DONNA. Must be . . . a raise in spirit . . . huh.

MASKED MAN. Wait, before you grow cynical . . . hear me out.

DONNA. Hey man, my spirit can only get as raised as my material conditions. Right now my spirit is urban innercity ghetto stretched out, huh, my spirit's in hock, and the part of it that's not is tied to this damned machine. Are you some kind of clown, labor psychologists tell you to walk around the plant depressing the workers . . . cause you damn sure can't cheer none up with the bullshit you belching.

CLARK. Oh you sposed to cheer us up, make us laugh . . . well you was funny except that last shit drug the hell outta me for one.

MASKED MAN. Money is not everything.

DONNA. Well give yours to us then!

MASKED MAN. If you understand how important the work is yr doing, then you'll be filled up with that pride of accomplishment.

DONNA. Why? We don't even own these machines. We don't own nothing but bills. Mister why are you here talking shit, it's bad enough we got to work, but we do not want to listen to and be distracted by no unfunny non-clown clowns.

REG. Ditto.

MASKED MAN. You have a stake in this system.

REG. What system?

MASKED MAN. The free enterprise system! You're free. You can do anything, go anywhere, because you live in a free society . . . you can't have this much freedom in a totalitarian country like—

DONNA. Crown Heights, South Bronx, Newark, Lower East Side, for instance.

MASKED MAN. Ahh that's just cynicism . . . you need really to have yr spirits raised Miss. We can't have that cynicism running loose in here. You make ten dollars an hour, a fantastic salary, same as the men.

DONNA. Yeh, but in the same hour I help make you five hundred thousand dollars. Plus got to give you the ten back the minute I get outta here.

REG. Groceries, rent, auto payments, clothes . . . all to the money masters huh?

DONNA. Ten dollars an hour . . . his boy the philanderer Henry Ford II makes only two dollars an hour . . . but two dollars an hour clear profit on each worker he owns. Two hundred thousand workers, that's four hundred thousand an hour clear profit.

CLARK. Philanderer?

REG. Womanizer.

DONNA. Male Chauvinist is more like it . . . and that bastard never done any real work in his life. Got people going down in the coal mines, tophatted white shirt wearing dudes snatching the wealth from the people who spend half their lives under the ground digging coal. Then while we working winter summer, six days a week, ten hrs a day. Dudes like our man here layin up in Bermuda, or Cannes or somewhere slick . . . rollin in dough that we made for them.

REG. True—but what is the gimmick with this dude tippin around in here?

MASKED MAN. Young lady, you're hardly being fair. You don't know anything about me.

DONNA. You said you own this factory . . . if that's true I know your class . . .

MASKED MAN. My class?? Now come on, you know in America there is no class system. Here we're all equal.

REG. Well how come you not working then . . . humpin at this machine?

MASKED MAN. I'm doing my job now, raising yr spirits—it's also sometimes called character guidance.

CLARK. So no raise just some more bullshittin. What kinda car you drive mister MM?

MASKED MAN. I don't drive, personally, my driver drives a modest Bentley to spread me around the place.

CLARK. I gotta chevy, to spread me around this factory and back home. Gotta have it too, public transportation closes down after you go back and forth to work. Excuse me, let me see your hands Mister.

MASKED MAN. You going to tell my fortune?

CLARK. Damn, smooth as a baby's behind . . . whatever work you doin mister its pretty slick.

MASKED MAN. The USA is still growing — expanding — The American Century goes on [*Snide aside*] contrary to the newspaper sensationalism of the mercantile interests. You all . . . all even the lowliest . . . the blackest the reddest the yellowest the brownest . . . all even we the whitest . . . all have a place in it.

DONNA. Korea, Vietnam, Cambodia, Guinea Bissau, Mozambique.

[MASKED MAN *shrinks like* HE *is being whipped*]

MASKED MAN. Cruel sensationalism. [*Leaping in the air*] We are still rrrricher than anybody!

[TUFFY *the union rep appears,* HE *is dressed like a "poor"* MASKED MAN, *cheaper versions of everything* MASKED MAN *has on*]

MASKED MAN. Ahh, here's my man, yr leader, stalwart Tuffy. He'll have some further clarifying word. What's the word friend Tuff?

TUFFY. [*Like Ojays*] Money-Money-Moneeeeeeee. [HE *is pushing wheelbarrow with a dead person in it under a tarp. As* HE *speaks* HE *unceremoniously dumps the body next to the machines*] Don't fuck with God! Niggers spicks greasers slanteyes broads all eat shit. You play you pay. America the beautiful, vote fusion and for god sakes no strike.

[WORKERS *look at the body, and at* TUFFY *and* MASKED MAN]

REG. Hey, a body what the hell's going on.

TUFFY. Instruction day friend woiker. (Hear my working class accent???) I'm your leader.

DONNA. You don't even want us to strike, misleader sounds more real . . . now killer out front . . . what's wrong with this dude you dropping on the floor . . . this is a crazy ass place alright . . .

CLARK. A dead man on the plant floor? What the hell is going on?

MASKED MAN. [*Laughs and snaps fingers*] Life has its lessons, and if you learn them you prosper, if you don't, still on the floor, or booted out the door?

DONNA. Or become a bureaucrat whore.

[The WORKERS *move to look at the dead body*]

REG. What's going on madass Tuffy now? What're you all crazy?

MASKED MAN. It's coming it's coming, be patient.

DONNA. What's coming . . . you murdering workers out in the open now??

TUFFY. We want to explain the game full up. We want you to know what side your bread is buttered on, or what side your butter is breaded on.

MASKED MAN. And so today we will reveal the totality of our establishment. Its grime and its rime. Its beauty and its booty.

TUFFY. This is undoubtedly the best system in the world.

DONNA. Capitalism and Racism you mean, women's oppression . . .

TUFFY. Whatever you call it . . . the rule of the cool is more like it. [*Aside to* MASKED MAN] Hey, chiefie, this broad sounds like a lefty . . . [*Sd in a dopey singsong*]

MASKED MAN. Don't call me Chiefie . . . Go on with yr demo Tuffy. I do the the-inkking around here.

TUFFY. No offense intended Chief . . . but watch it . . .

MASKED MAN. Go on!

DONNA. What kind of foolishness you guys running, you're even interrupting production, and I know you don't want to do that.

MASKED MAN. No, no, no we're not doing that. [*Like Bert Lahr*] We're not lady . . . we're raising yr, giving you, the spiritual food.

TUFFY. Yeh. [*Giggles*] yer gettin yer raise . . . for days . . .

CLARK. Whatta we crazy or you crazy . . . I never seen nothing like this during work hours, somea those union meetings come on nearabout like it tho, come to think about it . . .

DONNA. I'm interested in why you got this dead man in here.

TUFFY. To tell you the truth ahh troot . . . times is getting harder . . . very hard out there now . . . very hard. Jobs hard to come by.

MASKED MAN. MMMMMMMMMM [Smiling] indeed, indeed.

REG. Indeed? What's going on?

TUFFY. [Pacing, mock serious] Jobs, jobs, jobs, it's what our world lives by alright. And there's few of 'em, alright. Few of em . . .

MASKED MAN. MMMMMMMM [Smiling as before] indeed, indeed ., . .

REG. What's with this indeed? I knew I shdn't have gone for this overtime. Factory get a little deserted all kinds of ghosts and monsters come out.

DONNA. Yeh . . . whatta you dudes want . . . and why's this man dead?

TUFFY. You see there's no more jobs anywhere . . . [Sudden frenzy] None! none! [To DONNA] And don't let these commie bastids bullshit ya there's no jobs nowhere no more. Not in russia china or greasball coon fantasies of everybody bein equal bullshit.

REG. Tuffy you gonna get yr ass broke off and set afire you keep up with the nasty language, you hear?

DONNA. Russia is not a socialist country if that's why you mentioned it. It's the same shit going on there as here. Ghouls own the tools. And the people got nothin but a hard way to go.

MASKED MAN. Tuffy, Tuffy, will you go ahead with the presentation? I shd've done it myself . . .

TUFFY. [*Aside*] Yrself?? But chief you know I got to give the presentation because I'm a, scuse the expression, woiker like them dem. Right?

MASKED MAN. [*Looks drugged*] It sounds scientific . . . and don't think it's a rip off [*At audience*] it works too. And when you give the presentation tuf-guy think of the great ones of yr ilk, the great bribereenies of the past & present—and you can take yr place in the future . . . MEANY [*Looks ecstatic*] WOODCOCK.

TUFFY. MILLER, [*Does pirouette, spin*] REUTHER, [*Louder, more animated*] JOHN L. LEWIS.

MASKED MAN. [*An ecstatic peak*] SAMUEL H. GOMPERS!!!

TUFFY. [*Sweating and moved*] Yeh, Yeh, Yeh, Yeh, Yeh, I can do it Chief I can. Check me out right now.

[*Whirls . . .* WORKERS *standing staring with mixture of un-belief and cynicism*]

You woikers, Listen. Listen, I've got the word. I'm gonna raise yr spirits and tell you the troot, at the same time. Call me Archie Bunker if it makes you feel better.

MASKED MAN. Nice, nice . . . [*Beaming, cupping his hand around his mouth*]

TUFFY. You all, and all of us here, together . . . get that . . . to-gether, we're really lucky as hell lucky as blazes lucky as the dickens well we're very very lucky to be amuricans . . . lucky as shit lucky as pizza pie eatin lucky luciano lucky lucky lucky, to be amuricans. [*Hands up like tricky dick*] I hope you under-stand. I hope that's perfectly clear how fuckin lucky we are. Get it?? Get it?

DONNA. No [*Joined by* OTHERS] Nooo, you're drunk probably you acting crazier than usual.

REG. You always go out like this on the overtime shift? You won't catch me on this number again if I can help it.

CLARK. Yeh, but you can't help it, they want our ass for overtime we in overtime.

TUFFY. Right.

MASKED MAN. Well said my backward friend. Go on Tuffy.

TUFFY. Luck-keeee, that's the name of our game. Lucky to be in this great country. Lucky to be allowed in here some of us . . . my people were lowly potato pickin irish immigrants and look at me, baby look at me, now. Me and the Kennedys and John Wayne really made it big. Yeh. All courtesy of MM and his class mates.

[MM *bows modestly*]

And you greasers . . . [*A beer can flies past his head*] Excuse me, I didn't mean that, you PRs and Mexs you guys know you wdna hada chance to get through the gates, poor starving bastids, you wdna hadda chance except MM here, and kind word on yr behalf from yrs truly! We have to drag tons of greaseballs back across the rio grande tryin to sneak in here and take all the jobs every day.

DONNA. Sneak in where . . . California, Arizona, New Mexico, Texas is Chicano land.

TUFFY. [*In dopey singsong aside to* MM] A lef-ty. I'm tellin you boss! But listen to reason mates. You woogies . . .

REGGIE. [*Goes in his pocket and comes out with a blade which* HE *flicks open behind his back*] I told you . . .

TUFFY. I didn't mean it . . . you cullid guys you cullid people MM brought you from where? [*Shrinks up in gesture of extreme disgust*] Africa! Geez, think of it, the freakin dark continent, savages and shit.

REG. [*Moves forward*] God damn it.

TUFFY. Wait wait.

MASKED MAN. Please my good man don't get upset. Tuffy tends to be overly dramatic.

DONNA. Tuffy tends to be a racist, he always going around spreading those kind of bourgeois lies among us . . . that's part of his goddamn job.

REG. Yeh, well he gon lose parta his goddamn ass about it.

MASKED MAN. Wait, wait. [*Perturbed*] Tuffy come here, let me speak to you.

TUFFY. Yeh boss.

MASKED MAN. Look, you've got to be more subtle with your characterizations [*Whispers*] true tho they may be — discretion is the soul of valor.

TUFFY. Friends I'm sorry I've offended some of youse [*Looks over his shoulder for* MM's *approval*] check the language boss?? I'm sorry if I've offended some of you or somea youse — insert correct answer where indicated — But all I was tryin to say in my crude but innocent (wow!) fashion is that we've got to love MM. We've got to love MM.

[MM *does sex dance*]

We've got to love MM.

MASKED MAN. MMMMMMMMMMMMMM love me, love me, love me . . .

TUFFY. We've got to love MM because because because MM LOVES US yes. That's it now all repeat after me.

[*Only* CLARK *begins and then is stopped by* DONNA's *look. But* TUF *and* MM *shout as loud as* THEY *can*]

TUFFY AND MASKED MAN. WE'VE GOT TO LOVE MM BECAUSE MM LOVES US! WE'VE GOT TO LOVE MM BECAUSE MM LOVES US! WE'VE GOT TO LOVE MM BECAUSE MM LOVES US!

TUFFY. [THEY *are sweating and puffing*] You see how easy it is? All of us have got to develop a deep love for MM . . . because MM loves us and does so much for us. He brought us all here from backward places because he wanted us to make progress. He wanted to teach us to read and write. He wanted to give us culture and religion. He wanted to teach us to speak proper.

[MM *meanwhile is going through sex dance and alternating like highly moral xtian preacher figure*]

DONNA. If MM loves us so much why does he wear a mask?

MASKED MAN. What? What is she saying?

TUFFY. Mask? What Mask. MM don't wear no mask, you must be kidding. That's just a shadow from his hat.

DONNA. What? Where am I the crazy house? Is this really Colonel Motors or did I get a contact high when I took my kid to school this morning and walked through those halls?

TUFFY. MM does not wear a mask!

REG. What're you wastin our time with this bullshit now for Tuffy? The guy told us he wears a mask because he was like Superman and Spiderman a superhero. And first of all we see the fuckin mask so what's the bullshit?

MASKED MAN. I do not wear a mask I was humoring you with intellectual stimulation. I was reciting a highart poem. No wonder you don't understand it. I'll refrain in the future.

CLARK. [*Frowning*] Mask?

DONNA. Clark will you please stop fooling around.

[CLARK *screws up face*]

REG. Brother you got trouble seeing or you looking for some stale crumbs in your 8 year old sears roebuck refrigerator?

CLARK. I see it, for a second it didn't look like he had one on, really. It just looked like a shadow, really.

DONNA. I don't care about this dumb shit you all talking, you come in here with a body and then start rantin and ravin about how lucky we are. Who is that dead dude and why's he here?

MASKED MAN. Tuffy!

TUFFY. He's dead because he cdn't get a job so he killed hisself. Shot hisself in the personnel office. No jobs anywhere, nowhere in the world. So he's suffering, cdn't take it, so he killed hisself. Never seen nuthin like it before. He stood up and strangled himself to death.

REG. Strangled himself? What?

DONNA. I don't wanna hear that. Hey you all we need to get to the bottom of this. We need to get some more workers over here and find out just what's happening.

TUFFY. No, no, you have to hear the special presentation all by yr-selves.

MASKED MAN. It's best you hear the presentation together alone to-gether and alone. Everything always sounds better in isolation, remember that. Other people just confuse the issues.

TUFFY. Right Chief. And besides all those others who stayed out on break have been sent home.

REG. Sent home.

TUFFY. Yeh, yeh, let's say it's a temporary layoff. No more strikes. No more bullshit, no more nothin, but good clean honest work. Work work work overtime over over time and over over over over time. That's our goal more work, we gotta stay ahead of the com-mies, the krauts, the japs, the frogs, all of em, we gotta stay ahead and it means work. Woik for the american way. You remember when we added that to the Jack Armstrong promos, "he fights for truth justice and the american way"?

DONNA. Make sense Tuf. We're the only ones here?

MASKED MAN. MMMMMMMMMM Quaint isn't it. A new, so to speak, order . . . speak on it Tuffy lad.

TUFFY. Yeh, we taking some time, because there's no more jobs and we gotta get more work. We takin some time for a special character guidance. A special orientating session with THE NEW AGREES.

REG. Agrees?

TUFFY. Yeh, we givin out new agrees. New point of unity, a whole new contract for labor and management.

MASKED MAN. A whole new—uhh relationship!

DONNA. What? Make sense.

TUFFY. This is sense . . . We've selected you all to lead the way, because from now on [*An eruption of menace in his voice*] absolutely no work without a pledge to uphold the new agrees!

DONNA. What?

TUFFY. And so now, all over the industry we have management-labor leader teams getting smart cookies like yrselves to sign the agrees, make the first move to insure the new harmony between labor and management.

MASKED MAN. You see for too long there's been strife between us, but ultimately we have the same interests [*Tearfully*] to make this country a great place in which to live.

TUFFY. Right?

CLARK. Is that right, we have the same interests?

TUFFY. Right!

DONNA. Wrong.

TUFFY. This is the new détente!

MASKED MAN. [*Dancing*] Buy it buy it buy it! It's real! Peace in our time!

TUFFY. The New Agrees!

[REGGIE *begins laughing, almost doubling over*]

DONNA. Reg, it's not funny . . . as sick and silly as this shit seems, it's real.

[*A* POLICEMAN *is wandering slowly on the set from one side*]

TUFFY. Point one—MM is always right!

DONNA. Far Right!

TUFFY. And what he and his class mates do is done for the good of all of us! [*To* WORKERS] Cheer!

DONNA. Bullshit!

TUFFY. Point two. Tuffy and his Bribereenoes are the true servants of MM & company, and as such are the true leaders and benevolent hard-working brothers of workers everywhere. Cheer!

REG. Doublebullshit!

TUFFY. Point three. Working for MM is great and under no circumstances will we jeopardize this by complaining, bitching, or striking. Anyone urging these madnesses will be pointed out by all of us, isolated and fired for the common good!

DONNA. Yr crazy!

CLARK. Is this shit for real? They mean this?

DONNA. Yeh they mean it. It seem crazy? It is crazy. This whole thing, the whole society don't have to be this way. These money freaks run everything, got the world sick and crazy like this, like those weird pictures in the museums with 3 eyes and twisted up heads . . . that's them—that dead spooky music you hear in there is running through their brains. Dracula runs this country and that's Frankenstein bullshitting us right now.

TUFFY. That broad has got to shut up boss. She was a bad choice. Not that I'm against women. But . . . fucking bitches all they got is big mouths and complaints. We shdnta hired her in the first place. A cunt's place is on her back in the sack with a hard joint jammed up in her.

DONNA. Go to hell!

TUFFY. Point four. Woman's place is in the sack on her back with an erect penis inserted where appropriate. Post this, her place is in the crib minding the issue of such union. Hooray for the ERA!

DONNA. Go to hell. I don't have to stay around for such bullshit!

MASKED MAN. No, you don't . . . right you are . . . you have some rights . . . [Laughs nasty]

[DONNA thinks again about it. Another COP drifts slowly on scene, stands in background trying to be unobtrusive]

TUFFY. Point five. Coloreds, Mex's, PR's, Slants, Blanket Heads, All must make slightly less than the chump change paid to white workers.

REG. Fuck you.

MASKED MAN. Shut up and listen, it's for your own good!

DONNA. Bullshit!

TUFFY. Point six. Bourgeois Democracy has not worked well enough!

CLARK AND DONNA. What?

TUFFY. And so we must retreat for a short period . . . to a sterner form, a more gutsy style of government. Do-What-We-Say-Ism or as it is sometimes called Straight-Out-Ism where no one has to worry about choices—there is only one choice, ours.

DONNA. It's always been like that.

TUFFY. Oh no . . .

MASKED MAN. [*Miffed*] Fucking-a-tweety it has . . . But now it's straight out!!! We won't have this . . . this truculence. What we do we do for your benefit.

TUFFY. For our benefit!

CLARK. Our benefit?

REG. Clark will you wise up and stop taking this dope??

MASKED MAN. MMMMMMMMMMMM [*Mock smile*] for your benefit!

TUFFY. Point seven. Commies are poison and there is no such thing as socialism. Anyone talking that shit, thinking that shit, looking like talking like or smelling like a commie must be isolated and liquidated for the common good.

DONNA. You got the camps open yet Mr. Masked Man? Looks like you finally taking off your mask.

MASKED MAN. I told you I didn't have on a mask. Now you're beginning to understand.

DONNA. Like I said Dracula and the 30 vampires, you all run it all.

MASKED MAN. You don't understand . . .

DONNA. Whatta you holding us in here hostages while you got the rest of the workers locked out? Is that what's really happening?

TUFFY. Hostage??

MASKED MAN. Too dramatic my dear. Much too dramatic.

TUFFY. We know you all are a cross section of all the guys and dolls in this joint.

DONNA. Not really.

MASKED MAN. Really . . . the really backward are already with

Us . . . or the really advanced, however you choose to look at it . . . you see we present both sides.

TUFFY. We are making peace and prosperity for everyone, and we want you to join in the leadership . . .

DONNA. Have you finished with the agrees. Can we go?

TUFFY. Go? You haven't finished yr shift. You haven't said either what you think of the agrees.

REG. You haven't heard all the constructive criticism we been giving you guys. Like bullshit and go to hell. Fuck you was in it too I believe.

MASKED MAN. [*Hissing*] She told you one thing right, this is no laughing matter. There are no more jobs, either sign up with us or go starve.

[TUF *laughs almost uncontrollably*]

CLARK. If we sign those agrees what do we get?

TUFFY. You get to work . . . you get a steady slave my friend, a guaranteed income. Dignity. Prosperity for you and your families. All the things you need and rightfully demand. Those are the agrees. And I've got the contracts where you can sign on the dotted line.

MASKED MAN. Our little cross section.

DONNA. And the dead worker there. Shot, strangled . . . murdered by you.

MASKED MAN. Died of a broken heart, because he wasn't intelligent enough to sign the agrees. That hurt him so badly. Something burst within his head.

DONNA. [*Begins to move toward the body*] Who is this . . .

MASKED MAN. Yes, go ahead look . . .

DONNA. Aggghh. [*In horror*] It's Felipe . . .

REG. Felipe . . . goddamn, what bullshit you all talking here, Felipe didn't die of no goddam broken heart . . .

DONNA. A bullet in the center of his head.

MASKED MAN. Really? MMMMMMM things are getting serious . . .

TUFFY. We know you and this guy Felipe are around in this plant to upset things to organize the sweet workers against their own interests.

MASKED MAN. There were 3 of you in this section of the shop right . . . One we know is the woman. I'd make a guess and say the other is you sir. [*Pointing at* REGGIE]

REG. Whatta you talking about? You killed Felipe motherfucker you deserve to die. [HE *leaps at* TUFFY]

TUFFY. Hey Hey.

[*The* POLICEMEN *now run forward with guns drawn*]

DONNA. Reggie, cool it, this is just provocation . . . You bastids wanna accuse us of anything just do it. But dragging dead bodies around and the rest of the mad shit going on you can can all that. We ain't going for it. Let us out of here. It's after hours.

TUFFY. And the agrees?

REG. Fuck you and Fuck MM and Fuck the agrees, sabe??

MASKED MAN. Yes Kemosabe. I sabe. [*Looks off*] It all reminds me of how the last battle with my old companion went down . . . we were surrounded, backed up to the edge of Mass Line Canyon. Bullets whizzing around us, and flame tipped arrows. We battled down to our last ammunition, and suddenly Tonto was gone. [HE *is crouching as if firing . . . we hear war cries whoops and hollers now rising*] Tonto, I sd, Tonto, we're surrounded . . . but help is on the way . . . help is on the way good friend . . . and then he reminded me that I was the Lone Ranger, that there was no help, that I was a lonely superpower whose destiny was . . . was [*As if* HE *cannot bear to remember*]

[*Suddenly rising off the floor, in the midst of the fantasy with the lights dimming just slightly to give off the effect of being slightly removed from reality,* FELIPE *becomes* TONTO]

FELIPE (TONTO).   . . . a lonely superpower whose destiny is doom, doom.

MASKED MAN (NOW THE LONE RANGER). But you're with me . . . I can't be lonely and I won't be doomed alone . . . you're with me . . .

FELIPE (TONTO). Me, a scared house servant about to skip out the backdoor yr honor? I won't be with you. I ain't even with myself.

MASKED MAN (THE LONE RANGER). Don't talk like that . . . we're a team . . . we work together to keep the range free for democracy.

FELIPE (TONTO). Do you know Indian history, kemo sabe. All this was ours, the Indians' . . . and you bathed us in our own blood to get it . . . Your Manifest Destiny! Even Walt Whitman went for it. And if I ain't a house servant then I'm something better, a field hand, a worker, an oppressed nationality, spawn of an oppressed nation. And if I am not a house servant, if I am not a comprador or a traitor, then I am one of the millions who right now ride out there threatening you, whose arrows and bullets whiz ever closer to your frightened ass! And then even if I am in your field or factory I plot against you, I form nuclei of scientific revolutionaries to plan your downfall, your death or imprisonment, the destruction of yr system.

MASKED MAN (THE LONE RANGER). Tonto! Tontoooo! Don't make me kill you!

FELIPE (TONTO). Adios motherfucker.

[*A shot as the lights go down*]

MASKED MAN. You see he made me kill him . . . he made me . . . I thought he was my friend, my companion . . . I wd have let him fuck my sister any time . . . or me for that matter. He cd've lived in a nice neighborhood with hip stores and a mall, street musicians and foreign films. He gave it all up.

[*Lights back up* . . . FELIPE/TONTO *is back on the floor*]

CLARK. Whew . . . some strange shit alright . . .

DONNA. And now what, you bringing on fascism cause yr shit is exposed and all the Indians, black red people, white red people, brown red people, yellow red people, red red people, they all read your shit and hate it.

TUFFY. Shutup Willya. Ya'll get a fat lip.

REG. Fuck you Bureaucrat . . . you're the real tonto, the new tonto, a bribed goddam worker living off the extra blood Dracula can drip your way . . . a white chauvinist, a male chauvinist, a goddam dull ass assistant ghoul tied up to some dying shit.

TUFFY. Sign the agrees or be with your dead friend.

CLARK. You serious? You'll kill us?

MASKED MAN. Yr friend here is very slow.

DONNA. They will.

CLARK. But why me. I go along with all this shit. I put up with all of it . . . all I want's a raise, that's all. The other bullshit, all that talk about oppression capitalism and the like I don't know from nothing. I just need more money . . . to live . . . and for my family. That's all I want mister MM that's all.

MASKED MAN. But we have no more money for you . . . in fact we're raising yr spirits so we can lower your material . . . pay-cuts all around is the order of the day.

CLARK. Whatta you mean paycut . . . Hey paycut? You kidding can't get no paycut mister . . . don't have nuthin now. Can't make it on no paycut.

TUFFY. He told you Clark. MM told you, there's no money for you . . . you've got to take a cut, you'll learn to love it just like you learned to love everything else we've done to you.

CLARK. Yeh, yeh, but mister, I need more money. I don't want to make trouble really. I really do not want to make no trouble. I go home I just want to throw my feet up and watch the ballgame, but paycut I can't go for that. I ain't no trouble maker, you know that . . . Tuffy'll tell you that . . . but I can't live with this money you givin me and I just can't make no cut . . . that's the truth.

TUFFY. The agrees. Bullshittin times over.

MASKED MAN. Yes, the agrees . . . Sign, or disappear, join yr friend old Tonto.

REG. The shit has gone that far. Straight-Out-Ism pure and simple huh? You need to grow a halfa mustache Tuffy and pull yr bangs down over one eye. You'll look great with a goosestep.

MASKED MAN. How crude. We are much more modern . . .

DONNA. Whatever you are, however you package it, you'll get yr ass kicked again and again, no matter how many times you make trouble, you'll get yr ass kicked another time for the asking, and finally one day your ass will get kicked for once and for all, and you and your class mates mister MM and you Tuffy and yr bribereenoes, will be under our gun.

TUFFY. More lefty bullshit . . . hahahahaha.

MASKED MAN. Rave on, Lady Macbeth, but remember your time is running out . . . sign or lay on the floor with Tonto . . . Sign the agrees!

TUFFY. The agrees . . . Sign.

[*Now we hear the same war cries and whoops as during the* TON-TO *segment. They are at first like the Indians attacking but later they begin to change. Another* COP *runs in the plant*]

COP. Boss Boss, the workers are back. The streets are packed with em. They got signs.

MASKED MAN. What? Tuffy . . .

TUFFY. What're you talking about . . . There were supposed to

be cops guarding the workers' neighborhoods so they cdn't leave.
Cops and troops. They promised us.

DONNA. Time's running out for who?

[The WORKERS chant "Strike, Strike, Strike, Strike . . . Free
Donna, Free Reggie, Free Clark — Free the Colonel Motors Three!
Avenge the Death of Felipe! Free the Colonel Motors Three. Strike
Strike Strike Strike Strike"]

DONNA. We're walking outta here you two, call off your goons.

REG. Yeh get outta our way . . . you coming Clark??

CLARK. You goddam right. Whatta you mean am I coming? What
I look like to you a goddam fool?

REG. No brother . . . not that . . .

TUFFY. Boss you want to kill them . . .

[MASKED MAN turns to look at the window from which the chants
are coming]

DONNA. It won't do you no good, bloodsucker, to kill us
. . . they'll always be more . . . you'll have to kill all the workers all the oppressed nationalities to get rid of the likes of us
. . . and you can't do that.

REG. Before it's over they'll kill you.

DONNA. Let us out of here, we'll come back. But when we do, it'll
be to run this place for ourselves.

MASKED MAN. And so why let you go, so you'll help lead this
mess . . . oh no . . . you'll . . .

[At this point the door bursts open and WORKERS surge into the
factory chanting "Free Donna! Free Reggie! Free Clark! Avenge the
Murder of Felipe!" The WORKERS come in, some with clubs, and
sticks, some with pistols and rifles. They stand menacing MM,
TUF and CO.]

DONNA. See you later MM and Tuffy . . . we'll see you real
soon . . . we'll be back right after we finish our party . . .

REG. Yeh, we gotta party to go to . . . party of a new type . . .

DONNA. And then we'll be back . . .

[The WORKERS rush to greet them, the cry goes back up, "Strike" . . . the POLICE, MM and TUFFY line up on one side . . . the WORKERS, DONNA, REG and CLARK on the other. Some WORKERS rush over to TONTO's body . . .]

WORKERS. Strike! Strike! Strike! Strike!

BLACKOUT

Curtain

In the Tradition

(for Black Arthur Blythe)

In 1982, Baraka had this poem privately printed. It appeared in pamphlet form, with a handsome African-inspired cover by the painter Vincent Smith. The poem was later reprinted in *The Music*, but since I consider this pamphlet to be an autonomous work, the poem appears here, reflecting its original publication date.
                                                                  —wjh

> *"Not a White Shadow*
> *But Black People*
> *Will be Victorious . . . "*

Blues walk weeps ragtime
Painting slavery
women laid around
working feverishly for slavemaster romeos
as if in ragtime they spill
their origins like chillers   (lost chillen
in the streets to be
telephoned to by Huggie
Bear from channel 7, for the White Shadow
gives advice on how to hold our homes
together, tambien tu, Chicago Hermano)

                              genius bennygoodman headmaster
                              philanthropist
                              romeos—
                              but must coach
                              cannot shoot—

                              hey coah-ch
                              hey coah-ch
                              trembling fate wrapped in flags
                              hey coah-ch
                              you can hug this
                              while you at it
                              coah-ch
Women become
goils gals grinning in the face of his
no light

Men become
boys & slimy roosters crowing negros
in love with dressed up pimp stupidity death
hey coah-ch
wanna outlaw the dunk, cannot deal with skyman darrell
or double dippin hip doctors deadly in flight
cannot deal with Magic or Kareem . . . hey coah-ch coah-ch
bench yrself in the garbagecan of history o new imperial dog
denying with lying images
our strength & African
funky beauty

      nomatter the three networks idiot chatter

            Arthur Blythe
                Says
                   it!
            in the
            tradition

                2

            Tradition
            of Douglass
            of David Walker
            Garnett
            Turner
            Tubman
            of ragers yeh
               ragers
                      (of Kings, & Counts, & Dukes
                       of Satchelmouths & SunRa's
                       of Bessies & Billies & Sassys
                       & Ma's
            Musical screaming
            Niggers
            yeh
        tradition
            of Brown Welles
            & Brown Sterling
            & Brown Clifford
            of H Rap & H Box

Black baltimore sister blues antislavery singers
                countless funky blind folks
                & oneleg country beboppers
                bottleneck in the guitarneck dudes
                whispering thrashing cakewalking raging
                ladies
                & gents
                getdown folks, elegant as
                skywriting
        tradition
                of DuBois
                Baby Dodds & Lovie
            Austin, Sojourner
            I thought I heard Buddy Bolden

                say, you're terrible
                you're awful, Lester
              why do you want to be
              the president of all this
            of the blues and slow sideways
            horn. tradition of blue presidents
          locked up in the brig for wearing zoot suit
        army pants. tradition of monks & outside dudes
 of marylous and notes hung vibrating blue just beyond just after
just before just faster just slowly twilight crazier than europe or its
racist children

                bee-doo dee doop bee-doo dee dooo doop (Arthur
                tradition
                of shooters
                & silver fast dribblers
                of real fancy motherfuckers
                fancy as birds flight, sunward/high
                            highhigh
                            sunward
                            arcs/swoops/spirals
            in the tradition
¼ notes
eighth notes
16th notes
32nds, 64ths, 128ths, silver blue
presidents

of Langston & Langston Manifestos
Tell us again about the negro artist
& the racial mountain so we will not
be negro artists, Mckay Banjoes and
Homes In Harlem, Blue Black Boys &
Little Richard Wrights, Tradition of
For My People Margaret Walker & David Walker & Jr Walker
& Walker Smith Sweet Ray Leonard Rockin in Rhythm w/
   Musical Dukes,
What is this tradition Basied on, we Blue Black Wards strugglin
against a Big White Fog, Africa people, our fingerprints are
   everywhere
on you america, our fingerprints are everywhere, Cesaire told
   you
that, our family strewn around the world has made more parts of
   that world
blue and funky, cooler, flashier, hotter, afro-cuban james
   brownier
        a wide panafrican
        world

Tho we are afro-americans, african americans
let the geographic history of our flaming hatchet motion
               hot ax motion
               hammer & hatchet

       our cotton history
       our rum & indigo
           sugar cane
           history

Yet, in a casual gesture, if its talk you want, we can say
Cesaire, Damas, Depestre, Romain, Guillen
You want Shaka, Askia, (& Roland Snellings too)
      Mandingo, Nzinga, you want us to drop
        Cleopatra on you or Hannibal
        What are you masochists
        paper iron chemistry
        & smelting
        I aint even mentioned
          Troussaint or Dessaline
          or Robeson or Ngugi

Hah, you bloody & dazed, screaming at me to stop yet,
NO, hah, you think its over, tradition song, tradition
poem, poem for us together, poem for arthur blythe
   who told us again, in the tradition
                  in the
                tradition of

      life & dying
    in the tradition of those klanned & chained
    & lynched and shockleyed and naacped and ralph bunched

hah, you rise a little I mention we also the tradition of amos and
   andy
hypnotized selling us out vernons and hooks and other nigger
   crooks of
gibsons and crouches and other assorted louses of niggers that
   turn from
gold to shit proving dialectics muhammad ali style
But just as you rise up to gloat I scream COLTRANE! STEVIE
   WONDER!
          MALCOLM X!
          ALBERT AYLER!
         THE BLACK ARTS!

Shit & whistling out of my nkrumah, cabral, fanon, sweep—I cry
   Fletcher
Henderson, Cane, What Did I Do To Be So Black & Blue, the
   most perfect
   couplet in the language, I scream Moon Indigo, Black
     Bolshevik, KoKo,
   Now's the Time, Ark of Bones, Lonely Woman, Ghosts, A Love
     Supreme,
   Walkin, Straight No Chaser, In the Tradition
              of life
              & dying
           centuries of beautiful
              women
              crying
          In the tradition
              of screamed
              ape music
              coon hollers

                    shouts
                    even more profound
                    than its gorgeous
                    sound
            In the tradition of
all of us, in an unending everywhere at the same time
line
in motion forever
like the hip chicago poet Amus Mor
like the Art Ensemble
like Miles's Venus DeMilo
    & Horace Silver reminding us
    & Art Blakey sending us messages
    Black Brown & Beige people
    & Pharaoh old and new, Blood Brotherhoods
    all over the planet, land songs land poems
    land sculptures and paintings, land niggers want still want
    will get land
in the tradition of all of us in the positive aspect
all of our positive selves, cut zora neale & me & a buncha other
    folks in half. My brothers and sisters in the tradition. Vincent
Smith & Biggers, Color mad dudes, Catlett & White Chas & Wm,
    BT, Overstreet
& the 60s muralists. Jake Lawrence & Aaron Douglass & Ademola
Babatunde Building More Stately Mansions
We are the composers, racists & gunbearers
We are the artists
Dont tell me shit about a tradition of deadness & capitulation
of slavemasters sipping tea in the parlor
while we bleed to death in fields
tradition of cc rider
see what you done done
dont tell me shit about the tradition of slavemasters
& henry james I know about it up to my asshole in it
dont tell me shit about bach mozart or even ½ nigger
beethoven
get out of europe
come out of europe if you can
cancel on the english depts this is america
north, this is america
where's yr american music
gwashington won the war

where's yr american culture southernagrarians
         academic aryans
         penwarrens & wilburs
   say something american if you dare
     if you
     can
         where's yr american
         music
            Nigger music?

(Like englishmen talking about great britain stop with tongues
  lapped on their cravats you put the irish on em. Say shit
man, you mean irish irish Literature . . . when they say about
  they
you say nay you mean irish irish literature you mean, for the
last century you mean, when you scream say nay, you mean
  yeats,
synge, shaw, wilde, joyce, ocasey, beckett, them is, nay, them is
irish, they's irish, irish as the ira)

you mean nigger music? dont hide in europe—"oh thats
  classical!"
  come to this country
     nigger music?

you better go up in appalachia
and get some mountain some coal mining
songs, you better go down south in our land
& talk to the angloamerican national minority
they can fetch up a song or two, country & western
could save you from looking like saps before the world
otherwise
        Palante!
        Latino, Native American
        Bomba, Plena, Salsa, Rain dance War dance
        Magical invective
        The Latin Tinge
        Cherokee, Sonny Rollins w/Clifford Brown
        Diz & Machito, or Mongo SantaMaria

        Comin Comin World Saxophone Quartet you cannot
stand up against, Hell No I Aint Goin To Afghanistan, Leon

Thomas million year old pygmies you cannot stand up against, nor
Black Arthur tellin you like Blue Turhan Bey, Odessa, Romance can
Bloom even here in White Racist Land It can Bloom as Beautiful,
though flawed by our oppression it can
bloom bloom, in the tradition
    of revolution
     Renaissance
     Negritude
     Blackness
     Negrissmo
     Indigisme
   sounding niggers
   swahili speaking niggers niggers in turbans
  rna & app & aprp & cap black blacks
 & assembly line, turpentine, mighty fine female
  blacks, and cooks, truck drivers, coal miners
   small farmers, iron steel and hospital workers
    in the tradition of us
     in the tradition of us
     the reality not us the narrow fantasy
  in the tradition of african american black people/america

nigger music's almost all
you got, and you find it
much too hot

   in the tradition thank you arthur for playing & saying
    reminding us how deep how old how black how sweet how
we is and bees
when we remember
when we are our memory as the projection
of what it is evolving
in struggle
in passion and pain
we become our sweet black
selves

once again,
 in the tradition
  in the african american
   tradition
    open us

> yet bind us
> let all that is positive
> find
> us
>> we go into the future
>>> carrying a world
>>>> of blackness
>>>> yet we have been in the world
>>>> and we have gained all of what there
>>>> is and was, since the highest expression
>>>> of the world, is its total

& the universal
is the entire collection
of particulars

ours is one particular
one tradition
of love and suffering truth over lies
and now we find ourselves in chains
   the tradition says plainly to us fight plainly to us
    fight, that's in it, clearly, we are not meant to be slaves
it is a detour we have gone through and about to come out
in the tradition of gorgeous africa blackness
says to us fight, it's all right, you beautiful
   as night, the tradition
thank you langstron/arthur
says sing
says fight
in the tradition, always clarifying, always new and centuries old
says
    Sing!
    Fight!
        Sing!
        Fight!
            Sing!
            Fight! &c. &c.
                    Boosheee dooooo doo doooo dee
                      doooo
                    doooooooooo!
                    DEATH TO THE KLAN!

From *Daggers and Javelins*

The Revolutionary Tradition in Afro-American Literature

Speaking about the general ghettoized condition of Afro-American literature within the framework of so-called American literature, Bruce Franklin, a professor at the Newark branch of Rutgers University, had this to say in the *Minnesota Review*:

> If we wish to continue to use the term "American Literature," we must either admit that we mean white American literature or construe it to include the literature of several peoples, including the Afro-American nation. The latter course leads to a fundamental redefinition of American literature, its history, and the criteria appropriate to each and every American literary work. For the viewpoint of oppressed people can then no longer be excluded from the criticism and teaching of American literature. . . . The most distinctive feature of United States history is Afro-American slavery and its consequences. This truth is at the heart of our political, economic, and social experience as a nation state. It is also at the heart of our *cultural* experience, and therefore the slave narrative, like Afro-American culture in general, is not peripheral but central to American culture.

These words are so important because Franklin calls attention to not only the fact that what is called American literature is basically the literature of certain white men, but he also points out the importance to American culture and life itself of Afro-American life and culture in this country. But if we look at the standard history of American literature—Franklin points to the *Literary History of the United States* by Spiller, Thorp, Johnson, Canby, Ludwig, and Gibson, a college standard, in its 4th revised edition in 1974—we find, in its 1,555 pages of small print, four black writers, Chesnutt, Dunbar, Hughes, and Wright—and in the section on literature produced by the South during the Civil War, they devote three chapters, and discuss such literary giants as Hugh Legaré, William Wirt, and George Fitzhugh, author of *Cannibals All! or Slaves Without*

Masters. There is no mention of the slave narrative or slave poetry. There is no mention of William Wells Brown, the nineteenth-century black novelist and playwright. They do not even mention Frederick Douglass!! So we must face the essential national chauvinism of what is taught as American literature, even the "white part" of it, so that in many instances the anthologies and survey courses that we learn literature from are the choice of or have been influenced to a great extent by some of the most reactionary elements in American society. We have been raised up in literaure too often on right-wing anthologies and the standards of right-wing critics, pushing conservative and reactionary literature, playing down progressive and revolutionary forces, and almost outright excluding oppressed nationalities and minorities and women.

It was the rebellions of the sixties, explosions in 110 U.S. cities, that created the few Black Studies and Afro-American Studies departments that exist today. At the same time, these uprisings created the agonizingly small space that Afro-American literature takes up in the canon of academic and commerical written culture. A few authors got "walk-on" roles, to paraphrase Franklin again.

First we must understand the basic distortion that is given to all American literary history and official reflections of American life and culture. This is obviously because the literary establishment, and the academic establishment, far from being independent, represent in the main the ideas and worldview of the rulers of this country. These ideas, and the institutions from which they are mashed on us, constitute merely the *superstructure* of this society, a superstructure that reflects the economic foundations upon which it is built, the material base for United States life and culture, monopoly capitalism. So that in the main what is taught and pushed as great literature, or great art, philosophy, etc., are mainly ideas and concepts that can help maintain the status quo, which includes not only the exploitation of the majority by a capitalist elite, but also national oppression, racism, the oppression of women, and the extension of United States imperialism all over the world.

Afro-American literature as it has come into view, fragmented by chauvinism and distorted by the same reactionary forces that have distorted American literature itself, has indeed been laid out in the same confusing and oblique fashion. A method intended to hide more than it reveals, a method that wants to show that at best Afro-American literature is a mediocre, and conservative, reflection of the mediocre and conservative portrait that is given of all American literature.

In Afro-American literature for instance we have been taught that its beginnings rest with the writings of people like Phillis Wheatley and Jupiter Hammon. Ms. Wheatley writing in the eighteenth century is simply an imitator of Alexander Pope. It was against the law for black slaves to learn to read or write, so Ms. Wheatley's writings could only come under the "Gee whiz, it's alive" category of Dr. Frankenstein checking out his new monster! Also Wheatley's writing abounds with sentiments like "Twas mercy brought me from my pagan land," evincing gratitude in slavery—that the European slave trade had actually helped the Africans by exposing them to great European culture: which be the monster remarking how wise how omniscient be her creator!

Hammon is, if possible, even worse. In his stiff doggerel are such great ideas as slavery was good for us Africans because it taught us humility—so when we get to heaven we'll know how to act around God. Pretty far out! (Both were privileged Northern house servants reflecting both their privilege and their removal and isolation from the masses of African/Afro-American slaves.)

But these two are pushed as Afro-American literature simply as a method of showing off trained whatnots demonstrating the glory of the trainer. But this is not the beginnings of Afro-American literature as a genre.

The black people of this country were brought here in slavery chains on the ships of rising European capitalism. It is impossible to separate the rise of capitalism, the industrial revolution, the emergence of England and later America as world powers, from the trade in Africans. And from their initial presence as commodities initiating world trade through the triangular trade route of slaves to the New World, raw materials to England, and manufactured goods to Africa for the African feudal ruling class who had sold the other Africans into slavery, black life has contributed to and animated Anglo-American life and culture. But a formal, artifact-documented presence could easily be denied slaves. African culture was banned by the slave masters as *subversive*. Christianity was used first as a measure of civilization (if you weren't a Christian you weren't civilized—the papal bull states, it's cool to enslave non-Christians) but later it was used as a pacifier and agency for social control (its present function). The development of a *specifically* Afro-American culture must wait for the emergence of the Afro-American people, the particular nationality composed of Africans transformed by the fact and processes of slavery into an American people of African descent.

The most practical artifacts of that culture are the tools and environment of day-to-day living. In these practical pursuits are found the earliest Afro-American art — artifactual reflections of the life of that people. Music, because it is most abstract and could not therefore be so severely limited and checked by slave culture, must be the earliest of the "non-practical" arts to emerge (although a work song is to help one work!): the work song, chants, hollers, the spiritual, eventually the blues.

Afro-American literature rises as a reflection of the self-conscious self-expression of the Afro-American people, but to be an Afro-American literature, truly, it must reflect, in the main, the ideological and socio-cultural portrait of that people! The Wheatleys and Hammons reflect the ideology of Charlie McCarthy in relationship to Edgar Bergen. (Is that before anybody's time?)

The celebration of servitude is not the ideological reflection of the Afro-American masses, but of their tormentors.

In the slave narratives, the works of Frederick Douglass, Henry Bibb, Moses Roper, Linda Brent, William Wells Brown, the Krafts, Henry "Box" Brown, and others, Solomon Northrup, James Pennington, etc., are found the beginnings of a genuine Afro-American written literature. Here are the stirring narratives of slave America, the exploits and heroism of resistance and escape, the ongoing struggle and determination of that people to be free. Beside this body of strong, dramatic, incisive, democratic literature where is the literature of the slavemasters and -mistresses? Find it and compare it with the slave narratives and say which has a clearer, more honest, and ultimately more artistically powerful perception of American reality! (Yes, there are William Gilmore Simms, John Pendleton Kennedy, Augustus B. Longstreet, and George Washington Harris, touted as outstanding writers of the white, slave South. But their writing is unreadable, even though overt racists like Allen Tate and the Southern Agrarians prated about the slave South as a "gracious culture despite its defects." Those defects consisted in the main of millions of black slaves, whose life expectancy at maturity by the beginning of the nineteenth century in the deep South was seven years. One of the main arguments, as Bruce Franklin points out in *The Victim as Criminal and Artist*, for black slavery was that the blacks could do the manual labor "for which they were best suited . . . leaving their owners free to create a fine, elegant, and lasting culture" (p. 28). But check it out. At best such artistic efforts representing this so-called lasting culture are embarrassing satires, the efforts of the Southern Agrarians to represent them as something else notwithstanding.

The slave narratives are portraits of a people in motion, and they come into being as creations of the economic, social, and political life of the United States. The early part of the nineteenth century was marked by an intensification of slavery and by the taking away of the limited civil rights of free blacks as well. This was because slavery did not die out toward the end of the eighteenth century as was predicted. With the creation of the cotton gin, to the feudalistic or patriarchal slavery imposed on blacks was now added capitalist exploitation. Karl Marx points out in *Capital* that once cotton became an international commodity, no longer used only in United States domestic markets, blacks were not only tied for life to domestic slavery, but now had added to their inhuman burden the horrors of having to produce *surplus value*, as a kind of slave and proletarian in combination. The seven-year life expectancy came about "down river" in the black-belt cotton region because the slavemasters discovered that working slaves to death and then replacing them was more profitable than letting them live to grow old, less productive but still eating, wearing clothes, and taking up space!

This period of intense repression is when Afro-American literature emerges. It is also the period when the resistance of the Afro-American people intensifies. It is now that Gabriel Prosser, Denmark Vesey, Nat Turner, lead their uprisings and rebellions, and Harriet Tubman develops the underground railway.

At the approach of the Civil War, there is also another strong movement in Afro-American literature, the pre-Civil War revolutionary black nationalists: David Walker, the activists Henry Highland Garnet, Charles Lenox Remond, C. H. Langston, as well as William Wells Brown, an escaped slave who became the first black playwright and novelist. It is a literature sparked by protest, an antislavery literature, a fighting oral literature, that even when it was written was meant to be proclaimed from the lecterns and pulpits of the North and circulated secretly to inspire the black slaves in the South. These were black abolitionists, damning slavery in no uncertain terms, proclaiming death to slavery, and calling for rebellion from the slaves. This was not upper-class white abolitionism, morally outraged but politically liberal. (The most genuine of the white abolitionists was John Brown—he knew what to do about slavery, wage armed struggle against it!) These were black revolutionists, some like Langston even calling for black people to seize the land they toiled upon because it was only that land that provided a practical basis for the survival and development of the Afro-American people!

Usually in discussing Afro-American literature, teachers of literature combine the Wheatleys and Hammons with perhaps Douglass's narrative, and maybe Brown's novel, *Clotel*. The other slave narratives and the pre–Civil War black revolutionary nationalists are largely ignored or their importance diminished. Charles Chesnutt, who lamented that quality black folks had to be lumped together with the ignorant black masses, is pushed as a kind of father of black literature. Next, Paul Laurence Dunbar and James Weldon Johnson are raised to the top rank, but an analysis of the content of these men's works is made vague or one-sided. We are not aware perhaps that for all the positive elements of Dunbar's work, his use of dialect, which is positive insofar as it is the language of the black masses, is negative in the way that Dunbar frequently uses it only in the context of parties, eating, and other "coonery." Most of Dunbar's "serious" poetry is not in dialect.

Dunbar was deeply conservative, and his short story "The Patience of Gideon" shows a young slave, Gideon, who is put in charge of the plantation as the massa goes off to fight the Civil War. Gideon stays despite the masses of slaves running away as soon as massa leaves. Even Gideon's wife-to-be pleads with him to leave, but he will not. He has made a promise to massa, and so even his woman leaves him, alone with his promise to the slavemaster.

J.W. Johnson's quandary was how to create a "high art" out of Afro-American materials, not completely understanding that "high art" is by definition slavemaster, bourgeois art and that what was and is needed by all artists, or by those artists who intend for their works to serve the exploited and oppressed majority in this country, is that they be artistically powerful and politically revolutionary!

Johnson's *Autobiography of an Ex-Colored Man* tells of that quandary in social terms, with his protagonist existing in a never-never land between black and white and finally deciding because he is shamed and humiliated and horrified by the lynching of a black man that he cannot be a member of a race so disgraced. He disappears among the whites, forsaking art for commerce, pursuing the white lady of his heart!

The real giant of this period, the transitional figure, the connector between nineteenth-century Reconstruction and the new literary giants of the twentieth century and the Harlem Renaissance, is W.E.B. Du Bois. His *Souls Of Black Folk*, which issued an ideological challenge to the capitulationist philosophy of Booker T. Washington, is the intellectual and spiritual forerunner of the writings of the Renaissance. Du Bois's *Black Reconstruction* remains the most important work on the Reconstruction period done by an American. He was a social scientist, historian, as well as novelist, poet, and political activist. He founded black theatrical troupes like Krigwa Players, organized international conferences of black activists as leader of the Pan-Africanist movement, led social movements in the United States like the Niagara Movement and the NAACP, was a fighting literary editor, and his works of historical and sociological analysis are among the greatest written by an American. He studied and wrote about all aspects of black life and its connection with Africa and the slave trade. He was a socialist by 1910, and at the end of his life, inspired by and inspiring the African independence movements, residing in Nkrumah's Ghana, he became a communist. It is not possible to understand the history of ideas in the United States without reading Du Bois. Not to know his work is not to have a whole picture of Afro-American literature, sociology, history, and struggle and is to have a distorted view of American life in general.

Langston Hughes's manifesto, "The Negro Artist and the Racial Mountain" (1926), is not possible without Du Bois and his total rejection of American racial paternalism and cultural aggression. The Harlem Renaissance is simply the flowering of a twentieth-century Afro-American intelligentsia reflecting the motion of black people in America. It reflects a peasant people in motion out of the South toward the urban North to serve as cheap labor (a developing proletariat) for the developing United States imperialism cut off from its European immigrants by the coming of World War I. It is a literature of the new city dwellers having left their rural pasts. It is a literature of revolt, it is anti-imperialist, and fights the cultural aggression that imperialism visits upon its colonial and nationally oppressed conquests—first by reflecting and proclaiming the beauty and strengths of the oppressed people themselves. By showing the lives of the people themselves in all its rawness, deprivation and ugliness. By showing them to themselves. It is a revolutionary nationalist literature at its strongest, especially the works of Claude McKay and Langston Hughes. It reflects the entrance into the twentieth century of Afro-American people and the U.S. in general. It is the sensibility of the Afro-American Nation that developed after the destruction of the Reconstruction governments (and the period of Reconstruction was the most democratic period in U.S. life)—the sensibility that survived the dark repression of the 1880s and 1890s, when the northern industrial capitalists no longer needed blacks to stabilize the south while the Wall Street conquerors stripped the southern plantation aristocrats of economic and political independence, so now the northern capitalists sold blacks back into near slavery with the Hayes-Tilden Compromise of 1876, to crush black political life with the Ku Klux Klan lynching, the black codes, segregation, and outright fascism!

The Harlem Renaissance influenced black culture worldwide, but it all reflected the fact that all over the world, oppressed nations and colonial peoples were intensifying their struggle against imperialism. In Haiti, where the U.S. invaded in 1915, there was the *Indigisme* movement; in Puerto Rico it was called *Negrissmo*, in Paris, Senghor, Cesaire, and Damas called it *Negritude* and cited McKay and Hughes as their chief influences!

One aspect of the Harlem Renaissance in the "Roaring 20s" as part of "the Jazz Age" was the stirring anti-imperialism—another part (showing how the bourgeoisie tries to transform everything to its own use) was the cult of exoticism the commercializers and, often pathological, bourgeois "patrons" of the "New Negro" made of this cultural outpouring. This was the period, Hughes said, when "the Negro was in vogue."

But by the beginning of the thirties, after the crash of 1929 and the great depression—only one of many cyclical recessions, the bust part of the boom-bust cycle pointing toward the eventual destruction of capitalism—the exotic part of the Renaissance was over. The philanthropists turned to other pursuits and, just as in factories where blacks are the last hired and the first fired, the literary flowering as manifested by American publishers came to an end!

In the depression thirties the revolutionary ideas of the Russian Bolsheviks, of Marx, Engels, Lenin, and Stalin, had enormous influence on United States intellectuals. It was apparent that capitalism could not solve the problems of the exploited majority, let alone of black people, and that the United States bourgeoisie was unfit to rule society. Black writers also show this influence, mostly as it was transmitted by the then revolutionary Communist Party USA. The works of Hughes and McKay especially show this influence, and even though Hughes later copped out before the inquisitors of the HUAC, a collection of his thirties writings, *Good Morning, Revolution*, is must reading to get at his really powerful works.

Richard Wright was one of the most publicized and skilled black writers of the 1930s and 1940s. His early works, *Uncle Tom's Children*, *Native Son*, *Black Boy*, including the long-suppressed section of this book called *American Hunger*, are among the most powerful works written by any American writer of the period. Wright was, even more than Hughes, influenced by Marxist-Leninist ideology, though Wright's individualism and idealism finally sabotaged him. He joined the CPUSA when he got to Chicago. (He came in from the John Reed Club, an anti-imperialist writers' organization. And if one believes *American Hunger*, the careerist aspects of this move, getting his early works published by the communists, etc., are not insubstantial.) Wright had just come from Memphis when he joined and he remained a member of the CPUSA until 1944. It was at this point ironically that the CP, burdened by opportunist reactionary leadership, sold out the Black Liberation Movement by liquidating the correct revolutionary slogans "Liberation for the black nation! Self-determination for the Afro-American nation in the black-belt South!" The CP even liquidated itself, temporarily becoming the Communist Political Association, "a nonparty movement following the ideals of Washington, Jefferson, Lincoln and Tom Paine." But Wright's individualism and petit bourgeois vacillation had begun to isolate him from the party years before, though the errors and opportunism of CP leadership must be pointed out.

Many of the left, anti-imperialist, revolutionary, Marxist, and even pro-Soviet ideas that grew to such prominence in the thirties were sustained into the forties because the United States by then had joined a united front with the Soviet Union against fascism. But by the fifties United States world dominance (which was enhanced by the fact of its emerging unscathed from World War II) dictated that it launch a cold war against the Soviet Union to try to dominate a world market. World War II had allowed the insurgent colonial peoples to grow even stronger as the imperialists fought each other, and in 1949 the Chinese communists declared the People's Republic of China. This occasioned an attempted blockade and isolation of China as well by the United States and resulted in the Korean "police action." This was accompanied by intense ideological repression inside the U.S.A. itself, as McCarthyism emerged: the modern capitalist inquisition to purge all left and Marxist and anti-imperialist influences from American intellectual life!

Hughes copped out before HUAC, said he would not do it again, and told James Eastland that all United States citizens had equality. A tragedy! Wright fled to France and became an existentialist. Another event with tragic overtones. Du Bois was indicted as an agent of a foreign power and went abroad for an extended period. Robeson was persecuted and driven to his death as Jackie Robinson testified against him at HUAC. Powerful writers like Theodore Ward were covered with mountains of obscurity.

With the defection of the CPUSA to reformism, culminating in its 1957 pronouncement that it was now seeking socialism via the ballot in a "peaceful transition to socialism" and that the road to socialism was integration not revolution, the late 1940s and the 1950s were marked by a "reevaluation" of Wright's works. Both James Baldwin and Ralph Ellison spuriously condemned protest literature, and the general tone put out by well-published "spokespersons for black people" was that it was time to transcend the "limitations" of race and that Afro-American writing should disappear into the mainstream like *Lost Boundaries*. Baldwin of course later refutes his own arguments by becoming a civil-rights spokesman and activist, and by the sixties with *Blues for Mr. Charlie* he had even begun to question the nonviolent, passive pseudo-revolution put forward by the black bourgeoisie through its most articulate spokesman, Dr. Martin Luther King. And this is exactly the point in time when Ralph Ellison is put forward by the bourgeoisie as the most notable Afro-American writer!

Ralph Ellison's *Invisible Man* was the classic work of the fifties in restating and shifting the direction of Afro-American literature. The work puts down both nationalism and Marxism, and opts for *individualism*. This ideological content couched in the purrs of an obviously elegant technique was important in trying to steer Afro-American literature away from protest, away from the revolutionary concerns of the 1930s and early 1940s, and this primarily is the reason this work and its author are so valued by the literary and academic establishments in this country. Both Ellison and Baldwin wrote essays dismissing or finding flaws in Wright's ultimate concern in his best work.

But the fifties civil-rights movement was also superseded by the people's rapid intensification of the struggle in the sixties, and black literature like everything else was quick to show this. Malcolm X emerged to oppose the black bourgeois line of nonviolent passive resistance, which duplicates the reformist anti-Marxists of the CPUSA in their "nonviolent transition to socialism." Where the black bourgeoisie had dominated the Black Liberation Movement in the fifties with the aid of the CPUSA and the big capitalists themselves, in the sixties Malcolm X came forward articulating the political line of the black majority, self-determination, self-respect, and self-defense, and struggled out in the open against the civil-rights line of the black bourgeoisie, who could see black people beaten and spit on and bombed in churches, and whose only retaliation would be to kneel in the dust and pray.

Just as Malcolm's influence turned the entire civil-rights movement around, e.g., the student movement, which was SNCC, to the militance of Stokely Carmichael and Rap Brown, so the whole movement changed radically. The black bourgeoisie were no longer in control of the movement, and from civil rights we were talking next about self-defense, and then after Rap Brown about rebellion, to revolution itself.

All these moves were reflected by black literature, and they are fundamentally movements and thrusts by the people themselves, that the literature bears witness to and is a reflector of. The Black Arts Movement of the sixties basically wanted to reflect the rise of the militancy of the black masses as represented by Malcolm X. Its political line, at its most positive, was that literature must be a weapon of revolutionary struggle, that it must serve the black revolution. And its writers, Askia Muhammad Toure, Larry Neal, Clarence Reed, Don Lee, Sonia Sanchez, Carolyn Rodgers, Welton Smith, Marvin X, Henry Dumas, Gaston Neal, Clarence Franklin, Ben Caldwell, Ed Bullins, Ron Milner, Mari Evans, etc., its publications, its community black arts theaters, its manifestos and activism, were meant as real manifestations of black culture—black art as a weapon of liberation.

On the negative side, the Black Arts Movement, without the guidance of a scientific revolutionary organization, a Marxist-Leninist communist party, was like the BLM itself, left with spontaneity. It became embroiled in cultural nationalism, bourgeois nationalism, substituting mistrust and hatred of white people for scientific analysis of the real enemies of black people, until by the middle seventies a dead end had been reached that could only be surmounted by a complete change of worldview, ideology.

It is my view that this is exactly what is going on today in many places in the country. Afro-American literature is going through the quantitative changes necessary to make its qualitative leap back into the revolutionary positivism of the 1930s and the positive aspect of the black arts 1960s. For certain, the literature will always be a reflection of what the people themselves are, as well as a projection of what they struggle to become. The Afro-American nation is an oppressed nation, and its people, whether in the black-belt land base of that nation or as an oppressed nationality spread out around the rest of the nation-state, still face a revolutionary struggle. That nation is still oppressed by imperialism, and its liberation and self-determination can only be gained through revolution. The next wave of Afro-American literature, of a genuine people's literature, will dramatically record this.

Aimé Césaire

To study Aimé Césaire's work, especially his major work of poetry *Return to My Native Land*, it is necessary to look at the world the man and his work grow out of. Art is an attempt to describe the world, an ideological form, which also describes the mind of the describer. It is a projection of life; it is a projection of the particular life, of the artist, as well. Art can exist independently of the context of its creation only at the risk of obscurity.

Césaire was born in Martinique, a French colony in the West Indies, in 1913. His growing to consciousness at the beginning of the twentieth century happens within the framework of certain world-shaking, world-changing events (the culmination of certain processes, etc.) Early competitive capitalism was being transformed into imperialism, or the monopoly stage of capitalism. This transformation meant that capitalism had now to leap out of its national boundaries and pursue surplus value all over the world. It had inexorably to seek new markets, ever expanding, seek new sources of raw materials, new places to invest its surplus capital, and new spheres of influence. This transformation meant that the capitalists had to penetrate every land on the face of the planet searching for these things, its lifeblood for expansion. But wherever it penetrated, in order to suck its fill, rip out resources, steal with impunity, dialectically it had to (as a result of every process in the world being composed of contradictions, opposites, which give life itself its motion) also build railroads, mines, ports, factories, as Lenin pointed out in *Imperialism, the Highest Stage of Capitalism*. And because it had to build these means of production in order to steal, it had also to create a proletariat, workers, where before there were peasants — a working class, in fact, that one day would destroy imperialism. Imperialism also created a nationalist intelligentsia in these mainly Third World countries, where it practiced its superexploitation to extract superprofits. This nationalist intelligentsia finds itself inevitably in opposition to imperialism.

But if the twentieth century is the century of imperialism, it is also the century of proletarian revolution. Imperialism means war as well: wars between the imperialists themselves to divide the world. In 1884 the colonial powers had actually sat down in Berlin and divided up Africa like a cake, but by 1913, the same year as Césaire's birth, the First World War was about to break out as imperialist groups fought to redivide the world's spoils.

By 1917, socialist revolution was victorious in Russia, the most backward country in Europe, led by Lenin and the Bolshevik Party, and this set a concrete example not only for working people but also for colonial people all over the world. And as imperialism had intensified its rape of the colonial people, they had intensified their resistance. In 1919, led by Lenin, the Communist International, the Third International, a meeting and joining-together of communist parties all over the world, was effected, and the impact of this also shook the very foundations of the imperialist world. Lenin at this historic series of congresses also put forward a mighty slogan that summarizes the era of imperialism and the resistance of the people perfectly. Where Marx had laid out "Workers of all countries unite," Lenin now, reflecting the changed conditions of imperialism, said, "Workers of all countries and oppressed nations unite!," reflecting the mighty torrent of colonial peoples that was already in motion fighting against imperialism.

So the 1920s saw evidence of a continuously higher level of resistance. It also saw the widespread emergence of the nationalist intelligentsia in oppressed nations and colonies everywhere. As a reflection of world imperialism, there is world resistance, and the emergence of the native or colonial intelligentsia worldwide. We speak of the Harlem Renaissance as one flowering of such a native intelligentsia, focused directly around the arts. Langston Hughes and Claude McKay were its finest examples.

There were parallel movements in Haiti around the journal *La Revue Indigène*, associated with men like Jean Price Mars and Jacques Romain. Haiti's renaissance at this period came somewhat earlier, spurred on by the United States occupation in 1915. A movement to study Haitian folklore, a new self-consciousness born of a need to defend oneself against the cultural aggression and the bourgeois assimilation that imperialism always brings with it arose in Haiti, and a fiercely outspoken intelligentsia arose with this self-consciousness. In Cuba, Brazil, Martinique, there were parallel movements, part of the same outswell. In Cuba, it was called Negrissmo.

Paris was one center of colonial intellectuals. The imperialist countries themselves always draw the colonial peoples into them as cheap labor, but also they have become the "mother country," the beacons of civilization; the students and intellectuals as well flock to these fortresses of exploitation, some seeking merely to assimilate completely themselves and so become imitations of the conquerors, others seeking to answer questions that have been posed in the conqueror's language, by the conqueror's culture—but ultimately they answer those questions with a language of their own, resistance.

So Paris was one center for those intellectuals from the various countries the French had despoiled; as was London, for those oppressed by British imperialism; New York, for those ripped off by the U.S.A. Just as Amilcar Cabral or Augustino Neto could be found studying in Lisbon, before they returned to Africa to help destroy Portuguese colonialism, you could also find in Paris, at the same time, both Ho Chi Minh and Chou En Lai. Paris was a center for colonialized intellectuals from Africa, Asia, Latin America, the West Indies.

One important development of this collection of colonialized intellectuals in Paris, by the 1930s, was the movement represented by a booklet-manifesto called *Légitime Défense*, which not only verbalized the anticolonial feelings of young black intellectuals living in Paris but also launched a heated attack on the assimilationist native bourgeoisie and petite bourgeoisie in the colonial countries. It was a manifesto striking out against "this capitalistic, Christian, bourgeois world." *LD* was a cultural movement as well as a political movement, led by a young West Indian in Paris named Etienne Lero, a poet (also by René Menil, Jules Monnerot). The manifesto was directly focused on the French West Indian colonization process. And as often happens, it was put together by members of the very class of blacks it condemns: bourgeois, assimilationist, mulatto. In fact all the signers of the manifesto were specifically mulattoes, except for Lero. Ultimately the manifesto gave rise to an intensifying nationalism, a calling forth of a nationalist national bourgeoisie to replace the comprador assimilationist bourgeoisie, which helped to stabilize the earlier colonialism.

The manifesto begins with aspects of a Marxist analysis of island society and sees the West Indians as descendants of African slaves held three centuries. But it wants to use Marxism not only as a weapon of liberation but also surrealism! It lays out its intellectual leaders as Marx, but also Freud, Rimbaud, and Breton, and as such presents an intellectual pastiche not uncommon in the twenties and thirties. *LD* mentions for instance that "surrealism alone

. . . could liberate" the West Indian from his taboos and allow complete expression.

The reason that this essentially bourgeois and European intellectual and arts movement could have so much influence on these young black intellectuals, aside from the fact that they were in Paris, was the fact that surrealism purported to attack bourgeois values. It reflected the extreme disillusionment of Western petit bourgeois intellectuals with the emergence of imperialism, World War I, and the obvious drowning of Western lip service to human rights under a torrent of blood, slavery, and money.

But essentially it is the bourgeois and petit bourgeois class base of the writers of the manifesto that allows them to confuse bourgeois rebellion with revolution. Surrealism calls for a disordering finally of the bourgeois world, but even that is momentary, and it does not really call for its destruction.

Surrealism could attack bourgeois academic writing and art, and black intellectuals who wanted to attack the assimilationist tendency in West Indian writing felt common ground. *LD* attacks what they call "tracing paper poetry . . . stuffed with white morality, white culture, white education, white prejudice," a poetry of advanced mediocrity. It says that the West Indian intellectual "will stifle his originality in order to be considered civilized." He is afraid to "make like a nigger . . . in the world . . . or in his poetry." (See my essay "The Myth of a Negro Literature" for a parallel even in the 1960s. See my poem "Black Dada Nihilismus" for a parallel legitimization of the Dada-surreal utilization idea.)

The manifesto also picked up on Claude McKay and Langston Hughes, saying that "these two revolutionary black poets have brought us . . . the African love of life, African joy, and the African dream of death." It goes on, "Our distinguished writers never touch these subjects." The manifesto scathingly denounced West Indian poets still imitating the antiquated French Parnassian school, having not even moved toward realism, naturalism, and symbolism.

As poets, they denounced the imitation French literature created by the ten percent of the population that was literate, the same ten percent that was literate in French and hated Creole (this is in Haiti), when the ninety-percent majority who were illiterate spoke Creole.

This manifesto had a deep influence on the young student Aimé Césaire, then studying in Paris on a scholarship, as well as on two other writers important to the movement that would later be called Negritude, Leopold Senghor and Leon Damas. Senghor said *LD* reflected the "new Negro movement in the arts," the same phrase used by Alain Locke in the United States to describe the Harlem Renaissance.

These young poets were looking for a mode of expression, a method of saying what was uniquely theirs to say, and at the same time denouncing all sterile imitations of the colonial masters. Césaire said: "We have had no art. No poetry. Rather a hideous leprosy of counterfeits." Instead of Phillis Wheatleys and Jupiter Hammons they wanted an expression linked with continuity yet re-birth, indigenous and revolutionary, just as the Harlem Renaissance continued the legacy of the slave narratives, the pre-Civil War revolutionary black nationalists, by way of Du Bois's *Souls of Black Folk*, to sum up black America and America itself's entrance into the twentieth century.

But even the title of the manifesto is a title gotten from André Breton, and the *LD* mentions all the masters of surrealism, Breton, Aragon, Crevel, Dali, Eluard, Peret, Tristan Tzara. So that the con-tradictions in the manifesto should be evident on the surface. In a few years, many of the surrealists, who during this early period had joined the French Communist Party, left the party, and this seems obvious since communists see literature as primarily a functional weapon in making revolution, not as simply cunning artifacts in some salon rebellion, which will be celebrated, even housed, by the bourgeoisie itself once it understands the commercial value of shock and canned outrage. Duchamp's toilet seat supposedly intended to scandalize bourgeois art becomes itself quite soon a standard of bourgeois art, sitting calmly in the same museums it has declaimed it wanted to burn down!

The great influence of communist ideas on intellectuals through-out the world by the 1930s and the economic crisis should be noted again. The presence of Marxist ideas in *LD* can be thus accounted for. Lero, it should be added, saw himself as a political figure as much as a writer, and *LD* was clearly and openly political, although clearly flawed. There is mention of the Scottsboro Case in the Unit-ed States in the manifesto, and it asks quite openly, "When will American blacks really understand that their only escape from the American hell lies in communism." Jacques Romain of Haiti was a communist, Hughes was writing his Marxist-inspired poems, Guillén of Cuba had become a communist.

The return of the primitive, and the exoticism and primitivism that leaped through the West as part of the disillusionment with Western humanism, was very evident in the surrealist movement.

The raising of the word as magic, and the poet as magician, these ideas were picked up by people like Senghor, and these ideas when pursued become cultural nationalism and metaphysics. But the conflict between *socialist* realism and surrealism got clearly more obvious.

The blacks wanted to use surrealism a different way. For Césaire, it represented a destruction of French literary tradition, which he felt stifled by. "It was a weapon which exploded the French language. It shook up absolutely everything." Césaire even refused to write poetry and wrote the *Retour* as a prose-poem to get away from stifling form. He says: "Even tho I wanted to break with French literary traditions, I did not actually free myself from them until the moment I decided to turn my back on poetry. In fact, you could say that I became a poet by renouncing poetry." It was the only way to "break the stranglehold the accepted French form held on me."

The *LD* writers had declared themselves traitors to their class, openly breaking, at least on the surface, with the bourgeois assimilationist West Indian writers of the colonized mentality. The movement began as one of national (and racial—since blacks regardless of nationality are oppressed as a race worldwide) self-consciousness, and then self-affirmation. But at the same time it was a movement of social awareness and struggle, utilizing the language and forms of Marxism. The parallel in movements throughout the colonial world is striking. And the direct influence of the Harlem Renaissance on the writers of Negritude is readily acknowledged. The most important book of that renaissance to these writers was Claude McKay's *Banjo*, not only because of McKay's West Indian background and because he used in this book both Europe, the Marseilles docks, and the West Indies as his setting, but also because in *Banjo* there are ideas of resistance to colonialism, and statements about black people's situation, that are presented with the clarity of fire.

Both Césaire and later Sembene Ousmane were influenced directly by *Banjo*. Leon Damas of Guiana, one of the most important Negritude poets, was influenced by Hughes. Senghor translated Hughes and Cullen and Toomer. It was the openness, vitality, humanity, reality, of black life and feelings, and the passionate embrace of black people and black life and the will to struggle to raise it to a higher level, that attracted Senghor and the others to the Harlem Renaissance. The emerging national consciousness of the Afro-American people was being taken up and turned to good account by a similar nationalist intelligentsia. The United States was the most advanced capitalist country, and the illusion called bourgeois democracy was being pushed to its furthest limits. Within the state the Afro-American people in their struggle for development exploded in self-consciousness and self-affirmation. Whether it was movement of the twenties or the bashing entrance of big-band jazz, the shots heard around the world.

Another important influence on black French-speaking intellectuals in Paris and around the world at the time was the novel by René Maran, which was awarded the Prix Goncourt, *Batouala*. Awarded the prize out of a determined hypocrisy—bourgeois colonialist society had to congratulate itself as humane, but this book was at the same time denounced by the most important French critics and its author generally hounded into silence. Maran was the first black in Paris to tell the truth about colonialism and the true mentality of blacks rather than the pseudoscientific racism of the colonialists. Maran was a black who lived in French Equatorial Africa as a French colonial administrator. He lived among the Ubangis; Batouala was their chief. Maran said: "I showed blacks as they were. I had no intention of writing a polemic." And as one critic said, it was as objective as a police report—so objective that French critics associated Maran's name with *hate*, which is a favorite trick.

By 1934, Senghor, a Senegalese (in fact he is now the president of Senegal), along with Césaire, Damas, and some other West Indians, began to put out a newspaper called *L'Étudiant Noir*. Where *LD* showed the prevalence of politics, *LEN* showed the prevalence of culture. Obviously this is because of Senghor's influence. Senghor's relationship to Marxism he described as being "nondogmatic." In fact his relationship to it was so thoroughly cavalier that he could propose an "African socialism" parallel to what Negritude (blackness, niggerness) seemed to propose in one aspect, but this "African socialism" is, in fact, just black capitalism and neocolonialism.

In contrast to *LD*, neither Senghor, Damas, Diop, nor Soce were communists. Senghor related to the mystical and the magic, saying that his poetry captured invisible forces, and that it utilized "analogy images." Césaire did not share these concerns; to Césaire humanity was the most vital force. But there is little doubt of the enormous influence that Senghor's concerns with black culture and this general cultural nationalism had on Césaire.

It is important that we realize how clearly one breaks into two, how the contradictions in the Negritude movement and its different tendencies break it apart. Césaire reflects to one degree or another most of these tendencies, but he is in the main reflective, in *Retours*, of the revolutionary nationalist aspect of what is called the Negritude movement, rather than the negative or cultural nationalist aspect.

Oppressed by imperialism, colonialism, racism, Zionism, the oppressed nations and peoples fight back. To the extent that nationalism represents resistance to oppression it is revolutionary. Even where it focuses on culture, when it refuses to be wiped out by the imposition of colonial culture, when it raises up the history and lives of the oppressed people as part of the struggle for their future, it is revolutionary. That is revolutionary culture. When it sees that culture as some static, unchangeable, mystical phenomenon with certain eternal, metaphysical, nonmaterial, and nonmaterially derived values, it is reactionary; it is bourgeois nationalism; and finally it serves to raise a new bourgeoisie, the national bourgeoisie, to power. Senghor's Senegal is proof in living color of the reactionary nature of such cultural nationalism. The "eternal mystical values" of black communalism, supposedly raised in a modern African socialism, are the excuse for the most shameless bootlicking of French imperialism, and for one of the most relentlessly classstratified black societies in West Africa today.

For instance, Senghor's definition of Negritude (which is niggerness or blackness), "the total of black Africa's cultural values," proposes that there is a static cultural essence to blacks apart from the development of the specific material base of the culture itself. But culture reflects first and foremost the material, i.e., the economic and with that the political, framework of its being. Africa's cultural values when? During primitive communalism, slavery, feudalism, or capitalism? During ancient Egypt? In Songhai, enslaved by colonialism, or up under the well-polished fingernails of black neocolonialism?

Césaire, on the other hand, defines Negritude in 1959 as "the awareness of being black, the simple acknowledgement of a fact which implies the acceptance of it, a taking charge of one's destiny as a black man, of one's history and culture." Here there is self-knowledge, self-affirmation, and the move to liberation. Blackness is not a static, mystical, "eternal" cultural quality; it is concrete consciousness and with that, concrete struggle. It is not enough to understand the world; we must change it.

Sartre said, mistakenly I think, that the Negritude poets wanted a world without race, which is why they, dialectically, stressed race. But I think they want a world not without race but without racism (which is impossible without the destruction of its parent, imperialism).

The Negritude poets began publishing in 1934, with Leon Damas's work in the magazine *Esprit*, and his first book, *Pigments*. Césaire began publishing *Retours* in 1939 in the magazine *Volontés*. Senghor's first volume did not appear until 1945.

Césaire was born of barely lower petit bourgeois parents in Martinique, a "difficult childhood" sharing hard-earned bread, got to college as a scholarship student. Senghor was the son of a wealthy, African bourgeois family. Damas, who lived the life of a petit bourgeois *assimilado*, cried out against those values throughout his poetry.

In 1939 Césaire was still influenced enough by the struggle for liberation and examples like Guillén, Romain, Aragon, Lero, Hughes, McKay, to become a communist.

In 1945 Césaire went back to Martinique, under the banner of the Communist Party of France, became a communist deputy to the national assembly and the mayor of Fort-de-France. The position of the CPF at this point was that Martinique should be a department of France. There was no Martiniquais Communist Party; it was a department of the CPF, a wildly chauvinist position! Césaire supported these positions at first, but by 1956 he had totally denounced this policy of departmentalization for what it was, national chauvinism. In 1956, Césaire resigned from the CPF, not only charging the same chauvinism in the CPF relationship to the Martiniquais communists and the departmentalization, but also incensed over the CPF vote on the Algerian question, in which they upheld French colonialist policy in Algeria!

Césaire's letter to Maurice Thorez not only sums this all up but also reflects Césaire's own petit bourgeois vacillation between Marxism and class struggle led by the proletariat of all countries, and a comfortable petit bourgeois nationalism. His condemnation of Stalin, based on the traitor Khrushchev's opportunist denunciation of Stalin, shows this confusion, although Césaire says truthfully enough, "I think I have said enough to make it plain that it's neither Marxism nor Communism I repudiate; that the use certain people have made of Marxism and Communism is what I condemn. What I want is that Marxism and Communism be harnessed into the services of colored peoples, and not colored peoples into the service of Marxism and Communism . . . that the doctrine and the movement be tailored to fit men, not men to fit the movement. (See Mao, *On Practice*.)

Césaire condemns colonialism masquerading as communism, which is correct to do. The French Communist Party totally degenerated, as did many of the European parties and the American party in the fifties, swept away by revisionism. Ho Chi Minh, one of the founders of the French Communist Party, had also denounced it earlier for its chauvinism.

Césaire now looked to Africa to revitalize blacks and the Antilles, which carries the tendency of cultural nationalism and Pan-Africanism, both aspects of which can be found in *Retours*. The liberation of Africa will bring imperialism to its knees, but its many tentacles must be chopped off in each specific country by each specific people, based on their concrete conditions.

In the letter to Thorez, Césaire saw "two paths of doom: by segregation, by walling yourself up in the particular; or by dilution, by thinning off into emptiness of the [fake] 'universal.' " He says, "I have a different idea of a universal. It is of a universal rich with all that is particular, rich with all the particulars there are, the deepening of each particular, the coexistence of them all." (This sounds almost like Mao in *On Practice* and *On Contradiction*.)

Césaire's early poetry was influenced by the wild imagery of Rimbaud (*A Season in Hell*) and Lautréamont, but *Retours* goes beyond the scope of that imagery. Senghor condemned European poetry for using abstract words to explain images, whereas it is the power of the image itself which should do the "explaining." But William Carlos Williams was also explaining this to American poets who would not listen: "not in words but in things," he said. Césaire's thrashing images dig into the surreal in the sense that they are sometimes wildly unrelated elements, but juxtaposed they make a new dissociation that calls forth new associations and new meaning.

Césaire's poetry grows more traditionally surrealist in the volumes which follow *Retours*, like *Les Armes Miraculeuses* (1946) or *Soleil Coup Coupé* (1948). Wild imagery can cause brilliant new meaning. The power is in the focus on real life that can fuse into a new dialectic seemingly dissimilar elements. *Retours* abounds with this, but quite a bit of the poetry in the later books grows into simple abstraction, where dissimilar elements unfused by some powerful focus of life remain disparate and diffuse and obscure.

The language in *Retours* is rich, deep, and rhythmical, full of ecstasy, pain, introspection, celebration, but it is connected by feeling and the power of its focus. The language *rushes*, and this is my basic sense of it, it rushes, it leaps, it is a whirlwind, it literally sweeps us in torrents.

Even during the forties when Césaire was a communist his work proceeded in directions quite different from other well-known communist poets such as Neruda, Guillén, Aragon; it became more obscure, more solitarily flamboyant, more and more burdened with obscurity. (Read "Knives at Noon" and "Tornado." In "Tornado" again, rush of, unleashing of, the wild untamable, wind and blacks, the surreal—a twisting out of shape, a sudden violence too. But it is like an unfocused torrent of heat, which must be focused to blast steel. It is not the rebuilding we long for, the just transformation.)

In Martinique, Césaire has been the mayor of Fort-de-France for 27 years, except for a brief period when he resigned from the Communist Party. He participated in the First and Second World Congresses of Black Writers and Artists, and in the fifties began to focus on the question of decolonization. His *Discourse on Colonialism* (1955), and other essays with similar themes appearing in publications like *Présence Africaine*, are important.

He has written also *Toussaint Louverture* (1961), a biography which is as well a history of Haiti. In the sixties he began to write plays because, as he expressed it, the problems of decolonization and nation building, real problems for the liberation movements as formal independence began to come, needed to be widely understood. In 1963 he wrote *La Tragédie du Roi Christophe*, again focusing on Haiti and the black ruler who led Haiti after Toussaint and Dessalines. In 1967 he wrote *Un Saison au Congo*, about Patrice Lumumba's betrayal and assassination. Both plays were about decolonization and nation building. In 1969, Césaire's *A Tempest* appeared, which was an adaptation of Shakespeare's play, but dealing with blacks in the U.S.A.

Ironically, after Césaire went back to Martinique, he got deeper into surrealism poetically, coming more fully into the imperialist system as mayor of Fort-du-France, so that a "rearrangement of reality" seems more and more to suffice rather than the creation of a new reality after the destruction of the old. Politically he now advocates "autonomy" rather than departmentalization, i.e., a middle ground when talking about a people under imperialism. Césaire says there are too many benefits under French patronage to completely cut away with independence, and so he has come under increasing fire from the younger revolutionaries on the island.

Ngugi wa Thiongo

In Ngugi wa Thiongo we have modern African writing—i.e., writing that is and reflects the Africa in a real world of suffering and change. His book *Homecoming* is must reading. It is solid, politically sound, artistically valid criticism of modern African and Caribbean literature.

Like Ayi Kwei Armah's *The Beautiful Ones Are Not Yet Born*, Achebe's *A Man of the People*, Okot Bitek's *Song of Lawino*, Okello Oculi's *Prostitute and the Orphan*, Ngugi's *Grain* has begun to turn the full light of artistic analysis on the post-colonial period, and what it means. In the colonial period, the writers had to affirm the value, the strength of the vanquished. The colonial intellectual, the anti-imperialist intelligentsia first, as Fanon lays out so clearly, affirms, must identify with the culture, the people affirm this in the face of the colonial enemies and their *cultural aggression*.

In *Things Fall Apart* Achebe is affirming African society, describing its real chaos and anxiety, in the face of the rising colonial order. But as Ngugi points out, Africans are not the European Robinson Crusoe's man Friday . . . their lives cannot be summed up in *The Pacification of the Primitive Tribes of Lower Niger*; in their humanity, they are more complex . . . and what is more they will survive. Despite the dying, the craziness, of the old which is passing in the onslaught of the new.

The political reality of colonialism is not limited in some alleyway or tower called "politics"; it is the basis for the very shaping and process of the people's lives.

The facts of the Christian doctrine, the Christian church, Christian missionaries, are a lingering undercurrent and overcurrent in everything in Ngugi's *A Grain of Wheat* from its title . . . to the fixations of the characters torn between these and Ngai, the God of Black People.

The novel deals with the depths and levels and response to guilt, the mark of colonialism, the mark of slavery, and how the people react.

African writers have no choice but to deal with neo-colonialism, "imperialism ruling through native agents," as Cabral and Nkrumah informed us, no more choice than they had in dealing with colonialism. It is the actual life of the people, the reality. Only the colonialists, the neo-colonialists, or their apologists would have us *not* deal with these real-life shapers of our perceptions. And that is because they want to cover up to hide the real so they can pretend their hypes and lies, or the subjectivism and solipsism of their elitist intellectuals, are reality.

Ngugi's writing, like the most important of African writers', deals with colonialism and neocolonialism, or more precisely, African people up under the weight of, shaped by, these devilish systems. In *Grain of Wheat* he spoke about the transition from the colonial to what the people then did not quite understand, but a post-colonial consciousness. In *Petals of Blood*, his most complete statement to date, Ngugi hands us neo-colonialism. Not as a political sloganizing or abstract cliché, but as it is to be understood through its effect on real life.

Mere bitterness at neo-colonialism is not enough though. Some of the earlier works by African writers, e.g., Achebe, were bitter, but calling in the Army to end neo-colonial corruption—consider it in real-life terms—is hardly desirable, though it is also real, mostly real tragedy. And it abounds in Africa today, for the same reasons that Achebe has laid out. Ngugi, however, goes further. In *Grain*, he tried to deal with the general guilt that colonialism made, the weakness, the suffering. How all of African life was distorted and made ugly by it. The general theme is betrayal, as a result of weakness under colonialism. Domestic betrayal, political betrayal, and cultural betrayal. What Ngugi insists upon is that we learn to tell weeds from grain. That the grain's "death" is so it can bear fruit, but the weed will bear no fruit.

Ngugi tells us how the whole people are stained, broken, but some will survive, the many. He also implies that some of the biggest heroes to the people are their biggest betrayers or will be. In *Petals* the prophecy, the perception, has come into full and treacherous view.

Petals is the grand evocation of neo-colonialism, made so horrible that it could only be rendered as high art. Sembene Ousmane is another African writer/filmmaker impressive, profound, sharp in his continuous relating of African reality. Sembene also deals closeup with colonialism, and now neo-colonialism. Both also deal with the phenomenon of the multiple layers of culture that exist in African society, and their significance. Sembene, focusing on West Africa, and Senegal in particular, shows the original Wolof culture and its successive transformations under the Islamic invasion and then the Christian one. So that one can see the complex reality of contemporary African life where the animist African culture is overpainted with an Islamic coat, a Christian-colonial one, and these all spark and ignite in constant confrontation with the present neo-colonial regime, where black "Frenchmen" run the country for their own aggrandizement and profit, the complete exclusion of the people's needs. *Mandabi* is a classic teller of this sad and contemporary tale. A man receives a 25,000-franc money order and cannot benefit by it because he does not understand the neo-colonial bureaucracy, i.e., he does not know the "magic words," he is still caught back in a Wolof version of Islam. In fact a neo-colonial black "Frenchman" slickly rips him off and sends him back home to sit on the steps with his head in his hands. Yet, in the end there is a note of defiance, as the postman tells the sad protagonist who cries that the whole world is turned upside down and corruption is worshipped, he says well then you and I will have to change this. It is not hopeless.

Ngugi goes further. But he also goes deeper. *Petals* is a kind of murder mystery in one aspect, and this adds spice to it, but is secondary. It is primarily a "morality" tale, the measure of which is the needs of the many, the collective will. Three men are burned up in a whorehouse. They are three prominent Kenyans, but they are also three notorious (we find out as we get further and further into the novel) neo-colonialists. The black pigs who personally shove African people's faces into the muck of imperialist exploitation.

Four people are accused of the crime. Munira, the confused son of a similar black pig, high up in the Christian church. (And in this Munira reminds one of Mugo in *A Grain of Wheat*, who was similarly impaled psychologically on Christianity, as it was brought to Africa with colonialism.) Wanja, the granddaughter of a peasant patriot, who gave up his life struggling against European invasion. She is also the daughter of another African traitor.

Abdullah, a hero of the Mau Mau war, disillusioned and hurt by the rise of neo-colonialism, who flees into the countryside to lose himself. Karega, the young peasant who is thrown out of the university for leading a strike. These four cross each other's paths in a boondock peasant village of Ilmorog. Their reasons for coming to Ilmorog, which Ngugi raises again and again, and how their lives are intertwined, even unknown.

The three black traitors, Kimeria, Mzigo, and Chui, are also connected to the four accused. These connections spell out the suffering of modern Kenya under the black "Englishmen" and "nationalists" who run it now for imperialism. It is well known that Ngugi was taken off to jail for a year by Kenyatta's goons. They even arrested his library! And no charges were ever made, in what the *New York Times* refers to as "Kenya's liberal regime." Kenya is one of the most despicable of neo-colonial tragedies because it raised so much hope when the Mau Mau uprising took place and the British colonialists called an "Emergency." The retreat from all pretenses of independence and African popular government, not to mention socialism, by Kenyatta and company has been complete and ugly. Ngugi has recorded that retreat and the horrors it has wrought, so faithfully, and with such power, that you can see once you read this book why the nigger establishment went out to lunch and had Ngugi jailed. He portrays these neo-colonial functionaries, these government, church, business "leaders," for what they are, human carrion, feeding on African lives. He lets us see for once and for all that these are *monsters* . . . monsters.

Ngugi does not bite his tongue, he lays it out. He has upheld his responsibility so breathtakingly that one is given to putting the book down as one reads, standing up exclaiming, shouting out loud, that yes, yes, this is exact. A powerful book.

Munira is a confused petit bourgeois whose instincts have been ripped out by Christian gibberish. He comes to Ilmorog because he feels guilty that he has done nothing during the Emergency to bring about Uhuru. He goes to Ilmorog to head up the non-existent school. In this character, Ngugi shows a personality stunted by imperialism, a colored Hamlet who cannot get beyond stereotypes and emotional isolation from the masses because of his pathological upbringing. His father, whom he hates and wishes to impress, is a man who first denounces his parents and African culture to take up with Jesus and the colonial Christianity, outspokenly courting success. He is also a man who denounces the Mau Mau during the Emergency and has his ear cut off in payment. But he still comes up on his feet after the war, an amazing and successful landowner capitalist who can now even deny jobs to the patriots that fought in the liberation struggle. The power of Jesus still runs the land, just as Barclays Bank and Exxon do. This is a man who denies his daughter the freedom to marry Karega because Karega's family was "mixed up" with the Mau Mau! (And they were peasants.) The daughter commits suicide.

Kimeria is another Christianity-quoting fraud who while married seduces Wanja when she is very young and then refuses to marry her, leaving her pregnant and horrified. She disposes of the baby and becomes a barmaid. She comes to Ilmorog seeking her grandmother, and perhaps a new start.

Kimeria also betrays two Mau Mau freedom fighters to the British. One is Karega's brother N'ding'uri, who is hanged. The other is

Abdullah. Kimeria becomes a well-known rich businessman; Abdullah, the hero, a seller of fruits and sheepskins at the side of the highway.

Chui is the colonial hero who, once "independence" comes, betrays the people by becoming an instrument for the continuation of the same imperialist rule. The students strike to end British rule and cultural aggression at the university. They beg for Chui, the hero, to come and give them control of their own education in their own land, e.g., African studies, an end to the prefect system. But Chui mouths the imperialist clichés that education knows no nationality, while continuing to make them subservient to European history and culture. He also becomes a successful businessman, and board member for Theng'eta Breweries.

Mzigo is a government bureaucrat in charge of district education in the area where Ilmorog lies. He cares nothing for Ilmorog or the people themselves. Finally he comes to Ilmorog when it becomes a boomtown, to get a piece of the action, becoming a board member of Theng'eta as well.

Ilmorog becomes a boomtown first because Karega, ultimately the most politically advanced of the four who come to Ilmorog to live, convinces the people that they must go to Nairobi to see their MP to force him to help them in the face of a prolonged drought. A procession does go to Nairobi, in a really marvelous section of the book where the harassed peasants and the four travel to Nairobi, and for a time build a great solidarity amongst them because of their mutual participation in collective struggle. But they also come face to face with the grimmest of neo-colonial horrors. They are refused help by the quoting Christian churchman Jerrod Brown. They are intimidated from even entering the partying Chui's house. Kimeria makes Wanja accept his rape again, otherwise he will have all of the people jailed as robbers. And the MP, Nderi wa Riera, is a conniving slickster who has found that "Cultural Nationalism" will trick a few people and allow him to get over at the same time. He calls for changes of names of branches in foreign companies to African names, advocates "Africanization" Mobutu style, but opposes socialism as "sloganizing" and pushes for an African capitalism that will permit of the emergence of African Fords, Krupps, Rockefellers, etc.

Ilmorog also gets suddenly big because Wanja brings the Theng'eta beverage, a kind of African absinthe, into commercial use and with Abdullah's help builds a big restaurant and bar and hotel which is a center of the new Ilmorog, until the Kimeria's, Chui's, etc., rip it off, just as they rip Ilmorog off and just as the native agents ruling for imperialism are ripping African people off. Ilmorog is one microcosm of the new Africa. A new, i.e., neo-colonial, Africa, where the white folks have been run off from the top spots, at least cosmetically, (though in Kenya there's still a bunch taking money right on the soil), and the African domestic bourgeoisie and reactionary sector of the petite bourgeoisie do the managing of the rip-off.

The four accused of murder are the main focus of Ngugi's analysis of how this last stage of imperialism affects African people, but there are many, many other examples and personalities in this rich and agonizing portrait. Munira loses his mind; Abdullah becomes a whipped alcoholic and fruit peddler; Wanja becomes a prostitute and then Ilmorog's most successful madam, proprietor of The Sunshine Lodge, complete with red wig and miniskirt. Her main clients, Chui, Kimeria, and Mzigo. (She lets Munira christen her in her new undertaking because he has also helped ruin her life by forcing Karega out of his job.) Karega leaves Ilmorog, and drifts from job to job. He is a dockworker, works in a sugar refinery, sells fruits and sheepskins by the side of the road, and finally becomes a radical union leader. At the end of the book, even though he has been cleared of the murders, the officials keep him in detention because he is "a communist at heart." But Karega's evolution to this is one of the aspects of the whole of political developments in Kenya, and among African people, that Ngugi brings us face to face with, as the growth of a single personality by means of that character's exposure to Ngugi's thorough and cathartic revelation of reality.

Petals of Blood is a novel of grim reality for sure, but it is, at the same time, a novel of hope because it is a novel of struggle. At the end of the book, Karega, though imprisoned, is visited by a young woman worker, who tells him of the further radicalization of the workers' movement, and assures him he will be back. Karega's detention and Ngugi's, essentially for the same reasons, only shows us proof in the real world of the truth of Ngugi's staggering portrait.

Stylistically, Ngugi's prose is thick with portent, implication, irony, and battlefield humor. The novel uses flashback and flashback within flashback. It is circular, coming round to where it started, but actually it is a spiral motion, since its "circularity" is motion to a higher level of revelation and perception. Ngugi lays out with great clarity exactly what class struggle is in Africa today; only the dangerously naïve (or perhaps it is youthful idealism) or upholders of the status quo would even shape their mouths to deny the reality of Ngugi's blistering art.

He gives us Africa old and Africa new and Africa in transition, and the hope of Africa future. The book is also rooted deeply in East African life and culture; its telling is itself like the griot high up in his gig, with a social and political concreteness and again *clarity* that constantly astonishes. The book is a chronicle, an analysis steeped in sharply wrought dialectic; it is also an admonition, that we must choose sides, that perhaps we have already chosen sides, and that there remain only two sides, regardless of our subjectivism or lies or evasions and copouts, only two sides — one that of the people, the other that of the enemies of the people. Ngugi demands that we choose and his demand, as *Petals of Blood*, is high revolutionary art.

From *The Autobiography of LeRoi Jones/Amiri Baraka*

In 1979 Baraka was sentenced to 48 consecutive weekends in a Harlem halfway house for assault and resisting arrest. While incarcerated he wrote *The Autobiography*, and with this work he joins the great black autobiographical tradition that extends from Frederick Douglass and Harriet Jacobs to Malcolm X. His story begins with his birth in Newark, New Jersey, and ends with his conversion to socialism. "Error Farce" explores his time in the Air Force (1954–57), during which he initiated himself into the worlds of art and mind. He went into the service after flunking out of Howard University, "the capstone of Negro education." This first chapter, which is slightly condensed, takes up after his Basic Training. (Asterisks indicate omitted text.) The second chapter here, "The Black Arts," reproduced in its entirety, is an amazing and candid account of his stormy black-nationalist adventures in Harlem in 1965.

—wjh

Error Farce

* * * * *

I was sent for some reason to Chanute Field in Rantoul, Illinois. I was to be enrolled in weather school. Their aptitude tests said I was supposed to be a weather man. A radiosonde operator or rawinsonde operator to be exact. Which meant I was trained to send helium-filled balloons aloft and, looking through an instrument like the surveyor's transit, chart the airspeed and direction, air temperature and pressure. I was supposed to work at a weather station or at an airport, going out to check the little white weather shack with its latticed sides and slanted roof. (You can see these little white shacks at airports out near the runway.) I didn't mind this idea really. Weather men in the Air Force had weird kinds of hours. You usually worked three days on, two days off or something like that, so it was not the normal nine-to-five day. The three days you worked you stayed out at the airport or at the weather station and didn't go home and sometimes you would be at out-of-the-way places, Greenland or the Azores or somewhere wild. It seemed OK to me. Even the isolation, though I did not want to go to Greenland. Thule, Greenland!

But then, that was so legendary that I wouldn't even have minded that. But that did not happen.

There were only whites in my training squadron now. And some of the others, maybe all of them, had some college. I guess that's why they'd chosen us for weather school. And I guess that's why there were no other blacks in that squadron. And in some ways it felt like Barringer [High School] again. And, jim, that part of Illinois is a crime in itself. Flat and hostile, like the real South crept up on you. Southern Illinois: towns like Kankakee, Champaign-Urbana, Decatur. Stuck halfway between Chicago and St. Louis. (When I could I started to go to Chicago every weekend and stay at Kurt's house and roam around the South Side near the University of Chicago.)

But that was a strange place, and for me especially, altogether. The dead of winter, in little wooden barracks heated by coal furnaces. (It turned out later, in a heavy scandal, that the brother of the commanding general owned the coal company, which is why the base heating system had never been converted. Meanwhile they had one of us per barracks each week keeping the coal furnaces stoked, and if we let them go out we'd get court-martialed.)

The same disconnection and isolation [that resulted from Basic Training] characterized my stay at Chanute. And the first days were even worse, certainly now that I was just among white dudes again. As isolated and lonely as I might feel among bloods, to be the lone spot in the buttermilk is totally a drag. You have to assume a whole other character, just to communicate! You must speak a different language, adjust culturally, stay at a point of tension in which there can be no real relaxation.

Before our first test I went into the latrine and studied the materials. The next day I got a perfect paper, 100. It was pronounced with such weightiness the entire class looked around at me. I was surprised but better, it made me feel somewhat restored after my heavy defeat in school. Maybe I was not totally stupid.

After that there were a few white guys who'd come around the bunk to check up on why I'd gotten that perfect paper. A blond jock with a perfect German crew cut, a good-natured All American named Van Allison. Two ex–college dudes, one the hypertypical Ivy specimen, University of Maine, named Kreeger, and a short swarthy guy from the University of Maryland named Voster. (Hey, were all these guys German or something?) Kreeger, Voster, and I did some running close by the base. A few bars. We kept up a more or less steady conversation, though as I said, my conversational form had retreated somewhat. Kreeger had the classic "Princeton cut" and wore plain toes, gray flannel slacks, and blue button-down oxford shirts with the sleeves rolled up. He had a real Maine accent and was really a nice guy. He'd gotten tossed out for something and his obsession seemed to be to get back into the Ivy. Voster was a self-proclaimed intellectual, wanted to be a science major of some kind. I don't know how he ever got into the Air Force. (But then I don't know how I got in either.) It was a funny trio when engaged. Kreeger, off-the-top Ivy-isms; Voster, deep mock-probing philosophical; and whatever the fuck I was then. That was a college-type intellectual hookup, but bright enough and interesting in that context.

Later, I ran into a guy named Strassbaugh (another German?) who was in another squadron. He was the first hip white boy I met. Strass liked jazz and talked like a blood. He wanted to play saxophone and always talked about it. He was always looking for someplace to practice. And the "squares" and "farmers" that made up a large part of our companions-in-arms constantly drove Strass to distraction. Strass and I went into Champaign-Urbana looking for music one night, like trying to ice-skate in Death Valley.

There were two bloods I knew fairly well. One, a guy from one of the maintenance squadrons, was in the mold of my running buddies in Basic and Hillside Place. But he got further advanced in training and was gone in a minute. The other guy was really out. I met him one time at the University of Illinois library, where I started going from time to time. I even started taking a couple of courses, General Psychology 1 and 2, and got good grades. We walked back to the base talking. He was carrying a thick Dostoevsky under his arm, *The Brothers Karamazov*. I never saw him without that.

John Karamazov (I'm lying about his last name) saw me coming toward the library a few days later and the maintenance brother was with me, Jerry, in his civies, which were bright as tomorrow. Karamazov and I, of course, were dressed in less color—in honor of our training. We were headed for the university's weekly movie showing which some of the base intellectuals would make and John leans over and whispers in my ear, "Who is that *person*?" referring to Jerry. John was slender and stiff, he wore sweaters then but later he was always in a suit. John became very wealthy later in New York, after an early fling at a respectable bohemianism. I think he married four different white women and was last heard of (by me) living in a penthouse on Park Avenue (he'd made money in advertising, one of the first black advertising agencies) but rumor had it at last hearing that he'd lost his bux. But then he was roaming around in southern Illinois in the Error Farce too. I never found out why.

* * * * *

I would go up to Chicago as often as I could on the weekends. A bus from Rantoul up to Chicago or the train. The train was better. I might walk up under the El and check out the loud blues life. I went to see T-Bone Walker one night at the Crown Propeller. Kurt a couple times had some people over and he introduced me to some. We talked, the two of us, about Howard. The semester before his last one and he was trying to figure out what law school to go to. But I also ran a lot by myself as I was wont to. I snaked through the South Side and up to near North.

One time I was drifting around the South Side, near the University of Chicago, feeling alone, as usual, isolated, as usual, my usual emotional stock in trade, and I bump into this bookstore called the Green Door. It had a green door, and kind of orange plastic in the window so the sun wouldn't ruin the books. I came to rest staring into the window. There were books there I didn't recognize, a few I did. Like we'd had *Portrait of the Artist* my first year at Rutgers and I'd looked at it, but it was a *school* book and for that reason I didn't take it seriously. Though parts of it vaguely fascinated me even then. A copy of this was in the window, and next to it *Ulysses*, the book opened to the first page so you could see the words "Stately plump Buck Mulligan . . . " I stared at the words and tried to read them. I saw other books, Pound, Eliot, Thomas, philosophy books, art books, statistics, and poetry. Something dawned on me, like a big light bulb over my noggin. The comic-strip *Idea* lit up my mind at that moment as I stared at the books. I suddenly understood that I didn't know a hell of a lot about anything. What it was that seemed to move me then was that learning was *important*. I'd never thought that before. The employment agency I'd last gone to college at, the employment agency approach of most schools I guess, does not emphasize the *beauties* the absolute *joy* of learning. That is what came to me. Cut off as I was from the artificial concept of education, I suddenly appreciated what real education might be. I vowed, right then, to learn something new every day. It was a deep revelation, something I felt throughout my whole self. I was going to learn something every day. That's what I would do. Not just as a pastime, something to do in the service, but as a life commitment.

I went in and bought some books. *Portrait of the Artist* and Thomas' *Portrait of the Artist as a Young Dog*. In a couple of weeks

I bought *Ulysses*. But I went home this first time in a daze, having leaped past myself, to myself. All kinds of new connections yammered in my head. My heart beat faster my skin tingled. I could understand now a little better what was happening. I needed to learn. I wanted to study. But I wanted to learn and study stuff I wanted to learn and study. Serious, uncommon, weird stuff! At that moment my life was changed.

Another month or so and I was leaving Chanute. I was glad, even though I'd met some people, but I did not see myself remaining too long in the flatlands of middle America. Sometimes I felt like there were witches and devils out there. Plus every morning at about 4:30 the guy in charge of putting on the lights would throw them on and the switch was connected up with his own radio, which brought the "shitkickers," as Strass called them, at us full burst. At that time of the morning most of the city boys were not interested in country and Western.

But I had been elected Class Leader in weather training school because of the high marks I received consistently and one time Airman of the Month, for the academics, not the soldiering. I even began to look forward to tech school ending and being sent somewhere as a weather man, with lots of time to myself to pursue my newfound cause of learning, something every day! However, they pulled a trick on me of sorts. As the highest-finishing airman in the class I was given first choice, along with a few others, of where I would be shipped, out of a group of bases that needed weather men. The choices were right outside DC, which I seriously considered. If I had done that no doubt I would've gone back to Howard. Bermuda was also mentioned, plus Germany, Okinawa, and Greenland. But the one I wanted was Puerto Rico. Actually it was a tight choice between the DC base (Andrews AFB), Bermuda, or Puerto Rico. The enlisted man scam had it that "Puerto Rico was a country club" . . . "light duty and good weather . . . cheap prices and fine women." Hey, dudes was saying, you need to take Puerto Rico. And that was that, my choice was Puerto Rico. "A country club." But little did I know.

In choosing Puerto Rico I had then to sign up to go to gunnery school down there and become not just the normal weather man but a *weather gunner*. That is, I had volunteered to fly in B-36 bombers as a rawindsonde operator as well as a "right rear gunner." I thought, Hey, I'll be flying after all. Even the gun shit was part of an old romantic image of tail gunners in the Second World War, chewing gum, cracking jokes, and firing at the enemy. But reality, my friends, is always something else again.

Plus, the "country club" that I'd signed for apparently *was* a country club. Or at least *had been* a country club until we got there. The gargoyles at Strategic Air Command had also heard the airman scuttlebutt about Ramey AFB and they were determined to do something about it. So they chose to start doing something about it the same time I got sent down there. Talking about some bad luck! (I wrote something about this in a play, *A Recent Killing*.) The same time I arrived and a few other guys from Chanute, perhaps even the same day, the SAC commander sent his son-in-law (rumor had it) Bertram Harrison, a 38-year-old gung-ho brigadier general, to clean the joint up. It seems that Ramey had the highest venereal disease rate in SAC, the lowest efficiency rating on the mock bombing raids that SAC stages pretending to bomb large cities in the US and other places. So Harrison was sent down to gung-ho the base back in line and make us the efficient trained killers we were supposed to be.

I could see, once I got down there, how Ramey could and probably was being run on the casual side. The standard work uniform was white tee shirt and blue jeans and either the regular fatigue hat or, if you were in one of the flying squadrons, a baseball cap in your squadron's color. I was assigned to the 73rd Strategic Reconnaissance Squadron, which was later changed to the 73rd Bombardment Squadron. We wore blue baseball caps, though I never had one.

Puerto Rico was the first permanent base I was assigned to. My first permanent assignment (it turned out to be my last). Before I went down I was given a short leave and I went home. I remember going to Steve Korret's house in the Village. He had a new wife now, Charlene, a beautiful dancer—she's now a slightly older but still beautiful novelist. We had talked and he had introduced me to various people, white and black, streaming through his house. I remember talking to a white painter named Norman who painted strange unconnected quasi figures that had mystical significance. A tall black woman painter, Virginia. A short dark man, a poet whose name was Karl. At any rate, Steve and his wife had to leave and left me there. I was reading something. I was leaving from his house directly for the airport and thence to Puerto Rico. I was sitting alone reading and musing, then I looked at the time and I had to go, if I was going to catch my plane. I put the book down. My duffelbag, packed full, was standing in the corner. I made ready to leave. I grabbed the bag and went to heave it up onto my shoulder as I had done many times before. But this time I couldn't move it! The duffelbag would not budge! You'll say, it was psychological. You didn't want to leave. Your mind was playing tricks on you. Be that as it may, I couldn't move the bag. I strained to get it up onto my shoulder and it would not move.

I panicked for a minute, then sat down. My hands were shaking! I said, out loud, I've got to pick up this bag. I've got to get back to the base or I'll be AWOL. I went on cajoling myself, pleading with myself, and finally I tried again and the bag came up easily. I hefted it up to my shoulder and went out the door, down the stairs, and got a cab to Idlewild Airport.

Because Ramey was a permanent base and a big SAC base, I met a buncha people. And they were from the various classes and sectors of the base. One thing, if you are at all serious about understanding this country arrogantly called "this society," you'll see after any close investigation how absolutely structured according to class and caste it is in all areas. Nothing, no piece, of US life escapes! It is a class society in every nook and cranny of its total existence. Its material base and its ideas. Its economic foundation and its institutional and ideological superstructure. And this was clearer to me in practice than it ever was, until very recently, in theory. I always dealt with it as it came up, as I had to or was able to deal with it (just like you!) but I didn't always call it anything. But as I got older I recognized it more and more clearly for what it was, class and caste divisions. The rich the middle the poor. The white the light the brown the black. Everywhere in you America!

At Ramey, since I was in a flying squadron I was again with mostly whites. The flying squadrons were the "high class" groups on the base. Certainly the service makes all these things more obvious than ever before. There were officers and noncoms then enlisted men. That was the basic class structure, the fundamental hierarchy of the joint. And these were in all the squadrons, but the flying squadrons were tops, the upper class. Then came the maintenance squadrons and within that division there were divisions. Then underneath the maintenance squadrons the Air Police, then motor pool, then cooks or food service. Most of the blacks and other nonwhites were in food service, the motor pool, or maintenance. Only a few were in the flying squadrons. And this made some of the ones who were in them mad as all outdoors. Like the yellow madness of my childhood grew up and gone to college—now gone and joined the Air Force! I remember one Negro who never spoke to or was ever seen with any blood the whole time I was on that base. All he did was ride his motorcycle and sometimes ride his motorcycle with some white boys who rode motorcycles. I met the dude and he wasn't a bad dude, he was just crazy. He even talked like a white boy. But not the pursed-lip stiff-jaw of the academic white imitator. This guy "towked" like a working-class white boy from the Northeast. It amazed me. And even when the other bloods on the base would say funny things about this dude I would tell them (though I hadn't penetrated it down to theory level) that the dude was a nice cat, he was just out of his mind! I guess he talked to me because I was in a flying squadron too.

So again the relationships I developed were somewhat complex. I had friends, a lot of them white, in the flying squadron I was in as well as in the 60th Bomb and 301st Bomb. The 73rd, as I said, had blue baseball caps, the 60th red baseball caps, and the 301st had yellow baseball caps. Dudes in other bomb squadrons I knew because we would go to gunnery school together or target study (studying Russian cities from aerial photos so you would get familiar with the cities you were going to bomb from high up in the air). We sometimes went to embarrassing harassings like so-called Character Guidance. Where they would march us down to the theater and teach us how to be good airmen and stop getting venereal disease, &c.

So I got to know guys from the different flying squadrons, but especially gunners and other weather gunners. There was a little group of white weather gunners I hung with, and other crew members. They were mostly good guys, young like I was, some younger, naive about life and brash enough not to give a shit too much about our racial and national distinctions. They were the kinda guys who talked about "roaring into town." They'd go steaming off the base and get staggering, falling-down, singing drunk and not even know where they'd been the next day. That was one group and sometimes I'd be with them putting away watered-down beer like there was no tomorrow and cracking stupid jokes. These were the kinda guys they mighta shown in the war movies but not corny like that. Burke, a French Canadian from up in New England. Reilly, a big red-faced Irish lad from Boston. Goodsen, a freckled-faced All American Jew. Burset, a short funny-grinning perpetually joking and staggering Welsh American who aspired, he said, to the heaven of perpetual drunkenness. We greeted each other with shouts and there was always pushing and patting and horsing around. These guys were all good soldiers, good airmen, but they liked to have a good time and many times that's not possible playing war.

Another group was formed really around the painter, William White, a black dude from North Carolina. He was a weather gunner in the 301st and always wore the yellow baseball cap. Tall, introspective and serious, White had a barracks room full of paintings when I first met him. He later went to New York to continue painting after first going to Howard, even though I warned him continually not to go to that sorry joint. Except my protestations must have seemed to him like a simple case of unrequited love. White became one of my best and closest friends in life. He died, still trying to paint in New York, mixing methadone and whiskey.

But somehow one time I got to White's room. Oh, yeh, I'd met him in gunnery class not long after I came to Ramey. He'd come a little earlier. And the incident that brought us together was when some dude, a fat young white farm boy from Colorado I had known at Chanute (in fact it was he, Bodey, Clifton Bodey, who was in charge of snapping on the lights and hence the shitkicking sounds there in Illinois), pulled my chair out from under me one day in tech school, apparently thinking to make an impractical joke. I wheeled on his ass and fired right into his face (not a gun but my bony brown fist). He staggered backward, a big question mark on his face. I said, "You didn't think I could hit that hard, did you?" Really, at a loss for words myself and half expecting him to make a sudden counterattack. For sure he hadn't gone down and one of the old bits of folk wisdom I remember has always said, If you throw your best and they don't go down it's time to get in the wind. But Bodey only pulled himself up straight, other dudes in the class laughed, and White was among them laughing his ass off into his hands.

I guess Bodey was too surprised to do anything. He said some things designed to give battle but since he just didn't charge and start throwing me on my ass (he must've outweighed me by about 100 pounds) nothing happened and as it turned out Bodey and I never really became enemies, in fact he was closer to me than a lot of people. Because in a few months he had married a Puerto Rican prostitute about ten years older than he was (he was eighteen) and a lot of the dudes made fun of him for it, especially the white Southerners.

After that I would go to White's room a lot. Since I had weird roommates. We bunked three in a room, if you were lucky two, and all of that was considered luxury. I think my first roommates were Bodey and a white guy looked like Steve McQueen, named Cooper, from somewhere in Tennessee. Cooper was a buck sergeant (three stripes), Bodey and I two stripes (airman second class). Cooper was

the classic taciturn Southerner, probably filled with all the prejudice of that particular specimen but with the quiet dignity that
made acting nasty about it impossible. Bodey was loud and wrong,
naive and corny as the little Colorado farm he'd come from. He was
every stereotype you could think up and more. He collected gun
magazines and motorcycle magazines and girly magazines (Cooper
read these last ones too on occasion) but had nothing to do with
guns, motorcycles, or women. He claimed to know all about cars
and eventually he did get one, he got a motorcycle too (so did
Cooper), and when Cooper finally shipped out going to another
base I left Bodey there with a wife who spoke very little American
and no English at all and two kids, one on the runway and one in
the hangar (in airman talk), a stranger in a strange land, completely
ignorant of reality.

So I had to go to White's room to hang out when I wasn't on the
drinking bouts with Reilly and Burke and the others. White had collected a weird little group around him. They were mostly black
though there was one white dude who hung around us, Vincent, a
pudgy almost feminine Italian dude from the Bronx, with skin so
white he looked like he never got in the sun even though we were
in Puerto Rico. There was also an almost blond-haired Chicano
dude named Lopa who looked like a white boy even to the close observer. It was only when he talked that you could hear the halting
syllabics of his accent and it still always amazed me when I thought
that Lopa was a Mexican. This got Lopa in trouble before he got off
that base too. Once in a bar some "farmers" were talking bad about
"spics" and "greasers" in the charming official speech of the white
American and Lopa was leaning against the jukebox staring right
into their mouths. I think there were three of these farmers. It was
in Aguadilla, the closest town to Ramey, but in a bar frequented by
a lot of airmen. Lopa let them know he was Chicano and that he
didn't like what they said and that they were generally and unrecon-
cilably full of shit. One guy went to throw on Lopa and Lopa cut
him, across his face, sliced the shit out of him, leaving a scar, hideous and flaming, going from this farmer's ear down to the point of
his chin. Lopa did almost a year in the stockade for this shit and
when he got out he still had to do that year again in the regular service. But it was great when we walked across the base together and
we would see this little knot of Southerners approach us and we'd
see the one Lopa had cut, marked this motherfucker up somethin
terrible. Lopa would cut his eyes at the dude and smirk with utter
contempt and the agitators in our group would cut the fool.

The most way-out dude in this group was Yodo. His real name was something else. And people were always startling us by calling him that name, especially if they said Airman Lambert, because Yodo hadn't had any stripes (I think he might even have had three one time) in a very long time. Yodo's full name was Yodofus T. Syllieabla, "the high priest of Swahili, the czar of yap," he'd add, "and Phersona Figues is my pal." Phersona Figues was another one of the group whom Yodo had named. He named everyone of us, some odd name or another. Some of us he simply turned our names around. Like he would call me Yorel Senoj. White was Mailliw Etihw. Though he always called Vincent, Vincent, and Lopa, Lopa.

Yodo was absolutely committed to jazz, African American improvised music. His whole imaginative and creative life revolved around the music. You never saw Yodo without albums in his hands. Even during work hours. (He worked in the base dispensary.) White uniform and blue "cunt" cap, long striding somewhere. Yodo usually carried a cane, or some stick he'd fastened a plastic top to with a red ball or some such inside the top. He called the stick his "all-purpose" stick and named it too. The stick's name was Anacronobienoid. He was great for holding dialogues with the stick whenever it suited him. Like he might say, after holding a conversation with one of us about something, "Well, Anacronobienoid, what do you think of that?" Or he might say, if he disagreed with something we'd said, "Anacronobienoid disagrees." Or something. Once, a white noncom was giving Yodo a hard time about something and Yodo, without blinking, said, "Look, Anacronobienoid is laughing at you! Anacronobienoid thinks you're a joke." And he would stretch his eyes and make weird gestures with the stick. The poor noncom, rather than go on with it, just got in the wind.

Yodo was one of the funniest dudes I'd ever met. By the time I met him he'd been in the service about nine years. And during that time he'd floated around going from one base to another and re-enlisting simply because he didn't know what he'd be doing once he got out. Also, I think at one point he might have thought he could make some kind of career as a medical technician which he didn't think was possible in New Orleans where he'd come from and so he thought the service would give him a career then he could retire relatively young and just cool it. But he'd run afoul of the service, gotten into some trouble and had his stripes removed, and this had crushed him, though he never admitted it.

Yodo's dialogue or sometimes monologue about the music was almost nonstop. He'd talk about Bud and Bird and Brownie and Monk.

When he showed up at the door he'd swoop in with albums under his arm. On payday he'd buy whatever was in the BX, which wasn't much, and immediately come over to White's after work to play the side. He'd also write away for sides where possible. We'd play the sides and drink whatever was available to drink. Usually rum, since that was the cheapest in Puerto Rico.

Payday was only once a month, so that took on the character of a monthly bash, a big payday party. And much liquor and whatever else got bought. There was much going into town, usually Aguadilla, which was right down the road. Some would go further away to Ponce, Mayagüez, Arecibo, and the most ambitious would go all the way to the other end of the island to San Juan, usually by *guagua* (bus) unless you were a noncom or officer and had a car.

The music had always been a heavy part of my life, but Yodo raised it up in another way. Cut off as we were, and as he had been for so long, the music was a connection with black life. It was also a refuge, a way out of the agonizingly boring dreary white Cracker-oriented service life, especially in Puerto Rico, where one felt even more cut off from the normal channels of American and African American life. One could not shoot up to Chicago on the weekends or Rochester. Airmen piled into the Puerto Rican cities whenever they could and there were places in Puerto Rico full of adventure, beauty, all kinds of pleasure, but despite all this you knew you were away from home, on the real side. And what's more, stuck in some intolerable madness you now had almost no understanding of how you'd got sucked into.

We talked about that all the time. How silly we were, how dumb, &c., we had been to get hooked up in this bullshit. For one reason or another. Some without other opportunity. Some looking for a way out of a dead-end situation. A way into a career. Adventure and excitement. The claim of manhood. There were many reasons, but at this point, none of them were satisfactory.

There were some guys in the Air Force who did dig it. I have to believe they were a minority. Though there were a good number who'd signed up to do long stretches, some even to do a whole twenty, to retire. But these people were strange to us. They were among the "lames" we identified casually, squares and cornballs, gung-ho freaks and warcats who made us squirm for their simple-minded pleasure. We would always get on Yodo about the fact that he'd re-upped and had been in so long. We called him the oldest air-man basic in the service.

So White's room became a kind of haven. And once Yodo and

some of the others started showing occasionally at my room, which would send Bodey and Cooper out right smart, then sometimes we'd all gather in there for our record and booze and nonstop rap sessions. That was our basic life in the Air Force. We'd drink rum and play music and talk — project our desires or reminisce about what we'd lost or wanted people to think we'd had. And we became a kind of defensive unit for ourselves, a kind of salon.

White, of course, was the most serious painter. And when I first met him he was painting in mainly realistic style but occasionally veering off into surrealism. Later, in New York, under the influence of the abstract expressionists he developed a kind of surreal-abstractionist style that was very much his own. It was, of course, his nationality that slowed him down in his ascent in the world of fine art.

Yodo drew too, and painted some outright surrealistic pieces that revolved around the music. Bird with a duckbill Yodo named "Klacktovedisteen." Yodo said the duckbill made a sound "Klack Klack Klack," which is why Bird called his tune "Klacktovedisteen." He had a painting called "In Walked Bud," after Monk's tune. Yodo would enter the room sometimes, saying that, "In Walked Bud," and then dance in like Thelonious Monk danced next to his piano when the rest of the band was playing.

We met a couple of other guys in the Air Force who began to hang with us or hang with me. One was Jim Mitchum, from New York City, who walked around even then taking photographs. He was never anyplace without at least one camera. Jim Mitchum was kind of a snob and he talked in an exaggeratedly near-"proper" style, which was funny if you thought about it. He'd been in the service a while and his speech was meant to impress you that he was not just your regular airman deuce (two stripes), that he was some kind of intellectual.

Phil Peakes was another photographer with the bunch. He was white, Jewish. Apparently from some pretty heavily endowed suburb of Boston. Phil also was kind of snobbish, though he was still young enough for that not to have completely got the best of him. He was the kind of guy who needed to be an intellectual to pull it off and at the time hadn't got it all sufficiently together, so he was a mixture of nose up (he had a large one too) and nose regular. Phil and Jim and I would have the most openly arty conversations (according to our standards at the time) though on the real side Yodo and them were actually talking about some deeper questions, even casually.

Jim and Phil always felt slightly perturbed when Yodo was on the scene. And Yodo, sensing this, would pick at them in his not so subtle way. Having Anacronobienoid speak haughtily to them or chide them for their lack of knowledge about African American improvised music. Phil could cop by waving his latest acquisition, Glen Gould playing the Brandenburg Concerto or the Goldberg Variations or some such. But Phil didn't have such a heavy knowledge about that stuff either, not really. Jim would haltingly try to scoff at what Yodo might be asking, like for instance did he, Jim, like "Glass Enclosure" or "Un Poco Loco" best? Or who was playing drums on "Ornithology"? Or was he a Blakey fan (Yodo called him by his Muslim name, Buhainia) or did he dig Max?

Still, we were an enlarged salon and the contradictions inside that entity brought out all kinds of conversations and conflicts that were usually at least funny. We thought of ourselves as the base cognoscenti, the real hipsters or the base intellectuals, depending on what part of the group would be together. We all were unified by our hatred of the Air Force. Phil and Jim acted as if they had been kidnapped from their intellectual pursuits and now had been forcibly surrounded by unwashed idiots. Yodo, like Strassbaugh, thought there was too many squares, lames he called them, around the joint. And though he had re-upped before crossing our paths (and him losing his stripes) he confirmed that he would be leaving for good as soon as he could.

We had nothing but contempt for the "old soldiers," especially those who remained in the service for security, what they called "three hots and a flop." The sergeants who would counsel us that there was nothing outside for us, no jobs, no future, that we had better stay inside where we knew we had something going.

Something going? What? The fool, Harrison, was fanatical about trying to get all of us soldiering, like his brother-in-law wanted. He'd roam the base and show up without warning. He even came into my room one morning when I should have already been down at the flight line and scared the holy shit outta me. I thought it was my man JWT and I looked up at the one star on this guy's cap like the one-eyed Cyclops and babbled some shit trying to get outta there.

To check the VD Harrison even started passing out negative awards. To the squadron with the highest venereal disease rate on the base, he would announce this honor at the Saturday parade. (We started having weekly parades, Saturday morning, in full class A uniform!) This squadron then had the honor of marching to work every morning at seven, complete with the base band in front of them. The band members despised Harrison because before the VD marches, they had it mostly made. An occasional parade or officers' affair. But now they had to march every morning and play a full parade on Saturdays. We hung around with some of the band members, naturally. And they were death on Harrison.

The 73rd got the VD award one month and I think it really did cause some of the borderline VD cases at least to question the cleanliness of the *choche* before plunging in. I don't think it mattered too much to the wilder ones. When they got the little scratch each month they'd go charging off the base and lay down with the first *puta* they saw. "Hey, GI! $2 short time . . . $4 long time!"

But, God, could that shit make you feel sorry for yourself! Not even light out, line up, Atten-hup!, then some jive march music and go poking through the darkness down to the flight line. If you wanted to eat those mornings (that month you had the marches) you had to rise up still earlier. Though the food was so bad I changed my eating habits. A couple Sundays they had chicken in the mess hall and the shit was bleeding. Rare chicken! Sunday evenings they had some thick wet baloney. I gave it up. Found out I could get people's salads and desserts in exchange for that bleeding chicken. So I became a vegetarian. I was always walking around the base with nuts and raisins in my pockets. The wildest thing about the mess hall was when the maintenance dudes would come in. Some of 'em didn't want to wash up. You could see it especially on the white dudes (at least that's what we said) and the sight of somebody eating a slice of white bread with the black greasy fingerprints all over the bread could take your appetite. It helped reinforce the elitist tendency our salon took on.

There were a couple other members of the Ramey Air Force Base Intellectuals' Salon. Sid, a guy from Syracuse, who had gone to the University of Rochester, pre-med. He later got out and became a doctor. I guess he was drawn to some of us because we came on like intellectuals and I had gone to college. Jim to CCNY. Phil to Brandeis. Though we'd all dropped out for one reason or another. Sid smoked a pipe. He had a job in base supply or some such paper-pushing gig. Jim was in a maintenance squadron, open bay barracks, with the plebeians, and this bugged the hell out of him. "They're ignorant of everything important," he'd say. As stiff as an unused hardcover.

Another dude I got close to was a very short shriveled-up Jewish dude named Laffowiss. We called him Laffy, though he had usually a sad and forlorn expression on his face but it didn't stop him from constantly making jokes. His favorite entrance was bent over pretending to have a cigar in his mouth or fingers like Groucho Marx. Sometimes Laffy would stand like that or slightly modified even in the presence of a noncom or officer. He was from the Lower East Side old style. The Lower East Side that Mike Gold talked about in *Jews Without Money*. He was the true mensch, son of the Jewish working class. Cynical, full of a crystal-clear sardonic humor that cut through the crass bullshit of the Air Force with ease. But like the rest of us he was always running into trouble because of it.

Laffy was always complaining about the Air Force cuisine. He missed the East European specialties that characterized the Lower East Side. He was always loudly wishing for smoked herring, or pickles or pickled tomatoes, or whitefish. He was a nonstop questioner of everything. Slumped over, either pretending to be Groucho Marx or actually being Louie Laffowiss. He hung with us easily, laughing at us and with us and at himself. And the most common quality he had was an absolute and uncompromising hatred of the service, and the people who thought they were important because they had some kind of rank or status in it. Yodo and Laffy together would make a classic TV sitcom if TV was in the real people's hands instead of the few gimlet nitwits that run it now.

I guess the salon, I'm calling it now, but actually it was a defensive unit, a sanity-maintaining collective of aspiring intellectuals, taught us all something. We had the jazz foundation mixed with concern for the graphic arts—painting and photography—a couple of academics ensconced among us for laughs, and a few of us interested in literature. Laffy was a nonstop reader, as I had developed into being. The rest of the guys liked to talk about books, Phil and Sid were always talking about what they read. Jim always carried a book along with his camera. White read what he thought was serious and Yodo read *Downbeat, Metronome*, and any book on the music.

The high point of our salon structure came when I took a parttime job evenings in the library. The money was negligible, but I had spent quite a bit of time in there. And when this big WAF, a sister from Texas, who was the day clerk, let me know there was a parttime job at nights, I leaped at it. Joyce was about 6 foot 2 and I guess had some kind of undefined crush on me, but she was a good friend and earnest sister who'd gotten in the WAF to try to see the world. And she'd been to Europe and was now in Puerto Rico suffering under the shit like the rest of us.

The librarian was a little plump middle-aged career service librarian who saw that I not only knew how to run the library in the evening quickly enough, but enjoyed being around the books, so she gave me the run of the place. In a month or so she actually let me order the books and see to the stocking of the entire library. We had a hurricane in '55 and it blew every wooden structure on Ramey down and destroyed the town of Aguadilla. The rebuilt library was modern and even had a brand-new hi-fi set in it. The music library was mostly European concert music, but we were into that too. And for me it was really a learning period about this music and I was buying Bach, Mozart, Beethoven, Stravinsky, trying to fill in my knowledge, so that between our own collections and the library collection we were giving ourselves a collective education.

So that was smooth. In the evenings, a group of us from the salon would go into the library. This was after hours and we had the whole building to ourselves. And we would read and bullshit and drink and listen to music turned all the way up. It was the closest thing to paradise we ever encountered down there. Years later I met a guy who had also gone through Ramey and he said he'd seen my name in a bunch of the books there, A/2C L. Jones.

But in every way, like it or not, pleasant or not, the service was my graduate school or maybe it was undergraduate school. For one thing, I began to keep a journal, a diary, of what was going on. I can't find the thing now, though I guess it's still around somewhere. But it was the pain and frustration of this enforced isolation that began to make me scrawl my suffering to seek some audience for my effusive self-pity. As the journal went on it became more and more a listing of the various books I was reading. Because now, so completely cut off, I read constantly, almost every waking hour. I began reading the *New York Times*—you could only get it Sundays—and at the time 75 cents was an exorbitant fee, but I paid it. And that in itself was an adventure because I had never had much knowledge of the *Times* and its presumptions.

The best-seller list became a kind of bible for me. I tried to read everything on it. Ordering through either the library or the intellectual Readers' Subscription book club, which offered Joyce and Melville and James, &c. But I was in a very conscious and very agitated search for information, and it was focused more and more directly on literature. Later, I could see even how my handwriting changed in the journal. How it took on new shape and spoke of further comprehension and consideration of questions which before I could not have formed. I wanted to become an intellectual.

The world of Howard University and its brown and yellow fantasy promise had faded, leaving a terrible frustration and sense of deprivation. That I had through my own irresponsible acts deprived myself of something valuable. I thought the sharp and relentless striving to become intellectual was the answer. At some point I wanted to be back at Howard, at another point, and more and more consistently now, I was almost contemptuous of it and the people there, children. Though the constant self-pity I felt being there "among heathens" was an endless rebuke.

And then, on top of all this, I would actually, every once in a while, see some Howard people. Officers now. We were completely removed and separated from each other now. And the class realization I got from that, the class consciousness, was stunning to me. I could see that we were in different spheres. Of course I could not verbalize it as class, &c, but my perception of it as class, as a separation upheld by the society itself, was keen and staggering. Most of those Howard dudes who were officers in the Air Force avoided me. One I did meet at a base in the South and we talked in his room, and it was cold and frustrating. Our speech had been separated by reality. We no longer linked up. Our interests were different. I could hear the simplistic careerism. The prepared sheepdom of the readied-for-the-slaughter Negro pursuing his "good job" into hell itself. And "who was I?" was going through my head. Who was I? Where did I fit in? Standing now on the side of the road as the select browns and yellows marched by heroically, triumphantly, toward that shaft of gold leaned out the sky to call them home to yalla jesus. Some calendar shit! I mean it reminded me of the somber glories of the calendars one got in funeral parlors right across the street from the yalla folks' church.

There were a few black officers at Ramey. One was even on the same crew with me. N-45 "Not ready" was what the N meant. It meant we were a bunch of trainees, or ne'er-do-wells or misfits. Gadsen, the Negro officer on that crew, was classic, I guess, though I never knew many of them well. He was dark brown but absolutely yellow in his aspirations and kind of brownish despite it all. He was a link with the past, in some sense, for me. I think he'd gone to Lincoln. He had a big blue car with a plaid top, a convertible, and was considered, by whomever, the most eligible black bachelor on the base. He was young, not much older than me, a second lieutenant, so that he fit into the power structure in a commendable way, plus he was single and independent and could fly back and forth up the island pursuing what limited pleasures the island might offer to someone in the service. Though, for sure, we all surmised that those pleasures were much more than we would ever be exposed to. It was rumored that Gadsen always had one woman leaving the room as one was entering. And he enjoyed a kind of prestige among some of the base's blacks, a mixed love and hate. But the white boys, ever cognizant of the caste-class structure of the real America, constantly made Gadsen the butt of their jokes, so he could not be too uppity, at least in their heads.

One fat first lieutenant, a yellow Negro straight out, got caught up in some weird stuff that socked it home to me the sheepish quality expected of the careerist Negro. A fat white master sergeant got into a "game" being played by some of the younger officers near the flight line. They were tossing each other's hats around, which was questionable in the first place, what with the Articles of War, the so-called RHIP (Rank Has Its Privileges, the motto in the service that spells out the class structure of that society and US society in general clearer than I've ever seen it elsewhere). But they're tossing hats and fat Sergeant Mullarcy gets in it. Catches this black lieutenant's hat and tosses it, but too far for one of the other officers to catch. The black officer tells him to pick up the hat and the fat sergeant refuses!

A guy stood me up in front of the barracks one day. A white first looie, and made me salute over and over because he didn't dig the black salute (though Laffy saluted the same way). Black troops had a tendency to bend their heads sideways down to their hand when saluting rather than bringing the hand all the way up military style. This guy made me salute maybe 25 times until he was satisfied. I was determined in my sly way not to understand what he was talking about and went on saluting in the hot goddam sun and he stood there over me, the gung-ho sonafabitch! And it went on and on.

I knew what would have happened if I had just nutted out and refused to go through the saluting game. And at the end, I don't think I'd really changed my salute, but he was satisfied that he got me some extra duty or extra harassment for taking such liberties. But the fat sergeant refused to pick up the hat. I was squatting in the corner with some other airmen watching. And there finally was some compromise, like somebody else picked up the hat. But why? Why hadn't the officer just given the fat master an Article 15 or got one of his stripes? The fat sergeant was an old soldier, the yellow lieutenant a short-timer and probably in transition to his dentist's office in a few years. But still to me and the others that watched and heard of this, this was a clear display of the dickless stance such yellow status predicted.

But I never felt really part of all that. In it, I was, for sure, and it pained me like the great tragedies of my reading. And I began to scrawl my agonies into my journal regularly. My findings. The ideas that came out of the books. Proust and *Auntie Mame*. Hemingway and *The Man in the Grey Flannel Suit*. And Joyce, Faulkner, Melville, Dostoevsky, Hesse, Flaubert, Cummings, Lawrence, Pound, Patchen, Hardy, James, Balzac, Stendhal. I would read *Bonjour Tristesse* and Robert Graves in the same day. A book on Buddhism and *The Communist Manifesto* in the same afternoon. I enjoyed plunging into long books that I'd read were difficult to get through. The Proust and Dostoevsky were glad tasks for me. I'd find an author and read everything of his or hers I'd find. Puerto Rico made that difficult, but being the night librarian made it easier for me. And when I was given guard duty, which was always, I would squat out in the hot sun twelve hours trying to read clandestinely, because reading was not permitted during guard duty. Plus Harrison said we were to have nothing on display on our dressers or windowsills, so that after a while the books I began to amass had to be put inside my closet or otherwise stashed, though at times I got sloppy and put them on the dresser with a bookend like normal people.

I also began writing poetry more regularly. I'd written some light verse and some Elizabethan doggerel during my HU days, mostly hooked up with Liz. But now I was more serious (though still not altogether) with what I was doing. I was at least trying to put down what I knew or everything I thought I felt. Straining for big words and deep emotional registration, as abstract as my understanding of my life.

At the Green Door, I'd also stumbled into the literary magazine. *Accent*, a small magazine from somewhere in Illinois, impressed me most. With the strange abstruseness of doctrinaire modernism heretofore unknown to me. "Pity Poor Axel the Spinhead" was the name of one story, author now unknown. I tried to penetrate its murky symbolism. The poetry also swept past me. I had since been getting the *Partisan*, *Hudson*, *Kenyon* reviews, even *Sewanee* from time to time. I was getting beat over the head with the New Criticism and didn't know it. I strained to understand, to find something for myself in those words. I read Empson's *Seven Types of Ambiguity* and plowed into all the fashionable literary McCarthyism coming out then, as my entrance and baptism into the world of serious letters. All the time a radio would be screaming in hillbilly at the top of its voice and drunken airmen clattering through the hall goosing each other in memory of the most recent *puta* they'd banged.

I'd say the irony of all this is what someone far removed might think of as "delicious." The reality of my day-to-day Air Force life fairly terrified me—despite the collective resistance of our salon elitism. The daily grind of guard duty, or fortnightly "alerts," fake missions announced by the screaming of hellish sirens which sent us scrambling down to the flight line and up into the very wild black yonder, were literally driving me up the wall, or at least to drink. Yet the reality from which I wanted to escape was replaced by my reading, which often was the most backward forces in American literature, teaching me the world upside down and backwards. But despite the New Criticism and the word freaks and the Southern Agrarians and Fugitive propaganda, I imbibed as often as I could as a supposed antidote to the Air Force and it gave me enough solid reflection on real life so that it had to change me. That and the service.

I began to send poetry out to these magazines. And unerringly in a few days, rejection slips would come in. I wish I had saved these. For a time I did, but they disappeared somehow. I got rejection slips from all the quality magazines and *Accent* and some others I dug up. The *Saturday Review*, *The New Yorker*, *Harper's* and the *Atlantic Monthly*. They all showed the good taste and consistency to turn me down flat and very quickly. And these rejections only served to fuel the deep sense of despair, so ultimate and irreversible with a 22-year-old. None had any use for my deathless immortal words but I kept trying.

One afternoon I had gone to San Juan by myself. I had found some places in Old San Juan I could walk around. They had a tourist section, fairly arty. There was a painter there named Juan Botello and I would go in his shop and walk around that area trying to get close to some professional art. I had the *New York Times* under my arm. I was in civilian clothes and I remember I was reading *The New Yorker*. I'd stopped at a bench and sat down near a square. It was quiet and I could see a long way off toward the newer, more Americanized part of the city, the Condado Beach section, where I could only go if in uniform, so they would know I was an Americano and not a native. I had been reading one of the carefully put together exercises *The New Yorker* publishes constantly as high poetic art, and gradually I could feel my eyes fill up with tears, and my cheeks were wet and I was crying, quietly softly but like it was the end of the world. I had been moved by the writer's words, but in another, very personal way. A way that should have taught me even more than it did. Perhaps it would have saved me many more painful scenes and conflicts. But I was crying because I realized that I could never write like that writer. Not that I had any real desire to, but I knew even if I had the desire I could not do it. I realized that there was something in me so *out*, so unconnected with what this writer was and what that magazine was that what was in me that wanted to come out as poetry would never come out like that and be *my* poetry.

The verse spoke of lawns and trees and dew and birds and some subtlety of feeling amidst the jingling rhymes that spoke of a world almost completely alien to me. Except in magazines or walking across some campus or in some house and neighborhood I hadn't been in. What was so terrifying to me was that when I looked through the magazine, I liked the clothes, the objects, the general ambience of the place—of the life being lived by the supposed readers and creators of the *New Yorker* world. But that verse threw me off, it had no feeling I could really use. I might carry the magazine as a tool of my own desired upward social mobility, such as I understood it. I might like some of the jokes, and absolutely dig the soft-curving button-down collars and well-tailored suits I saw. The restaurants and theater advertisements. The rich elegance and savoir-faire of all I could see and touch. But the poem, the *inside*, of that life chilled me, repelled me, was inpenetrable. And I hated myself because of it yet at the same time knew somehow that it was correct that I be myself, whatever that meant. And myself could not deal with the real meanings of the life spelled out by those tidy words.

I made no dazzling proclamations as a result of this crying into the *New Yorker* experience. I still felt sad as I took a *publico* back. I still wrote the same kinds of deadly abstractions about love, death, tragic isolation. I still went on reading whatever I could get or find out about. Sartre, Camus, de Beauvoir, anthologies of poetry. I learned about Apollinaire and Rimbaud. I read every novel of Evelyn Waugh's I could find and wondered often how to pronounce his name. I thought Sebastian Flyte in *Brideshead Revisited* was marvelous! I still got the reviews and stiff magazines. I even subscribed to *Partisan Review*. And I went on scribbling nightly or whenever, but regularly, in my journal. Writing haughty reviews and deep analyses of what I read. I was aware of an intellectual world—it had existed all this time—people were walking around knowing about it, knowing these various ideas, books, phrases, histories, relationships, and I didn't. Why hadn't I caught on in school? That there was an intellectual *life* that could be pursued. A life of ideas and, above all, Art?

I brought no great selectivity to my reading, though I began to understand after a while that some literature was more serious, more probing and thought-provoking than other, lighter stuff I might mash on myself as a result of reading the *New York Times Book Review*. But I found signposts and guides, references and printed directions. I might see a certain reference in a book or magazine—for instance, I saw the word "Kafka" in *Esquire*. What was a Kafka? I looked in dictionaries, no Kafka. Finally I stumbled on an article in some literary review about his work. The stiff abstruse language of the article only bade me rush harder after its sense. And all the sub- and counter-references, the foreign words and jargon of the New Critics, I tracked down like Sherlock Holmes, but it was not elementary.

During this period I also went home over another Christmas break. Again, I went to the Village and visited Steve Korret and his beautiful golden-brown dancer wife. Their apartment on Bedford Street was stark white, except for the kitchen, which was orange. The books ranged up and down one wall now pulled me to them and held me there. Steve laughed at me standing by his bookcase hungrily gobbling up titles. A lot of them Eastern and Buddhist. Steve had become a Zen Buddhist. I did not know how fashionable this was becoming in the Village and its counterparts elsewhere. It was still the middle '50s ('56) and the tremendous popularity of the East in bohemian circles had not yet reached its full peak. Steve was an early acolyte. He even worked in an Eastern bookshop called Orientalia, around 12th Street. I came to the bookstore before I went back and I was transported by the hundreds of scholarly books on various schools of Buddhism and Eastern thought in general. I bought two of R. H. Blythe's books on Zen, analyzing Western art for parallels with Zen consciousness. I was swept up.

Dylan Thomas was also very heavy in those days downtown. People passing through Korret's house talked of "Dylan." One black poet there lilted some of Thomas' verses and then some of his own which were amazingly similar.

Korret was a writer! The idea of this made me drunk with wonder. A writer! What a thing to be—so weird—so outside of the ordinary parade of gray hellos and goodbyes I could begin to measure my life with. A writer. In the mysterious jumble of Greenwich Village.

Steve and his friends treated me like a little boy, which I guess I was. A little boy off in the goofy hopeless world of the Army? No, the Air Force. How comic. How tragic. How odd. How romantic. How petty. I thought the last myself. These painters, dancers, writers, thinkers, witty makers of brilliant statements, and here I am on the fringe again. Unconnected and without note once again, just like at Howard.

But I did get back to Ramey on time. Even sadder and more hopeless. I still had almost two years to go on my four-year enlistment. And my new intellectual life made soldiering harder and harder.

I had been moved to another crew, R-32, a "Ready" crew, which meant we were among the actual strike force of any bombing mission. It meant I had to go regularly to gunnery schools on base and in Tampa, Florida; Mobile, Alabama; Shreveport, Louisiana. In Tampa I met the Howard officer. In Mobile, I shot down the drone aircraft during the gunnery sessions, because an old gunner told me in Puerto Rico that the shit was fixed and that the sight was rigged so you couldn't hit the drone cause the drones cost $10,000 apiece. So you had to use "Kentucky windage"—just shoot a little ahead of the thing, like deer hunting. And I brought it down, which meant I was supposed to go to a "Select" crew or at least a "Lead," but I didn't.

In Shreveport, Reilly, Burke, and I tried to go off the base together, but the locals discouraged it. I ended up two days AWOL. I had gotten lost and laid up with a sister down in the Bottom (one black community of Shreveport—see *The System of Dante's Hell*) and finally came back rumpled and hung over and absolutely broke.

But I was trying to become an intellectual. I was becoming haughtier and more silent. More critical in a more general way. More specialized in my concerns. More abstract and distant. I was being drawn, had been drawn, into a world that Howard prepared me for on one level—blunt elitism. Though the deeper resolves of intellectualism I knew mostly nothing about, even though I'd been prodded to hook up self-consciously with the profoundest art of the African American, black music, by one man, titillated by another, I knew nothing consciously when I got out and went into the death organization—error farce.

Yet my reading was, in the main, white people. Europeans, Anglo-Americans. So that my ascent toward some ideal intellectual pose was at the same time a trip toward a white-out I couldn't even understand. I was learning and, at the same time, unlearning. The fasteners to black life unloosed. I was taking words, cramming my face with them. White people's words. Profound, beautiful, some even correct and important. But that is a tangle of non-self in that for all that. A non-self creation where you become other than you as you. Where the harnesses of black life are loosened and you free-float, you think, in the great sunkissed intellectual waygonesphere. Imbibing, gobbling, stuffing yourself with reflections of the other.

Finally, I am an internationalist and it is clear to me now that all people have contributed to the wealth of common world culture — and I thought that then, if only on the surface! But I had given myself, in my quest for intellectualism, a steady diet of European thought, though altered somewhat by the Eastern Buddhist reading. That was what intellectualism meant! To me. It was certainly not conscious. But I had never been warned. (An old man in the South one time had said to me, "Some folks speaks too clear," talking about my clipped Northern speech. But, hey, that never registered.) Be careful in giving up the "provincial" that you do not include the fundamental and profound.

I was being drafted into the world of Quattrocento, vers libre, avant-garde, surrealism and dada, New Criticism, cubism, art nouveau, objectivism, "Prufrock," ambiguity, art music, rococo, shoe and non-shoe, Highbrow vs. Middlebrow, and I didn't realize the deeper significance of it. I reacted to some of it, emotionally, like the New Yorker crying incident, but even that, the realization it brought, didn't reach consciousness.

I was going down a road. Positive in the overall, but just now I was taking a twist and I'd answer for it, you bet.

The letter said I was a Communist. One day I got a message to report to the first sergeant and the adjutant and they said I had been removed from my crew, taken off "flying status," and my "secret" clearance rescinded. I knew what was happening, I'd known from the giddy-up. In a week or so I had to go back again and they told me I was being transferred out of the 73rd Bomb to Air Base Group.

In Group I was put on a gardening detail with other troops, who had mostly been busted down for various infractions. We were supposed to be planting flowers to beautify the base. One ex–tech sergeant I met, his arms bare except for the traces of his removed five stripes, was planting collards next to the flowers.

I was a gardener for a month or so and the salon regulars thought it amusing, but I didn't, in the hot sun digging holes for flowers. At least on flying status I got to sit in the hot sun guarding and reading.

I was then moved to another job, in the registration office at the Visiting Officers' Quarters. I also had been moved to an open bay in the Air Base Group barracks, which was like the torture of Chanute and Sampson. But with the move to the V/BOQ, I was moved into a room there, in the back of the joint. This was really the best job I had except for the library. I slept in a small room and came out to the front office to work my eight hours. Giving out blankets and pillows, making up beds, then going back in my room to read and drink.

The guy in charge of us (three of us) was an Italian dude, short, plump, perpetually smiling, named Cosi. That wasn't his real name, but it's OK *Cosi* is an Italian word which means "like," used like the blood use of "like," like you understand? Like this and like that. Cosi had an accent and had been born in Italy. He'd come over and after a few years of seeking opportunity had finally settled for the Air Force.

He was a sweet guy, a nonstop talker, always laughing and making jokes and saying "*cosi.*" We sat up talking on his shift or mine. He went out occasionally, but almost as seldom as I. He marveled constantly at my reading. He'd come in and whistle, "Hey, reading again? . . . *Maron' a mia!*" And start kidding me. Once he came in and I was reading *For Whom the Bell Tolls.* I was at the part where the hero, Roberto, is killed by the Fascists and I was weeping like a baby. Cosi said, "A goddam book can make you cry? *Maron' a mia!*"

I was in limbo for months and heard nothing from anyone about my case. Then suddenly, one day, I was brought in and questioned. I was shown a sheet which listed organizations and they asked me had I ever belonged to any. I put down the Civil Rights Congress because I had once gone to a meeting where a guy had talked about this organization. I wrote about this meeting in the space provided on the form. I was shown a copy of the accusatory letter, which had been sent anonymously. I got a chance to glance at a sheet which said that among the artifacts the Air Force was amassing as to my offense were copies of the *Partisan Review!*

I was asked if I belonged to an organization called the Congress of Cultural Freedom. I said, "No," and was shown the magazine which they'd gotten from my room. I hadn't known the publishers. I had letters in my drawers with rejection notes and that address. It was lucky my ass wasn't on the line. Shit, I *wanted* to get kicked out of the service.

The thing dragged on and I began writing letters home about headaches I was having. I had received a couple letters from Steve Korret, one in particular made reference to Zen and quoted Thomas. Korret said in answer to one letter I'd written him that I "was always crying. Cry, Poet!" And that was the first time I'd ever been called that. Poet. It dug into me. I had a photo he'd given me on my last leave. Taken at a party, with various of Steve's friends, in particular a slim-faced white girl with a long ponytail and heavy eye pencil

sending her eyes around the corners of her head. This flick fascinated me! Not just the wild-looking woman in black stockings, but
the whole scene. A Village party with all the hair let down, all the
cultivated wildness on display. This was the Village. Weird! Something else was happening other than what I knew about. Wild stuff.
Free open shit. Look at that weird-looking woman. I bet she'd fuck.
I bet she knows about all kinds of heavy shit. And I bet she'd fuck.
Not like them stuck-up bitches at the Capstone. Wow!

The shit dragged on for months with me still in limbo, still making beds at the V/BOQ, and at last I got orders to leave. We were sitting where we could see the flight line, drinking vodka ($1 a fifth)
and cackling about the Commander of all Strategic Air Command
(Curtis LeMay) driving face down on a go-cart back and forth, back
and forth, on the flight line like a juvenile delinquent!

We kept saying, screaming really, "This is the motherfucker in
charge of us?" It made us hysterical!

Cosi brought me the orders. He was breathing hard and grinning,
like he knew it was important. It was just that Special Orders
were an event for any airman. You didn't know what the hell was
happening.

I had been discharged. *Undesirably!* What? UNDESIRABLY! I
was to be discharged in thirty days. Being shipped to South Carolina
in about two weeks, then undergoing two weeks' processing.

The guys there whooped and hollered. What the fuck, Undesirable or up your ass & gone, getting out was what was happening. That
news shot around to the salon members and other folks. The hip
folks were happy for me. I was getting the fuck out. The squares
were sorry I'd gotten a funny discharge. UNDESIRABLE!

Hey, I wanted to get out. It didn't matter, long as I was sane &
healthy. I wanted out. Out! Undesirable or Not, here I come.

And in a few weeks I was on my way to South Carolina. While I
was being processed I got a chance to go up to Columbia to see my
relatives. My aunts and uncles and grandmother. I spent most of the
time talking to my tall, thin, dark, fast-talking aunt.

I was happy to see everybody else, including my tall, light-brown,
light-eyed, slender aunt everybody agreed was beautiful. But to the
tall dark aunt I poured out my heart, such as I could muster. I had
been kicked out. My parents wouldn't like it. Would they understand? I wanted help and she gave me that by listening, commenting
on the obvious and reserving comment on the abstruse. I stayed

there talking a week or so and then got discharged formally and got a bus to ride twenty some odd hours back to Newark.

My Air Force career was over.

The Black Arts (Harlem, Politics, Search for a New Life)

The arrival uptown, Harlem, can only be summed up by the feelings jumping out of Césaire's *Return to My Native Land* or Fanon's *The Wretched of the Earth* or Cabral's *Return to the Source*. The middle-class native intellectual, having outintegrated the most integrated, now plunges headlong back into what he perceives as blackest, native-est. Having dug, finally, how white he has become, now, *classically*, comes back to his countrymen charged up with the desire to be black, uphold black, &c. . . . . a fanatical patriot!

When we came up out of the subway, March 1965, cold and clear, Harlem all around us staring us down, we felt like pioneers of the new order. Back in the homeland to help raise the race. Youth in their fervor know no limitations, except they are celebrations of them. Narrow, because they lack experience, yet fervent, super-energetic, super-optimistic. If we had known what faced us, some would've copped out, some would've probably got down, to study, as we should've, instead of the nowhere shit so many of us were involved with.

The building on 130th Street was an old brownstone, like you can find in Harlem. Right off by Lenox with its crab sellers, the permanently out of work taking a stroll or in knots, summing up USA, its working people going and coming. Gray with black is the dominant color. Brown gives it flair, the yellow an edge to its conceits. The occupation army of white police beady-eyed and ubiquitous.

We set up shop and cleaned and swept and painted. We got a flag, White designed, the "Greek" theater masks of comedy and tragedy, rendered Afro style, like a shield, with spear behind, all in black and gold. The Black Arts Repertory Theater/School.

Malcolm's death had thrown people up in the air like coins in a huge hairy hand. Even before I'd left Cooper Square people had showed up. Carrying various perceptions. Some crazed or halfway there. John Ferris, the poet, showed for the first time, like he was Malcolm's bodyguard, and told stories about imminent revenge.

The Mosque on 116th Street burned up and took the edge off, but people were vowing to go to Chicago and kill Elijah.

Whatever Malcolm had laid out was now just in the wind to be grabbed on the fly. The OAAU, the united front structure Malcolm wanted to build, styled after the Organization of African Unity (OAU), was not completely put together. There was no doubt it would soon be gone. The fact of Malcolm's death meant, for us, that the Nation, of Islam, had also died. Though there were arguments about who was right: Malcolm or Elijah? But up close to us, Malcolm, Malcolm, Semper. . . .

The mood? I came downtown one time during these early days and was sitting in the Orchidia Restaurant, down on Second Avenue. We had just come from the St. Mark's Theater, Vashti and I, where I'd been talking about plans to stage my plays *The Toilet* and *The Slave*. Lonnie Elder and Douglas Turner Ward were sitting there, loud in conversation. Elder said something about Malcolm. "Why did Ossie [Davis] call him a prince. He wasn't no prince."

I came out of my chair like the black plague. "Don't ever say anything about Malcolm. Nothing. Don't let nothing come out of your mouth ever about Malcolm." Whatever the rage did to my face made them quiet. They only stared. I got Vashti and we went back uptown.

What was really interesting during this period is who came up and who didn't. Some, of course, the smaller core, augmented by a few uptown heads, were at the Arts every day and night trying to do whatever they thought they were doing. Others constantly came by and helped, many artists from various disciplines who contributed what they could. Doing programs, being in forums, helping us with our major arts project in the streets that coming summer. Still others we saw from time to time who wanted to help in deeper ways, talking to us, trying to counsel and help us. There were others whom we very seldom saw and then mainly downtown. There were others we never saw who nevertheless, in being true to the vanity of illusion and dubious social distinction, were also there, invisible except for their inadequately disguised disdain.

A basic core was the Hackensacks (Shammy definite, Tong most of the time), Jimmy Lesser, Dave, McLucas, a friend of Tong's who came along, Tub, a largish, sourly succinct dude; and after work, Corny and Clarence, plus Leroy McLucas and, a little later, Clarence Reed, the poet, who was hanging around on Lenox Avenue at the Progressive Labor Party offices, due in large part to his friendship with their black organizer, Bill Epton.

Larry Neal was one of those who were always in and out, helping with programs and giving us some rational counsel. Askia was there a lot in that same role and from time to time Max Stanford. Vashti was there all the time, trying to deal with some of the people who started acting like "crazy niggas," as she called them, often at the top of her voice. Tong was married, but I don't think his wife ever came around. She was always at home or at work. But I think Tong never encouraged her to come by the Arts or else it was her own idea. All the rest of those brothers had various, often frequently changing, lady friends, but I was the only one of the core who had a regular, fairly stable relationship, with Vashti Lowns.

I developed a great deal of affection and respect for Larry Neal, but I think Larry knew a little more about the nature of some of the more nutty dudes the Arts was to attract, so he was in and out, but constantly on the scene. We picked up a lot of people in those few months. It was a socially and intellectually seismically significant development, the leaving of some of us (and more we didn't even know) from downtown and the implied and actual cutting of certain ties, and the attempt to build a black arts institution, and that in the heart of the past capital of African American people in the US, Harlem. The reality set many fresh and needed ideas in motion. The idea set even more ideas in motion and more concrete realities. In many ways it was something like the period of the Harlem Renaissance. Black intellectuals drawn to a common spot out of the larger commonality of their national experience. A rise in black national consciousness among the people themselves is what set both periods in motion, and whenever there is a high level of black national consciousness, a militant affirmation of the African American national identity, the whole of the American society takes off.

But even more than the Harlem geography the Black Arts movement reflected that black people themselves had first moved to a political unity, despite their differences, that they were questioning the US and its white racist monopoly capitalism.

The emergence of the independent African states and the appearance of African freedom fighters, fighting guerrilla wars with white colonialism, was destined to produce young intellectuals (and older ones too) who reveled in the spirit of defiant revolution and sought to use it to create art. An art that would reach the people, that would take them higher, ready them for war and victory, as popular as the Impressions or the Miracles or Marvin Gaye. That was our vision and its image kept us stepping, heads high and backs straight.

Sun Ra and Albert Ayler were always on the scene. For some, Sun

Ra became our resident philosopher, having regular midweek performances in which he introduced the light-show concept that white rock groups later found out about and got rich from. When Ra would play his Sun-Organ, when he played low notes, deep blues and dark colors would light up on it. When he played high notes, oranges and yellows would light up, and we sat, sometimes maybe with fifteen or twenty people in the audience, and thought we were being exposed to the profundity of blackness. Jim Campbell directed the bigger plays at the Arts and that's where I first met Yusef Iman. When we got our regular programs going, concerts, readings, plays, in the downstairs auditorium we made by tearing down a couple of walls, black artists flowed through those doors. Some for single performances, some for longer relationships, some to absorb what it all was. We were all trying to grow together.

Milford Graves was another regular, and Hugh Glover, who was just starting. But Andrew Hill, soft-spoken, blinking, sometimes in disbelief, behind his cool glasses, was our music director for the summer program. Overstreet became our director of graphics along with Betty Blayton.

One of our first official actions was a parade across 125th Street. With Sun Ra and his Myth-Science Arkestra leading it, Albert and his brother Don blowing and Milford wailing his drums, the core of us, as it had grown, some other black artists from downtown and those in Harlem who'd now begun to come in, plus Baba Oserjeman and his Yoruba Temple. We marched down the street holding William White's newly designed Black Arts flag. I've seen one photo that survives of this (in a magazine put out by Asian activist, Yuri Kuchiyama, North Star). A small group of sometimes comically arrogant black people daring to raise the question of art and politics and revolution, black revolution!

We had little money. But the mortgage on the brownstone was only about $100 a month and it was in generally good condition. I was the main source of funds. I had a couple of plays running downtown at the St. Marks Theater, and we had put on a benefit just before we left, doing The Toilet; Charles Patterson's Black Ice; another play of mine, which I directed, Experimental Death Unit #1; and a play by a guy named Nat White called The Black Tramp. We charged $20 a ticket, the audience was mostly white, and we used the money to pay down on the brownstone and help put the building in some shape.

Tong was supposed to direct my Experimental Death Unit #1, but, after a few days, he had slapped the star, Barbara Ann Teer, so I took over and directed it. The slapping situation unnerved me. The problem was to get the play directed, not to make Barbara Ann Teer "submit" in some kind of way. But that was the kind of shit that Tong got into, with all kinds of people, many people I felt kindly toward or who were my friends. He even got into a hassle with my sister during our Operation Bootstrap summer program because my sister was given an office which Tong thought was too large for a woman, plus my sister smoked. That was a major battle.

What began to be obvious to me before too long was that Shammy was volatile and unpredictable, but he had a basic respect for me as a writer, certainly for the downtown huzzas. But he was unpredictable. His brother had a deep malady, probably some kind of advanced paranoia. What was predictable about him was the negativity he carried with him, no, *wore*, like a wet suit.

Dave was younger than the other two, and influenced by both, but he was closer to Shammy. Dave and I were alike in a number of ways. Dave wrote poetry and music criticism. He was steady and assumed a lot of the daily arts programming and scheduling. He handled the artists and was a serious student of Sun Ra.

The first forum we had at the building was about which way the arts were going and the responsibility of the black artist. Tong, incensed by some point Sun Ra was making, leaped up and tried to walk toward him before being forcibly restrained, calling Sun Ra "an old woman." I was shocked and deeply embarrassed. Certainly Dave didn't like it either, but he could never be openly critical of Tong. In some ways Tong resented anyone who had leadership qualities. For one thing, any intellectual who might shine in his younger brother Shammy's eyes, Tong was *jealous* of. He was against Sun Ra because Sun Ra, in Tong's mind, was alienating Dave.

The only person to try to give Tong what he needed as far as African American street therapy, a good ass-kicking, was his brother Shammy, and once, during the middle of an exhibit of painting, suddenly Shammy and Tong rolled into view, fighting each other, rolling on the floor, till the rest of us separated them. The two of them became the new talk of the Harlem nationalist and Black Arts community.

Shammy had a love-hate relationship going with me. He envied me, I think, the celebrity of the well-known writer, and liked, I think, being associated with me. But at the same time he did not like to be in my shadow and secretly he thought he could write as well as I. His brother Tong hated me, because Shammy emulated me in many ways, even down to mannerisms and the way we dressed. So not only would they fight, I had to struggle with Tong because of his craziness, often directed at me. I also had to stop the wild-acting Shammy from getting jumped on by any number of Black Arts regulars and Harlem citizens who wanted to kick his ass. Finally, there were more people wanting to kick the two Hackensack brothers' asses than you could kill with a submachine gun without a lot of extra clips. They were a major problem at the Arts.

After we had first moved in, one morning I see this tallish, long-striding figure coming down the street with a suitcase and a red tarboosh on his bald shaven head. It was the bony-faced, acid-looking Tong. He had not come up *with* us; in fact, he was, in our deliberations, against the move. We even thought he might just drop out and not hang with us. (I was hoping.) But then there he was, asking could he have an office and work with us. He touched the red tarboosh, which at the time I was unclear about, and said only, "Yeh, this is me." Then he went inside and Dave found him an office. The fighting and other backwardness started not long after that.

Cornelius, as the various struggles between the Hackensacks or between them and any number of other people would go on, used to ask why I put up with it. He would say, "Goddam, LeRoi, these mf's must have something on you." Later, it got so bad that Corny and the others would come in with plans for the two brothers' destruction, which I would naysay. They even came in with a smiling bespectacled murderer friend of theirs (who was a very sweet dude) who would have left either or both of the brothers in an alley perforated in some deadly manner.

Dave was all but frozen stiff trying to function rationally and get the real work we wanted to do in motion. He was always caught between the two brothers, ideologically and factionally. And there were different factions throughout the Arts. For one thing, Shammy would work. And he would do most of what we agreed on, though he might come up with some improvisation or alternative reading of it that would be puzzling. He wrote plays of some real value and was ready to direct them and find actors and do the work necessary for us to get an audience. Tong did nothing. He would sit in his office with a small court that quickly developed. Jimmy Lesser, who looked like a Muslim and talked Elijah Muhammad's program up a storm. He was sort of Tong's left-hand man, because Lesser had a relationship with Shammy, but Lesser would always hook up with where he thought the momentum was careening, which he assumed to be Tong. Tong's right-hand man was Tub, about 6 feet 3, 200 pounds of muscle. Tub was actually a good man, dependable, but he had been swept up all the way by the red tarboosh rhetoric of Tong Hackensack and he functioned mostly as Tong's yea-sayer and enforcer. When I last saw Tub, he had become a Hanafi Musulman, a small sect of Islam associated by some with religious fanaticism.

At the time I knew little of Islam, either the orthodox, Sunni kind or any other kind. What I knew of the Nation of Islam, the so-called Black Muslims, I had picked up, like most people, through Malcolm X. The religious practice interested me less than the black national-ism. It was only after I left Harlem that I became more interested in the religion of Islam. But, apparently, in Tong's office the study of orthodox Islam became the central focus and people were warned that they could not smoke in Tong's office. What went on in that office mostly was discussion, we used to call it bullshitting, but I don't know if the aspirers to Sunni truths bullshit or not. Maybe it is called something else.

With the smallish Majid, a pleasant, smiling, little brown intellec-tual with horn-rim glasses, the basic Tong faction was formed. What they did was mostly criticize and undermine whatever went down in the Arts. They opposed most programs if only by doing nothing. Yet they were even more arrogant than the most arrogant of the rest of us. But they never proselytized for their faith in front of me, for some reason. So I knew even less of the formal mechanisms of their "worship" than I needed to. They were content, in the main, to talk bad about and undermine the rest of us, any way they could.

Perhaps what Tong had in mind was to become the de facto "leader" of the BARTS. I sensed that often enough. He thought he was a superior person. He had not been downtown wasting his life as a traitor to black people. He lived downtown, yes, but he was married to a black woman. A light-skinned proper-acting lady from Philly. I think she was a Philadelphia social worker. But all during the time I knew Tong I saw him with his wife socially perhaps only once.

Tong had not been downtown married to a white woman. He had not just hung around with white dudes trying to screw every white woman who had been turned away from the Miss America pageant. I know that the light of Islam helped that rhetoric, scowling at the swine-eating, wine-drinking dudes the rest of us were. But I have never met a person as violently male chauvinist as Tong. He would make women (at least black women) walk several feet behind him, and he was consequently always getting into struggles with most of the women around the Arts who didn't even know what the fuck he was talking about (i.e., the religious "justification" for his bullshit); they just wasn't buying it.

Vashti was slick enough to stay away from Tong. Though she would light up most of the Arts dudes when they were bullshitting, which was often. But with Tong, Vashti just smiled her slightly lop-sided smile and would say to me, nodding her head, "Tong is crazy, Roi, really pretty crazy." And I'd look at her and roll my eyes.

The first large rally we held, out on Seventh Avenue in front of the House of Proper Propaganda, created the first major open conflict between Tong and me. The older black nationalists always talked on their ladders across the street in front of the Hotel Theresa. Larger forums were held in front of Mr. Michaux's bookstore, called, affectionately, the House of Proper Propaganda. Malcolm had spo-ken in front of the store often and there was a sign in front of the store ringed by Pan-African leaders from everywhere in the black world. There was a major reason for our rally, mobilizing people against police brutality. We got out the literature, even got a car to use a sound system. But just as things were ready and we were about to proceed down the one long block to Seventh and then down to 125th, Tong declared to a small group of us left at the building that he opposed the rally.

The people were already assembled, new music was playing out of the speakers, which was the trademark of our rallies, the use of the most avant-garde black music, and our people were there wait-ing. I was momentarily speechless. I didn't believe he had said that, and certainly I had no understanding of why he had said it. "What?" I said, staring as if at a monster. "Why are you saying that?"

"Suppose it's a setup. Suppose the cops just let us put this together so they can attack."

I must have been sputtering. "What?" I wanted to keep saying it, but it would've betrayed my absolute lack of understanding of what was going on. Finally, I got myself to say, "That's a pretty wild idea."

Tong said, "You just want to get black people killed!" And his face twisted into the acid scowl it always threatened to be.

"I just don't believe that it's any setup," I said. "I think we should have the rally. We planned it and did the work to get the people out. We've got to get over there and do it."

Tong stepped close to me. We were in the hallway, readying to go out onto the street. "You're a wise guy," he said, the terminology temporarily nonplussing me.

"I *am* wise," I said. He had his face just an inch or so from mine, though he was taller and seemingly tougher. But I stuck my face close to his like in a cartoon.

"You know what I mean," Tong went on. But after the freeze-frame face-to-face I walked around him, and the few of us went on to the rally.

I heard Vashti's words echoing and this confirmed it for me on one level, though now I knew I would have to deal with this Tong openly and quietly as well. He was mad as the maddest goddam nut I'd ever met. Or was he just that intent on undermining my "leadership" and "taking over" the Arts? Tong's faction held him as the real moral and spiritual leadership of the Arts, but even they had to retreat partially in the face of the reality of trying to set up a functioning black arts institution. His faction did very little of anything but sit around. Plus the artists, mostly, did not relate to them, plus the staff of folks that we took on when we did our summer program not only thought Tong and friends the lunatic fringe of the Black Arts, but despised them because they didn't even think they were serious artists. Tub and Lesser made no pretensions of being artists, but neither did Cornelius. But Cornelius was our greatest propagandist. He probably talked to thousands of people a day and handed out literature. People running into Tub or Lesser or Tong would be put off from even wanting to be around us. Shammy had that charming way about him as well, but he was not in the Tong faction because of their conflicts.

Tong was so mad that he would try to disrupt the rally probably to become the real decider of direction in the Arts. As it was, he was constantly initiating little bullshit Islamic-related "rules" for his office. As hat-wearing a bunch of bloods as we were, Tub would announce when you came in Tong's office, "Take off your hat. No cigarettes." While the rest of us, informality's children, would be wandering around trying to get stuff printed, or see that there was enough space for a rehearsal or a class, or talk to some artist about doing something with us or for us. While Tong and company scowled either behind the closed door or with the door left open, sitting back in tilted chairs, a red tarboosh on the desk, upon which not one speck of any productive labor crossed. So that when people would come up to the Arts you could figure out after a time where they were coming from by who they hung with. The Arts types would be swinging with Dave. Sometimes he and Sun Ra would stay holed up for hours. The Arts/Politics dudes and the Political dudes would crowd into my narrow office, like Larry Neal or Askia

or Ted Wilson or Overstreet and the others. The weirdo-mystical ir-
ritators would gravitate to Tong.

What Tong wanted, I don't really know. Leadership of the Arts,
perhaps. Though once, when he was borrowing some money, because he had no job and his rent was not paid, he told me that I was
the quarterback and I ought to keep my fullback (him) in good
shape. He was a strange, often deadly quiet man who probably fancied himself many things, but the only thing I knew he was good at
consistently was making trouble.

The Supremes' "Where Did Our Love Go?" and Mary Welles' "My
Guy" reached me in 1964. And Dionne Warwick's "Walk On By."
These tunes seemed to carry word from the black for me. Monterey,
the downtown streets of the forming Black Arts core, the dazzle that
black women presented to me now. Marvin Gaye's "Stubborn Kind
of Fellow" was playing when we got uptown. "Keep On Pushing,"
which poet David Henderson made into a great poem, was one of
our themes, and all of us would try for Curtis Mayfield's keening fal-
setto with the Impressions. Plus their "We're a Winner" also moved
us and spoke, it seemed, directly to our national desire.

It was as if I had a new ear for black music at that point in the middle '60s. I was a jazz freak, though we rhythm-and-bluesed to Ray
Charles' "I Got a Woman" and "Drown in My Own Tears" at our
downtown loft sets. But now the rhythm and blues took on special
significance and meaning. Those artists, too, were reflecting the
rising tide of the people's struggles. Martha and the Vandellas'
"Dancing in the Streets" was like our national anthem. Their "Heat
Wave" had signaled earlier, downtown, that the shit was on the rise.
But "Dancing in the Streets," which spoke to us of Harlem and the
other places, then Watts and later Newark and Detroit, seemed to
say it all out. "Summer's here and time is near / for dancing in the
streets!"

We did the Philly Dog and the Boston Monkey, whirling and being as revolutionary in our dancing as we were in our own thoughts.
Somebody told me that Tong had said that I "danced like a white
boy." I guess that was part of the reason he thought he should run
the Arts. I used to dance pretty well back home, but when I heard
that, I figured maybe my living downtown had cooled my cool.
Ruined my rhythms. That was part of the whole sense of myself that
I carried at the Arts as well. I *was* guilty for having lived downtown
for so long with a white wife. I think that was the kind of trump card
that Tong and them thought they held. And it did make me reluc-
tant at times to come down hard on people who obviously needed

exactly that, because I was still insecure and tender-headed about my recent life. So certain people could play off that, and probably did. Certainly, Tong and company did.

I even stopped going downtown, and I'm sure certain aspects of the stances I took were based on my feeling of revulsion when my Greenwich Village days were focused on. Others in that Harlem community mouthed similar kinds of charges. Though most of what they said, on the legitimate side, was that most of us were from downtown and knew next to nothing about Harlem, which was very much correct.

An opportunity presented itself that we were lucky enough and hip enough to seize upon. We had no money for any really well-advertised programs at the Arts, but we did the best we could. We turned out flyers and little booklets which Dave had designed and circulated them, building up our audience. We did *Dutchman* again and a new play of mine, *Jello*. I also wrote the play *A Black Mass* in my office at the Arts. It is a work that dramatizes the Nation of Islam's mythology about the origins of the white man, having been created by the mad scientist Yacub. Patterson's *Black Ice* was another of our staples. In trying to get money to put on programs we searched for various sources. One very successful set was a benefit concert which was recorded by ABC Impulse. I knew the producer of Impulse, Bob Thiele, fairly well, having done liner notes for him, on the enormously important *Live at Birdland* album, for which I interviewed Trane in the little telephone-booth dressing room in the back. So Thiele liked the idea of doing an album dedicated to the avant-garde in black music, which he could then market as an anthology and as a sampler of albums he would bring out later. He called the album *The New Wave in Jazz* and it featured Trane, playing the beautiful and frightening "Nature Boy," and groups led by Albert Ayler, Archie Shepp, Grachan Moncur, Bobby Hutcherson, and Charles Tolliver. The only person left off the tape, which infuriated me, was Sun Ra. Dave did one section of the liner notes and I did the other. So we got some money for our programs and also got a very hip record out.

Then we heard about the Haryou Act programs around the corner functioning out of the Hotel Theresa. Haryou was the first anti-poverty program set up by Lyndon Johnson in his continuing assault on the Great Society. They were trying to set up a stop-riot program for the summer of '65, the summer after the "long hot summer" of '64. There was to be an Operation Bootstrap functioning that summer in Harlem out of Haryou. What it would be was anybody's guess and we found out when we started coming around there that most of those folks at Haryou didn't know either.

Livingston Wingate, now a judge, was the director of Haryou. He was Adam Clayton Powell's man, I was told, and a very popular dude uptown. However, the guy running the summer program was an egg-shaped, light-skinned man named Frank Stanley, who tried to be likable but seemed just a trifle on the slick side. Some said, more greasy than slick. My job was constantly to rush back and forth between Stanley and Wingate and a few other folks trying to get some money. Finally, we hit on the idea that we could do a summer arts and culture program. I wrote up the proposal with help from my old HU buddy Shorty, who was now an accountant with some firm. Shorty was also married to a white woman in the Bronx, but that spring of '65 when we met I was talking so much shit that Shorty soon moved out of his situation and was at the Arts as our accountant. Shorty knew a couple of Bronx operators on the semi-legal side, Ricky and Tony, so they became the triumvirate of our financial dealing and accountability, which, with all the headaches, crazy niggers, crazy government, crazy whiteys, they did remarkably well.

There were always many versions of how much money we got out of Haryou that summer for our Arts & Culture sector of Operation Bootstrap. But we must have got away with a couple hundred grand and even more in services when it was all over. It was really a great program, running that entire summer. We brought paintings into the street with outdoor art exhibitions. Overstreet designed the easels we used to show the paintings and he brought artists with him to oversee and contribute to the shows. Each night the show would move to a new location in Harlem.

We brought new music out in the streets, on play streets, vacant lots, playgrounds, parks. I think perhaps the Jazzmobile came from our first idea. We had trucks with stages we designed from banquet tables, held together by clamps (another Overstreet design). And Pharoah, Albert, Archie, Sun Ra, Trane, Cecil Taylor, and many other of the newest of the new came up and blew. The only bad incident was when a white media famous tenor man came up with an integrated group and someone threw an egg at him. We told the musicians we wanted black groups and boycotted them if they refused to make their groups all black. But there was music at these different sites every night moving all over Harlem.

We brought drama out in the street as well. We set up our improvised stages and with a little fanfare we quickly got a crowd. One evening we sent Shammy with a pistol chasing one of the characters in *Black Ice*. The bloods seeing a brother with a gun chasing somebody who looked like a white man made a crowd instantly, and the show began! Or just the sight of us unpacking and setting up would be enough. We performed in projects, parks, the streets, alleys, playgrounds. Each night a different location, five nights, sometimes six, a week.

We brought street-corner poetry readings, moving the poets by truck from site to site. So that each night throughout that summer we flooded Harlem streets with new music, new poetry, new dance, new paintings, and the sweep of the Black Arts movement had recycled itself back to the people. We had huge audiences, really mass audiences, and though what we brought was supposed to be avant and super-new, most of it the people dug. That's why we knew the music critics that put down the new music as inaccessible were full of shit. People danced in the street to Sun Ra and cheered Ayler and Shepp and Cecil and Jackie McLean and the others. It was a great summer!

We set up crews for each of the arts, each with its own truck, sound equipment, stages, or whatever else was needed. Harlem residents were our technical staff and quite a few of the more sympathetic folks from downtown who came up, like Overstreet and White. All those beautiful people who did come together that summer whose names I cannot recall have that sweet memory as their final unspendable paycheck.

Getting paid at Haryou was always a drag. There was always something happening which slowed the checks down. What we would do is simply unleash our staff and crew on the Haryou bureaucrats and they'd sail over there and talk so bad and threatening to the Haryou crowd that our checks, though late, would get there before the other projects'.

Hanging out in front of the Theresa was hip anyway, because people always gathered there, plus the old Garveyites would be there on their ladders with the red, black, and green flags beating the white man to death every evening.

It was a great place to argue and I had some furious mouth shootouts. One of the most memorable was arguing with Robert McBeth, who later became head of the New Lafayette Theater, about black art. McBeth told me that there was no such a boogie man. That art was simply art, that it could not be black. I said there's Russian art, French art, Spanish and Chinese and English art, &c., but not black art? My problem was that "black" is not a nationality and I wasn't clear on that.

Barbara Ann Teer and I got into a similar argument, I think out in front of the Black Arts, slinging the pros and cons of black art. Though I think Barbara Ann was convinced, as her National Black Theater now attests.

Being able to hire people that summer gave a big plus mark to our cry of Black Arts! It was a powerfully constructive program and word of it spread not only through the city, up and down town, but across the country. Not so weirdly, when I had done *Dutchman* downtown I had got an Obie award, but uptown it was called by some newspapers "racist drama." From the "fair-haired black boy" of Off-Broadway, as Langston Hughes called me with his tongue stuck way up in his cheek, I got to be a full-up racist. So strange, that the victims, once they began to scream and shout at their oppressors, can now be termed the oppressors. We accuse whites of racism, so—Presto! Chango!—"black racism" is the real problem. "Hate-whitey dramas" were what I and my colleagues on West 130th Street were writing. And, the white god help us, when we were trying to find out how we would carry out our all-black aesthetic when most of our plays had at least one white in them, it was Shammy who came up with the idea that we should do them in whiteface. We loved the idea and it became a tack one associated with the black arts. Blacks in whiteface! What racism! My God!

We also gave classes in playwriting, poetry, history, music, painting, and martial arts. A young black poet named Ojijiko was our resident martial artist. Harold Cruse was our history teacher and at one time he had two FBI agents in his classes. One, Donald Duncan, was later implicated in framing Max Stanford and Herman Ferguson for some bullshit attempt to assassinate Roy Wilkins and Whitney Young. Another one of these agents had also penetrated Malcolm's OAAU. One guy was tall and light-skinned with red freckles. I'd see him going back and forth to Harold's class. Later we put out flyers and circulated them to many cities with these dudes' pictures and one of their lady friends, alerting people to these agents' presence.

Bringing art to the people, black art to black people, and getting paid for doing it was sweet. Both the artists and the people were raised by that experience. But we were just going on instinct and our own skills at what we did best, arts. We knew next to nothing about bureaucratic games or the subtlety needed to preserve so fragile a program as we had erected. We had no funds of our own and no correct understanding of the economic self-reliance needed to push a program calling for black self-determination, even in the arts.

We met a lot of people, many who had our best interests at heart, but we did not take some of the best advice. We did not benefit from the wisdom of our elders. We met Bumpy Johnson, the grand old man of organized Harlem crime. Bumpy was one of the first to insist that black dudes run their own rackets and stop paying off the white boys. He was a respected elder, straight as a board, with an office in a warehouse that sold *exterminator*, a legit front for his widely known and widely respected operations. For an hour or so Bumpy talked to me like my father, telling me I had to meet different people and get hooked up really to the community and not get too far out so that negative folks could shoot me down. I listened and was proud to be there with the bald-headed dignified Mr. Bumpy Johnson, but I couldn't really hear what he was saying. I didn't really understand. But Bumpy could see we were heading for trouble if we didn't get fully conscious in a hurry, but I was too naïve to dig. I thought that if I roared and roared and took it all straight ahead, as hard as I could, relentless in attack, we would get over, we would win. The question was, would we survive?

Sargent Shriver, Kennedy's brother-in-law, was head of the anti-poverty program. He came to New York to tour Haryou's various programs. When he came with his entourage to the Black Arts building, we wouldn't let him in. Bad us! Dave came up to my office and told me Shriver was outside waiting to get in. I could peek out my front window and see the crowd of white DC bureaucrats along with some of the Negroes from around the corner. I told Dave, "Later for them motherfuckers."

"It's Shriver," Dave told me.

"Fuck Shriver." And Dave carried the message back. And looking out of the window you could see the white faces turning red and the Negro faces turning Negroier.

So it was about this time that word of the "racist" Black Arts program began to surface in the media—"teaching racism with government funds"! In retrospect, that obviously wasn't cool. With a good grasp of skating on the thin ice of government grants and with a smart grantsman around we could have not only bit deeper into the federal pie, we could have gotten some of the foundation money. But we were too honest and too naïve for our own good. We talked revolution because we meant it; we hooked up programs of revolutionary and progressive black art because we knew our people needed them, but we had not scienced out how these activities were to be sustained on an economic side. Later, after the word "black" had cooled out some and the idea of even "black art" had sunk roots deep enough in the black masses, where it could not simply be denied out of existence, the powers-that-be brought in some Negro art, some skin theater, eliminating the most progressive and revolutionary expressions for a fundable colored theater that merely traded on "the black experience," rather than carrying on the black struggle for democracy and self-determination. Then the Fords and Rockefellers "fount" them some colored folks they could trust and dropped some dough on them for colored theater. Douglas Turner Ward's Negro Ensemble is perhaps the most famous case in point. During a period when the average young blood would go to your head for calling him or her a knee-grow, the Fords and Rockefellers could raise themselves up a whole-ass knee-grow ensemble. But that's part of the formula: Deny reality as long as you have to and then, when backed up against the wall, substitute an ersatz model filled with the standard white racist lies which include some dressed as Negro art. Instead of black art, bring in Negro art, house nigger art, and celebrate slavery, right on!

But we made it easier for them to take us off — we acted so wild and woolly. News of our publicly nutting out on Shriver, news of our "black racism," steadily accelerated. And the funding of the most obviously successful arts and culture program any poverty program ever had was made "highly controversial." But we thought we could simply trample the racist rulers with the sincerity of our feelings. We hated white people so publicly, for one reason, because we had been so publicly tied up with them before.

There was, however, a positive overall effect of the Black Arts concept that still remains. We showed that we had heard and understood Malcom and that we were trying to create an art that would be a weapon in the Black Liberation Movement. In August of that year, while we were still conducting our nightly black art in the streets, our Operation Bootstrap program, Watts went up in flame and blood, a war raged in Watts for five days. That's what we thought, that it was out-and-out war. When Malcolm was murdered we felt that was the final open declaration of war on black people and we resolved to fight. The Harlem move was our open commitment to this idea. In our naïve and subjective way we fully expected the revolution to jump off any minute, Watts or Harlem style. There had been rebellions in many cities since the year before, when Jacksonville and Harlem went up. For us, it meant black people had taken the offensive and we despised those who did not equally commit themselves to the struggle. Young writers and other artists were drawn to this stance and its furious patriotism and outright despising of whites. Poets Sonia Sanchez, Clarence Reed, Clarence Franklin, playwright Ronald Drayton were among those that flowered out of the Black Arts. Sonia, then a wide-eyed young woman, quiet and self-deprecating, was herself coming out of a bad marriage and she came to our programs announcing very quietly and timidly that she was a poet. The two Clarences had walked the streets of Harlem all their lives, but the Black Arts saw them flower as poets. Sam Anderson and Ed Spriggs developed out of that Black Arts movement, participating in the readings we gave, at places like the Club Baron and the Celebrity Club or in the small Black Arts RTS auditorium. We had one hugely successful reading at the Baron, Milford Graves on drums, plus the African dance company from Oserjeman's Yoruba Temple.

Some of us were very much influenced by the Yorubas. When we first arrived in Harlem, Oserjeman's group was very political. They dressed as traditional West Africans from Nigeria, but upheld the right of black self-determination, declaring that Africans in Harlem must control it. We gave many rallies at which Oserjeman or some other speaker from the Yoruba Temple spoke. I had known Baba Oserjeman through a host of image changes. He was Francis King from Detroit, a friend of Steve Korret's, where I first met him. He was always spoken of then, by his friends, as a kind of con man-hustler. He wore English riding outfits and jodhpurs and affected a bit of an English accent. He then became Francisco Rey, Spanish for a minute. Then he became Serj Khingh, a little Indian, and he opened one of the first coffeehouses on the Lower East Side, called Bhowani's Table, where some of us used to go. The next I heard of Oserjeman, he had become Nana Oserjeman of the Damballah Qwedo, "practicing the religion of our fathers." And finally (?), Baba Oserjeman, chief priest of the Yoruba Temple.

I had no formal definition of cultural nationalism. I didn't even correctly know what it was. But certainly it was all around us then, the Nation of Islam the most known. But Malcolm's death ended any would-be hookup with the Nation for me and most of my friends. Lesser stoutly maintained he was a follower of the honorable Elijah Muhammad, but he belonged to no mosque and his commitment to the Nation seemed to be the carrying of a Qur'an and the wearing of the funny little suits and bow ties popularized by the nation, plus carrying a briefcase and standing slue-footed ("45 degrees") the way he thought a good Muslim should.

All of our politics were confused. Tong and his boys thought they were focused on a kind of Islam, but the only results I saw were negative. Some of us were influenced by the Yorubas because we could understand a connection we had with Africa and wanted to celebrate it. We liked the African garb that Serj and his people wore. The lovely long dresses, the bubbas and lappas and geles of the women. After so much exposure to white women, the graceful dress of the sisters in their African look, with their hair natural, turned us on. Plus, Oserjeman and the rest talked about and practiced polygamy, and certainly for some of us who were used to ripping and roaring out of one bed and into another, this "ancient custom of our people" provided a perfect outlet for male chauvinism, now disguised as "an ancient custom of our people."

All of the various influences focused on white people as enemies, devils, beasts, &c., and our thinking fell in perfectly with this. One question white reporters never seemed tired of asking me was, if I hated all white people, were all white people the enemy? When the last question was asked I would say, well, I haven't met all white people. It was our intention to be hard and unyielding in our hatred because we felt that's what was needed, to hate these devils with all our hearts, that that would help in their defeat and our own liberation.

So if "Hate whitey" was our war cry, it was also reason for me to be attacked. That was Tong's main method of undermining and attacking—to point out how a few months ago I lived downtown with white folks, now here I was directing black people. Plus, the press and the white power structure had definitely set us up, exploiting my recent fame to turn it to infamy. Larry Neal and Eddie Ellis had articles on this phenomenon in the *Liberator* magazine, but I still slept what they were saying, that I was being propped up so I could become an all-purpose whipping boy to show the absurdity of our cries of Black Art.

We faced both internal and external conflict. Every day was the revelation of one aspect or the other. One day Shammy got into a struggle with a dude from the Yoruba Temple over a woman that Shammy wanted and the Yoruba dude did too, plus Shammy had talked wise to one of Oserjeman's wives. When I looked up, the entire Yoruba Temple, which numbered a couple hundred in those days, came over to the Arts. They had come, they said, "for satisfaction." One of their priests' wives had been insulted and it must be rectified.

At first our people wouldn't let the Yorubas in, but I came downstairs and let them all file in. They stood silently around the wall, some with walking sticks, a couple, I suppose, with heat. Shammy wanted to act mock-heroic and defiant, but finally I got him to beg the priest's pardon and so his face was saved and likewise Shammy's ass. But Oserjeman lectured us on our bad manners and our lack of African perspective. We could not come up to Harlem and act like Europeans. I was boiling mad and embarrassed again by one of the Hackensack brothers.

The program that summer built a great rapport in all sectors of the community, especially since we were able to give out some jobs. We worked constantly to agitate the community and to further inflame it against the white racist system. But it seemed that fools like the Hackensacks did everything they could to break down that rapport and isolate us. When the program was over, we faced the bleak prospect of trying to raise money to continue our programs at the level to which we'd grown accustomed. I went downtown one night, backstage, to see Sammy Davis in *Golden Boy*. He made me a gift that night of $500 in brand-new $100 bills right out of his pocket. We also got Sammy to come uptown and do a benefit for us. It was at a Haryou facility on 125th Street. Sammy appeared with his entire entourage and made those surroundings seem even more spartan than they were. It was wild how white Sammy's act seemed in Harlem. But he did all right by us, whatever his motives.

There was one school of thought, not wholly shared by me, that we could simply gorilla the bux out of anyone, that we needed not only black celebrities but the government as well. That proved wrong on both counts. We pulled some thoroughly juvenile delinquent shit on Harry Belafonte — after demanding some money which he wouldn't give up, writing his name on some paper and then tearing the paper up as if that signified his imminent disposal. But it didn't work, Belafonte wasn't cowed by such shallow theatrics.

Our trips down to the various regional offices of the Office of Economic Opportunity, which was the funding agent for Haryou, were legion. We still have photos of Dr. Proctor (now pastor of Adam's Abyssinia) sitting with his head in his hands listening to our frantic spontaneous treatises on why we had to have some money, or some more money, &c. We felt that we had a right to demand money for our operations — some of us, I guess, felt we had a right to demand money for our personal lives, but I never had that problem.

So this gorilla attitude did permeate one aspect of our public image. While I did not think such an image was an absolutely correct one, there were only a few things I could do about it. I mean, I thought it was all right to present that image to the state, i.e., to the white racist government and those linked up with it ideologically or through employment. But I did not think that that should be our image as far as black people were concerned. With the Hackensacks and Tong's clique on the scene, that problem was also a constant. They were always having some confrontation or other with someone and then justifying it in the name of blackness. So that I spent a lot of my time cooling out that image, trying to rectify it or in hassles with our own perpetrators.

What our image was at large, outside of Harlem, I can only guess. Though the large motion in black communities to set up Black Arts equivalent institutions meant to me that the image was, in the main, creative.

Downtown some people still smarted over the disrupted social organization that the "mass" move uptown had caused them. (Fifteen years later a white woman came up to me in a bar and talked to me in a bitter accusing tone about how I had personally estranged her black husband away from her. With my wife, Amina, sitting there listening to her. It *was* sad.) The downtowners who came up to work and contribute to the Arts, I guess, had some contradictory words to put out against the straight-out maniac line that was being run by some. We heard fragments of the tales and emotional dislocation coming from downtown, from both black and white, and it was curious to me, like listening to one's obituary. Perhaps like Cross Damon in Wright's The Outsider.

One night a group of the black downtown residents had come up for a reading at the Arts. Ishmael Reed and Calvin Hernton among them. Vashti gets into an argument with this one poet, Luther Rupcity, about the nature of the Arts, what we were trying to do. What we were trying to be would have been Rupcity's phrasing. He and Hernton were very close and Vashti had little use for either one. Calvin had a problem with black women downtown and up that year because he had come out with his book Sex and Racism in the USA, which roots the problems of black national oppression in sexual conflicts and psychological antagonism stemming from those sexual conflicts. Interesting that both Cleaver and Jimmy Baldwin, to varying degrees, have also made this analysis. Calvin's statement that lit many sisters up was that many sisters are lesbians because black men do not relate to them sexually.

Rupcity was spouting some aspect of Hernton's theories and Vashti lit into him and Hernton with such ferocity that everyone else in the small gathering suddenly stopped to check out what was happening. Vashti was gesturing and backing Luther up, when Luther stops talking to her and turns to me with his hands palms up and says, "Will you get this lesbian off me?"

There were at least a dozen persons in that room who would have gladly and without remuneration beaten Calvin, Ishmael, Rupcity, and entourage into fragments and slivers of confusion and foolishness. But obviously I had been called. As I stepped toward Luther, he began crying, like real tears formed and rolled. My jaw was tight and my fists obviously shaking with anticipation. Rupcity says to me, "Don't hit me. What do you want to do, hit me? I know you've got those big hands. You want to hit me?" And he was quite right, that idea did cross my mind. But his display was further out than I expected and it unnerved me. I felt sorry for them. I jawed at him, talked bad to him, and then they all dragged out of there.

Vashti and I were living on Seventh Avenue right up near 145th Street. After struggling with the Arts all day I would walk up Seventh Avenue to our little three-room flat which overlooked a courtyard full of new, middle-aged, and ancient garbage. It was a fifth-floor walk-up, up over a West Indian bakery. So I was always eating them hip meat pies smoking hot, but I could never deal with the ginger beer. We went to the Zambesi bar across the street and around the corner was the Lagos, African named even before our new African consciousness. We hung out up and down Seventh Avenue. Count Basie's and Wells', home of the famous chicken and waffles, were our special hangouts. We'd fall by the Red Rooster, the stakeout joint of the black middle class. For special meeting meals with whites or certain kinds of Negroes we'd go to Frank's on West 125th Street, which had, at the time, white waiters who circulated playing Gypsy violins! Occasionally we might go by Shalimar, across the street from Sugar Ray's, or Small's (which Wilt Chamberlain had bought). I saw Redd Foxx in there one night and he made a joke about black militants and I said something to him from my table. It was a brief exchange but I could see his embarrassment come out from under those red freckles. They made a Sammy Davis film, *A Man Called Adam*, about a weird Louis Armstrong-Miles Davis combination, at Small's, and we got some of our actors on as extras. I even met Cicely Tyson and exchanged pleasantries while Vashti smirked just off camera.

Not just Vashti and I, but some of the dudes from the Arts and myself would hang out. We were always in the Apollo. I even went backstage and talked to Dionne Warwicke, who I fancied I had a crush on, trying to get her to do a benefit for the Arts. Some brothers opened a coffeehouse right around the corner from the Arts called The Truth. It was meant to cater to the Black Arts and those with similar tastes. There had been a rush of folks from downtown up to Harlem, but also from outside New York. People had come into New York as usual, but now there was a very special magnetism.

Harlem had its share of nuts and bolts. Not all of them came with us, but we did bring more than our share. There were resident paranoids and schizophrenics we ran into as well as sane people reacting normally to our abnormality. Most people were not running away from white people and a "shadowy" life as King(s) of the Lower East Side. So sometimes we probably confused some people's normal reaction to our nuttiness as nutty reactions to normality! But, all things considered, like they say, there were some bona fide nuts we ran into and some of the best people we have ever met in life.

Around us, at this point, there were people from RAM and also from the *Liberator* magazine, run by Dan Watts. There were the Garvey people, young and old. The neo-Garveyite followers of Carlos Cooks, like the AJASS society led by Elombe Brath, who first featured the "Naturally" programs that made natural hairstyles popular among some advanced groups of black people. They also modeled African clothing styles with their "Grandassa" models.

There were all kinds of other nationalists. The street-corner variety, which included not only the Garveyites but folks like Eddie "Porkchop" Davis, who was on the ladder daily giving white people hell. There were the cultural nationalists like the Nation of Islam, the Yoruba Temple, and even smaller cults and the orthodox or Sunni Muslims, who also had many variations, and the black Jews or Hebrews, the Egyptian Coptics, and various other "consciousness-raising" religious cults and sects. There were black militants of all persuasions and those on the left like Bill Epton around the corner at the Progressive Labor Party. Epton got arrested during the '64 rebellion and charged with "criminal anarchy." Bill was a soft-spoken likable dude whose relationship with the black community, from a little ramshackle office over a restaurant on Lenox Avenue, gave PLP a little credibility before it came out with its bullshit position that "all nationalism is nationalism," negating the revolutionary aspect of liberation struggles against imperialism which are not direct struggles for socialism.

Bill and I appeared on programs together and got along all right, but I was a nationalist and he a Marxist. We argued about whether PLP would come to his defense adequately. I told him I thought they would leave his ass to rot, while letting him take the weight. PLP did get him out, though I think he later resigned from the organization and is now part of a mainly black organization still based in Harlem. PLP did, however, leave another of its black cadres in prison to rot and take the weight and expelled this brother as a "nationalist." I never found out what Epton thought of this.

There were also the basic working people, moving out of Harlem most times to work and struggle and then returning at night to the indignities of ghetto life. There were Harlem office workers and bureaucrats and politicians. There were other cults like Democratic and Republican blacks. We disrupted several of their rallies, one at which Mayor Lindsay was to speak. There were right-wing nationalists like James Lawson who acted as bodyguards for the white and black politicos and we had constant run-ins with them. There were people like Charles Kenyatta around who got great notoriety as "Malcolm's former security." Kenyatta spoke on the ladder every day as well. But our comment was terse: "Motherfuckers who say they was Malcolm's bodyguards need to be killed. They shoulda died along with Malcolm." And Haryou, because it had got some dough, drew all kinds of hustlers and con men, religious and secular. There were people like baldhead Omar, who wanted to talk his way up on some money and power, or Donald Hassan, who got a reputation for being as crazy as Shammy, trying to gorilla his way up on same. There were the good-timers who wanted to hang out all day and night. Corny would lead us around to the various after-hours joints, where he would hold forth and introduce me to everybody and we would argue about Shammy and Tong and whether there was a black middle class or not. Corny said there wasn't. (Years later Cornelius was shot to death in just such an after-hours joint by some gunmen who, when robbing the place, turned for no reason and suddenly filled Corny full of lead!)

There were the gangsters and hoodlums and people in "the life" and all kinds of people who had been overlooked or peeped and popped. There was, as in any large urban black community, all kinds of promise and all kinds of frustration and bitterness. The sickness, the pathology that Fanon talks about in the communities of the oppressed, it was all full out and openly roaring around and over and through and within us. The Black Arts itself was a pastiche of so many things, so many styles and ideologies. We had no stated ideology except "black," and that meant many things to many people, much of it useful, much of it not. But we shot from the hip, came always off the top or near the top of our heads. Our sincerity was our real ideology, a gestalt of our experience, an eclectic mixture of what we thought we knew and understood. What we wanted. Who we thought we were. It was very messy.

Vashti and I were a pair for those times. She young and aggressive, so full of her own sense of what everything was (even as she was in the act of finding out) that she was intimidated by nothing. Probably some white women hated Vashti (some black ones too) because she was not just a symbol of something new, she was the whole drum set. People must have thought, this young girl, how'd she get into so much? But the brash young lady from DC was just what the doctor ordered and she knew it. Whoever it was—nuts, nationalists, Muslims, Yorubas, artsy types, politicians—Vashti handled them. "Hey, you betta get outta my face!" was one of her favorite statements. And our struggles were many and varied, for whatever reason. But we took all that in stride because we knew we had something deeper, we knew we actually dug each other, that we were *friends* as well as lovers.

Even my waywardness and roving eye she tried to deal with straight up and straight ahead. She'd say, "Roi, you gonna make me kill this bitch," of any object of my dalliance she would perchance to spy. And there were those. At Dolores Soul, the actress, Vashti merely laughed. "That old bitch!" And at Maria Cuevas, the writer, she just put her hands on her hips and when either of them was around the Arts she'd stand and watch them so intensely they felt a laser on their intentions that cooled them into distance.

One time we fought about my intentions. Vashti wanted to know when I was going to get a divorce. She said, "You think I'm just living with you for my health?" And we went off. I stalked out the door, headed for somewhere. The next day I went to the bank. Goddam Vashti had withdrawn all the money and split for somewhere. Then she calls me up at the Arts, laughing. "Fooled your ass, didn't I?" I was rising in smoke like the Phoenix. I get home and she's bought a goddam antique rocking chair.

We had a real falling out another time about something very similar. She says she's tired of my bullshit, she's going home to DC. When I get up to 145th Street that evening she has taken most of her shit and gone. I was depressed not only with this personal wipe-out; the day-to-day shit at the Arts could be extremely depressing with that cast of nuts to deal with. I was trying to figure out how we were going to sustain the program now that the federal moneys had been stopped. The phone rings and it's Brandy, a friend of Vashti's she'd met through Shammy. Shammy's female thing was astonishing. He ran through so many women so quickly it was impossible to keep track. They'd appear, be on the set a few minutes, and then disappear as if Porto Rico, the dude with the hook at the Apollo amateur night, had pulled them off accompanied by crazy music.

Brandy was a Shammy ex and she'd got real tight with Vashti. But now she's on the phone and I tell her that Vashti is not in. She says, "I know. Do you want me to come over?" In truth, the only reason I said I was busy, some dudes were coming over, was because suddenly I got the image of Shammy and that crazy-ass Vashti converging on me with waving swords and I couldn't handle it.

A few minutes later, Vashti calls from Washington. She asks me what I'm doing. She says, "I bet you got some woman over there, don't you?" It was funny now, so I told her about her friend Brandy and Vashti goes up in smoke right on the phone. "That bitch. I was the one who told her I was going to DC and to watch out for my interests. That bitch. Wait till I get my hands around her throat!"

But when she didn't come back I got into all kinds of dubious shit. For one thing, during the summer cultural program, the Yorubas had sent people over for some of the jobs. One of them, a young little girl named Olabumi, caught my eye. She was tiny but built like a dancer, with, as the nationalists say, an impressive history (a shapely behind). I started watching her go up and down the stairs at the Arts wondering what was under the long African lappa she wore.

At a program we had at the Baron, the Yoruba dancers are wailing and then Olabumi, or Bumi as we called her, falls out. One of the Yorubas then spreads the story that I was staring at her so intensely that it made her faint. At any rate, I found myself going by her place, but then I found out she lived with two other women and one of the Yoruba, a dude who sold incense. I didn't know what it meant, but I didn't care. Maybe I was interfering with some of their polygamy. Anyway, we found ourselves in one of the worst flophouse hotels in Harlem, but once getting in there she said she had no intention of doing anything. She said that Olatuni, whom she lived with, was her guardian, nothing more. But she would not give it up. So this became one focus for my after–Arts hours, trying to catch up with this little teasing Bumi.

I met another woman at the same time, a little light-skinned woman with glasses who walked like she thought she was a musician or at least a street hipster. This Lucille had been downtown and had moved up, but she was living in Harlem and hanging downtown and had come uptown before most of us. When I ran into her she was staying with some girlfriend and implying she might be going to lead a life of Lesbos.

The influence of the cultural nationalism on all of us at the Black Arts was real. For instance, when I finally succeeded in getting Bumi to come up to 145th Street and spend the night, I immediately got the idea that both Bumi and Lucille could move in, that I should begin to live as the Yorubas at Serj's temple. As an obvious justification for male chauvinist bed rambling there is little to discuss, but the extent to which these ideas had penetrated my thinking on the real side is what is interesting. But not only my thinking. I did convince the two of them to move into 145th Street. Bumi, a teenager, an African dancer, child of the new age, seeking some new revelation of changed black reality. Lucille, an office worker who loved the music, whose quest for blackness was made all the more ironic (but necessary) by her very light skin.

Lucille, the office worker, liked the idea (but maybe she just wanted to get next to little Bumi), but Olabumi, who was associated in the temple with polygamous marriages, seemed less impressed with the idea. The three of us sat and discussed it, with Lucille marveling at Bumi's sewing machine, a portable she was carrying with her to make bubbas and lappas for wearing and for the temple's performances. But why had I found it necessary now to offer such a relationship to these sisters? I had never asked any of the white women I had been with to enter into some polygamous relationship. Though that is just a formalism, since the many affairs and one-night stands that went on amounted to something like polygamy. Engels says adultery is the partner of monogamy. None of that went through my mind, the idea of polygamy was "new" and "black," so we went for it.

After a day or two, this relationship, such as it was, got reported back to me by Lesser, who said, "I understand that you're living according to one of the most illustrious traditions of our ancestors." But by the time he said that shit, it was already just about over. Vashti had decided she was coming back, so these other sisters had to cut out.

Things at the Arts were getting dire. When the summer program was going and money was flowing in, things were great, there were conflicts but they could be handled. The noise Tong and Co. sold, the antipathy the community people, professional artists, and the like felt for them, I could cool out somewhat, at least keep the shooting war off. But without the cash flow, raising money here and there with handouts and our programs, people started to get more sullen.

People kept coming to me with plans to dump Tong or Tong and Shammy in the river or off the roof. One old friend of Tong's from childhood sat in on one of these frenetic discussions and he agreed that the dude was dangerous and needed to be took off. Then he slips a note to Tong telling him to watch out.

Tong bursts into my office and says he understands somebody is planning to do something to him. That he is ready and that no one would survive. I had a huge blue-steel cowboy-style .357 magnum I used to carry in my briefcase. And while he is woofing I run my eye over the briefcase and his eyes drift in its direction as well. He knows full well what is in there. But I kept scribbling notes for a play I was trying to write and looked up at him only barely. "I don't know what you're talking about." And he goes back into his office. But the tension between us and his mob after that was unbearable. It was like you couldn't do anything for fucking around and being fucked with by these unproductive nuts. One little dude took Tong out in Mount Morris Park and kicked his ass one afternoon after Tong kept woofing at him, and that made me feel much better. Tong thought he was bad bad, but the little dude was a boxer and jabbed and hooked him dizzy. We stopped it. Why? I don't know.

Our politics, first and ultimately, was the reason the program and its development were in such disorder. Our politics which flowed from our mix-matched and eclectic ideology. We had straight-out white supremacy bourgeois opinions mixed with mass felt revolutionary ones. We wanted to destroy a system and didn't realize that we still carried a great deal of that system around with us behind our eyes.

In one of our confrontations, for instance, Jimmy Lesser, one of Tong's black blacks, confessed that he could not get as deep into the militant thing as we could. (I didn't quite understand the difference then between bourgeois nationalism that just wanted to get in on the exploitation and a revolutionary democratic view that wanted to destroy it, so-called revolutionary nationalism. This is the reason so many of us slept on what it meant that Malcolm and Elijah had split. That split between the politics of an oppressed bourgeoisie and the politics of the exploited and oppressed revolutionary black masses.) Lesser then says, "Look, man, I have to admit I'm a traditionalist. I need a snowy blond white woman at my side, whatever I'm going to do."

I was so horrified because I realized I had been, was being, vilified by motherfuckers that wasn't even as straight as I was, who had problems even much deeper than my own. The fact that I couldn't believe there could be suckers much sicker than me was what had left me open to these clucks. And I resented it, deeply. It made me even more sardonic and terse in dealing with these dudes.

The reason this conversation had come up was that all the lights had blown out in New York City, I guess for the first time. In Harlem this Great Blackout had a special effect. Suddenly, at the corner of Lenox and 125th, a group of white people were being taunted and robbed. The police swung into action — saving white people is their second most important function after their most important function, saving white rich people's property. They had to do some property saving too. Windows were getting smashed and commodities were disappearing at an alarming rate, well below their established exchange value.

We got the idea that we should agitate for more of what was going on, as if people needed us to tell them what to do. By the time we got our sound truck in action one piece of 125th had been stripped as clean as most bloods' pockets. But we started speaking over the loudspeaker, riding up and down Lenox and Seventh. "Now's the time," we shouted. "They can't see you. Rip these stores off. Take everything. Come on out and get it!"

We had just come back up the hill near 130th Street when police cars hemmed us in. White cops leaped out, guns drawn. They dragged us out of the seat, sticking a gun to my head. We were running off at the mouth, driving their temperature up even higher. They were dragging us to their car. I think it was me and Dave in the car. But just as they are getting us into the car a crowd forms. They came together instantly, those bars and corners emptied, and suddenly, yeh, the surrounders were themselves surrounded. And, jim, if they thought my mouth was bad, they hadn't heard nothing. Bloods lit them up on all sides. One old sister, her hands on her hips, stood between us and their car calling them "White motherfuckers! You white motherfuckers need to be killed! Leave them young boys alone, goddamn it!"

And the others joined in. There were maybe a half dozen police and now, very quickly, about fifty or sixty people. The police had to decide what to do. They were caught between training their guns on us or the crowd, which was getting louder and louder and prettier and prettier (the cops would say "uglier"). Plus, the people were closing off the space, drawing the circle in tighter. But one cop gets on the radio and starts calling. The goddam precinct house was right around the corner at 135th and Seventh and they push us toward the car, pushing the confrontation toward its explosion

point. But then some colored cops arrive. That's why they were calling. The Buffalo Soldiers were needed once more and they arrived
riding their trusty backwardness. We get smashed into a police car
and talked bad to with a gun at our heads by the white cops. They
are threatening to kill us. "Like Gilligan did? Huh?" we screamed.
(Gilligan was the cop who had shot the young black boy in an incident that helped set off the Harlem Rebellion and wanted posters
appeared the next day with the caption WANTED FOR MURDER:
GILLIGAN THE COP! The PLP was reputed to have done it and that's
why the police wanted to bust Epton.) The cop tried to strangle us.

When we got to the precinct they were pushing us into the back
room, where they said they were going to finish us off, but as we entered I spied the newly appointed black commander of the precinct,
Eldridge Waithe, a West Indian dude with a fairly good reputation,
for a black cop. He came over, and we started screaming that these
freaks were gonna kill us. So Waithe intervenes, questions the cops,
questions us, and after an hour or so in which many of the Black Arts
people had come over to the precinct or were calling the precinct
over the phone, Waithe cut us loose.

That's what Lesser meant. He wasn't as militant as us. He thought
the revolution had to do with wearing bow ties and standing slue-
footed. But at least that involved some activity. Some did even less.

I was growing sick of most of these people, because even some
of the more productive brothers and sisters would only come
around at times when they thought they didn't have to put up with
the Hackensacks and the rest of that crew. Corny sat and broke
down in tears one night because Shammy had said something to
him and Corny wanted to kill him and, because he couldn't, the
frustration ate him up, and he wept, trying to threaten Shammy
still, but at the same time wailing like a child.

Askia, Dave, and I sat up all night after we got released from the
joint, talking of revolution. The blackout itself was an agitating element of romance in our concept of revolution. We were still so unclear. We still did not even understand in anything approaching a
scientific way what were the purposes or the methods for making
real revolution. We were angry and we had heart. We thought those
were most of the prerequisites. But the Hackensacks turned people
like Larry Neal and Askia off. Larry thought they were seriously
ill—"counterproductive," he called them. But Larry was going
through some personal problems himself. One of his close political
comrades had run off with his wife. He'd told me in that same narrow little office. That seemed shitty and ugly, like it was happening

in another world. The wild ins and outs of our various relationships I could take as they came, but something like that seemed, somehow, foreign. Like a bourgeois movie.

After that, Larry had gotten involved with a sister that Tong had some design on, and that put even more distance between them, as if there needed to be any more. Plus, Larry had been openly critical of the way the Hackensacks, in general, liked to fuck things up. So there was bad blood between them.

The screwy Tong, in what he conceived as some secret strategy, tried to get his young disciple, Majid, to follow me around. He was supposed to report on my activities, where I went and whatnot. I guess because he thought that allowed him to undermine even more, interfering with stuff he didn't like. But then, also, I guess I was his meal ticket. There was no money changing hands anymore. The little money I got, from royalties and readings, I needed to support myself. But I did give up some few dollars to keep the Arts functioning. We did programs that brought in a little money and contributions, but we were just barely paying the bills. Tong and his nuts might have resented the fact that I did have some money, and they chose not to work, at anything, and that was yet another edge between us.

But now the bullshit was rising so high that I was getting more and more distracted. When Vashti found out about my nutty liaison with the two sisters she went up in smoke, started throwing plates and pots, a steam iron, her fists, then she repacked her bags and split. She moved downtown with a girlfriend, or at least down to the East Nineties.

I guess I was wasted. When she'd been in DC, that was one thing. I figured she'd be back and the separation didn't seem permanent or the final solution. But this walkout had bodings of finality, termination. Plus, now, I felt naked. It was the kind of loneliness that can descend on you at the end of some personal relationship or phase of your life. Vashti had been for me, no matter my craziness, a real companion, an extension of myself, as I was, I guess, an extension of her. We'd always felt like two hip young things against a crazy world, and we were time enough for it. There was a groping tenderness to our relationship that came from experiencing sweetness in the midst of the unknown and clinging to that sweetness as life itself.

So the days passed now with an edge of gloom to them, and the weight of the growing madness at the Arts weighed even heavier on me. For now, I literally could not stand the asshole Tong or his unpredictable brother. I hung with Corny and Clarence in and out of the Harlem bars or holed up in my office drinking cheap orange wine. The goings and comings of Tong and his litter of nuts did not interest me. The programs we put on, Dave and I took care of. The artists that came through, the two of us talked to. We regarded Tong &c. as bad weather and dealt with them as little as possible.

We had a public image. We still spoke at rallies and programs, firing away intensely as we could against the white beasts who oppressed black people. Earlier in the year I had finally published the book *The System of Dante's Hell*. The moiling twisted experience of my youth still moiled and twisted as an aesthetic form of rhythmic images, searching for a voice that finally begins to emerge at the end of the book and its "fast narrative" of a perpetually gloomy reality. But I had already gone past that stage in my life. (I hoped!) When I had, at the end of *Dante*, "woke up with white men, screaming for God to help me." I had served that apprenticeship to my own real spirit. I had left the Village and that education I had given myself, reading and feeling myself through great parts of the Western world. I had dashed out at full speed hurling denunciations at the place of my intellectual birth, ashamed of its European cast. Arriving full up in the place of blackness, to save myself and to save the black world. Ah, the world-filling egos of youth.

But now I felt more alone than ever, bereft of Vashti's kindred spirit and love. Facing dumb dissembling motherfuckers who wasted time conspiring against advance and productivity. My head was a swirl of images, disconnection and new connection, its focus vague, dulled by my own subjectivism. Most of our intentions were good. We wanted to help free black people. We, ourselves, had got back a self-consciousness of our nationality, but we were bogged deep in nationalism, a growing, ever more deepening cultural nationalism it was to turn out. Malcolm's death, certainly, had left many people scrambling and unprepared. There was no revolutionary party we understood. No science we could relate to. Those people calling themselves Communists, we despised. They were stupid-ass white people — shit, they were part of the enemy. Hadn't they even come around saying that "the nationalism of Malcolm X was just like the nationalism of the KKK" and that "Malcolm was a police agent?" Shit, they needed to be fired on.

But we were a clutch of kids, some of us never even got past that and remain kids even to this very day. We needed to be directed, we needed guidance. We needed simple education. There were next to no black institutions where we could learn, that's why we had tried to put one together. We could understand what it was to be uneducated in a world of airplanes and skyscrapers. I, certainly, knew what it was to be suddenly conscious and then be made ashamed of your own unconsciousness which had ended only a few seconds before.

When I finished whatever tasks I had given myself at the Arts I would take off, unless I was talking to some of the artists or Corny or Clarence or a few of the other people or Dave. But now there was little to say to the others, who had their own powwows, which produced nothing I could see but metaphysical double-talk and empty leers pretending consciousness.

I discovered where Vashti was holed up and started calling her. You could tell that she hadn't frozen up on me completely but she did think that I was too much trouble. There was too much wear and tear on the neurons. And was it worth it? But a couple of phone calls and we were at least sitting in some bar sipping drinks and staring out at the world trying to put something back together.

The first night I slept over where Vashti was staying proved to be the beginning of the end of the beginning. We ate breakfast and talked. I was restless and she wondered why. I was supposed to show up at the Arts around ten o'clock, but I didn't feel like it. It was nothing formal, just a bedraggled, out-of-it feeling.

We went out to a bar, then we decided to go downtown to see a flick. They were doing Evelyn Waugh's The Loved One and we sat through that. When we came out I told Vashti to call the Arts and see what was happening. She said they were wondering where I was. Tong had asked Dave and Dave passed it on. At that point I felt, "Oh bullshit, fuck them . . . " I had Vashti by the hand and told her simply, "Hey, it's finished. Fuck those people. I'm not going back there."

I went to the old apartment and packed a few clothes. I called Shorty and told him to watch my shit—I was cutting out for a while. Then we went to Vashti's place and got her clothes and took off. At first I didn't know where we were going, I just didn't feel like seeing those gloomy nuts on West 130th Street. Finally, after several bars and another flick, I decided we should go home, to Newark, to my parents' house. I called up, made arrangements, and then cut out. A couple of young people who had started coming up to the Arts were from Newark. We contacted them through Shorty and got them to help us move out our clothes and most of our belongings. Except I left a huge record collection, with Shorty supposedly minding it, that I never got back. Shorty let Corny and Clarence and some others know where we were, but that's all. We didn't even tell young relia-ble Dave, because Dave was always the object of manipulation by the Tongs and Shammys.

When Tong and Shammy found out I had split, moved out with Vashti, they got nuts, I guess. They went running up to the apart-ment and threw whatever was left around. Then they stormed around Harlem, claiming they were looking for me. For a couple of months, whenever I came to New York, I carried a sawed-off shot-gun inside my hunting jacket in such a way that I could put my hand on it, open the coat, and fire almost simultaneously. But happily I had no confrontations.

In the first heat of that split, there was a casualty. Apparently Larry Neal, Askia, and some others went to inquire of Dave about my whereabouts and were met with even more hostility from the now thoroughly lost and desperate survivors at the building. Now there was no money, the programs had stopped. Of those still around, only Dave would do anything consistently to put together the programs, and now there were no resources. Shammy was frus-trated and angry because I had split. Tong was now free to run amuck and that amuckness ended up with Larry being shot as he emerged from a subway by Shammy. It was a small-caliber weapon and Larry was hit in the leg. But now it seemed a war threatened to jump off, of forces colliding in the vacuum of my sudden removal. But I didn't care, except for some twinges of feeling about my failed responsibility. When I saw Larry he questioned me and said that some other folks wanted to know why I had brought those nuts into the community and then left them up there.

But now I had other things to think about. Like, what was I doing back in Newark? I had just completed a book of essays called Home, which meant coming back to one's self, one's consciousness, com-ing back to blackness. I ended the introduction to the book: " . . . by the time you read this, I will be even blacker." That was true, albeit the grand stance. But I could also have said: " . . . and confused like a motherfucker." But, at least, I was, literally, Home.

From *The Music*

███████

Primitive World: an Anti-Nuclear Jazz Musical

PRIMITIVE WORLD was first performed at Sweet Basil, New York City, in January 1984.

Characters

MAN/ BLACK MUSICIAN

WOMAN/ BLACK MUSICIAN

HAM/ STATESMAN

SADO/ MONEY GOD

MASO/ MONEY GOD

HEART/ DRUMMER

WOMAN/ BLACK MUSICIAN, Heart's Wife

WHITE MUSICIAN, LATINO MUSICIAN, Heart's Companions

[A MAN carrying a tenor saxophone which is in parts comes running into his space. A shack, a mixture of future and primitive beginnings. In the background a kind of wind music, like voices in pain, like people seeing their world blown apart. And across the back of the stage, faded red- and death-colored slides sweep across, sporadically — in some kind of out rhythm. Suddenly — and just swifter than clear identification — an image of horrible suffering blows by — in the rhythm of the music, the sharp broken glass shreds of sound.

There are lights, like fires, that come up, then fade. Flicker bright.

The MAN has apparently been bitten by something. Blood is streaming down his arm. HE is wearing some kind of metallic *jump suit-looking garment, and a helmet that seems to have an oxygen mask fitted into it.*

HE *is wrapping up his arm, and placing the horn on a table where* HE *can look at it and work on it.* HE *works on his arm, sprinkles powder on it.* HE *is concerned about it, but not panicky. But still* HE *tries to fit the horn together; but some of the parts are warped and* HE *is having some trouble making them fit. Occasionally,* HE *will pick up the mouthpiece part of the horn and make some sounds on it. Simple, then more ambitious. But then, this will simply drive him back to trying to fix it]*

At one point, HE *seems to* SMELL *something, and rises quickly to go to the window and tries to seal it even more tightly.* HE *sniffs at the bottom of the door.* HE *goes back to the horn, and fumbling with it, sings snatches of a song.*

MAN.
    in the mountains
    in the valley
    in the ruins
    in the dead blown-up city

    Poison death
    fire left
    Cloud of horror
    Silent memory

[Repeat first stanza.
HE *stands and picks up a pile of records and weighs them in his hand.* HE *shuffles through them. Then looks at a record player that is in parts.* HE *shuffles them around, singing the song, a blues ballad, quiet and precise]*

Where are you
Where are me
Where are life
Where are sun

poison death
fire death
blow up death
murder death

in the mountains
in the valley
even niggers in the alley
all blown up destroyed

Poison death
Fire left
Clouds of horror
Silent tongue, silent memory

[*Upstage, from the darkness a spot illuminates a* STATESMAN *talking. A tall, aging man with spinning eyes. His hair plastered down like Superman.* HE *is in a dark business suit, but has a red cape. There is a dollar sign on the cape.* HE *is surrounded by garbage cans full of money—big bills bulge out of each can so that the tops sit slightly askew.* HE *is making a speech, and every once in a while looking at a script* HE *has in his inner pocket, trying to memorize. The* MAN's *dialogue must be in rhythmic, musical relationship to the song the* MUSICIAN *sings, a kind of counterpoint. But, of course,* THEY *are not in the same place—*THEY *are separated by time and understanding. The* MUSICIAN, *when* HE *is frustrated with his attempted repair job, blows on the mouthpiece, making a hard music.* HE *sings in many styles—Bluesy old, Bluesy-Stevie, Jazzy like Joe Lee Wilson, cool like Johnny Hartman*]

HAM. Therefore, since we have tried to live with everybody and they didn't want to live with us. [HE's *memorizing, repeating, missing and coming clear*] Since we tried to live . . . with everyone . . . and they won't have it. They won't have our peace. [HE *is reading, but the thought of what* HE *is saying animates him*]

[*The* MAN *is making wild sounds with the mouthpiece.* HE *is beating on floor and walls like a drum. It is a weird music, as accompaniment for* HAM's *speech in the process of being memorized.*

There is a banging on the door in the MUSICIAN's *space. It is tentative, but it gets harder, as if the person were trying to act forceful. At first we cannot see where the noise comes from, then we see it is a* YOUNG WOMAN, *slender, dark.* SHE *is also looking over her shoulder.*

The MUSICIAN, *hearing the knocking, does not respond. The* WOMAN *is getting bolder and bolder, knocking.*]

The STATESMAN, *memorizing the speech, postures and speaks, at the same time doing a kind of dance. It is a dance of slow rising murderousness.* HE *is gesturing and pointing, like a tribesman dancing a bitter challenge, in some anonymous clearing a million years ago. But we see his surroundings are more modern than today in the hard technology.* HE *is speaking, but also* HE *gives the speech some rhythm, some music emphasis, drawing out and shortening the lines, so that it is poetic, musical, and frightening]*

HAM. We pleaded with them. We showed them light. We told them we were better than the world. More holy. More red and white more blue. We said Holy mother of profit, make these people, these all these people love us as we are. But today . . . yes today [HE *repeats, picks out certain words and lines* . . .]

[The MUSICIAN *is trying to see who is out there. The* WOMAN *begins to call softly. Then more loudly]*

WOMAN. Is there anyone in there? [Knock knock knock] ·Is there anyone in there?

[The MUSICIAN *is frozen, but curious,* HE *hears,* HE *draws closer to the door.* HE *is still fiddling with the horn, but more quietly, obviously looking at the door, but continuing to do something as if nothing was happening.* HE *is still singing quietly, more quietly, his song.*

Now the WOMAN *is knocking, and falling back from the door, looking around, but also, checking out the shack, the windows sealed, the bottom of the door sealed, but* SHE *thinks she detects a light]*

Is anyone there?

Is anyone there?
Is anyone there?
Don't ask again
Someone waiting for you
Is anyone there?
Is anyone there?
Alone in the . . .

[Suddenly the MUSICIAN *gets up and pulls the door open]*

MAN. Shit! Hey. Ain't nothing bad enough to put me out past whatever it is. Yeh? Who is it? A monster? Red smoke? Death on a motorcycle? Ancient shit. New horror? Hey. Dig this. [HE *holds up his horn, still unable to put it together*] This is me!

[WOMAN, *her head around the doorway. The* BROTHER *has taken some stance like* HE *is going to defend himself, if necessary, by blowing the horn. The* WOMAN *pokes her head around, still tentative, amazed at the stance of the* BROTHER. HE *has worked himself up, to where* HE *is "going to town," squatting suddenly with the horn in some kind of karate pose extension of himself* . . .]

Yeh . . . [*Gesturing with the horn, not even seeing the* WOMAN . . .] Yeh, dig this — this is me, horrible shit all together — crazy life — this is me!

WOMAN. Well. [HE *looks, and finally, sees!*] You all right?

MAN. Oh? [*Digs himself, like someone not used to people or other eyes*] Oh? OK, hello . . . hello and shit.

WOMAN. You all right? [SHE *edges forward.* HE *is trying to welcome her, but still not certain of what and how, etc., edges backward*]

MAN. All right? What you mean? Who're you? Out there in the dark. Asking me am I OK, all right? What about you? Shit, you might be a ghost, some ambitious smoke. I might be dead . . . [HE *is admitting her to the house and retreating at the same time*] Am I all right?

WOMAN. All right?

MAN. Yeh.

WOMAN. Well, are you inviting me in?

MAN. Yeh, I opened the door. [HE *is gesturing with the horn, now somewhat embarrassed at his wildness*] Am I all right? [*Sings and toots on mouthpiece*]
Am I all right? Am I cool?
Am I all right? Am I well?
Am I all right? Do I have what I need?
Am I all right? Am I still breathing fine?

I'm all right, sure I'm great. It's the world
That's blown, I'm cool. It's the world
That's smashed, I'm in perfect shape.

It's just the world
It's blown apart
It's just the world
I'm doing fine.

WOMAN. [SHE *stands looking at the* MAN *and over her shoulder, etc.*]
He's doing great
It's just the world
He's in perfect shape
It's just the world
Wow, it's so profound
he's cool, he's hip
it's just the world
he's all right, it's just the world

[SHE *laughs, and the laughter while ridiculing his unrealistic stance, at the same time relaxes him.* HE *smiles, half grudging*]

MAN. That does sound out, don't it? I'm all right, it's just the world that's fucked up. Wow! Wow is right!! [*Then focusing on her*] Well, come on in anyway. You know so much about how we connected with the world, how come you running around in it?

WOMAN. [*Relaxing, unzippering the jump suit enough to get some air*] Hey, you don't want the whole story now, do you? [*Laughs, a mixture of lightness and bad memory*] I was part of a good thing . . [*Heavy pause*] and it got . . . blown . . . wasted . . .

[HAM, *the* STATESMAN, *with congealed hair, is doing his cave dance surrounded by the garbage cans overloaded with money*]

Cans marked

HAM. [*Sings*]
We told them, you read it
We warned them, don't dread it
We were right, you knew it
We were white, we were rich

You poor ones, don't worry
We represent your suffering too
You black and red and brown and
Yellow ones, don't worry, we are
Absolutely in touch with you

Don't do it, we screamed, don't
Try to live. Don't try it, we sung—
We won't allow any life but ours.

Holy Mother of profit, you know
We are always true. Money Lord
we are more white, more red
more blue.

[Pause, looking around at the garbage cans as if for response]

HAM. (continued)
And now,
what is the pleasure of the
center of the earth, what is
the will of the money gods?

[The light has been raised to show the section of the stage where
the STATESMAN, like from a past age, a fading nightmare,
continues to perform a life exorcism, a death ritual to bring the
dying on.

The song is a poem/chant of rising death feeling. A rising strangle
on light and love.

The STATESMAN, as HE SINGS and DANCES, makes motions from
time to time like HE is playing a violin. HE plays an imaginary
violin, sometimes, uses different parts of his body, arms, legs,
head, as an imaginary violin, and saws away, spitting out the
doomlike song]

And now? And now? And now?
We've begged and pleaded
Compromised and defended
But now? But now! We'll have no more
of this. But now? But now!

We'll right the world for good.
But now! But now! But now, and now,
and now.

[*His dance turns into a "blowup" mime, his arms and body making explosion gestures, each larger and larger, and more devastating*]

So what is the word
From the Money Gods?
What is the word of Boss
Divine? Now, and now and now!!

What is the word
of the Money Gods?
What does eternity
speak? And now and now and now!!

[*Suddenly, the garbage cans begin to move. They wobble like they're going to fall over, and as they tilt, the* STATESMAN (HAM) *shrieks his doom chant more intensely, like Ra & Yma Sumac*]

HAM. (continued)
Begged and pleaded, pretended to
be mortal, acted humble like humans
but none of that worked, none of it
made them see who we were. And now

And now, Money Gods, answer, Money
Gods, speak to us, now and now the time
is now, we've acted like humans and other
passive things too long, now and now we've
come to another time, it's passed into

another clime. And now, they'll know
we'll show, the depth and breadth
of our power. We wait, only for a sign
let the money gods roar out their pleasure!

[*The cans rocking, and one at a time, but rapidly, the tops of all four of them pop open — and out of two of the cans, there are* TWO MEN *with top hats on who rise up, the money that has covered them, flying everywhere.*

The STATESMAN (HAM) *is ecstatic,* HE *leaps in the air, for his prayers have been answered. The* MONEY GODS *have appeared.* HE *leaps, and saws the imaginary violins crazily. The* MONEY GODS *also have violins, real ones, and* THEY *play as* THEY *sing and speak and chant.* ONE's *face is painted into a smile, the* OTHER *into a frown. But* THEY *have no faces, rather* THEY *are wearing layers and layers of masks. And every so often, at indi-*

cated moments, their singing and chants take on more significance as THEY discard one of the masks only to reveal the mask under it is the same as the mask the opposite is wearing. So the SMILING GOD takes off a mask to reveal a frown as the FROWN-ING GOD takes off his mask to reveal a smile.

The MONEY GODS play the violins like telegraph messages from all over the world. The dit dit dit of world news tonight. To the heightened razor craziness of their violin playing, their voices in bizarre song, which seems to combine stock exchange jargon and atmosphere and the entire range of television, radio, and billboard commercials—one after another, and intermixed, the national anthem of commercials is their lyrics.

These commercials and violin playing must be delivered in much the same rhythm as the telegraph message violins. As THEY emerge from out the cans it is a ritualized dance, which at the same time reveals their lives as merchants and controllers of society. It is a power-mime dance THEY do as THEY emerge shouting the crazed commercials]

[The MUSICIAN and the WOMAN are standing closer in the room, talking quietly about each other's lives. HE is still trying to fix the horn, to make it play, and still occasionally playing the mouth-piece blues and rags, singing snatches of "Am I All Right," humming it, now scatting it lightly, punctuating with the mouthpiece, or the horn's keys pressed rapidly like subtle percussion runs]

WOMAN. You know I can fix that horn?

MAN. Well how come you didn't fix it when you first got in here?

WOMAN. Because I was waiting for you to admit that we'd met before, that you knew my name and that you had known me before, out there with the people of disaster!

MAN. Why would you say that? This is the first time I ever saw you.

WOMAN. The explosions took your memory.

MAN. Why are you saying this?

WOMAN. That I can fix the horn?

MAN. No. That too, but the other stuff.

WOMAN. Then who are you?

MAN. I only tell who I am to people I am in love with. [*A pause, an uneasy smile*] Who're you?

WOMAN. You really don't know me?

MAN. Why are you talking like this?

WOMAN. [*Shrugging, like an unexpected delay*] What is that pile in the corner over there? Extra wood for the fire?

MAN. [*Blowing into the mouthpiece*] It just might be . . . [HE *goes over and pulls back the tarpaulin*] It's a piano . . . wasted . . . I can't do nothin' with it anyway. But it's out past Cage right now. It's been prepared by violent reality!

[*The sound of the* STATESMAN/MONEY GODS *in their wild dance is heard from time to time, like sound effects, percussive bits and pieces, and a spotlight—reminds you of flashing neon signs in which flashes of the killer statesman ritual dance, with the speaker,* HAM, *transfixed like a true believer and worshiper, are seen*]

[*The* WOMAN *sits down at the piano on a box,* SHE *dusts it off, rubs at it to clean it, removes boxes and bottles from around it,* SHE *pokes at it, a few smooth runs, her voice trailing the notes swooning up and down the keys.* SHE *does very little, but what* SHE *does makes the* MUSICIAN *stop and look at her*]

MAN. Uhhuh. [*Acknowledging*] What you gon' do? You can play that?

WOMAN. [*Nodding at the horn*] About as well as you can play that. And yours is broke!

MAN. You said you can fix it!

WOMAN. Then remember me, lover man! [SHE *begins to play the piano. It is a sad little ballad, at each break of the line,* SHE *almost hums tears, tears, tears*]

MAN. You can sing too?

WOMAN. [*Extending the melodic little piece, sings*]
As it is with the world
so it is with love
as it's light or dark
so it is with love

under the stars
is more than astrology
it has some influence
on your psychology

so let's change our lives
for a change let's make our world
beautiful. So let's change our world
for a change let's make our lives
beautiful!

[SHE *finishes the piece with a slowing, brooding introspection, humming and slipping in and out of the lyrics, the piano poignant, but panging and banging slightly out of tune*]

MAN. Hey. [HE *holds the horn up looking at it*] That was nice — some real music for a change.

WOMAN. [SHE *wheels around off the box*] You think I wasn't serious about fixing this horn? I can play that horn too.

[HE *looks at her*]

But that ain't my specialty. My father and grandfather could play — they built bridges and played music. They never was on television, but they swung harder than most of them that were! There was always horns and instruments, a piano around our house. Not to be looked at, like a pretty piece of furniture, but to be low down played.

MAN. I don't know why I can't fix it myself. [*Pause*] Goddam, I can play it. And can't fix it. But where I was you could send 'em out to be fixed.

[*The* WOMAN *has the horn, looking at it.* SHE *pads it, pushes the keys in silent rushing scales. Looks at the mouthpiece*]

[*Now the dit dit dit madness is brought up in the lights. The* MONEY GODS *are frozen in their maniacal dance posture.* THEY *are trembling and jerky like* THEY *still must play, play, but* THEY *are fixed and staring, eyes rolling around*]

HAM. Ah, masters of reality, creators of the future, you've responded.

SADO. [*Smiling face*] Yes, of course. [*Loose sing-song, like one of Snow White's dwarfs, Dopey*] Of course, yes. We're like that. Always generous to a fault.

MASO. [*Frowning face*] We must respond. We know how absolutely powerful we are. How we run everything. [HE *breaks into a song*]
If it's run
We run it
If it's fun
We own it
If it's valuable
We define it
If it's rebellious
We confine it

HAM. Now that you've come, to give me my words. My thoughts for the year. How to deal with weird events, invasions and such, bombings of reactors and fundings for bad actors. Overthrowing governments, assassinating patriots.

[HE *is taken by his speech, swaying back and forth like a drunk getting ready to have an orgasm.*

Suddenly MASO *and* SADO *go into wild violin duet.* HAM, *picking up on it, starts to pick up his sway, the* TWO VIOLINISTS *are "competing" with each other, one-upping, snarling, jumping*]

MASO. Uhh, Uhh.

SADO. Umm Umm.

[THEY *jump toward each other, and away like a boxing match.*

HAM *dances to their playing*—HE *has a smaller violin which* HE *scratches at, puts in his pocket, spinning, eyes crossing*]

HAM. [Sings]
Knowledge
and death
everything
and death
jungle lights itch
and death
all of it is life
all of it is death
and death

[MASO and SADO pick up death chant, sawing away at their axes.
HAM now begins on flute, accompanying the MONEY GODS, singing and grunting and dancing.

Every so often the TWO exchange masks and change the key THEY
sing in or the tempo to show the change]

MASO.
and death
the answer

SADO AND MASO.
and death
and question

nothing anywhere resembles
great death, nothing

in or outside
the sun

the bloody
moon

we know, we do know
what's great

immortal
death.

SADO. [Abruptly] What . . .

MASO. Do you want?

[*A stock market board bell rings and we hear ticker tape, when* THEY *laugh*]

SADO. Sell!

MASO. Sell? Sell? Sell? [*Looks around wildly*]

SADO. Sell!

[*The sound of chains being dragged somewhere, slave moans like the blood market of king cotton*]

HAM. [*Spinning, looking out at audience*]
You hear that
Sell, Sell, Sell!

[*The* THREE *like spastic madmen go through the act of selling—Freeze—*]

HAM (*continued*). And the prophecy, the future? Today is the day when all that is settled! When the things worldwide are set. Have they come? Will they survive? Who will wake? The powerful Gods.

[*Gestures at the mad* MONEY GODS *grating Sell.* HAM *goes back into dance, a trio, with two violins and flute*]

[*Lights up on the* MUSICIANS—*the* WOMAN *is still bent over the horn, playing it in pantomime, checking her embouchure, etc.*]

MAN. So what's the problem? Thought you had no trouble with such as this. You played it and repaired it and come in out the night—some black lady beautiful wizard—gonna fix my horn.

WOMAN. [*Looking up, wistfully, not saying anything at first*] It's fixed!

MAN. [*Laughing, light disbelief*] Ah, yes, fixed. Could you fix the world as easy?

WOMAN. Fix the world? [*Half-laugh, then silence*] You remember that old song, "If This World Was Mine"? . . . [SHE *sings the first stanza of it . . .*]

MAN. [HE *is listening and not saying a word for a long time*] If This World Was Mine . . . If it was either one of ours, if it had ever been . . .

WOMAN. But it never was . . . and if you think of times ancienter than these last few decades of destruction. If we go back beyond the scene of this crime. If we go back to where the black nation dwelt across the seas, years and years before our slavery . . . you'd see more destruction. A nation committing suicide . . . kings and queens selling farmers to merchants . . .

MAN. A world of destruction, now it comes round, there it goes, now it comes round again, now blood smeared on stone. Now bombs and bullets, now death flesh ripped. [*Straightens up*] But we had no say in this last million murders . . . we had no say . . .

WOMAN. No? No way . . . [SHE *is looking at the horn* . . . SHE *slowly holds it up for him* . . .] You wanted this?

MAN. Oh, it's still fixed? [*Laughs*] You mean you can really fix . . .

WOMAN. Can you really play?

MAN. [*Tentatively seizing the horn*] Can I play? [*Pause*] If I can't play—the world will end now!

SADO. What . . .

MASO. Do you want? [*Staring stupidly at* HAM, *who, bathed in their madness, has drawn up as large as* THEY—*their stares shrink him*]

HAM. Yes . . . Want? [*Lower key*] The future—

SADO. That's it, Bucks, that's it, of course. That's what distinguishes us, the Money Gods, from the . . . rest!

MASO. Our money—of course, dear Dough . . .

SADO. Of course, but all the others . . . *want*! They're always wanting—wanting stuff. Always wanting.

MASO. Of course, yes, that's it—always wanting.

SADO. Of course, that's why this crazy path—this whining about Mars, this refusal to see our greatness-power.

HAM. [*Illuminated*] Want—Of course . . .

SADO. [*Screaming*] They want food! [*Screaming—sawing*]

MASO. [*Screams*] Why, Why, Why, they want LIFE!

SADO. SELL!

HAM. Yes, yes, that's it. They be talking 'bout . . . all these. [*At audience*]

MASO. Wanters—out there! Wanting! All The Time Wanting!

SADO. Crazed with Desire. While we are Wholly cool, coolly whole. A buck!

MASO. Hey, wanters!

[ALL THREE *take up their instruments and shoot them at the audience, sawing and screaming!*]

ALL THREE. Hey, WANTERS! WANT ALL YOU WANT! WANT WANT WANT! [*Crazed laughter*]

SADO. (*To* HAM) Now what calls us through your mouth?

MASO. Your teeth—your armpits.

SADO. SELL!

MASO. Trace the faces negative all impinge upon us as our conquests—[*Waves*] These faces!

[*Violins*]

SADO. They want stuff, don't they?

HAM. Yes.

[*Flutes, flutes, whistles, kazoos, etc.*]

MASO. [*Accusingly at* HAM] The future, you wanted.

HAM. Why—Yes—I thought—My job was to—tell these—[*Harshly*] miserable wanters—what they wanted was wanting!

MASO AND HAM. [*Howling*] HaHaHaHaHaHa.

SADO. Veddy good. What they wanted was—Ha Ha.

MASO. [*Grabs them*] But this is serious, Bread. There are evil forces everywhere. Stronger forces—than these tie-wearing weaklings who also want [*Trancelike*] who at this very moment conspire to back us against the wall.

SADO. Our rocket

[*Breathy rhythm on flute underscoring*]

MASO. Their rocket

SADO. Our triple nuke

MASO. Their triple nuke

SADO. Our dirt killing bleed-more

MASO. Their dirt killing bleed-more

SADO. LASERS

MASO. LASERS

SADO. A million niggers with razors

[MASO *and* HAM *look*]

MASO. What?

HAM. Not that?

SADO. Well, in a manner of speaking. [*A joke*]

HAM.
    They're called something
    else in the Eastern
    steppes.

MASO.
    But they're darker
    and starker
    always wearing
    our parka
    Our enemies
    got niggers
    Too!

    [*Amazed*]

MASO/SADO/HAM.
    Wow!
    The really secret
    Weapon

    [*Song*]

    But here with us they're
    wanting
    throughout this land
    like a
    haunting

MASO. Always!

SADO. Always! [*Sawing.*

    HAM *whistles, blowing things, throwing them away*]

MASO. Buy. [*Reverse motions, clacking of stock board*] Buy! [*Making buy motions, changing masks*]

SADO. But they can't get nothing. All over there—depths of jungle—dying folks—you'll never—never

HAM. They'll, You'll, never! That's it—They'll never! Never! That's it, Sirs, Never [*Sawing and humping up and down*] uh uh

[The SISTER *is handing the horn toward the* BROTHER, *the antics of the* STATESMEN *are quiet in pantomime*]

WOMAN. So you were saying about the world ending . . .

[The MAN *takes the horn, laughing, begins to play. A solo piece* — "From the Old to the New"! *Drawing somewhat closer*]

So you can

MAN. I can

WOMAN. That was . . .

MAN. "Out of the Old into the New."

WOMAN. [*Turning toward window*] Out there, in that poison dark. Where the dead rule all that is left of a world.

[BROTHER *plays behind her. Repeat*]

MAN.
All that is left of
a world

[SHE *plays behind him*]

Destroyed
by idiots!

WOMAN.
But play some more — Hey, it's dark —
Light up the world.

[The MAN *plays up tempo* "The World Destroyed By Idiots Can Yet Rise Again"!

Second chorus, SHE *gets in, sharp fertile chords.*

Tableau: The MADMEN — *the* MUSICIANS *in Flashing Lights.*

THEY *take turns singing and accompanying each other*]

MAN.
All that I am
All that I own
Nothing it seems
Nothing but dreams

WOMAN.
  Dreams can be real
  Make life what you feel
  Be all you need
  A blue spirit freed

MAN.
  Here in the dark
  Death kills the spark
  You brought light with you
  You brought life with you

WOMAN.
  Dreams can be real
  Make life what you feel

MAN.
  You brought light with you
  You brought life with you

[*Instrumental duet. Instrumental and vocal duet, saxophone, piano, vocals*]

MAN AND WOMAN.
  But we are alive here together
  This is no dream, as grim as it is
  This is our lives, our broken world
  We meet tonight, like lovers in a book
  But this is no dream, we are alive
  in love, here together, to remake
  our world, our lives, together
  This is no dream, our hearts know
  it's real, remake our world
  broken hearts of dreamers
  the madness of screamers
  But this is no dream, broken
  world crying. This is no dream
  millions are dying. Remake our
  hearts, like lovers, together.
  This is no dream. Our lives
  reality. Let life go on
  Let life go on go on
  This is no dream!

HAM. So today—News for the Wanters

MASO. The Screamers

SADO. The Pleaders

[The sweep of the MUSICIANS' love song comes up like a breath of air and the MADMEN visibly shiver, pull up their coats]

MASO. Ah . . . what's that?

[Instrumental duet]

SADO. Crazies protesting the bomb.

MASO. Or protesting our beautiful nerve gas.

HAM. PEACE FREAKS.

SADO. Or Niggers complaining.

MASO. Women exclaiming.

SADO. But it does no good—we own the world.

MASO. Yes, bux, you got that very right.

HAM. Right! Right!
 Far Far Far Right!

MASO. WHITE ON!

HAM. The News today will be awesome. I've set up an all-Universe broadcast, a universal fact layout session.

SADO AND MASO. [Duet]
 They think
 they can
 threaten us

 They think
 we can
 be scared

They think
it's flesh
and blood here

When it's coin,
and legal tender
silver certificates

instead of organic
parts. No feelings

No Souls
No memory
and most of all no hearts

Back us against the wall
These wanters. Whole countries
of them.

[*A rock through the window hits* HAM]

HAM.
    The News is why they
    Wait. The Big News
    The End News. Anchor
    of Anchors.

MASO. Tell Them we've tried.

MASO AND SADO. [*Duet*]
    That cannot be
    denied.   But
    no one can
    back us
    against
            the wall
                    no one
                        not at
                            all

    These wanters
    These taunters
    These marchers
    Draft Dodgers

They stomp us with their
desires.

These rioters
Cities on Fire

Fiends and criminals
Non-white idlers
Begging nations
insatiable cravings

They want
just want
and want and
want
and want

They want to rule
They want to be
They want love

[Smirks]

Like cries in the mist
these wanters want to be
all this

[Gestures ALL]

MASO. But tonight the stand will be made

SADO. No further steps these wanters will take

MASO AND SADO. We are the final takers!

HAM. [Applauding] Yes—The News! What speaks as future?

MASO AND SADO. [Laughing maniacally, trying to saw as THEY
    roll] Future?

MASO. How presumptuous of you.

SADO. How presumptuous indeed.

MASO AND SADO. We are in charge of the past.

SADO. And the Future.

MASO. And as punishment for this wild wanting, this aggression all around.

SADO. We have decided not to let them *have* a future!

MASO. No future, after all . . .

HAM. [*As if* HE's *hearing something grand and mysterious*] No . . . Future . . .

MASO AND SADO. No future at all!

HAM. And That is . . . the News.

MASO. The News.

SADO. The last News anybody will get!

[*Lights up on the* TWO MUSICIANS]

WOMAN. You don't recognize me—because you don't even recognize yourself.

MAN. [*Musing*]
Lightning in the sky
The building shaking
The ground like water

[*Musical background: the violins, flute, etc. Piano and sax*]

WOMAN. What do you remember?

MAN.
A wave of lost souls. The Blinding
Light. A world full of screams.
Oceans of Fire.

[*It becomes like a reenactment. Lights—slides*]

WOMAN.
Explosions Explosions. You were running.
The sky behind you was white with Horror.
A figure alone. You were running

Toward me. I was fixed in the
heat storm, the thrashing on all sides.
I had screamed myself into a silence
of jagged edges.

MAN.
A ring of the murdered flashing across
the sky. The murderers' voices whining
over radios televisions newspapers
blown by with their lies screaming

WOMAN. I saw you race past me.

MAN. I escaped alone, the dirt on fire.

WOMAN.
You carried the horn in two pieces
Like I found it. The survivors had
scattered. I hid in the shadows.
You paused to look around. I
could barely see your face.

MAN.
The world seemed midnight permanently
Hell uncovered to Burn
hideous like that in an eternal night.

WOMAN.
You stood there staring
into red darkness
as if fixed yet
already flying

MAN.
It had been an evening
of music, amusing
conversation
The Money Gods were

whining we
tried to change
the station

They said there'd be
no future
That the world
had been
canceled

(*Tableau of* MONEY GODS *as* THEY *approach their last press conference.*

Violins and Flute come in as death imminence sound. The MONEY GODS' *voices:* BUY SELL *are a rhythm form for the song.*)

WOMAN.

Remember that ending
Blind death mounts light
Blackness and fire the
Blown-up world weeping
as it flies out into
emptiness

MAN.

The panic The death—Yes
I ran ran. [*Covers eyes, then looks*]
    And where
were you then? When
they blew up the world?

WOMAN.

I was there as you came
flying out the fire.
I was there in the shadows
weeping for the world.
Too tired to run farther
I lay there watching as you decided
I felt your mind searching
But I heard a music in you then
that lifted me
and moved me toward
you.

MAN.

And what did I do? Just run
half mad, afraid . . .

WOMAN.
> And I ran
> in your direction
> I followed you
> I led you
> I advised you
> like nature

MAN.
> And I never
> saw you

WOMAN.
> You always
> saw me

MAN.
> Always?
> Then what
> did
> I do?

WOMAN.
> What you're doing
> now, what
> we're doing
> now
> Reconstruct
> till fresh winds
> blow your brain
> clear again

> At that moment
> you go back
> to the Fire
> The mad night
> they blew up
> the world

> Then you stare
> like a mad thing
> and cover your mouth
> with silence

Then you wander out
into
the dark
trying to
find the old world
like a Zombie

MAN.
Dreams
Hideous Dreams
The horn
in pieces
The world
on fire
my hands
burning
the ground
screaming

WOMAN.
Where I lived
we were close
to each other
My family and
me.

We worked
and fought
them
worked
and made
love
and picketed
worked
and sang
Made beautiful songs
out of poems
we danced
we painted
we spoke the words
of genius
we also

worked
struggled with
the Money Gods
with their stooges
and hatchet persons
Yes, the Money Gods!

I knew you then
I'd heard that sound
that beautiful horn
Carrying memories and humanity's
future
I'd heard you
You'd seen me
You'd looked in my eyes
I thought
or were you staring
past me into
this

Like a black
crazy bird
scrambling out of
Smoke

They'd blown up
My home
my city
my family
my life . . .
all our lives

All our futures
I'd come East
toward the
water
Then you flashed
out the black fire
night

A broken horn
in your
hands

Trying to sing, [SHE *comes closer*]

You were standing there
peering into the hot
dark, trying to find
a song.

MAN. [Sings]
Another life
like this, caught
a life looking for
your kiss

There must be
another life
somewhere

Someone take me
there

WOMAN.
Yes, like that
A romantic thing
Why, I wandered
In this craziness . . .

You saw me then and fled
You thought I was a nightmare
An illusion. You had not
tasted me
then

MAN.
The shadows
were
warm
Like humans
lived
there

Now a soft face
the brown skin
lovely under
some sudden
moon

The lips there
I touched
them

WOMAN.
We were running
together. A wind
caressed us. I
hadn't felt a
breeze like that
so gentle
full of Music

All loveliness
seemed alien
in that
world

MAN.
This world

WOMAN.
Except

MAN. [HE *reaches for her, takes her to him*]
Except even without that memory you are
all that loveliness
means!

WOMAN.
Except, remember!

MAN.
I do

WOMAN.
What's my name?

MAN.
Naima

WOMAN. [*Begins to play that tune on the piano*]
You remember nothing.

[*Lights up on the* STATESMEN]

HAM. [*Slowly accelerating rhythmic speech*] No future . . . What
a coup!

MASO AND SADO. Of course — This'll teach them

HAM. It will It will

MASO. And you, Ham, will go down in
history

SADO. Ha Ha. If there was any more
history! We've canceled it,
remember

MASO. Oh, Yes, Ha Ha! Canceled
History. I always wanted to do
that.

HAM. I'll announce it!

SADO. Be Firm

MASO. But Loving

HAM. Tell Them The Buck Stops Here [*Points at the* MONEY GODS]
Right here!

MASO. You see this little pink button I wear around my neck?

SADO.
I, of course, have one too. Simultaneous
Inspirational Destruct Switches.
For Him and Him.

HAM.
Oh, how thrilling. But, sirs, ahem,
In my ignorance I thought such
buttons were red!

MASO.

Fiction writers' conceit. We hate
anything red!

SADO.

Better Dead! Ha Ha

MASO.

You might say it's our message
to the world. Ha Ha

SADO.

But let us be serious   [THEY pose]

MASO.

As befits world creators

SADO.

And world destroyers

[*Flashing flicks identify them seriously*]

HAM.

This will be a special bulletin?

SADO.

Of course. Stop all transmissions
and fire away

HAM.

When?

MASO.

Now—It's now the whole thing goes [*Imitates studio*]

HAM. Special Bulletin! We interrupt this program—all programs
—all activity of any kind—with this special bulletin

[*A rap*]

The Money gods have
decided because there's too much Wanting,
and Needing too I might add, that
society itself has become a pest!

The MG's are sick of it. Life
with you boobs. You people You
nations You countries. So
because you continue to make your silly demands
for life, liberty, sovereignty,
independence, liberation,
heaven forbid, revolution,
and various rights of all
sorts. Because you complain
and make noise. And Strike. And Vote
and Fight. And will not go peacefully.
Or die
The MG's have decided to
  Cancel the World—
  Until Further Notice!

[*A roar of anguish—from the people—heard over a TV monitor*]

MASO. [*At monitor*]
  Look at them out there, scrambling
  Crazy with Fear!

SADO.
  Turn it forward slowly
  so we can see the Approach
  of death to them all!
  Let us watch the end—how
  Thrilling

HAM. Awe-inspiring

MASO.
  Slow Forward—Look
  Suicides, mobs searching
  for us. Flags. Committees.
  Nasty people cursing.
  Look as it gets later
  they're trying to rush the
  Gray House looking for you,
  Ham. Ha Ha.

  How vulgar. They're
  Shooting cops. Drowning

politicians. They think
they'll take over—but
the world is done.

We've decided

SADO.
Fast forward. Let's look at
the very very end. The madness
and explosions.

[*A big monitor shows explosions, agony, blood, dying*]

MASO. Now! Now! Now!

SADO. Even the Gray House went up!

HAM.
Wonderful! Wonderful!
They thought I was still in it!

[MASO *and* SADO, *looking at each other meaningfully, laughing harder still*]

Is the whole world blowing up?

MASO. Of course.

HAM.
Where do we hide—um retreat
till the old world's blown up and
a new one is created?

SADO. A new one?

HAM.
Yes, isn't that the plan, to create
a new world?

[SADO *and* MASO, *laughing like at a child*]

SADO.
Why would we want that? A New World
Full of what? New complaints?

MASO.
New wants and New Wanters?
No, enough is enough.

HAM.
Enough—yes—of course
is enough. And . . .

SADO.
And . . . you mean yourself and
property

HAM. Uhuh

SADO.
Are you asking what about, Bux
and I?

HAM. Uhuh

MASO.
As for you—you have ultra
super bomb shelters five hundred feet
under the soil. You'll survive
of course.

HAM. [*Dutifully smiling*] Yes—but

SADO.
If we told you you'd find it hard to
believe. We're serious. We're through
The World's too old too full of
rotten wanting

MASO.
We've found a way to change into the
very stuff of the universe, the very stuff
of the world!

SADO. [*A bloodcurdling scream*] The Insect Is Supreme!

MASO. [*Secret admission*] Ants Are the Hippest!

SADO AND MASO. [*With violins screeching . . .*] The Energy

[*. . . up mad screech sound!* THEY *begin to babble, like a vac-tic scat abstracting the facts the reality, to a tale of their own mak-ing. Instruments used to accent their deteriorating sense of real-ity. A voice and violin with flute piece—The voice screamed, moaned, growled, screeched, sung, etc.*]

MASO.
The ultimate energy—Computer mind
insects.

SADO. The Holy Scarab!

MASO. [*Clack Clack*] Buy!

HAM. Ultimate . . . Energy.

SADO.
Time is energy—power—wealth
  control
Nobody would ask an ant for anything.
Ha Ha Nobody could want anything from
an ant.

MASO.
Eternal Master Glorious Warrior
Gloriously beautiful

[SADO, *like* HE's *been turned on by the* OTHER's *rhetoric—a love song to insects*]

[*Waving photos*]

The complex eye
ultimate historian

SADO. Most of all, survivor!

[*A sudden blow*]

MASO. [*As if praying*]
Master of Creation
  . . . I Shall Not Want . . .

HAM. Freedom—The Transparent Responder. [*Crawls, bumps into monitor*]
Ohh! But what's this—fast forward the world's blown up
the fire cross the sky. Dead people
toe up everywhere. Skeletons and
desolation—What fire didn't
kill, radiation and disease—
But still I see—shadows—
Shadows—No, what is this?
Money Gods, What is this we see?

MASO.
Prayer to the Insect Master

SADO.
You see only insects the holy ant
building beyond the
rationalization of broken human desire

HAM.
I see the ants—
But the future—these shadows—
like living—humans

MASO. What?

HAM. Look here

MASO. [*Moving to the monitor*] There is somebody

[*The MUSICIANS*]

MAN. I do remember . . . life. You are life to me

WOMAN. From no knowledge to life itself

MAN.
No, the nightmare defined it
     What was
          alive.

(*Closer to her, SHE is running randomly up and down the piano.*)

Lost in the dark I thought
    I cd not grow
    Now I live
       among the
         stars

WOMAN.
What memory A kind of
   being there when you
     enter yr self
      conscious
       yr very senses
       demanding
    all of what Life is
     every minute

MAN.
We're lucky to be alive
   Is that a Song?

[HE *bends to kiss her.* SHE *plays a brief very melodic ballad*]

But we cd be a Song
   two poems
  in search of a
    home

[*Piano*]

MAN. You smell like life! [Musing]
       That light beyond—[Remembering]
      was you
     That flow of lovely
      words
     The tremble the air is
     as it sings
      to us
     as quiet
      beauty
    was you
I remember we lay there whispering
    under the music
  I said I loved you
you smiled and let me

caress you slowly—
   it was like
      a song

WOMAN. What name did you call me then?

MAN. Naima

WOMAN. Then you remember

MAN. I always remembered

WOMAN.
   That word I tossed at you
      yr eyes upon me heating
         the air
      through which
   I returned yr stare

MAN. [*Playing lightly, the same ballad, humming the end of some phrases*]
   It seemed we were below
      the surface
      of the earth
   A black sky with holes
      Music seeping everywhere
      It was Sun Ra

WOMAN.
   If there were scientists of this
      life as lived
      measuring that space
         we came to each other
            in
         They'd measure the
            heat
          & music
         Their dials wd say
            MAGIC!

MAN.
> All of that you said
>> to me
>
> It was Africa
> I said to you
>> Naima

WOMAN.
> Yes

MAN.
> I said, "Naima
> can you
> love me?"

WOMAN.
> I said, "Yes," I remember
>> I sd, "Yes,"
>>> and you breathed
>>> the air into harmonies

MAN.
>> My blood the
>> rhythm
> I remember . . .
> I was warm and
>> dark

WOMAN.
>> We were already in each other's
>>> language
>>> Passion Eyes
>> You said, "Come
>>> with me"

MAN.
>> You smelt like
>>> music

WOMAN.
  It was
   like a
    Song

[*Duet out, lights dim to suggest lovemaking*]

[*In the Chamber, the* MONEY GODS *watch ever more frantically. But* THEY *are already Mad. Though the Madness has been already made to seem the "norm"*]

MASO. [*Exchanging masks as rhythmic device—a bizarre game*] Hey, it's only niggers! No people. Ha, you scared me for a second. The Ants survive. Forrrrrrrrr—everrrrrrrrrr—Insect Deities.

HAM. Niggers? Will They not . . . reproduce?

SADO. I see your point!

MASO. You mean, these blobs of distorted protoplasm would have the nerve . . . to survive.

[MUSICIANS *repeat Song and Playing*]

SADO. We cannot permit it.

HAM. It seems contradictory—[*Musing*] Five Hundred feet below the earth!

SADO. Send heavier waves of death—

MASO. But even better, kill them before they arrive.

HAM. Death Music Future!

SADO. Of course

[THEY *begin to get various instruments axes out to wail against the living future*]

MASO.
  So we prepare The Final Assault.
  As Death is launched. The bombs.
  The Fire

SADO. Even beyond that!

[Song like shrieking—like a mad person humming mood music out of tune!]

[The eerie trio gets together, the expressionist masks of faces contorting, a happening of craziness attacking!]

[We see now a music war begin. The MONEY GODS and HAM, like invading Monsters. Blow a piece called "War of the Worlds" which sounds like laser death beams from alien maniacs!]

[The MAN and WOMAN MUSICIANS suddenly feel the presence of the MONEY GODS and HAM. THEY are attempting to destroy them. At first, the TWO stagger under the attack. It is danced by the weird TRIO like ballet and burlesque; showing their ass, then leaping crude pas de trois! tour jetés, etc.]

MAN. What's happening. Of a sudden, this air is clawing at me.

WOMAN. [Touching her throat and eyes] Juke Box Death Ray!

MAN. [Closing eyes]
In Boats. A horse.
The Whip. He's . . . galloping
Crown Prince . . .

WOMAN. Like Bela Lugosi's theme song

MAN. [Shouts!] FRANKENSTEIN!

[They are making ready to play.

The WOMAN—An explosive piano run, like machine-gunning colonialists from the high ground, on a very clear day!

The MAN—a solo, like the horn is talking! It's trying to identify the MONEY GODS and attack them murderously]

[The MONEY GODS jump around, attacking, retreating. Sneak attacks, deadly rockets launched.

We see a tableau of struggle. The music: an extended piece.

The struggle seems a balance, back and forth—like a surreal cutting session—with death as the penalty for losing!

The three dance around to get better leverage, advantage. THEY *try to spread out and then gang up. But it is clearly a war, all out, with exchanged solos and wincing on both sides like they're hit.*

But then from the dark, a thumping, a deep and thunderous rumbling—the drum(s).

The MONEY GODS *notice, the* BROTHER *and* SISTER *are animated, get down harder, at the sound.*

The drum sets the music from Africa, to Latino, to low-down Blues, to traditional New Orleans, to Big Band to Bop to Hard Bop to a throbbing dynamic solo, with the bombs rocking the MONEY GODS!

Now a straight-ahead, impossible tempo piece, which is the beginning of

A Suite: 1. Tension 2. Explosion 3. Terror 4. Death 5. Silence 6. Time

SILENCE—*weeps of violin—horn snorts—like temporary quiet on the battlefield—and suddenly a pounding on the* MUSICIANS' *door]*

MAN. *[Instinctively]* The Drummer

WOMAN. Who's that?

[The MAN *swings open the door. Violin screeching wind poison wafts in. Black jump-suited goggles, carrying all kinds of percussion instruments, and, of course a brace of congas under wraps]*

DRUMMER *(Heart).* I saw lights, I heard . . . music . . . two musics fighting back and forth.

MAN. A drummer?

WOMAN. Who are you?

DRUMMER. *[HE thumps an answer, the talking drum which accompanies the verse/song]*
They try to blow up
the world
Turn night
to poison

day to fire
But I am Man

MAN.

  If the world survive
    A drummer
      must be in
        it!

WOMAN.

  Man

MAN.

  Yes, they try
  to turn the world
  back to animal
  rule
  Gorilla time
  Ape era
  Monkeys' business

WOMAN.

  Even past that
  before that
  Crazier than that
  they in the past
  killing our future

[*The* MONEY GODS' *laughter spits in eerily. Their faces for a second are creeping across a wall.*

Drum accompanying — Drum popping]

MAN.

  And they here around us
  now. Blowing Mickey Mouse
  as vampire insect

WOMAN.

  Yes, like they worship
  some hideous . . .
  insects

DRUMMER.
Yes, I've heard
recently the cries
of Killer insects

WOMAN.
We've heard them
praying in their
craziness—to insects
to be insects
and to kill off
human life

DRUMMER.
No one can kill
life. It live
Its heartbeat
It live!

WOMAN.
Yes, you survive
the lonely darkness

DRUMMER.
I'm not alone
My name is Heart
I search for lovers
. . . like you

What's a drum
without a horn and
box

[They laugh]

I search for more life
to go with that
I've found

MAN.
Life, out there, still?
More life?

WOMAN. Life?

DRUMMER.
Every day, more life
We're hiding out there
Waiting for the air
to clear

A giant *orchestra* building
all of us, rainbow people
blowing more life in
the world

WOMAN. [Musing]
Like there could be a world
after all.

MAN.
But that mad shit
we heard
that screeching
like Mickey Mouse
hatchet murder

WOMAN.
Madness of the past
trying to kill
our future

DRUMMER.
Yes, we know them
death figures
We heard you
Fighting them
Knew you was life
I come
You heard me
Coming [DRUMMER *plays licks* HE *played*]

MAN.
Life go on go on [*Plays note of direction, then goes to the corner*]
and look my man

Black Heart [HE *uncovers yet another instrument, the bare frame
of trap drums*]
I found these—
Knew I'd need
some Heart music

DRUMMER. Heart music! [*Rushes to set up*]
Heart here.
I need to call
some of the others
be with us
when the final
go down
get down

WOMAN.
When the war
gon start
you need
your heart

MAN. [*Touching her*]
Lovers' music
the soul
of the
world . . .
Naima, my name is . . . [*About to embrace*]

WOMAN. I know your name, Mtu, I know your name. [THEY
embrace]

The screeching of the MONEY GODS *begins again. We see them.*
THEY *look like* THEY've *been attacked, faces raw, wounded, background in shambles*]

MAN. Get ready

DRUMMER. [*Calls*]
Music Lovers
Soul People
Heart Companions
Ready To Get Down

WOMAN.
> This the final go
> Life or death [*Kissing her* PARTNER, *sitting at piano.*

> *But as* MONEY GODS *begin their screech*, Death Attack of the
> Money Gods, THEY *look changed. Their faces are altering, chang-*
> *ing to insects, large hideous insects, buzzing (violins), chirping,*
> *etc.* HAM *jerks around like some weird gorilla*]

DRUMMER.
> The Past versus
> The Future!

WOMAN. Yes

DRUMMER.
> Yet I am the past
> that lives to be
> future

MAN.
> But not
> the dead past
> the past of horror
> terror
> madness
> stupidity
> the past will
> die and stay
> dead

WOMAN.
> You are no past
> man, you are
> only
> tradition

> [MONEY GODS, *now raising their axes in combat.* The Final
> Conflict]

DRUMMER. [*Calling to his* COMPANIONS]
> Music Lovers
> Heart Companions
> Soul People!

All Who Love Life better than death!

[BLACK WOMAN, HEART's WIFE, a WHITE and LATINO, push warily through the door. They have instruments in their hands, the Life Orchestra formed meets this final challenge. The Music War, a long final suite beginning with:

1. Tension
2. Explosion
3. Terror
4. Death
5. Silence
6. Time

But then, as a kind of ReBirth, like a history of music, the whole suite, but particularly the Life Orchestra plays:

1. ReBirth
2. New Life
3. Lovers
4. Sweet World
5. "Great Peace" (Reds and Blues)

The last music confrontation shows the insects turning in circles, made mad by the music, their monitors and machines smoking and exploding.

MUSICIANS finally are playing, embracing, and dancing, life victory movement. Final chorus is all together and get audience to sing/chant gigantic:]

ALL.
YES TO LIFE!
NO TO DEATH!
YES TO LIFE!
NO TO DEATH!

[And at each chant, MONEY GODS and HAM, dead feet straight up in air, shrink and die deader. And finally ending in unison joy laughing shouts]

ALL. [Continued]
YES!
YES!
YES!
YES!

New and Previously Unpublished Work

Jimmy!

On December 8, 1987 Baraka, along with Toni Morrison and Maya Angelou, eulogized James Baldwin during a funeral service for him at the Cathedral of St. John the Divine in New York City. More than 4,000 people attended the event. In his tribute Baraka called Baldwin "God's black revolutionary mouth." But if anybody is "God's black revolutionary mouth" it is Baraka, whose entire career has been devoted to bringing the revolution to the word.

—wjh

We know, or ought to know by now, that what we call 'reality' exists independent of any of the multivisioned subjectivisms that nevertheless distort and actually peril all life here. For me, one clear example of the dichotomy between what actually is and what might be reflected in some smeared mirror of private need, is the public characterization of the mighty being for whom we are gathered here to bid our tearful farewells!

You will notice, happily, or with whatever degree of predictable social confusion, that I have spoken of Jimmy. And it is he, this Jimmy, of whom I will continue to speak. It is this Jimmy, this glorious, elegant griot of our oppressed African American nation who I am eulogizing. So let the butchering copy editors of our captivity stay for an eternal moment their dead eraser fingers from our celebration.

There will be, and should be, reams and reams of analysis, even praise, for our friend but also even larger measures of non-analysis and certainly condemnation for James Baldwin, the Negro writer. Alas we have not yet the power to render completely sterile or make impossible the errors and lies which will merely be America being itself rather than its unconvincing promise.

But the wide gap, the world spanning abyss, between the James Baldwin of yellow journalism and English departments (and here we thought this was America), and the Jimmy Baldwin of our real lives is stunning! When he told us *Nobody Knows My* (he meant Our) *Name,* he was trying to get you ready for it even then!

For one thing, no matter the piles of deathly prose citing influences, relationships, metaphor and criticism that will attempt to tell us about our older brother, most will miss the mark simply because for the most part they will be retelling old lies or making up new ones, or shaping yet another black life to fit the great white stomach which yet rules and tries to digest the world!

For first of all Jimmy Baldwin was not only a writer, an international literary figure, he was man, spirit, voice—old and black and terrible as that first ancestor.

As man, he came to us from the family, the human lives, names we can call David, Gloria, Lover, Robert . . . and this extension, is one intimate identification as he could so casually, in that way of his, eyes and self smiling, not much larger than that first ancestor, fragile as truth always is, big eyes popped out like righteous monitors of the soulful. The Africans say that big ol eyes like that means someone can make things happen! And didn't he?

Between Jimmy's smile and grace, his insistent elegance even as he damned you, even as he smote what evil was unfortunate, breathing or otherwise, to stumble his way—He was all the way live, all the way conscious, turned all the way up, receiving and broadcasting, sometime so hard, what needed to, would back up from those two television tubes poking out of his head!

As man, he was my friend, my older brother he would joke, not really joking. As man he was Our friend, Our older or younger brother. We listened to him like we would somebody in our family—whatever you might think of what he might say. We could hear it. He was close, as man, as human relative, we could make it some cold seasons merely warmed by his handshake, smile or eyes. Warmed by his voice, jocular yet instantly cutting. Kind yet perfectly clear. We could make it sometimes, just remembering his arm waved in confirmation or indignation, the rapid fire speech, pushing out at the world like urgent messages for those who would be real.

This man traveled the earth like its history and its biographer. He reported, criticized, made beautiful, analyzed, cajoled, lyricized, attacked, sang, made us better, made us consciously human or perhaps more acidly pre human.

He was spirit because he was living. And even past this tragic hour when we weep he has gone away, and why, and why we keep asking. There's mountains of evil creatures who we would willingly bid farewell to—Jimmy could have given you some of their names on demand—We curse our luck, our oppressors—our age, our weakness. Why & Why again? And why can drive you mad, or said enough times might even make you wise!

Yet this why in us is him as well. Jimmy was wise from asking whys giving us his wise and his whys to go with our own, to make them into a larger why and a deeper Wise.

Jimmy's spirit, which will be with us as long as we remember ourselves, is the only truth which keeps us sane and changes our whys to wiseness. It is his spirit, spirit of the little black first ancestor, which we feel those of us who really felt it, we know this spirit will be with us for "as long as the sun shines and the water flows." For his is the spirit of life thrilling to its own consciousness.

His spirit is part of our own, it is our feelings' completion. Our perceptions' extension, the edge of our rationale, the paradigm for our best use of this world.

When we saw and heard him, he made us feel good. He made us feel, for one thing, that we could defend ourselves and define ourselves, that we were in the world not merely as animate slaves but as terrifyingly sensitive measurers of what is good or evil beautiful or ugly. This is the power of his spirit. This is the bond which created our love for him. This is the fire that terrifies our pitiful enemies. That not only are we alive but shatteringly precise in our songs and our scorn. You could not possibly think yourself righteous, Murderers, when you saw or were wrenched by our Jimmy's spirit! He was carrying it as us, as we carry him as us.

Jimmy will be remembered, even as James, for his word. Only the completely ignorant can doubt his mastery of it. Jimmy Baldwin was the creator of contemporary American speech even before Americans could dig that. He created it so we could speak to each other at unimaginable intensities of feeling, so we could make sense to each other at yet higher and higher tempos.

But that word, arranged as art, sparkling and gesturing from the page, was also man and spirit. Nothing was more inspiring than hearing that voice, seeing that face, and that whip of tongue, that signification that was his fingers, reveal and expose, raise and bring down, condemn or extol!

I had met him years before at Howard, when Owen Dodson presented his *Amen Corner* there. But it was not until later confined by the armed forces that I got to feel that spirit from another more desperate angle of need, and therefore understanding.

Jimmy's face, his eyes, the flush of his consciousness animating the breath of my mind, sprung from earlier reading of his early efforts in literary magazines, and the aura those created — stretched itself, awakened so to speak, when I stared newly arrived in New York from my imprisonment and internal confusion to see this black man staring from the cover of *Notes of A Native Son* at me unblinking. I looked at that face, and heard that voice, even before I read the book. Hey, it was me — for real! When I read those marvelous essays, that voice became part of my life forever. Those eyes were part of my instruments of judgment and determination. Those deliberations, that experience, the grimness and high art, became mine instantly. From the moment I saw his face, he was my deepest hero, the agent of consciousness in my young life. Jimmy was that for many of us.

What was said of him, the so called analysis, often reeking of the dead smell of white supremacy and its non-existent humanity, made no difference. All of that did not really register, except as re-call for dull conversations with fire plugs or chairs or stone steps when abroad in the practiced indifference called U.S. society.

What he gave me, what he gave us, we perceived instantly and grew enormous inside because of it. That black warm truth. That invincible gesture of sacred human concern, clearly projected — we absorbed with what gives life in this world contrasted as it is against the dangerous powers of death.

Jimmy grew as we all did, but he was growing first and was the measure, even as we claimed understanding and transcendence. Just as he wanted to distance himself from a mentor like Richard Wright, better to understand more clearly where he himself, his own self and voice began and Richard's left off.

Happily for some of us, when we distanced ourselves from Jimmy, it turned out that this not only let us understand ourselves more clearly, but it allowed us finally to come to grips with the actual truth power and beauty of this artist and hero.

It was Jimmy who led us from Critical Realism to an aesthetic furthering of it that made it more useful to the still living. He was like us so much, constantly growing, constantly measuring himself against himself, and thus against the world.

It was evident he loved beauty — art, but when the Civil Rights Movement pitched to its height, no matter his early aestheticism and seeming hauteur, he was our truest definer, our educated conscience made irresistible by his high consciousness.

Jimmy was a "civil rights leader" too, *at the same time!*, thinkers of outmoded social outrage. He was in the truest tradition of the great artists of all times. Those who understand it is beauty AND

TRUTH we seek, and that indeed one cannot exist without and as an extension of the other.

At the hot peak of the movement Jimmy was one of its truest voices. His stance, that is our judgment of the world, the majority of us who still struggle to survive the bestiality of so called civilization, (the slaves) that is true and not that of our torturers, was a dangerous profundity and as such fuel for our getaway and liberation!

He was our consummate & complete man of letters, not as an unliving artifact, but as a black man we could touch and relate to even there in that space filled with black fire at the base and circumference of our souls. And what was supremely ironic is that for all his aestheticism and ultra sophistication, there he was now demanding that we get in the world completely, that we comprehend the ultimate intelligence of our enforced commitment to finally bring humanity to the world!

Jimmy's voice, as much as Dr. King's or Malcolm X's, helped shepherd and guide us toward black liberation.

And for this, of course, the intellectual gunmen of the animal king tried to vanquish him. For ultimately, even the rare lyricism of his song, the sweeping aesthetic obsession with feeling could not cover the social heaviness of his communication!

The celebrated James Baldwin of earlier times could not be used to cover the undaunted freedom chants of the Jimmy who walked with King and SNCC or the evil little nigger who wrote *Blues For Mr. Charlie!*

For as far as I'm concerned, it was *Blues For Mr. Charlie* that announced the black arts movement, even so far as describing down to minute fragments of breath, the class struggle raging inside the black community. Even as it is menaced by prehuman maniacs.

But attacked or not, repressed or not, suddenly unnews worthy or not, Jimmy did what Jimmy was. He lived his life as witness. He wrote until the end. We hear of the writers' blocks of celebrated Americans, how great they are so great indeed that their writing fingers have been turned to checks, but Jimmy wrote. He produced. He spoke. He sang, no matter the odds. He remained man, and spirit and voice. Ever expanding, ever more conscious!

Gratifying to me in the extreme was that each year we grew closer, grew to understand each other even more. Ultimately I did understand, as I feel I always did, but now consciously, that he *was* my older brother—a brother of the communal spirit!!

One day I took him to Newark's Scudder Homes, the toilet bowl of the world, with a film crew. Seemingly deserted at first, the streets, once the vine got to graping, filled quickly and Jimmy found himself surrounded by black people eager only to look at him, ask him questions, or tell him he was still their main man. At the nadir of social dislocation one young brother his hat turned half way around said, "I just read *Just Above My Head*, Mr. Baldwin. It's great! How you doing?" Jimmy's smile of recognition alone would have lit up even the darker regions under the earth.

We hung out all night one time lurching out of Mikell's after talking to David, and the next morning, Jimmy still leading and gesturing, clear as a bell, was still telling me some things I really needed to know, and I was still giving him feedback that yes there were a bunch of us who knew who he was, and loved him for it, since it was one of the only ways we could ever really love ourselves!!

Jimmy was one of those people whose celebrity is recognized whether by name or not, by the very aura that accompanied him. Whose intelligence is revealed in the most casual gesture or turn of apparel and bearing. We were aware at once that such dignity was the basis and result of great achievement of serious regard for the deep, the heavy, the profound.

Yet because of this deep and deeply felt by us integrity Jimmy carried like his many hats, his film of Malcolm X was rejected, reviews of his later works began to appear on page 2 because he could not be permitted to tell the truth so forcefully. Finally, great minds even forbade him to publish his last work, *The Evidence of Things Not Seen*, exposing the duplicity of the legal machinations obscuring the real killers of the black Atlanta children. He had to sue the publisher in order to get the book out. When he told me this last outrage, I remember the word *Weimar* flashed through my head. Reading this formidable completely mature and awesome work I could understand the terror of White Supremacy and its worshippers at its appearance. It is important that I include this quote from the work as his man, spirit voice, flesh of his soul speaking to us with the clarity of revelation

The Western world is located somewhere between the Statue of Liberty and the pillar of salt.

At the center of the European horror is their religion: a religion by which it is intended one be coerced, and in which no one believes, the proof being the Black/White conditions, or options, the horror into which the cowardly delusion of White supremacy seems to have transformed Africa, and the utterly intolerable nightmare of the American Dream. I speak with the authority of the grandson of a slave, issue of the bondswoman, Hagar's child. And, what the slave did—despised and rejected, 'buked and scorned—with the European's paranoid vision of human life was to alchemize it into a force that contained a human use. The Black preacher, since the church was the only Civilized institution that we were permitted—separately—to enter, was our first warrior, terrorist, or guerrilla. He said that freedom was real—that we were real. He told us that trouble don't last always. He told us that our children and our elders were sacred, when the Civilized were spitting on them and hacking them to pieces, in the name of God, and in order to keep on making money. And, furthermore, we were not so much permitted to enter the church as corralled into it, as a means of rendering us docile and as a means of forcing us to corroborate the inscrutable will of God, Who had decreed that we should be slaves forever.

The Evidence of Things Not Seen, pp. 82–83

But it was Jimmy's life that puts such demonic tragedy in ever tightening jeopardy world wide. He would not be still, he would not and never could be made to be just a mouthpiece for the prettily obscene. He sang of our lives and our needs and our will to triumph, even until his final hour.

Jimmy always made us feel good. He always made us know we were dangerously intelligent and as courageous as the will to be free!

Let us hold him in our hearts and minds. Let us make him part of our invincible black souls, the intelligence of our transcendence. Let our black hearts grow big world absorbing eyes like his, never closed. Let us one day be able to celebrate him like he must be celebrated if we are ever to be truly self determining. For Jimmy was God's black revolutionary mouth. If there is a God, and revolution his righteous natural expression. And elegant song the deepest and most fundamental commonplace of being alive.

If we cannot understand our love of Jimmy Baldwin it is too late to speak of freedom or liberation, it has already been lost!

But it is his life that was confirmation of our love, and our love that is continuing proof that Hey, did you see Jimmy last night . . . you hear what he told so and so . . . part of our long slave narrative—

as we speak to ourselves from within ourselves
and it is Jimmy's voice we hear,
it has always been!

Black People & Jesse Jackson II

Here are Baraka's unique black radical reflections on Jesse Jackson and the July 1988 Democratic Convention in Atlanta; they are refreshingly different from the views of the tv news pontiffs who covered the same event. This is a long essay and there is space to publish only one section, so I have chosen Part II, because it focuses on Jackson. He is a figure, it seems, that every contemporary black intellectual has to come to terms with; for example, both Gerald Early and Stanley Crouch have written long meditations on Jackson, which are included in their recent collections. Part I focuses on the convention in general. This is the first publication of the essay.

—wjh

By this time, as well, the center piece of the extravaganza had begun formally. And people began scurrying to be where they were supposed to be to get their instructions their inspiration their salaries or whatever the case was.

The big boys are so accommodating of our frustration they had even put out two sets of tee shirts one with the Dukakis Bentsen regulars and another with Bentsen's face x'd out and Jesse Jackson's face unmarked and supported. I thought by now I should try to get to Jesse directly to find out what was on his mind and what he was going to do. Not just as a reporter for *Essence* magazine, but for my own and our own edification and self-defense.

But of course getting to Jackson in that maze of indirection and disinformation was difficult, even though I had been given his suite numbers by people very close to him. Finally I succeeded in getting an agreement that I could ride over to the convention with him the night he was to speak. I wanted to hear what he was going to say, how he summed up life among the Dems rat now!

So that evening my children and I gathered at the appointed place and waited. And as secret as that point of embarkation was supposed to be there was a tiny knot of people standing there with us. As it got closer to the time we were told Jesse would appear, the secret service men in the lobby came over to me, one bumping me the way they do if they think you have some heat somewhere and are liable to grab for it on sudden surprising impact. We were asked to move back. A crazy woman danced and made nutty remarks at the edge of the little knot seeming to focus on one gent who left later after conversation with Jesse's aides.

Then one woman I knew to be with the Jackson campaign came

over to me and asked me why was I waiting. I told her she shuffled through her papers and told me that there must be some mistake, that my presence was not on the schedule. Of course I protested, I had spoken with the top scheduling person who had talked directly to Jesse—I could hear her doing it—and it was she who had told me what to do.

But now it was not on the schedule. I was wondering was this just the usual criss-cross of bureaucracy, or what, when the crazy woman started dancing just behind me. "Oh, is it my turn?" I told her and in a few seconds she withdrew. At that point C. Delores Tucker, former secretary of state of Pennsylvania, chairperson of the black Democratic caucus, appeared through the door helping Mrs. Rosa Parks. I greeted them, introduced them to the children and chatted while we waited for Jesse.

In a few minutes the main group appeared. The first through the door, leading the way, was Inner City Broadcasting chairman and former Manhattan borough president, Percy Sutton. And then Jesse and his family. When I approached Jesse, "Hey, man what's happening?"

Jesse bent in my direction saying, "I'm sorry, Imamu, but there's no room." As indeed there could not have been. At that point my daughter, Shani, armed with a tiny Polaroid camera I had given her to take pictures of the notables, snapped our picture. Later, the children would tell their mother that Jesse must have known me a long time to call me by the organizational title I held during the '60s, Imamu. History is filled with details.

The kids and I then had to scramble to get over to the convention center in time. Riding on a bus especially set up for carrying delegates and whoever back and forth. I took the kids and several other old friends I'd bumped into who were going over to the viewing rooms equipped with tv monitors. This is where the people close to delegates or officials or whoever watched. Then I took off across the street to the convention center.

But when I got there a few steps away there was a huge crowd of people outside and much weeping and wailing. There was no room in the convention either. Not even for many of the delegates. People waved their delegate badges and the press, including myself and many others, waved their various sets of credentials but the police said the place was overcrowded and no more people would be admitted. Not even the delegates!

Well if the delegates weren't going to be admitted, then who the hell was that inside taking up the space? This argument rumbled around at the tops of many people's voices all around the convention center. There was no room? Well who was there room for?

Thinking about it now such a situation could only be produced by the theatrical atmosphere such conventions produce normally, but now with the addition of the Jackson factor and the question which hung in balance above that convention and city and above us all. What would Jesse say? What would Jesse do? And this question had a celebrity to it and a show business quality that brought out audience, not just delegates, just whoever had the whatever to make it.

At one point I saw Atlanta's mayor, Andy Young, walking behind the glass walls with full entourage a picture of special pleading or was that importance. Enraged I could not get in I began to beat on the glass walls to get Young's attention.

He probably didn't see me but a host of secret service chaps did and a small group came over waving at me to stop banging on the door. I didn't so one pushed the door open and told me to stop. I banged again, Young hadn't left and I was determined to get inside. This brought the fellow half way out the door. He told me if I banged the door again he'd arrest me. It seemed outrageous to me, I wasn't banging at him in the first place. A loose now sparser crowd of the unadmitted looked on, one black radio reporter stepped forward with me. I banged again.

Now the secret service dude stepped forward outside the doors, "I'm gonna arrest you," he was screaming.

"Hey, man, you don't control shit out here . . . this is Atlanta. You need to take your ass back inside and be important somewhere else."

There were two or three black Atlanta policemen standing a few steps behind me watching. I saw one's hand go up to his mouth and I knew it was cool. They were not going to arrest me for this dude. And when he left they let it all come out in a big roar. "What's your name, man?"

They could appreciate my argument. And they laughed like hell as the ss man went on his way scowling and talking at his wrist radio as he departed to show us we were still savages.

Coming around to the other side of the building still looking to get in the crowds of the left outside milled and trailed around like myself looking for a way in. I came upon a television newsman interviewing Rev. Ralph Abernathy, one time second in command to Dr. King in SCLC. Now he was also standing on the outside. (Martin Luther King, III was also kept outside, it made the next day's papers.)

The newsman was asking about Abernathy's being refused entrance to the convention. "What do you think Rev Jackson would think about you being kept outside the convention tonight?"

"Oh, he wouldn't like it at all. No, he wouldn't like that at all. And I know this was a great speech, one of the most important speeches ever made."

Abernathy went on describing the complete inappropriateness of his being shut out, and as the newsman finished he said, "And what is your name sir?"

I leaped into it, "You don't know Rev Ralph Abernathy? Well how did you even get this job, you're obviously not qualified if you don't know who Ralph Abernathy is. He was Dr. King's second in command in the Civil Rights movement." But I was just covering my own embarrassment and pain at what was happening, that Abernathy could be here standing anonymously in the crowd disconnected from wherever this big top was going.

And as bizarre as this actual indication this had been one materialization of a general perception that the negroes were being asked to be the tail on the donkey or one main negro and the other "necessaries," and for all the swirl and roar, the bravado and even sincere commitment of the rest of whoever . . . "us" or "them" that the only room on the donkey's tail was for the tiny insects that live there.

I moped up the stairs in the large hall directly opposite the convention center and brooded as the various entertainers and conpersons were introduced. This was the night of the presidential nominations and Jesse would be one of the speakers. I drank Courvoisier and watched the show unfold.

Jesse's whole presence had a magnetism about it that has diminished so rapidly it seems a long time ago already. The campaign, particularly after Super Tuesday, had given him real world statesman status. And as an independent presence, someone representing a specific constituency who had very concrete interests and the will and information to protect them. He had to be recognized and like it or not . . . like him or not, he must be given the weight of our claim, the respect for the implied power of his position.

Jackson's response to Dukakis missed telephone message racism had done damage to that projection. It had brought a mumble of antipathy from the black masses and turned his image around in a way that made him seem very finite and vulnerable. You don't let nobody insult you (us) like that. Bump Dukakis!, the oath.

But there was still the mystique of the well known, and Jesse had been our hope, even those of us who knew him when and who might even have put him down a decade or so ago for being a petty bourgeois opportunist. All of us had taken hope at the courageous picture Jesse made in opposing and exposing the gunbearers of privilege and imperialism he was running against, besting them at every turn. Our man, big good looking, smart nigger.

But not just the question of the insult, that was just the answer to the question of when the white folks was gonna get to whiting. Where were *our own* priorities? Our own self determined agenda? What was it that we should be doing, armed with the actual dismissal of our humanity as "a problem"? Where was our agenda?

It was the argument that went on in the hotels where the black delegates and political activists and intellectuals were holed up. The line that kept emerging from the sincere and the others not publicly sold, "What are black folks going to get out of this?" The majority of black folks. Not just Sly and the Family Caucus.

The screen I watched the speech on was as big as a four or five story building, in glorious pseudocolor. There was a roaring all around like a sports event. It was not rock concert glitter serrating the edge of the picture but maybe Madison Square Garden one night forty years ago, when The Brown Bomber or Sugar was getting ready to come into the ring. I had my own view of what was going on, based on what I'd run into but also based on a long resident activism in the Black Liberation Movement, including a thorough knowledge of Jesse Jackson. So I was backed away from total submersion in the event. But the whirlwind of this heavyweight bout between fact and mythology, this gaudy class struggle on the big screen, had such a giant roaring rhythm it caught me up in the amazing spectacle.

It is a kind of grandiose arrogance that hits first, the glitter and shine and sparkle and overblown self importance of the importantly manipulated. From the television it seemed a telethon for some new disease, a mass religious conversion or pretension. Circusy and carnival like, but for all that restrained and formal. Everything was fixed and plotted. There was no spontaneity given off just used up labor high polished for resale.

When I focused directly so I could also hear, Jackson was into his speech. What I wanted to know before was what ideas had led to this speech, what real objectives for the African American people, the Rainbow? But now the words were rolling out, the entire space held in breathless tension at our hero's magnetic voice and rhythms.

"We meet at a crossroads," he was saying. The camera panned incessantly getting the white folks' reaction and the few others. There was a rapt attention widespread. These people, for *whatever* reason, were interested in what he was saying.

"Shall we expand, be inclusive, find unity and power, or suffer division and impotence?"

But this question seemed to have been answered. And its answer was now being read to the whole. When the lefts I'd felt closest to had first come upon me it was to assure me that they were passing out literature among the Rainbow folk readying them for the Vice Presidential nomination. Dukakis' nomination of Bentsen, the Democrats' George Bush, was actually a violation of the people's constitutional right to select a vice presidential candidate separately from the presidential candidate. People, according to the U.S. Constitution, voted for people, not parties or party choices.

These lefts' job, they said, would be to circulate the vice presidential nominating instructions and get the necessary petitions signed so they could spearhead the vice presidential nomination. But the rally, and the mounting evidence on all sides seemed to project that not only were black people to be transformed into bugs so they could ride safely in Dukakis' tail, but even the so called anti revisionist (i.e., anti the US Communist Party and Soviet Union) Left was being transformed into a tail pinned to the tail, and they were proud as hell of it for that matter.

But the other shoe had not hit yet, and Jesse was readying to drop it now. "Common Ground," he was saying. "Think of Jerusalem . . . the birthplace for three great religions" (Do the Israelis know that? ran through my head.)

"Common Ground! That is the challenge to our party tonight. Left wing. Right wing. Progress will come not through boundless liberalism nor static conservatism, but at the critical mass of mutual survival. It takes two wings to fly." (Our preachers excel in metaphor.)

"The bible teaches that when lions and the lambs can lie down together and none will be afraid, there will be peace in the valley. Lions eat lambs; lambs sensibly flee from lions. Yet, even lions and lambs can find common ground. Why? Neither lions nor lambs want the forest to catch fire. Neither lions nor lambs want acid rain to fall. Neither lions nor lambs can survive nuclear war. If lions and lambs can find common ground, surely we can."

When I heard this it broke my heart. Why? Because he had answered the question. Lions eat lambs. But then went on to unanswer it and make it metaphysical and transparently opportunistic. Though at the end of this speech people hailed it widely, the media hailed it. But even some who were genuinely moved by the speech, if not by its pronouncements, then certainly by the gleaming aesthetic of its form, the deftness of handling of its content had to blanch at *what* Jesse was saying.

"Now we must build a quilt together." He was likening U.S. society to one of his momma's quilts. The one he spoke of now would be a quilt of lions and lambchop bones, of donkey's tail and insects, of the rich and the poor working together to keep both that way.

"Blacks and Hispanics, when we fight for civil rights, we are right—but our patch isn't big enough," suddenly everything was expendable if its expendability, the flexibility of its survival would provide an entrance into that craziness he was publicly aspiring to be accepted into. Even the liberation of the people who had borned him into the world, and upon whose very backs he had ridden into Atlanta for this convention like Jesus came into Galilee riding on another ass on a palm sunday long ago, a few days before his rubout and later triumphant return from the dead. Jesse after the Atlanta debacle can be said to have experienced two thirds of the Jesus trip. Though his return from the dead remains in the mouth of speculation.

"Conservatives and Progressives, when you fight for what you believe, you are right—but your patch isn't big enough." You mean both the slave and the slavemaster are right? Both slavery and freedom are right? Is this what is required to qualify for the nomination as president of the United States, double talk and submission to the will of the mighty?

He would confirm this for us later by quoting a poem that began, "I am tired of sailing my little boat / far inside the harbor bar / I want to go out where the big ships float. . . . " But the living historically valid part of Jesse Jackson his real life ties with black working class life he would also make reference to. At best the living memory of himself necessary for what Du Bois called, "true self consciousness" (as opposed to the "double consciousness" of the negro, who sees nothing directly but only sees himself and the world through the eyes of people who hate him). At worst though this living matter can be used to deceive, grass roots camouflage for anti grass roots ideology.

For instance when Jesse said near the end, "Most poor people are not on welfare. They work hard every day that they can. They sweep the streets. They work. They catch the early bus. They work. They pick up the garbage. They work. They feed our children in school. They work. They take care of other people's children and cannot care for their own . . . " you could see black people openly weeping and whites too moved to some measure of understanding by this impressive, poetic brother. And yet . . . and yet . . . was it all for naught?

I know he broke me down near the end. Only the coldness of my perception and rationale of what all this was prevented some open weeping. The whole was a compendium of many of Jesse's speeches throughout the campaign, and I had heard this part before as well. But it was still cutting, transporting, "Don't give up. Hold on, for the morning comes. How do I know?

"I understand. I am the son of a teenage mother, who was the daughter of a teenage mother. I understand. I was not born with a silver spoon in my mouth. I understand.

"You see Jesse Jackson on television. But you don't know the me that makes me me. Jesse Jackson is my third name. I am adopted. I never spent a night in my daddy's house. I really do understand.

"Born in my mother's bed. She couldn't afford hospital care. I understand.

"Born in a three room house. Bathroom in the back yard. Slop jar by the bed. I understand.

"I am a working person's person. I wasn't born with a silver spoon in my mouth, but a shovel in my hand. My mother was a working mother went to work with runs in her stockings so that I could have new socks and not be embarrassed in school. I really do understand."

It was not just skill he maintained, but it was also feeling, real feeling. And that is Jesse's danger to the Democrats and to white supremacy that he does feel the needs of the people but now in his personal quest for "acceptance" or "significance" or even Jesse-Power (which is not the same as Black Power) he was willing to use the real to cover the deal.

For instance in the very next paragraph of that speech Jesse shows that he knows but also that he is willing to stall to get hold of the ball. But that ball is never coming his way except like those balls fixed to chains that are standard issue for many African Americans inside various joints, the Democratic party included.

Jesse was blowing hard and pretty, like a rhythm blade cut through most of us. "We didn't eat turkey on three o'clock on Thanksgiving day, because Momma was off cooking someone else's turkey. We'd play football to pass the time till momma came home. Around six we would meet her at the bottom of the hill carrying back Du Carcass."

Yes, I swear I heard it, and then in the hotel a black minister had verified it for me. The two of us telling everybody how Jesse had "laid on symbol" as the ancestor jailees used to say. "Lay on symbol." In the transcript of the speech that has now been changed to "leftovers." But he and we who heard know what he said and what he meant. That indeed this merriment was much like a holiday, and yes there were those of us down here who weren't involved in the real business, we were just the marginalia the bubbles rising off the heady brew. We wanted to eat now, but all we were gonna get was Du Carcass, some leftovers. The white men and quite a few white women had already et.

It was a weird weird aura that gripped this country just after that speech. In the huge open hall where I sat, and later the media-peoples' bar there was a mixed expression it seemed to me. There had to be simple dismissal by the white majority since that is what their white supremacy instructed them to do, as far as consideration of Jesse's candidacy or even comprehending his stand on the various issues. Jackson had pushed the whole of the electorate to the left, however, made them consider questions and stances that simply would never have been raised without him running in the primaries. So that there was also, along with the automatic dismissal, a stubborn sympathy, at Jackson's courage?, his aggressiveness, his typical nigger problematic maddeningly continuous assertion of his (our) humanity.

Like the quick to snicker cynical media bar types. Forget the fact that I was fixing them in a clearly analytic stare from the beginning of the broadcast, until the end. Still, the quality of their response to what was coming off the tube was easy dismissal crossed with a shadow of fresh consideration perhaps, like blowing pollen every several minutes would blow up their unsuspecting noses and there would be a lean, a curl, a certain coloring to their digging that carried a rumor of something human and common.

Talking to various people during the next few weeks brought that same cross reference, especially from whites. The need to diminish, but at the same time, the need to put that in perspective, to claim after all that Jesse did "Have something."

At the convention however the speech was a blanket air that pinned all of us together in some posture. And those evaluations were paradigms for what I would encounter once I got back home. For the most advanced, the speech was a pastiche of everything Jesse had said during the primaries, except now he was intoning the tragic words, the invitation of public buggery that always prefaced the negro's rise to the bottom.

At the other end of the political spectrum mention of the speech brought religious ecstasy and demonstration of the power of zombification. One would see throughout the rest of the convention the ossification of the Rainbow into a transportable herd of Jessephiles, most who did not understand that Jesse had already given the farm away. The others were the opportunists who benefit from peoples' misinformation and pain.

One of the central topics that began to surface in the cross convention discussions was just who was it negotiating with the Democrats, if indeed negotiations were going on? Since the whole credibility of what Jesse was doing hinged on just what he was gonna get. Since the independent posture the primaries fostered had been generally if not totally dispelled, what Jesse was gonna get, the payoff had taken up much of the conversation since. This was the essence of what Walter Fauntroy, long-time civil rights activist, was saying when I first ran into him. And a host of others, it was obsessional but right on it. What, indeed would be payment for giving up your self-determination? Even in the closed context of black American relationship to the major imperialist parties. You had to get something. So what was it you was getting? In exchange for us, in exchange for these peepas behinds which you done give to the man.

This was the essence of what Farrakhan was asking, and the dissenters at the split rally. The Dukakis negroes' press conference had even broken down into that. And Mayor Hatcher, an old friend since way back in '72 and the National Black Assembly meeting in Gary, had even put the whole discussion in perspective by citing what Dukakis could not do, legally, so we could think more clearly about what he needed to do. In terms of demonstrating to the African American community that our support for him was not just an act of giving up our self determination!

So it was one late night after many meetings that talking to an old political friend might give deeper insight into this whole process. This brother had been with Jesse since before Gary, in fact as far back as Operation Breadbasket, which was the Jesse breakoff Chicago hook-up ostensibly a SCLC chapter but mostly Jesse. Probably even back before that. But certainly when Hatcher became 1st black mayor of a major US city, this brother was there, and so was Jesse. That's when Jesse and Hatcher got tight as well.

But now in a discussion of what we was gonna get, or what Jesse was asking for and what it meant to the rest of us the brother started telling me that Jesse had gotten rid of all his old comrades in arms on his negotiating council with the white folks. He said the campaign structure had not only excised many of the old heads, but replaced them with folks who were almost the antithesis of what Jesse was saying earlier. The apotheosis of which was the white campaign manager, Gerald Austin, who personally fouled up a huge rally we put together at SUNY Stony Brook, in which several thousand students waited at the perimenter of our outside amphitheater while Gerald Austin, a few minutes before Jesse was to appear, and just a few miles away from Stony Brook decided not to bring Jesse in. He put out some garbage about Jesse being ill, but he had spoken at several stops on Long Island before the Stony Brook cancellation and a few stops afterwards.

This is the same manager who a few weeks after the convention was bragging about how much money he had made while he was in the campaign, but how he never believed in the campaign or agreed much with Jackson. But that the money had made it all worthwhile. One wants to know in the first place why was this dude even there? There are black electoral technicians across the country by now, who have been hugely successful. What is the Why? to that one wonders?

And now standing in the half lit rising quiet of last straggler hotel lobbies talking earnestly and quietly to an old friend, there is a sense of grim wonder. Is it a hollowness in us, that we cannot sustain what is required for our own self determination? What is it in a white campaign manager that says so much about the whole process of Jesse Jackson's run for president, once it really got to be that and his own mind was infected with that real fantasy, that he *was* running for president.

But it must be the Double Consciousness Du Bois spoke of, it cannot be anything else. So we must embrace any poisonous confection as "good for us" when actually it's good for somebody else, it's just that we're seeing the world through that somebody else's eyes and not our own. Otherwise the question of Self Determination would be less misunderstood among us, and there would be less "misdefining" it so it seemed fantastic or oppressive to somebody else, or generally without merit.

So now I was being told that Jesse had stripped his inner circle of those forces who knew him from the Gary/Black Power days. From the days when Jesse had risen in the National Black Convention making a resolution that the assembled pursue the idea of putting together a Black political party.

"Even Mayor Hatcher is gone now," the brother was telling me.

"Hatcher?" I couldn't believe it. There was nobody anywhere who was more of a Jesse supporter than Richard Hatcher of Gary, Indiana. In fact, in the last few years when one mentioned Hatcher, one thought of Jesse Jackson.

"Why?"

"They said he was 'too strident'," the brother was saying.

"Too strident? What the hell you talking about? You know Hatcher, he doesn't even talk loud . . . "

"Well, that's what they said . . . He was too strident."

"Who the hell said that?"

"Bentsen," the brother said, and this was someone who certainly would know.

"Bentsen?" I remember there in the darkening hotel lobby I actually started to weep.

Had it gone that far? Was it really, literally about mass denial and opportunism, again? Surely Jesse could not stand up in front of these millions and be seen as the committer of such an outrage. Hatcher?

This is the first time I was given any rundown on Ron Brown, like Dukakis himself, a product of the Special Products Division of Teddy Kennedy, Inc. Any checkout of the RB vita will show that Ron ain't been around too many bloods in his rise to we know now. In Atlanta I simply wondered how he had got so far so fast, but with this fill in it became clearer. And certainly with Brown's helicopter like rise to Democratic party chairman, the plot not only thickened it congealed into something ugly and nasty.

But dig this, Brown is sent into Jesse's camp very late as the connection needed to raise up the Jackson (Negro & Black/Progressive) demands to the level of human understanding. All that grunting about Self Determination and Black Power wouldn't do. We all saw where that stuff leads. Next thing you know, niggers be walking around talking about what they think and shit . . . !

But then once Brown gets the colored imprimatur, viz the "wit Jesse" then he shows up as leading contender for the Dem party chair's job, whereupon the first thing he says is that he don't represent no niggers in the 1st place, never has and never will! Whew! Slick as a derringer.

Then we see him later speaking at the New Orleans summit a sad reprise of the '72 Gary convention and he is there selling the Democratic party and actually has the mammy tappin temerity to mention Fannie Lou Hamer's name and how he is standing on her shoulders. No, he is defiling her memory and insulting all the rest of us, that's what he doin.

To add insult to injury the Lefts I had been running with sent a person to see me saying they had to talk to me. There was some further bric-a-brac through a phone call, and finally late late at night they, about five, arrived at my room for pow wow. From the outset of the convention I had not been close to them. Their whole stance seemed to me too much of a tail of the tail on the stumbling racist donkey. And this after years of struggling with them to see that electoral politics is relevant in the U.S., that it is a suitable arena for the genuine Left. That this is bourgeois democracy, unlike China or Russia. And that the legal struggle, voting &c., as Mao taught must be carried all the way to the end. For instance all these black mayors and black politicians ought at least to be passing Anti-Klan laws in these cities of black plurality and majority and even where we are the minority. They should be passing Anti-Racism laws, making it a jail offense with a fine, say, for practicing racism. Even the calling of names should be treated like assault, and the Anti-Racism law would see to these folk doing some time. I mean it is absurd to me for people to talk about revolution and can't even elect someone to a local school board!

But climbing into the dirty arena of bourgeois politics, whether electoral politics or trade union work does not mean you are converted to bourgeois politics. But so much like the classic definition of the middle class, these folk were going from one extreme to another, just like an unbalanced middle.

So now fresh from nixing electoral politics altogether for the last eight years they now wanted to worship the sacred behind of political mediocrity. At the '80 convention in San Francisco they were made tail-ready, and now here they sat trying to get me, in the name of "democratic centralism" to turn into the tail's tail, and they themselves had become sad tales of opportunism.

The gist of their jive was that now they would not nominate Jesse as Vice President. Their evaluation of the Dukakis-Bentsen nausea was that the main tails were going to get Bentsen to change his position on some of the key issues. For instance they thought that he would change his position on Contra aid as well as aid for the notorious South African puppet Jonas Savimbi.

As far as tailing the tail the transformation was almost complete. The group sat there trying to convince me that being a tail's tail was revolutionary work.

I caught up to Jesse that next day finally at an SCLC event at one of the hotels, presided over by Rev Lowery, SCLC's current president. The dais bristled with SCLC bigshots, plus Ben Hooks, head of the NAACP.

Waiting for Jesse to enter, I went up to the dais to talk to Hooks and Lowery. I asked about the tv program where Dukakis came to speak after the Bentsen nomination and missed phone message racism. Hooks had maintained his invitation to Dukakis for this major NAACP function and many black people criticized him for it. Many even carried signs at the dinner itself criticizing Dukakis and putting Jesse's name forward. So many that Hooks had to scatter them to save a little face.

But Hooks had made some statement in his introduction that his constituency wanted Jesse but that Bentsen should not fear because they were open minded, &c. That was smooth, I began, how you handled the Dukakis appearance at your dinner. Hooks was acknowledging his smoothness when Lowery piped in, "That's because he's such an expert at Tomming . . . ." Lowery was cracking up.

"But I learned everything I know about Tomming from you, Reverend." And the laughter got bigger. It was all loose and friendly, but at the same time there was a worn out spot of contention lingering easy to spot, from several paces away.

These were rivals, contenders, in a sense. And they both reveled in the fact of their being that, that there was such a field in which to "rival" each other, but at the same time each had a body of real experience and information about the world, and a serious position in human society to show for it.

I suppose also, since I was a licensed militant, this was Lowery keeping his franchise warm at Hooks' expense. Though it should be said now, that given the nature of that gathering, Jesse coming to claim the ex officio throne of SCLC, not any formal position, simply the most worshipful spot, Hooks acquitted himself one of the bunch in a way I hadn't known. After Lowery and Fauntroy singing his standard, "The Impossible Dream" and Rev Willie Barrow, Jesse's associate preacher at PUSH and before that Operation Breadbasket, Hooks came on like Zora Neale's Rev Lovelace. Mean he actually, like they say, low down preached. But then he knew that he was setting the stage for Jesse.

When Jesse came in, I was making all kinds of gestures and sending notes telling him I wanted to talk to him, and finally though I could see he did not seem particularly overjoyed about it he was nodding his head from the stage up and down, yes.

Secret Service folk were collected like they do. And after Jesse's speech getting up through them to the stage was a major piece of work. We shot out the back door, and while photographers were taking his picture, a large group of note employees, kitchen workers, waiters, all gathered in the tiny space just behind the hotel where we stood as Jesse's picture got taken. Jesse was posing and didn't see them at first, but I pointed at the people there and he turned and lit up like a Christmas tree. He began talking to these people, answering questions, the cameramen snapping away. And it was real, 1st that the black masses do or did adore Jesse. I say did because I do not think that adoration is as high today as it was before the Dukakis insult or before the convention. 2nd, Jesse does genuinely feel what he says when he would sing out, "Yes, you domestic workers, truck drivers, cab drivers, waiters, workers on the assembly line, when I get to be president, you'll have a friend in the white house!"

And that is a powerful implication in this land of corporate domination and workers exploitation, for a presidential candidate to say and mean that . . . a friend in the white house for working people, particularly black working people. And gradually over the campaign when the zig zag smoke screen of color was occasionally pierced, you could hear the establishment complaining as much about Jesse's "leftist — radical — non-mainstream" position on the issues as about his color. It was Paul Robeson, I think who summed up his position, and the position of black activists in U.S. society in general, saying, "Two things the establishment doesn't like about me are my nationality and my opinions!"

But it was just this legitimate and authentic relationship between the black masses and Jesse Jackson that was his real strength, no matter what the dull candidates or the corporate stooge media had to say. From Super Tuesday on, all the black masses wanted was someone to stand up for them or stand up with them. Someone to speak on their behalf, some leader who genuinely had their interests, all of our interests at heart.

And Jesse has always had the problem of balancing his genuine feeling for black people with his own personal needs and projection. He said elsewhere he wanted to be a workhorse not a showhorse. But how to keep those priorities and principles on top and straight ahead, not compromised into submission and nonexistence. This is one of the abiding contentions about Jesse, that his candidacy this last time had seemed to put to rest. So that even though the "hustler" slander was dropped on Jackson by the legalized dope now in the white house, made you wanna call his momma the real hustler, still to be for real that put down has plagued Jesse since Operation Breadbasket.

And the question now was how did all this get finally to be about the Democratic party? It didn't begin about them. Certainly in the 1972 Gary Convention, calling for a black political party, it wasn't about the Democrats or the Republicans, it was about Self Determination for the African American people. This is the question that was rising through that community now: was there something Jesse was getting to go along with Dukakis and company? Dukakis had been nominated and aside from Jesse's speech, a glittering anthology of Jesse's greatest hits, what had we gotten? Had Jesse gotten something, and the rest of us, as usual (like the Democratic convention in Miami in 1972, or any other time) been left in the dust blown up by our politicians gum bumping?

And now tonight, the vice presidential showdown was roaring towards us. What would Jesse do now, where would all of us be, as a result of this? These things were blowing through my mind as I stood watching Jesse be photographed with the workers exchanging words and banterings in a kind of breathless joy.

In the limousine, with Jesse and Ron Walters, the Howard University political science teacher, and one of Jesse's key advisors as well as an old comrade in struggle from the National Black Assembly, and Walter Fauntroy. I rode in the jump seat facing Jesse, my questions scrawled on a steno notebook. This was going to be the interview, on the way to wherever on Jackson's monstrous schedule.

Nothing was said directly about last night's intro to Mainstream American Mythology via the speech or its fallout. Although the 1st ecstasies were already giving way to a coarser evaluation in terms of the old form vs content saw. As the car sped through downtown Atlanta, people recognizing Jesse and the ss folk in their accompanying cars would smile and wave, or jump up and down and point, or stare relevantly.

I had to talk fast because of the way this was going down. In the car on the way to somewhere else. I came on like a reporter, Essence Magazine, the magazine for Black Women. Although our relationship, all of us in the car, could not be leapfrogged so that the dialogue was completely tactful or completely tactless. "What effect do you think Dukakis' naming of Bentsen as his vice presidential running mate will have on black voters?"

All of us had thrown that question around, and had come up with many answers. Even in the Black Dukakis Democrat press conference I had asked that. That night when Dan Rostenkowski, the Chicago congressman was begging for white Democrats to come back and I had sneaked up behind Moynihan and asked him if he thought that strategy would work? His "We think so", sounded extremely white breadish.

Our opening cross banter had centered directly on What was we gonna get, as a very fat and bottom line question I had relayed to him directly from the folk. So as I whipped out the pad and told him I had about four solid questions I wanted to ask, He began by answering the exchange knowing exactly what was on my mind. "You know the question in the street is what are we gonna get, what is Dukakis gonna give up in exchange for our support?"

"Well, you know it can't all come out, and a lot of people don't understand the process of political negotiations. But we have got something, something real. For instance, Conyers' On site voter registration bill was passed (in the Democratic platform committee) you know that is important, and will put thousands of new voters on the books, bring thousands of new Democrats into the fold."

He talked about this bill as if I didn't know that Conyers had put this together as far back as the 1972 convention. In fact as he cited the legislative pluses black folks were receiving I was struck by how much of it did come right out of that historical 1972 meeting of 8000 black people. It also brought Dick Hatcher back to my mind, and my own tears of the night before.

"The Dellums South African sanctions. This would knock 50 to 100 billion dollars out of that racist economy. That's what we can do.

"The D.C. bill will mean two senators from the District of Columbia, and thousands of jobs, and increase our ability to influence domestic and foreign policy."

"But what effect will Dukakis' choice of Bentsen, someone directly opposed to both these planks, and a whole lot of other things you've talked about have on black people?"

"Dukakis will have to earn black people's vote. I earned it. I convinced them I would represent their interests. But Dukakis will have to go to the areas. Gain a certain comfort level. Learn to speak to black people . . ."

I wanted to press him on the main question. "But what about the Vice Presidency. A lot of people want you to be nominated, think that's the only way we would a real voice . . ."

Jesse did not pause, "If I run tonight (for VP nomination) I would win."

So it was not that he didn't think he could win. I thought perhaps it was that . . .

"But win in July lose in November . . ."

It sounded now like he had put both feet down in the Democrat party ark.

"You wouldn't run independently? People don't know anything about any Bentsen."

"Bentsen would be able to recover lost Democrats. I have a block of voters, assured. He has to revive his."

Yes, now its clear we both know that. And the others riding in the car. And a whole bunch of other folks. So why this direction, this going along with the Donkeys?

"But we have a legislative agenda. Bentsen in the senate supporting D.C. statehood. Things do change. His record does make us uneasy. But we think we can get him to pledge no Contra aid (in Nicaragua) and the support of D.C. statehood. It would mean a net shift of 2 senate votes. That's real power.

Plus, you don't make Thursday decisions on Sunday. We have to deal with now. The power available now. And we have to use it in a mature way. Zogman raising the Palestinian question. So that becomes a reality on the planks. We can get support on that now. There's a price for winning."

"But talking about Bentsen. Suppose the Democrats lose in November, anyway?"

Without batting an eye, "If the Democrats lose in November, I'm running in 92."

"But don't you think the Vice Presidential nomination would be a means of consolidating some real power?"

"I'm not encouraging the Vice Presidential nomination." This was an absolute reversal of what the preening Lefts had told me previously. I was sure too that they knew it, that they had been told. And in response simply zipped up their tail suits all the way up around the ears and eyes.

Jesse was giving his justification. "That would play directly into Reagan & Bush's hands. I think its a political option we should avoid. We would have no access to Bush."

The question of What? jumped into my mouth again. But Jesse went on. "We have Democratic party leadership within our grasp. Eight at large seats on the Democratic National Committee Friday? Now that's different!" He was laughing and the rest in the car laughed. Different meaning that was real power, that was the great What?.

"Black folks gave the U.S. Senate back to the Democrats. We have to study politics as a science, not emotionally or romantically, or trading our integrity."

It seemed the last statement was aimed at not only the unhip black masses but for militants like your reporter who was still wanting to know what all this had to do with real self determination.

"But there has to be a tension between your platform planks and Bentsen's . . ."

"South Africa as a terrorist state." He was reciting the Whats? again. Conyers' Voter Registration bill. Make the anti terrorist bill applicable to South Africa. Companies can be ordered out of a terrorist state. We don't trade with a terrorist state. And all the definitions of a terrorist state must now apply to South Africa.

"Our plank about no first use of nuclear weapons. Our plank about fair taxes. Taxing the rich not the middle class and the poor. We're developing the power of negotiation. The tax plank is gaining favor with the convention. Eleven out of fourteen of the minority planks will be accepted. Eighty percent of our delegates have reached the convention. We have to show consistency not schizophrenia. But we have to be Eternally Vigilant," he was putting a heavy emphasis on it because we had reached the hotel. "Otherwise everything could turn into garbage. Any contract is only as good as your ability to enforce it."

There was more, ends and threads, in the main a boastful declaration that Yes, indeed, black people and progressive people were going to get something out of Jesse's decision to go along with the Democrats. It could even be rolled around in your mouth to sound like it had something to do with Black Power. But I felt nothing. I had been talking to a politician. One I had known a long time, one I even loved in many ways, but now what he said was not convincing to me. Also, I had noticed as the convention came up and certainly afterward on the confused trail toward the November election, Jesse talked less and less directly about the issues: Comprehensive Budget, Fair Taxes, Military Spending, The middle east, Central America, Africa, Women, Education, Health Care, and began to compact all of his inspirational platform to the throwaway slogan "Up with Hope, Down with Dope!" As if that was the key to black self determination and equality. As if it was crack that had brought us here on the slave ship. Dope that had stripped us of self determination and put us on plantations and now the big city ghettoes which were just continuations of the plantation slave quarters. As if it was dope that deprived us of education, employment, housing; dope that made us victims of police brutality and white supremacy.

Certainly in a Dukakis Bentsen world Jesse claiming he was the general in charge of the war on drugs was preferable to Jesse talking about the U.S. one sided pro-Israeli policy in the middle east, or U.S. corporate support for fascist South Africa or no contra aid. And Jesse had already begun to comply, at least it seemed that way to me and some of the other kindred sourpusses I held my non-stop discussions with.

Earlier in the year, in Iowa, Jesse had pleaded with me to come with his campaign, to be one of his fighters. I was one of his fighters, but I didn't think then I could be part of the campaign. I wondered what would have happened had I accepted his offer and worked with the campaign, I would suppose in the capacity of a writer and organizer. What would it have been like facing these questions with answers very different from the ones I was getting from Jesse? But that seemed a long time ago now, and our concerns had pushed us apart I thought. Was this same process going on with the large masses of black people? And how would that be registered?

With some more banter and back and forth and a promise to get back together I got out of the car with them at the Marriott and we went our separate ways. Tonight would spell it all out much more clearly.

So "tail" was the name of the game that black folks and the Rainbow were supposed to play. I had heard it from the horse's mouth. However it was described to me, what it still seemed like was like those slaves before they let us fight in the civil war trailing behind Sherman's soldiers. They thought that was the safest place.

Even worse, the so called Left had approached me late that night, even after my weeping fit over Hatcher and in a tiresome and chauvinist display of opportunism demanded allegiance from me to their careerist cavorting. Since the chosen few of these folks had already gotten jobs with the campaign or elsewhere the Rainbow touched and these jobs seemed their goal, their reinforced importance.

At one point I wanted to know why only the nonblack folks had gotten such jobs, but that is the subject of another very serious contemplation. I asked at another point what did they think the Palestinians must think of these so called progressives who openly betrayed them on the floor and agreed not to raise the Palestinian question, so as not to upset the backward racists who ran the Democratic party. "The Palestinians agreed", they shot.

"The Palestinians got a bourgeoisie too." was all I could say. Even as oppressed, even as the African American people were oppressed and still at the same time had a bourgeoisie like as not willing to joyfully cavort with the instruments of their oppression squealing with bought pleasure.

What it all did reveal was that already there was a built in lie for this truth we sought. Just as in every development of black music, there was always a commercial shadow, a paid lie to cover it, to hide the history and meaning, the philosophy of that aesthetic that might help change the whole society, so Jesse's campaign, the rainbow, all of it, already had a coopt factor, a false aspect, a contradiction, that grew up with it, that would try to make us believe that there was nothing possible but nothing and as usual, our enemies owned that, and would give us a taste if we promised to play dead.

At the convention the next night I went from delegation to delegation pushing the line of nominating Jesse for VP and thus overturning the sad line of cooptation and opportunism white supremacy had put together for us to swallow.

I went to those delegations that had the largest concentrations of black people. And from each almost in rote I heard, "Jesse told us not to". Just as he said he had. Urging them to nominate him anyway did no good. From Jersey, New York, Mississippi, South Carolina, Michigan, on and on, came the same answer.

"If you ever see me one night dead drunk and naked walking up the middle of the street babbling out of my mind", I told two ranking folks in the New Jersey delegation and some of the New York folks who were passing anti-UNITA leaflets around, as opposition to Bentsen's pro-UNITA, pro-Savimbi (a South African puppet) position, "Take me inside, off the street, no matter what I tell you, hear?"

But then there are street coaches of drunken naked foolishness, who are slick tonight, who sparkle tonight, whose names are colored names, whose skin is colored, whose teeth are very white though and send signals to their masters on call. Look, they are here amongst us shaking hands, skinning and grinning, clean as new money. There as Wonder Woman tries to sing ". . . the rocket's red glare" while Donna Felisa Rincon de Gautier, former mayor of San Juan, awaits to be recognized. While George McGovern whiffs and pumps like speech after the medley by the high school bands. The Democrats are using John Philip Sousa so we will not understand at first that these are not picnic band songs but the invitation to the same conflagration "The Reag" urges us to. Picnic Martial.

Negroes named Ron and Willie and Sharon and Charlie and Percy have our lives in their hands amongst the Babbits who look like

Donald Sutherland as elegant yuppie of the breadbasket. There's Bill Bradley a jock yup, he's a good guise used to play remember with the nigs. Hey, and there's Superman, I mean Clark Kent, uh, Gore in mufti glowing like an ubermensch.

Then Barbara Jordan in to praise Bentsen and the Democrats her elegant baritone now somewhat shaky, beaming on the 100 foot screen. Two weeks later she almost died from the effort.

"Barbara, Barbara," they're calling. I'm standing among a group of paraplegics in wheelchairs poised at the edge of the huge crowd.

She sounds like Jesse, like what is rhetorically appropriate, "We must take the moral highground. Lloyd Bentsen is sensible, logical, rational . . . We must temper our emotions"

James Forman talks to me like a distant ghost. He is saying, "Support the party . . . " I'd wanted a hotdog, and there was a line. But " . . . the party"? No, he'd said, ". . . the ticket." But there was no ticket.

Jesse had told me, "Imamu, there's no room . . . " And it was not just to me he was talking.

Forman was saying, "I support Dukakis because of his firm position on peace in Central America." This was an old comrade in struggle. He was smiling like it beat memory away from him, in stiff stubborn geometrical curves. Walking away he was even more shadowy, and I loved him for it, for just being in the lobby fading into the hotdog buyers and not on the starry platform among the Dutch Moriels and Tom Bradleys. There's my old friend Micky Leland, Texas congressman, used to be in the N.B.A. He's introducing . . .

Maybe it was Senator Glenn who said the separation of church and state was what the people needed not Matthew, Mark, Luke and John as interpreted by Bush, Meese and Reagan . . . Swaggart and Baker. He said if they wanted more years maybe they could get ten to twenty"

That was funny, but I forget just how it was said. There were billions of red, white and blue balloons, crepe paper, signs, hats, raps, images, and most of all lies. Swinging, being blown and waved. Covering the truth then being the truth. There was nothing else. That was the truth. The black people mostly grinned and were beat down overwhelmed by the cardboard box and ribbon, the noise makers and their brothers and sisters clean as Ho's teeth in charge of the charge backwards.

And finally that is what it was, by the Democratic party certainly and by those black folks charged by us all with coming away with some direction some indication some clue as to where we move for self determination, without which there is no democracy.

Throughout the night both lifting toward the Bentsen bomb, his appearance, Rostenkowski heralded at least as vulgar as the racism that made it necessary, and all that came after, heading toward the supposed orgasm of Dukakis coming, live, it all seemed a rising tinsel of swelling scream, but on a tin horn. A cheap horn. Maybe because of the endless J. P. Sousa caress that makes all thought cheap.

And I had already seen on the front page of the Atlanta newspaper young black militants crying when Jesse spoke, and I knew if you talked to them about it they would have explanations. A shrug that acknowledged raw emotion and backhanded political clarity and principle. But this was this time and not another. A time when backwardness clogged all entrances and only death was alive and well.

I remember Ted Kennedy and the balloons being released. A stage full of banners and big Jennifer Holliday singing The Battle Hymn of the Republic. Jackie Jackson inside the sea of flags and Jesse next to Mrs. Bentsen. And Mike and Kitty looking at each other. I remember Jesse's family arrayed the night he spoke the deference to the children yet it is not too out of line to suggest that the worst weight of all this long march has been on his wife. You could see it when you talked to her and when you saw her that night on tv, or this night among the white stars of this tacky firmament.

And then Dukakis was speaking. He was laying out his cold curt remedy for paper illness and paper regard. His cold cereal and cold supper. Of high standards and justice of the Ayatollah and Bentsen and Jesse's children being intelligent (unlike most of black ours!) and of his new grandchildren and of Bush and Reagan and of a new era of greatness in America, which now we know is to be drum majored in by Bush and Quayle, when here we thought vaudeville was over a long time ago.

Dukakis was saying, "We will never bring disgrace upon this country, by any act of dishonesty and cowardice . . . " but hadn't it all been done already? It was dishonest to suggest that Dukakis was a better candidate than Jackson and it was cowardly for the party not to acknowledge Jesse as a legitimate Vice Presidential candidate. And since Jesse insists on valorizing the Dems with his "me too" ism he is implicated as well.

The question of a black presidential candidate and even a black president is not so much at issue as the question of black democracy, self determination and equality in the United States. The ex slave is still displaced after emancipation and without reconstruction. The 30,000,000 African Americans still have not even a representative in the Senate, though many now question whether there should even be a senate with two senators for Utah as well as New York, that's hardly one man one vote.

Jesse's decision to go along with the Democratic party's description of him as a non-being means that the will and self determination of the African American people is still being suffocated under the weight of white supremacy.

The peculiar description of Jesse's role during the Dukakis-Bush campaign, problematical and racially polarized is clear indication of this. Jesse's retreat from the issues to just the servant's yodel of "Up with Hope, Down with Dope" is more.

But our push for Jesse is part of our push for ourselves. We do not just want another famous Negro famous for being with white folks. We want democracy in America, we want equality. Jesse represented our desire for Self Determination, the shaping of our own lives with the same opportunity possessed by any other American. But Jesse's great run ended with the ignominious confirmation of our continued slavery. The convention finally, I could understand, was just the big house during a holiday season. And now the house negroes did sing and dance and clap their hands. And were it not for the fact that there was an outside to the house, and the night real and moving away in all directions, in which real people lived and desired, all of those goings on would not seem like utter foolishness. But there is, and they did.

July 1988–June 1989, Atlanta/Newark

Why's/Wise

Why's/Wise is a long poem in the tradition of the Griots[1] — but this is about African American (American) History. It is also like Melvin Tolson's *Liberia*, William Carlos William's *Paterson*, Charles Olson's *Maximus* in that it tries to tell the history/life like an ongoing-off-coming Tale.

I've been working on the piece now for almost two years, there are already some twenty-five to thirty parts, which are just now beginning to appear.

—A.B.

Wise 1

If you ever find
yourself, some where
lost and surrounded
by enemies
who wont let you
speak in your own language
who destroy your statues
& instruments, who ban
your omm bomm ba boom
then you are in trouble
deep trouble
they ban your
oom boom ba boom
you in deep deep
trouble

humph!

probably take you several hundred years
to get
out!

Wise 2

I was of people
caught in deep trouble
like I scribe you
some deep trouble, where
enemies had took us
surrounded us / in they
country
then banned our
oom boom ba boom

the confusion
the sickness

/What vision in the blackness
        of Queens
        of Kings

/What vision
  in the blackness
 that head
  & heart
 of yours

   that sweet verse
   you made, I still hear
   that song, son
    of the son's son's son's
         son
         I still hear that
          song,
         that cry
         cries
         screams
         life exploded
         our world exploding us
         transformed to niggers
What vision
in the blackness
your own hand sold you
"I am not a king or queen," your own hand
if you bee of the royal catch
or the tribes soulwarped by the ghoulishness

I still hear those songs, and cries
of the sons and sons and daughters and daughters
I still bear that weeping in my heart
that bleeding in my memory

And I am not a king
nor trader in flesh
I was
of the sufferers
I am among those
to be avenged!

Wise 3

Son singin
fount some
words/Son
singin
in that other
language
talkin bout "bay
bee, why you
leave me
here," talking bout
"up unner de sun
cotton in my hand." Son
singing, think he bad
cause he
can speak
they language, talkin bout
"dark was the night
 the ocean deep
 white eyes cut through me
 made me weep."
Son singin
fount some words. Think
he bad. Speak
they
language.

'sawright
I say
'sawright
wit me
look like
yeh, we gon be here
a taste

Wise 4

No coat has I got
nor extra chop
no soft bed or favor
no connection w/ the slaver

dark was the night
our eyes had not met
I fastened my life to me
and tried to find my way

talk did I hear
of fires and burning
and death to the gods

on the dirt where I slept
such talk
warmed me

such talk
lit my way

I has never got nothing but hard times and punishment
Any joy I had I made myself, and the dark woman
who took my hand and led me to myself

I has never got nothing
but a head full of blood
my scar, my missing teeth,

I has never got nothing but
killer frustration/ yes dark
was the night
cold was the ground

I has never got nothing, and talk
of rebellion
warmed me

Song to me, was the darkness
in which I could stand

my profile melted into the black air
red from the flame of the burning big house

in those crazy dreams I called myself
Coltrane
bathed in a black and red fire
in those crazy moments I called myself
Thelonious
& this was in the 19th century!

Wise 5

I overheard the other night
standing by the window
of the big house

a nigra say, through an alabaster
mask, "the first negro
was a white man."

Slanty red darts angulate the darkness
my hands got cold, my head was sweaty

like a mystery
story
like a gospel
hymn
like the tales
of the
wizards
and the life
of the gods
I did not know
who my father
was

I only barely
knew
my mother

But I knew something that night
about a negro
something even
the tv cant wash
away

I fount out something
about the negro

the wind may blow
the train dont come
the mayor might belch
his mistress might gain weight

But I fount out something that night
about the negro
& the world
got clear

you can hurray all you want to
you can kiss an elephants ass

But I fount out something
that night, before I slid
back to the field hands quarters
I fount out somthing
about
the magic
of slavery

& I vowed not to be
a slave
no more

Wise 6

Has we come far?

We has come far.

How we got there

How we got where?

Who we talkin bout?

What they name?

Oh, the slave peepas
you the slave peepas

Who the slave peepas
Just the same.

Struggle in dark, come down
the road. Knew your life
your sorrow. Knew your singing
in the dark. Knew the whip

that scarred you. And the century
change, alright, alright, the
years go by in light in darkness

there's white peepa voice behind my air
claim I should be free. They peepas hang out
in the north somewhere, dont need no bread
from the big house man. They voice hang
in the air.

But thas alright, alright wit me.
I preciate all of that.

Thas alright, alright wit me
But I been gone, naw, I been gone

my shape look like black on black
and fading

Wise 7

Back in the forest

the maroons laid

outraged by slavery, & split

from it, when the bombs burst

across the air, and fire tore

mens hearts, they knew some new

joint change was upon the time

and so emerged, a gun in one hand,

something funky, in the other.

Wise 8

From the country
to the city, we left
where things
were pretty—to get away from
the klansmen, and race freaks who
hung with the Slavemasters' cause
who could not believe in democracy
who would not let life be beautiful
who howled moon shadows screaming
for the primitive. Who climbed the trees
for past centuries, hollering for caves
and blood. From the country, to the city
we left where things were
pretty. Got city life, got city bred
wanted rights and services (get to that,
we thought) when all the time
it coulda been better, when all the time
new cdda been, built cdda been, progress

cdda been, and all the great notes of peace
all the great notes of peace
  all that
      cdda
          been

Wise 9

our war
was for
liberation
to end
slave times
now war
is over
we free
they say

who they
who say
what free
gone be?

there are cities
we can go to

there are cities
of light and newing

So what these faces laws hover
these swine wind law death people
these death time rebs return to crow
these slavemaster corpse leap off the flo
these sheet face coward monster haints
these death word carriers and slave lovers

there was war
before
be war
again
died before

will die again
but not gone die
not gone leave
not gone cry too long
not gone grieve
free is who we are and be
love who what will lift us we
struggle love struggle—against primitive death
while you walking round
spirit death tie you down
slave death and servant death and let me work for us to be

Wise 10

So in 1877 the lie grew
we all knew
the heart dead
the lie instead

They talked blood
They put on hoods
They paid for murder
They closed the books

No democracy
No light
primitive times
returned

across the road
the horse men prowled
American guns for African American lives

You'll never vote
you'll never grow
you'll never never never
be free   never
be free

        never

be free

　　　　never
　　　　never
　　　　never

　　　　　　　　Enter Booker T.

Rough Hand Dreamers (Wise 11)

You was a country folk, on the
land. Farmers before farmers
founders of cities, ile ife,[2]
where the world began. Was creator
of university, I trumpet timbuctoo
because I cannot bear to think
you think Banneker was wilder
than the breed. It was the woman
conceived of familiar cows and
architecture. Yon drummers know
how they are hide curers & musicians.
Now they enter the cities to enter future
reality. Now death, now blood, now hooded
criminals, resistance in its human dimension
like electric theories, post all abrahams.

What was it we wanted = Ourselves!
And why? We had been inside others being alive
for nothing
and worked to death
　　　our murders
　　　were circuses
　　　our murderers
　　　something like
　　　clowns

A farmer come to the city (Wise 12)

dirt growing in his mind
songs black land come in to
curl your poetry blind.
Banjo

waves and sinking bones
play eyes on sky
blood music

heaven people
say see heaven
they seeing
up side down

now they say we fought for evil
took our guns, the wise ones hid, say you
never was to be here
you never was to be

kept to edge of city
alleys behind the bossman's
house. got a job, you got a space,
you got a bond to heal your face

changed from slave
to convict, gone
from lazy to vagrant
jail lost boy in sleep
jail house/plantation moan
jail, was how they changed it
we
vote among roaches

Wise 13

And now you know
how "ghettoes"
grow

                                    (you knew
                                    (how ghettoes)
                                    grew?   )

                (Reality
                        for "you"
                is minstrelsy.)

N O T E S

1. Griots were the African Singer-Poet-Historians who carried word from bird, mouth to ear, and who are the root of our own African-American oral tradition.
2. Ile Ife was an ancient holy Yoruba city.

Select Bibliography

WORKS BY AMIRI BARAKA
(in chronological order)

Preface to a Twenty Volume Suicide Note. New York: Totem Press, 1961.

Blues People: Negro Music in White America. New York: William Morrow and Co., 1963.

The Dead Lecturer. New York: Grove Press, 1964.

Dutchman and The Slave. New York: William Morrow and Co., 1964.

The System of Dante's Hell. New York: Grove Press, 1965.

Home: Social Essays. New York: William Morrow and Co., 1966.

The Baptism & The Toilet. New York: Grove Press, 1967.

Tales. New York: Grove Press, 1967.

Black Music. New York: William Morrow and Co., 1968.

Four Black Revolutionary Plays. Indianapolis: The Bobbs-Merrill Co., 1969.

Black Magic: Collected Poetry, 1961–1967. Indianapolis: The Bobbs-Merrill Co., 1969.

In Our Terribleness. Indianapolis: The Bobbs-Merrill Co., 1970.

It's Nation Time. Chicago: Third World Press, 1970.

Jello. Chicago: Third World Press, 1970.

Raise Race Rays Raze: Essays Since 1965. New York: Random House, 1971.

Spirit Reach. Newark: Jihad Productions, 1972.

Hard Facts. Newark: Congress of Afrikan People, 1975.

The Motion of History and Other Plays. New York: William Morrow and Co., 1978.

Selected Plays and Prose of Amiri Baraka/LeRoi Jones. New York: William Morrow and Co., 1979.

Selected Poetry of Amiri Baraka/LeRoi Jones. New York: William Morrow and Co., 1979.

The Sidney Poet Heroical. New York: I. Reed Books, 1979.

reggae or not! New York: Contact II Publications, 1981.

Daggers and Javelins: Essays, 1974–1979. New York: William Morrow and Co., 1984.

The Autobiography of LeRoi Jones/Amiri Baraka. New York: Freundlich Books, 1984.

The Music: Reflections on Jazz and Blues. New York: William Morrow and Co., 1987.

WORKS EDITED BY BARAKA

The Moderns: An Anthology of New Writing in America. New York: Corinth Books, 1963.

Black Fire: An Anthology of Afro-American Writing. New York: William Morrow and Co., 1968 (With Larry Neal.)

Confirmation: An Anthology of African American Women. New York: William Morrow and Co., 1983. (With Amina Baraka.)

UNCOLLECTED ESSAYS

"How You Sound??" In *The New American Poetry: 1945–1960,* edited by Donald M. Allen. New York: Grove Press, 1960. 242–52.

"Philistinism and the Negro Writer." In *Anger, and Beyond: The Negro Writer in the United States,* edited by Herbert Hill. New York: Harper and Row, 1966. 51–61.

"Confessions of a Former Anti-Semite." *The Village Voice,* 17–23. December 1980, 1, 19–23.

BIBLIOGRAPHIES

Dace, Letitia. *LeRoi Jones: A Checklist of Works by and About Him.* London: Nether Press, 1971.

Harris, William J. *The Poetry and Poetics of Amiri Baraka: The Jazz Aesthetic.* Columbia: University of Missouri Press, 1985. Pp. 164–171.

Hudson, Theodore. *From LeRoi Jones to Amiri Baraka: The Literary Works.* Durham, N.C.: Duke University Press, 1973. Pp. 198–209.

Inge, Thomas M. *Black American Writers: Bibliographical Essays, Volume 2: Richard Wright, Ralph Ellison, James Baldwin, and Amiri Baraka.* New York: St. Martin's Press, 1978. Pp. 121–178.

Sollors, Werner. *Amiri Baraka/LeRoi Jones: The Quest for a "Populist Modernism."* New York: Columbia University Press, 1978. Pp. 301–28.

BIOGRAPHICAL AND CRITICAL STUDIES

Allen, Donald, ed. *New American Poetry: 1945–1960.* New York: Grove Press, 1960.

———. and Robert Creeley, eds. *New American Story*. New York: Grove Press, 1965.

Baker, Houston A. "Generational Shifts and the Recent Criticism of Afro-American Literature." *Black American Literature Forum*, 15, no. 1 (Spring 1981): 3–21.

———. " 'These Are Songs If You Have the/Music': An Essay on Imamu Baraka." *Minority Voices*, 1, no. 1 (Spring 1977): 1–18.

Benston, Kimberly. *Baraka: The Renegade and the Mask*. New Haven: Yale University Press, 1976.

———. ed. *Imamu Amiri Baraka (LeRoi Jones): A Collection of Critical Essays*. Englewood Cliffs, N.J.: Prentice-Hall, 1978.

Boundary 2 (including a supplement on Amiri Baraka) 6, no. 2 (Winter 1978): 303–442.

Brown, Lloyd W. *Amiri Baraka*. Boston: Twayne Publishers, 1980.

Brunner, Richard W., "Interview with Amiri Baraka," 1970. (Housed at The Schomberg Center of Oral History, New York, N.Y.)

Fischer, William C. "Amiri Baraka." In *American Writers* (supplement 2, part 1), edited A. Walton Litz, pp. 29–63. New York: Charles Scribner's Sons, 1981.

Fox, Robert Elliot. *Conscientious Sorcerers: The Black Postmodernist Fiction of LeRoi Jones/Amiri Baraka, Ishmael Reed and Samual R. Delany*. New York: Greenwood Press, 1987.

Gibson, Donald B., ed. *Five Black Writers*. New York: New York University Press, 1970.

———. ed. *Modern Black Poets: A Collection of Critical Essays*. Englewood Cliffs, N.J.: Prentice-Hall, 1973.

Gwynne, James B., ed. *Amiri Baraka: The Kaleidoscopic Torch*. New York: Steppingstones Press, 1985.

Harris, William J. *The Poetry and Poetics of Amiri Baraka: The Jazz Aesthetic*. Columbia: University of Missouri, 1985.

Hudson, Theodore. *From LeRoi Jones to Amiri Baraka: The Literary Works*. Durham, N.C.: Duke University Press, 1973.

Jones, Hettie. *How I Became Hettie Jones*. New York: E. P. Dutton, 1990.

Klinkowitz, Jerome. *Post-Contemporary American Fiction* (Second Edition). Urbana: University of Illinois Press, 1980.

Knight, Arthur and Kit, ed. *The Beat Vision*. New York: Paragon House, 1987.

Kofsky, Frank. *Black Nationalism and the Revolution in Music*. New York: Pathfinder Press, 1970.

Lacey, Henry C. To Raise, Destroy, and Create: The Poetry, Drama, and Fiction of Imamu Amiri Baraka (LeRoi Jones). Troy, New York: The Whitson Publishing Co., 1981.

Melhem, D. H. Heroism in the New Black Poetry: Introductions and Interviews. Lexington: The University Press of Kentucky, 1989.

Neal, Larry. Visions of a Liberated Future: Black Arts Movement Writings. New York: Thunder's Mouth Press, 1989.

Ossman, David, ed. The Sullen Art. New York: Corinth Books, 1963.

Pickney, Darryl. "The Changes of Amiri Baraka." New York Times Book Review, 16 December 1979, p. 9.

Rampersad, Arnold. The Life of Langston Hughes: Volume II: 1941–1967, I Dream a World. New York: Oxford University Press, 1988.

Rosenthal, M. L. "American Poetry Today." Salmagundi, nos. 22–23 (Spring–Summer 1973): 57–70.

———. The New Poets. New York: Oxford University Press, 1967.

Sollors, Werner. Amiri Baraka/LeRoi Jones: The Quest for a "Populist Modernism". New York: Columbia University Press, 1978.

ABOUT THE AUTHOR

Amiri Baraka (LeRoi Jones) was born in the industrial city of Newark, New Jersey, in 1934. After attending Howard University in Washington, D.C., he served in the United States Air Force. In the late fifties he settled in Greenwich Village and was a central figure of the bohemian scene there. He became famous in 1964, with the New York production of his Obie Award-winning play, *Dutchman*. After the death of Malcolm X he became a Black Nationalist, moving first to Harlem and then back home to Newark. In the mid-1970s he became a Third World Marxist-Leninist. Baraka has produced over twenty plays, three jazz operas, seven nonfiction books, a novel, and thirteen volumes of poetry. He has been the recipient of grants from both the Rockefeller Foundation and the National Endowment for the Arts. Currently he is a professor of Africana Studies at SUNY–Stony Brook. He lives with his wife, the poet Amina Baraka, in Newark.

ABOUT THE EDITOR

William J. Harris is Associate Professor of English at SUNY–Stony Brook where he teaches American and Afro-American literature and creative writing. Author of numerous scholarly articles, he has published a critical study, *The Poetry and Poetics of Amiri Baraka: The Jazz Aesthetic* and two books of poetry, *Hey Fella Would You Mind Holding This Piano a Moment* and *In My Own Dark Way*. He was an Andrew W. Mellon Fellow in the Humanities at Harvard University (1982–1983). Currently he is at work on a study of the experimental fiction of Ishmael Reed.